Building Open World Landscapes with Unreal Engine 5

Create stunning open world environments with foliage, lighting, and materials in UE5

David Ignacio García
Ramón Olivero

Building Open World Landscapes with Unreal Engine 5

Portfolio Director: Rohit Rajkumar
Relationship Lead: Tanisha Mehrotra
Program Manager: Sandip Tadge
Content Engineer: Shreya Sarkar
Technical Editor: Tejas Mhasvekar
Copy Editor: Safis Editing
Indexer: Pratik Shirodkar
Proofreader: Shreya Sarkar
Production Designer: Vijay Kamble
Growth Lead: Namita Velgekar

First published: November 2025
Production reference: 2081225

Published by Packt Publishing Ltd.
Grosvenor House
11 St Paul's Square
Birmingham
B3 1RB, UK.

ISBN 978-1-83508-557-8
`www.packtpub.com`

The ability to acquire and share knowledge is an inherent human trait, but it truly flourishes when we are surrounded by individuals who ignite our imagination, creativity, and a perpetual curiosity for learning.

We consider ourselves incredibly fortunate to have collaborated with an exceptional team of professionals in every aspect discussed throughout this book. Our thanks go to the instructor team at UT-HUB: Néstor, Alba, Natalia, Alejandro, and José Carlos, who supported us throughout this creative journey and helped transform our initiatives into tangible projects. This would not have been possible without you.

We also extend our gratitude to those who have fostered our personal and professional growth throughout our lives, our parents. They are the foundational pillars upon which we have relied to continue growing as professionals: Tahís and Ramón J., Marisa and José Ángel.

This achievement is yours as well.

- David Ignacio García, Ramón Olivero

Foreword

As Unreal Engine 5 began transforming digital environment design a few years back, my students — and myself, to be honest! — sought a structured and complete guide to creating expansive and immersive open worlds. Unfortunately, readily available resources offering such comprehensive instruction were scarce. Most of the time, my students got lost in a maze of not-so-complete video tutorials on the internet, with scarce results, I should say...

I wish they had had a book such as this in their hands back then; it would have saved them countless hours of trial and error!

Building Open World Landscapes with Unreal Engine 5 provides a comprehensive guide to mastering the engine's complex terrain system and its related features. Authors David Ignacio García and Ramón Olivero have done an amazing job structuring it to provide a systematic introduction to the core principles and advanced techniques essential for effective environment design. Starting from the basics, they have meticulously deconstructed many of the intricate processes, transforming them into a series of manageable, easily reproducible steps. This approach is particularly beneficial for people approaching the software for the first time.

What's more, this book offers several key benefits for experienced Unreal Engine users looking to enhance their skills, as it fosters a deep understanding of the underlying methodologies rather than merely providing a superficial overview.

This book is not just a technical manual; it is a thoughtfully designed educational resource, empowering readers to engage critically with the vast creative potential of Unreal Engine 5's environment system.

I wholeheartedly recommend it.

Marco Secchi,

Freelance Game Developer, Academic Lecturer at NABA, Nuova Accademia di Belle Arti

Contributors

About the authors

David Ignacio García is a real-time 3D technologist, entrepreneur, and educator focused on building robust Unreal Engine pipelines and solutions, with a long-standing commitment to the real-time ecosystem. Trained as an architect, he transitioned from architectural visualization into interactive simulation and virtual production, leading teams that design scalable Unreal Engine workflows for AEC, entertainment, and enterprise.

He is the founder of BaboonLab, an Epic Games Service Partner specializing in Unreal Engine consulting, education, and project development, and the creator of IdealTwin, a SaaS platform that brings data-driven digital twin experiences to the web and Unreal Engine. A Gold Unreal Authorized Instructor, David has trained hundreds of students and professionals through UT-HUB and Epic programs, including the Unreal Fellowship, where he has served as TA, Mentor, and Senior Instructor. He also serves at Epic Games as Partner x Education Advisor across Europe and the Middle East, strengthening the partner and education ecosystem and accelerating adoption of production-ready workflows.

David's work spans city-scale visualization, procedural worldbuilding, performance optimization, and pixel-streaming deployments, with a consistent emphasis on maintainable, production-ready practices. His goal is to bridge creative intent and technical execution so teams can deliver expansive, real-time worlds with confidence.

Ramón Olivero is an architect and 3D visualization enthusiast who evolved from architectural visualization to large-scale worldbuilding. This trajectory led him to specialize as a technical artist focused on procedural tools, real-time environments, and virtual production. With years of university teaching experience, he centers his career on bridging creative vision and technical execution. As an Unreal Engine instructor, Ramón has trained hundreds of students and professionals through academic programs and industry initiatives, including Epic Games' Unreal Fellowship.

His work empowers artists and developers to adopt production-ready workflows, optimize pipelines, and bring expansive worlds to life in real time. Ramón serves as Head of Studio and instructor at UT-HUB. His commitment to teaching and lifelong learning continues to inspire creators to explore the possibilities of interactive worlds.

About the reviewers

Omar Costa is a cybersecurity specialist and independent game developer with an IT management degree and an MBA in product management for the metaverse. He has technical experience with languages (C#, C++, Python, JavaScript) and building projects with Unreal, Unity, and Godot engines. Professionally, he is part of a multidisciplinary GRC team focused on cybersecurity supplier risk assessment. He has led complex innovation and technological transformation projects, leveraging technology as a strategic differentiator. His generalist profile and distinct mix of experiences allowed him to apply a creative, analytical, and technological perspective to his review, focusing on verifying this book's accuracy and architectural integrity.

I would like to extend my sincere thanks to the authors and the entire Packt publishing team. It was a pleasure and an honor to contribute to this book and collaborate with such dedicated professionals.

Simone Destro is a 3D developer and technical artist specializing in real-time applications built with Unreal Engine. With several years of experience in the 3D industry, he has worked on a wide range of projects across architecture, automotive, fashion, and virtual experiences. Simone combines technical expertise with a strong artistic vision, developing interactive environments, configurators, and immersive visual storytelling for clients and studios in diverse creative fields. His background bridges art and technology through immersive digital design.

Table of Contents

Chapter 2: Quixel Bridge, Megascans, and Fab 27

Chapter 4: Project Structure and Naming Conventions 103

Part 2: Creating and Detailing Your Open World 129

Chapter 5: Managing Levels and Layers 131

Chapter 6: Building Your Landscape 167

Chapter 7: Populating Your World with Foliage 199

Chapter 8: Introduction to Materials 227

Chapter 10: Setting up your Post Process Volume 301

Part 4: Blueprints, Testing, and Optimization 329

Chapter 11: Understanding Programming Logic and Blueprints 331

Chapter 12: Optimizing and Testing Your Scene 361

Preface

Creating natural and believable open worlds has always been one of the greatest challenges in game development. The vast scale, fine detail, and technical complexity they demand often make the process overwhelming for artists and designers alike. The goal of *Building Open World Landscapes with Unreal Engine 5* is to make that journey approachable. It provides a structured and practical framework to help you understand how **Unreal Engine 5 (UE5)** equips you with the tools needed to design, build, and optimize large-scale environments with confidence and artistic intent.

Throughout the book's chapters, we will explore every key stage of world creation from initial project setup and efficient asset management, through level organization and **World Partition**, to terrain sculpting, material creation, foliage workflows, lighting design, and performance optimization. Each topic connects seamlessly to the next, guiding you from core principles to advanced techniques for building production-quality environments.

This book follows a hands-on learning methodology: each concept is introduced through real-world examples and step-by-step exercises that reflect professional studio practices. The focus is not only on gaining expertise at using the tools, but also on understanding the reasoning behind each decision, helping you develop both technical proficiency and creative judgment.

By the end of this journey, you will have built your own optimized open world environment in UE5. More importantly, you will understand the complete workflow required to take an idea from early reference gathering and world planning to a visually rich, efficient, and scalable environment. Whether your goal is game development, cinematic production, or virtual production, this book will provide you with the insight and skills to transform your creative vision into a compelling world.

Who this book is for

If you want to use UE5 to create convincing open world environments, this book is for you. It's a practical guide for aspiring level and game designers, environment and technical artists, indie developers, and educators or students who need a clear, production-ready workflow.

You'll learn studio-relevant skills: sculpting terrains, building landscape materials, painting vegetation and foliage, setting up lighting, and optimizing large levels. Along the way, you'll work with **World Partition** for streaming, tap into Quixel Megascans for high-quality assets, and apply profiling techniques to keep performance on target. The result is portfolio-ready worlds you can iterate on for gameplay, cinematics, or virtual production.

No prior expertise is required, only a basic familiarity with Unreal Engine and core 3D concepts. The book takes you step by step from first principles to confident execution, so you can ship environments that look great and run efficiently.

What this book covers

Chapter 1, Starting a Project in Unreal Engine, establishes the development environment and core terminology. It walks you through installing UE5, creating a new project from templates, and navigating the interface, viewports, and essential panels. By the end of the chapter, you will be able to configure basic project settings and understand the key tools needed to begin building environments.

Chapter 2, Quixel Bridge, Megascans, and Fab, maps the UE5 asset ecosystem and shows how to source and manage production-ready content. It introduces Fab as a unified marketplace, then demonstrates using Quixel Bridge inside the editor to browse, import, and organize Megascans assets, including surfaces, 3D models, and digital humans.

Chapter 3, Ingestion and Static Meshes, focuses on importing and validating static meshes for real-time use in UE5. It covers clean ingestion workflows, scale and orientation checks, common import issues, and optimization techniques, including Level of Detail (LODs), mesh simplification, and efficient UVs. The chapter also applies materials to meshes and demonstrates practical exercises that balance visual fidelity with performance.

Chapter 4, Project Structure and Naming Conventions, establishes a clear folder hierarchy and consistent naming to keep UE5 projects scalable and team-friendly. It references the Allar style guide as a practical baseline, then shows how to apply conventions to assets, actors, and code. The chapter also introduces version control options (Git, Perforce, Plastic, and SVN) and best practices for repositories, enabling reliable collaboration and safer iteration.

Chapter 5, Managing Levels and Layers, explains how UE5 organizes game worlds and why that structure matters for scale, collaboration, and performance. It introduces levels, lighting scenarios, and layers, then contrasts traditional level/sublevel hierarchies with **World Partition**, detailing streaming, region-based editing, and multi-user workflows.

Chapter 6, Building Your Landscape, moves from planning to hands-on environment creation in UE5. It introduces practical methods to translate ideas into a playable scene, covering project/template selection, early scene blocking, and validation techniques, then guides you through **Landscape** and **Sculpt** tools for shaping natural terrain.

Chapter 7, Populating Your World with Foliage, introduces UE5 tools for adding, managing, and optimizing plant life to shape mood, narrative, and atmosphere. It explains foliage terminology, demonstrates **Foliage Mode** for rapid painting and editing of large areas, and outlines procedural options for broad coverage. The chapter concludes with performance tips for density, LODs, culling, and instancing to keep rich scenes efficient at scale.

Chapter 8, Introduction to Materials, explains how surfaces respond to light and how to build physically based materials in UE5. It orients you to the Material Editor interface, common nodes, and texture inputs, then walks through Physically Based Rendering (PBR) workflows for creating consistent, reusable materials and material instances. The chapter also highlights practical tips for organization and performance when authoring shaders at scale.

Chapter 9, Create Your World's Atmospheric Lighting, focuses on building believable, performant open world lighting in UE5. It introduces the **Environment Light Mixer** and key actors for physically grounded ambience, then explains **Lumen, Virtual Shadow Maps**, and **Nanite** considerations for quality and performance, including tuning exposure, shadows, and time-of-day for consistent results.

Chapter 10, Setting Up Your Post Process Volume, shows how to control a scene's final look using global volumes. It covers setup and tuning of core effects: color grading and tonemapping, **Bloom**, and **Depth of Field**, plus blending, priorities for consistent art direction. The chapter closes with best practices for dynamic changes and performance in large open world levels.

Chapter 11, Understanding Programming Logic and Blueprints, introduces UE5's visual scripting for building game and tool logic without writing code. It explains the node-based workflow, core concepts (variables, events, functions, and the **Construction Script**), and common Blueprint types. The chapter then walks through creating a Blueprint Class and shows how to prototype reusable tools that streamline environment creation and iteration.

Chapter 12, Optimizing and Testing Your Scene, reframes world-building with performance as a continuous design constraint. It explains the real-time rendering pipeline and shows how to profile scenes to locate bottlenecks, then applies best practices across meshes, materials, lighting, collisions, and LODs for open world scale.

To get the most out of this book

You should feel comfortable with basic 3D concepts such as meshes, UVs, textures, materials, and lighting, as well as with Unreal Engine's navigation and interface. If you've already opened a project, moved the camera, and placed a few Actors in a scene, you're ready to begin.

Recommended knowledge (helpful, but not required)

Some familiarity with asset management tools such as **Fab** or **Quixel Bridge**, project organization, and real-time performance concepts (LODs, draw calls, and culling) will help you follow along more easily. A basic understanding of Blueprints will also make the exercises more intuitive.

Additional skills that accelerate learning

Knowing how to use version control systems such as **Git**, **Perforce**, and **Tortoise** can make experimentation safer. Building and maintaining mood boards or visual reference folders helps define a consistent artistic direction. Understanding scale, proportion, and composition supports better design decisions in large environments, while a grasp of PBR materials and texture maps **(Base Color**, **Normal**, **Roughness**, **Metallic**, and **Ambient Occlusion**) ensures that surfaces react to light realistically.

Software/hardware requirements

To follow along smoothly, make sure your system meets or exceeds the following specifications. All examples and screenshots in this book were developed and tested on Windows 10/11, which is the recommended platform. While macOS users can complete most exercises, minor interface differences and some performance variations may occur.

Software covered in the book	**Details**
Unreal Engine 5.5 or later	Available for free through the Epic Games Launcher. Ensure that the Starter Content and Quixel Bridge plugins are installed
Epic Games Launcher	Required for downloading Unreal Engine, managing updates, and accessing Fab (the unified marketplace)
Quixel Bridge / Fab integration	Required for asset browsing and importing from the Megascans library

Software covered in the book	Details
Visual Studio 2022 (Community Edition) or Rider for Unreal Engine	
Version Control Client	Git, Perforce, or Plastic SCM is recommended for managing project iterations
Image editing software (optional)	Adobe Photoshop, GIMP, or Substance 3D Sampler for creating or adjusting textures
Web browser	Required to access online references

Hardware covered in the book	Specifications
Operating System	Windows 10/11 (recommended) or macOS Monterey (or newer).
Processor (CPU)	6-core or higher (Intel i7 / AMD Ryzen 7 or equivalent)
Memory (RAM)	Minimum 16 GB, 32 GB recommended for open world projects
Graphics (GPU)	NVIDIA RTX 3060/AMD RX 6700 XT or better, 8 GB VRAM or higher
Storage	SSD with at least 100 GB of free space for Unreal Engine, project files, and assets
Display	1080p minimum; 1440p or higher recommended for comfortable workspace visibility
Internet Connection	Required for downloading Unreal Engine, Megascans assets, and updates.

Note for macOS users: Unreal Engine 5.5 runs on macOS, but some GPU-dependent features, such as **Nanite** and **Lumen**, may be limited or perform differently compared to Windows. Where relevant, equivalent workflows will be noted, but all examples and optimizations are demonstrated on Windows.

To make the most of the book, work chapter by chapter, take notes, and profile your scenes regularly (in fps). Keep your project well structured and under version control. Good organization saves time and helps you iterate efficiently as your world grows.

Note that the authors acknowledge the use of cutting-edge AI, such as ChatGPT, with the sole aim of enhancing the language and clarity within the book, thereby ensuring a smooth reading experience for readers. It's important to note that the content itself has been crafted by the author and edited by a professional publishing team.

Download the color images

To help you follow the Unreal Engine 5 workflows more easily, we also provide a PDF file containing all screenshots in color. This PDF allows you to zoom in and view settings, parameters, and UI elements. You can download the PDF file here: `https://packt.link/gbp/9781835085578`

Conventions used

There are a number of text conventions used throughout this book.

`CodeInText`: Indicates code words in text, database table names, folder names, filenames, file extensions, pathnames, dummy URLs, user input, and X (formerly, Twitter) handles. For example: "After creating our level, it's a good time to save it in the `OpenWorldLevel` folder created in the previous step before starting to work on any modifications:"

Bold: Indicates a new term, an important word, or words that you see on the screen. For instance, words in menus or dialog boxes appear in the text like this. For example: "The next step is to add the **Scale** variable and connect it to the **Relative Transform Scale** of the **Add Static Mesh Component** node. This will allow us to configure the global scale of all Static Meshes created from the editor."

Warnings or important notes appear like this.

Tips and tricks appear like this.

Get in touch

Feedback from our readers is always welcome.

General feedback: If you have questions about any aspect of this book or have any general feedback, please email us at `customercare@packt.com` and mention the book's title in the subject of your message.

Errata: Although we have taken every care to ensure the accuracy of our content, mistakes do happen. If you have found a mistake in this book, we would be grateful if you reported this to us. Please visit `http://www.packt.com/submit-errata`, click **Submit Errata**, and fill in the form.

Piracy: If you come across any illegal copies of our works in any form on the internet, we would be grateful if you would provide us with the location address or website name. Please contact us at `copyright@packt.com` with a link to the material.

If you are interested in becoming an author: If there is a topic that you have expertise in and you are interested in either writing or contributing to a book, please visit `http://authors.packt.com/`.

Share your thoughts

Once you've read *Building Open World Landscapes with Unreal Engine 5*, we'd love to hear your thoughts! Scan the QR code below to go straight to the Amazon review page for this book and share your feedback.

`https://packt.link/r/1835085571`

Your review is important to us and the tech community and will help us make sure we're delivering excellent quality content.

Free Benefits with Your Book

This book comes with free benefits to support your learning. Activate them now for instant access (see the "*How to Unlock*" section for instructions).

Here's a quick overview of what you can instantly unlock with your purchase:

PDF and ePub Copies

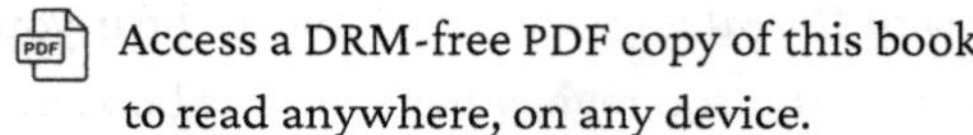

Access a DRM-free PDF copy of this book to read anywhere, on any device.

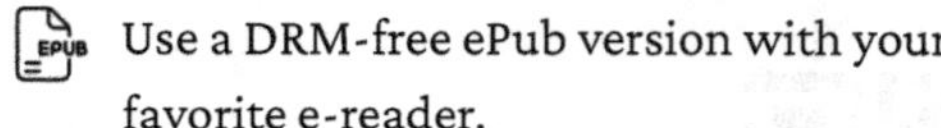

Use a DRM-free ePub version with your favorite e-reader.

Next-Gen Web-Based Reader

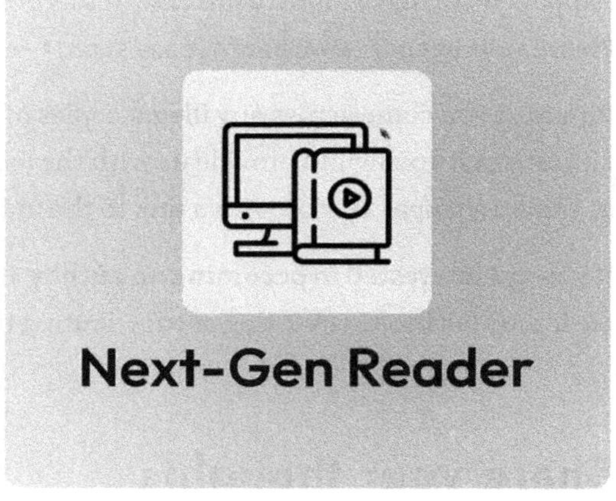

Multi-device progress sync: Pick up where you left off, on any device.

Highlighting and notetaking: Capture ideas and turn reading into lasting knowledge.

Bookmarking: Save and revisit key sections whenever you need them.

Dark mode: Reduce eye strain by switching to dark or sepia themes.

How to Unlock

UNLOCK NOW

Scan the QR code (or go to `packtpub.com/unlock`). Search for this book by name, confirm the edition, and then follow the steps on the page.

***Note:** Keep your invoice handy. Purchases made directly from Packt don't require one.*

Part 1

Setting Up Your Scene in Unreal Engine

This part focuses on the initial setup and foundation of your Unreal Engine project. It begins by helping you establish the development environment, install Unreal Engine 5, and navigate its core interface. You'll then explore how to access and manage production-ready assets using Fab and Quixel Bridge, followed by importing and validating Static Meshes to ensure correct scale, orientation, and optimization for real-time use.

The part concludes with best practices for organizing your project through naming conventions, folder hierarchies, and version control systems, laying a structured base for building larger, more complex environments later in the book.

This part of the book includes the following chapters:

- *Chapter 1, Starting a Project in Unreal Engine*
- *Chapter 2, Quixel Bridge, Megascans, and Fab*
- *Chapter 3, Ingestion and Static Meshes*
- *Chapter 4, Project Structure and Naming Conventions*

1

Starting a Project in Unreal Engine

Welcome to the fascinating world of **Unreal Engine 5 (UE5)**. Within the pages of this book, we will explore the art of crafting stunning landscapes and immersive environments by utilizing the array of tools provided by Epic Games for Unreal Engine.

Before setting off on our journey to construct breathtaking worlds, our first essential task is to set up our development environment. Unreal Engine is readily available for free download. In the ensuing sections, we will learn about engine installation and project creation, acquainting ourselves with the interface and the many tools available at our disposal.

Within this chapter, we will explore the following key topics:

- Learning the Unreal Engine terminology
- Installing Unreal Engine
- Setting up the project and templates
- Exploring the Unreal Engine interface

Technical requirements

Unreal Engine has minimum and recommended hardware requirements for **version 5.5**, and there are special hardware requirements related to its advanced rendering features.

These special requirements ensure that the advanced rendering features in UE5 can deliver their full potential and provide the best possible visual quality and performance. It's crucial to meet or exceed these requirements if you plan to utilize these features extensively in your projects.

Here's an overview.

These are the minimum hardware requirements:

- **Operating system:** Windows 10 64-bit version
- **Processor:** Dual-core Intel or AMD, 2.5 GHz or faster
- **Memory:** 8 GB RAM
- **Graphics card:** DirectX 11 compatible graphics card with at least 1 GB of VRAM
- **Hard drive:** 100 GB of free space (SSD recommended)

Important note

Please note that these are the minimum requirements for running the engine and working on basic projects. More complex projects or the use of advanced features may require better hardware.

These are the recommended hardware requirements:

- **Operating system:** Windows 10 64-bit version 1909 revision .1350 or higher, or versions 2004 and 20H2 revision .789 or higher
- **Processor:** Quad-core Intel or AMD, 2.5 GHz or faster
- **Memory:** 8 GB RAM
- **Graphics card:** DirectX 11 or 12 compatible graphics card with the latest drivers

Note

These recommended specifications will provide a smoother and more efficient experience when working with Unreal Engine and UE5, especially for larger and more complex projects.

Special hardware requirements for UE5 rendering features

UE5 introduces advanced rendering features such as **Lumen Global Illumination**, **Nanite** virtualized geometry, and more. These features may have additional hardware requirements to fully utilize their capabilities.

These are the **Lumen Global Illumination** and **Reflections** requirements:

- **Software Ray Tracing**: This feature may require a video card using DirectX 11 with support for Shader Model 5
- **Hardware Ray Tracing**: Requires Windows 10 build 1909.1350 or newer with DirectX 12 support and specific compatible graphics cards (e.g., NVIDIA RTX-2000 series or newer, AMD RX-6000 series or newer, Intel® Arc™ A-Series graphics cards or newer)

These are the Nanite virtualized geometry requirements:

- Windows 10 build 1909.1350 or newer, or Windows 11 with support for DirectX 12 Agility SDK
- DirectX 12 (with Shader Model 6.6 atomics) or Vulkan (VK_KHR_shader_atomic_int64) is necessary
- **SM6** (**Shader Model 6**) must be enabled in **Project Settings** (enabled by default in new projects)

Other rendering features

UE5 may have specific hardware requirements or recommendations for other advanced rendering features, so it's essential to check the official UE5 documentation for the most up-to-date information.

Important note

At the time of writing, an earlier version of Unreal Engine was in use. However, the screenshots, examples, and exercises have since been reviewed to reflect changes introduced in version 5.6. You may still notice slight differences in menus, layouts, or naming conventions due to ongoing updates to the engine's interface. These variations will not affect your ability to follow the instructions or complete the exercises. For additional context on recent interface updates, the official Unreal Engine documentation may be useful: `https://dev.epicgames.com/documentation`.

Learning the Unreal Engine terminology

In this section, we'll explore key terminology commonly used in the context of Unreal Engine, shedding light on fundamental concepts:

- **Project**: An Unreal Engine project serves as the container for all the elements within your creative endeavor. It allows you to structure your work by organizing content into folders. Each project is represented by a `.uproject` file, which is essential for project creation, opening, and saving. This concept distinguishes Unreal Engine from other **digital content creation** (**DCC**) tools, as it embraces a project-based approach, particularly relevant due to its origins as a game engine where compilation plays a vital role.
- **Blueprint**: The **Blueprint Visual Scripting system** is a comprehensive gameplay scripting tool within Unreal Editor. It employs a node-based interface to construct gameplay elements. Objects created using Blueprint are often colloquially referred to as **Blueprints**. This distinction sets Unreal Engine apart, offering non-C++ programmers a powerful way to implement programming logic.
- **Object**: Objects represent the fundamental building blocks within Unreal Engine. In essence, they encapsulate essential functionality for assets. Objects, or UObjects as referred to in C++, serve as the parent class from which all other Unreal classes inherit. In other words, every element or class within Unreal is derived from UObject.
- **Actor**: Actors form the backbone of any Unreal Engine project, embodying all objects that can be placed or spawned within a game level. This broad category includes a variety of elements, such as cameras that capture the game world from different angles, static meshes that provide the physical structures and objects within the game, or player start locations that define where a player enters the game world. Actors are versatile and support 3D transformations, enabling them to move (translate), rotate, and change size (scale) within the game space. Their lifecycle is dynamic; they can be instantiated or removed during gameplay through scripted code, allowing for interactive and responsive game environments that can change over time or in response to player actions.
- **Pawn**: Pawns are a specialized subclass of Actors designed to serve as the in-game representations or avatars of players or AI entities. They are essentially the characters or entities within the game that can have some form of agency. Unlike the broader `Actor` class, Pawns are specifically meant to be controlled. They can be directed by human players, providing a direct interface for player interaction within the game world, or be automated and driven by the game's AI, acting as **non-player characters** (**NPCs**) with varying degrees of complexity and autonomy. This duality allows for a rich interaction between the player-controlled characters and the game environment, including AI-controlled entities.

- **Character**: Within the hierarchy of Unreal Engine's class system, Characters are a further refinement of Pawns, tailored for more complex, player-controlled entities, typically those that walk on two legs or require sophisticated movement dynamics. This subclass is optimized for bipedal movement and includes preconfigured setups for collision detection, which is crucial for a realistic interaction with the game world, and input bindings that map player actions to character movements and behaviors. Characters are designed to facilitate the creation of player avatars with advanced capabilities, including running, jumping, and other actions that player characters commonly perform, supported by additional code that enhances the interactivity and responsiveness of player-controlled characters within the game.
- **Brush**: Brushes are a type of Actor and define 3D shapes, such as cubes or spheres. They find utility in level geometry design and are known as **Binary Space Partition** (**BSP**) brushes. While useful for fast level blocking, they are not typically employed as a final method of level design. Instead, they are often replaced with static meshes as the project progresses. Unreal Engine also offers modern methods for geometry modeling and level blocking, which will be discussed later in *Chapter 6*.
- **Level**: Although we will talk about levels in *Chapter 5*, it's an important concept to know from the beginning of this journey. A level in Unreal Engine is a self-contained environment or scene where gameplay takes place. It is a composite of all the elements that make up the game space, including the geometry that forms the physical world, the Actors and Pawns that populate it, and the various interactive and static objects that define the player's experience. Each level is crafted to deliver a unique set of challenges, narratives, and aesthetics, encapsulated within a `.umap` file. Levels are the stages or worlds within which the game unfolds, designed by developers to create immersive and engaging environments. They are the canvas on which the game's story is painted, allowing for the seamless integration of gameplay mechanics, narrative elements, and the visual and auditory experience of the game.
- **World**: The world acts as a container for all the levels constituting your game or project. Typically, worlds are organized into specific levels, each serving a unique purpose, such as lighting, events, or geometry. The organization of worlds and levels varies based on project requirements, emphasizing the importance of tailoring this structure to your project's specific needs. Understanding the scope of your project is paramount in making these organizational decisions.

Now that the technical requirements, including technologies and key concepts within Unreal Engine, are understood, let's explore where we can find the installers and the installation process.

Installing Unreal Engine

To begin, you need to install the Epic Games Launcher by following these steps:

1. Go to the Unreal Engine website by opening your web browser and navigating to `https://www.unrealengine.com/`.
2. Register and download the Epic Games Launcher. Look for the option to register or create an account on the website.
3. Complete the registration process by providing the required information.
4. After registering, you will have the option to download the Epic Games Launcher. Click on the **Download** link to start the download.
5. Sign in to the Epic Games Launcher.
6. Once the Epic Games Launcher installer is downloaded, run the installer.
7. Follow the installation instructions to install the Epic Games Launcher on your computer.
8. After installation, launch the Epic Games Launcher.
9. Open the Epic Games Launcher that you've just installed on your computer.
10. You may need to sign in using the account you created earlier.
11. Inside the Epic Games Launcher, you will see various tabs on the left-hand side. Click on the **Unreal Engine** tab. This is where you will manage Unreal Engine installations.
12. At the top of the Epic Games Launcher, you'll see several tabs. Click on the **Library** tab. This is where you can view and manage your Unreal Engine installations.
13. Under the **Library** tab, you'll find a section called **ENGINE VERSIONS**. To install a specific version of Unreal Engine, click the + icon next to **ENGINE VERSIONS**.
14. Unreal Engine provides several versions to choose from. Choose the desired version you need to install from the list of available options.

    Depending on your computer's specifications and internet connection speed, the download and installation of Unreal Engine can take 10 to 40 minutes or more.

15. After selecting the version you want, click the **Install** button. The launcher will start downloading and installing that specific version of Unreal Engine.
16. Once the installation is complete, click the **Launch** button to start the Unreal Engine you've installed.

    Several versions of Unreal Engine can be installed on your computer. Remember to select the preferred version on the top right **Launch** button drop-down list; a version of Unreal Engine 5.5 or later is recommended. You will only be able to select from the installed versions.

In *Figure 1.1*, you can see the **Library** tab from the Epic Games Launcher, where the **5.6.1** version is already installed and assigned as the default engine:

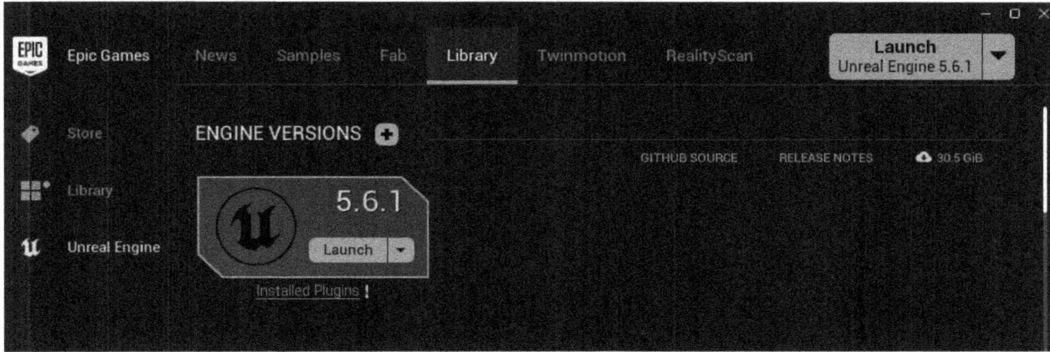

Figure 1.1 – Unreal Engine section in Epic Games Launcher

You are ready to start creating and working on your projects. Make sure to keep your Unreal Engine installations up to date to access the latest features and improvements.

Setting up the project and templates

When you launch Unreal Engine without specifying a particular project, the Unreal Project Browser automatically opens, as shown here:

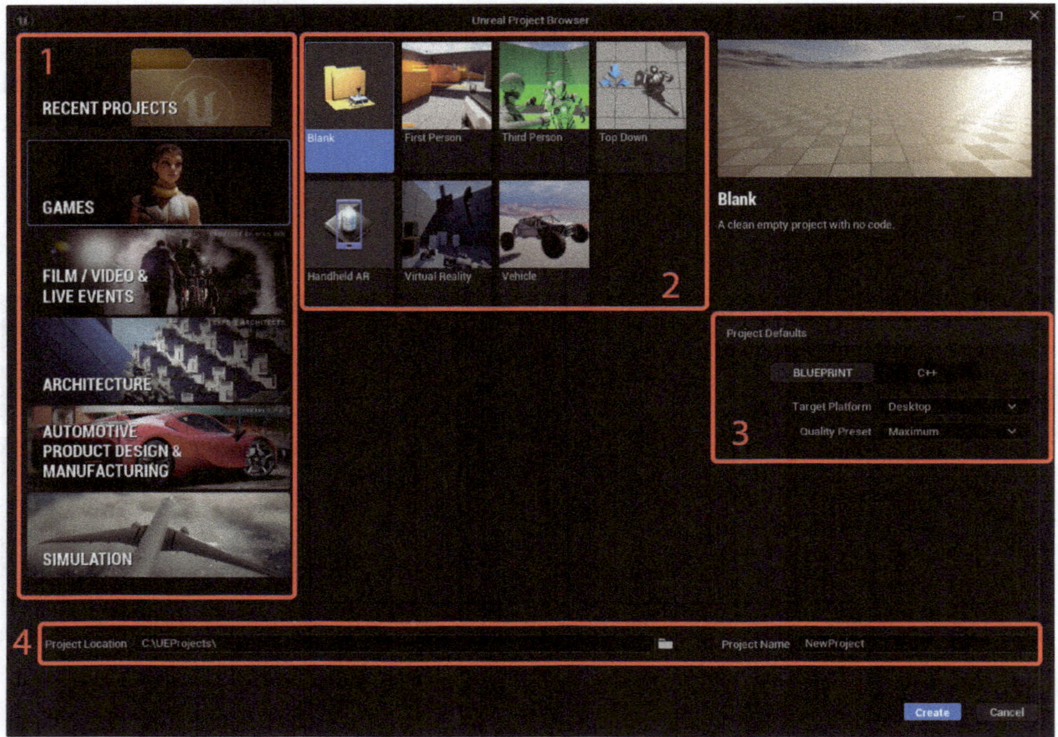

Figure 1.2 – The Unreal Project Browser

Figure 1.2 shows the following sections:

1. In this browser, you can choose the category (**1**) for templates. If you've previously created projects in Unreal Engine, you'll have a **RECENT PROJECTS** category, allowing you to reopen any of your recent projects. The available categories include the following:

    - **GAMES**
    - **FILM / VIDEO & LIVE EVENTS**
    - **ARCHITECTURE**
    - **AUTOMOTIVE, PRODUCT DESIGN & MANUFACTURING**
    - **SIMULATION**

2. The category templates (**2**) serve as foundational frameworks containing files and a level, providing a starting point for various project types. You also have the option to begin with an empty template. Within the **GAMES** category, you'll find the following:

    - **First Person**: This template is designed for games with a first-person perspective. It features a player character represented by arms holding a gun. Players can move the character within the level with the help of a keyboard, controller, or virtual joystick on a touch device.
    - **Third Person**: This includes a playable character with a camera that follows it from behind and slightly above. The character comes with walking, running, and jumping animations. It can be controlled with the help of a keyboard, controller, or virtual joystick on a touch device.
    - **Top Down**: This features a character controlled by mouse input, with a camera positioned high above. Players control the character by clicking on their desired destination, utilizing a navigation system to avoid obstacles. This top-down view is commonly used in action role-playing games.
    - **Handheld AR**: This is designed for **augmented reality (AR)** applications on Android and iOS devices. It provides runtime logic for toggling **AR** mode on and off. It also provides example code for hit detection and handling light estimation.
    - **Virtual Reality**: This is equipped with essential features for **virtual reality (VR)** games, including teleport locomotion, grabbable objects, interactive elements, and a VR spectator camera. This template includes a level where players can move around and interact with objects.
    - **Vehicle**: This contains both regular and complex vehicles with suspension systems. The template includes a simple track and various obstacles.

3. In the **Project Defaults** section (**3**), you can set your project's specifications, including the target platform (the hardware where your game or application will run), quality settings, ray tracing options, and more. You will find these options in **Project Defaults**:

    - **Implementation**: Choose how you want to implement your project's logic, either through Blueprints or C++.
    - **Target Platform**: Specify whether your project targets **Desktop** or **Mobile** platforms.

- **Quality Preset**: Select the maximum quality level based on your project's target platform, choosing between **Maximum** (recommended for computer or game console projects) or **Scalable** (recommended for mobile device projects).
- **Starter Content**: This includes simple static meshes with basic textures and materials, useful for quick learning and experimentation.
- **Ray Tracing**: Decide whether to enable or disable ray tracing for your project.

4. In **Project Location (4)**, you can indicate where you want to save your project and provide it with a name.

   In the following figure, you will see the configuration we used in our project: template category **(1)**, template file **(2)**, **Project Location (3)**, and **Project Name (4)**.

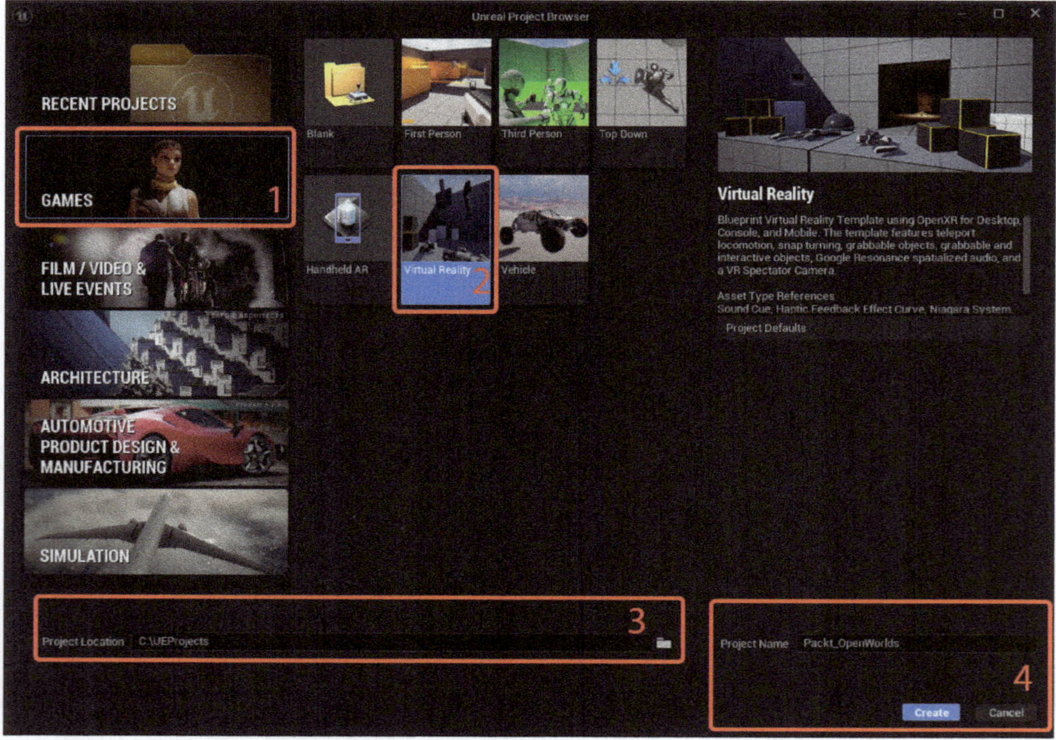

Figure 1.3 – Project creation from VR template

Important note

We will utilize the **Virtual Reality** template found in the **GAMES** category to leverage features such as teleport locomotion and the VR spectator camera.

5. Finally, click **Create** to initiate the project creation process. Unreal Engine will automatically open your newly created project.

The process may take a few minutes, but once the shaders have finished compiling and the project has loaded, the main Unreal Engine interface will open, giving you access to the tools and panels you need to begin your development journey.

Exploring the Unreal Engine interface

After your project loads, upon launching UE5 for the first time, you'll find yourself within the Unreal Engine Level Editor interface, as shown here:

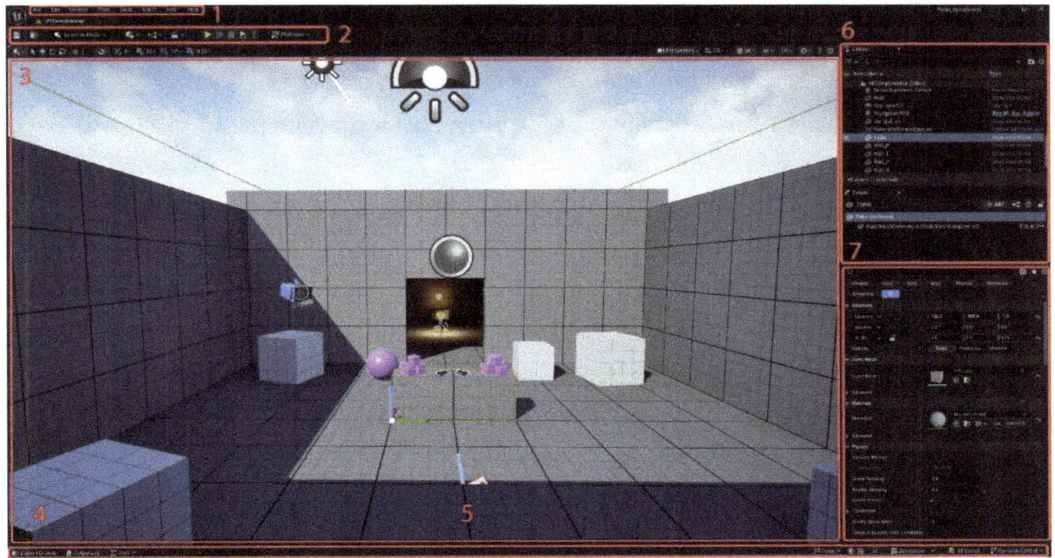

Figure 1.4 – An overview of the Unreal Engine Level Editor

It's essential to acquaint yourself with the general purpose and functionality of these components, particularly if you're new to game and application development using UE5. Let's see them in more detail.

Menu bar [1]

The menu bar, as shown in *Figure 1.5*, is a crucial navigational hub within the Unreal Engine Level Editor, offering a wide range of tools and options to help you create, edit, and manage your projects efficiently.

Figure 1.5 – The menu bar

Here's a brief overview of the different tabs on the menu bar and their functions:

- **File**: This menu typically contains options for creating new projects, opening existing projects, saving, and exporting your work. You can also find project packaging and deployment options here.
- **Edit**: This menu offers various editing functions, including undo and redo, copy and paste, and the ability to find and replace elements within your project. It often contains keyboard shortcuts for these actions as well. This also provides access to the settings and preferences of the Unreal Engine editor. You can configure editor-specific preferences, project settings, and other customization options.
- **Window**: This menu allows you to manage open windows and panels within the editor. You can arrange and customize your workspace by docking or floating windows, and you can also access different layout presets.
- **Tools**: This menu allows you to open many different tools made for analyzing and helping you get a better understanding of your project. These new panels or tools are usually more developer- or optimization-focused than the ones you can open from the **Window** menu.
- **Build**: In this menu, you find options related to building different elements of your project. It includes functions such as building lighting, rebuilding levels, navigation, and landscape.
- **Select**: This menu allows you to choose between different selection options that can help you gather the elements you specifically want in bulk, instead of selecting individual elements one by one.
- **Actor**: This menu offers you a list of tools and options to manipulate the Actors in your level – from opening the sub-editor to working with snaps or optimizing the asset.
- **Help**: This menu contains resources and information to assist you in using Unreal Engine. You can access documentation, tutorials, and community support from here. It may also include information about the editor's version and updates.

Main toolbar [2]

The main toolbar is a highly useful interface component within Unreal Editor, offering shortcuts to frequently used tools and commands. It is thoughtfully divided into distinct areas, each serving a specific purpose:

Figure 1.6 – The main toolbar

Here's a closer look at some key features you'll frequently use from the main toolbar:

- **Save**: This button serves as a quick means to save the currently open level. However, it should be noted that it only saves the progress made within the current level and not any new assets created during your work.
- **Selection Mode**: Within this section, you'll find shortcuts that enable rapid switching between different editing modes tailored for specific content within your level:
    - **Selection**: Used for selecting and manipulating objects
    - **Landscape**: Specifically designed for terrain and landscape editing
    - **Foliage**: Focused on vegetation placement and editing
    - **Mesh Painting**: Ideal for applying and editing textures or materials on meshes
    - **Modeling**: For detailed 3D modeling and object creation; requires the **Modeling Tools Editor Mode** plugin to be enabled
    - **Fracture**: Designed for fracturing objects and dealing with destructible elements
    - **Brush Editing**: Primarily used for shaping and sculpting geometry
    - **Animation**: Dedicated to animation-related tasks
- **Content Shortcuts**: This segment provides shortcuts for adding and accessing common types of content within the Level Editor:
    - **Create**: Offers a list of frequently used assets for convenient addition to your level. It also grants access to the **Place Actors** panels, facilitating quick asset placement.
    - **Blueprints**: Enables the creation and access of Blueprints, a vital aspect of Unreal Engine's visual scripting system.
    - **Cinematics**: Streamlines the creation of cinematic sequences, including Level sequences and master sequences.

- **Play Mode**: Here, you'll find shortcut buttons that allow you to initiate and experience your game directly within the editor. It's a valuable tool for testing and previewing your project's functionality.
- **Platforms**: This section contains an array of options for configuring, preparing, and deploying your project to various platforms, including desktop, mobile devices, and consoles. It streamlines the process of ensuring your project is compatible with your target platform.
- **Settings**: This category encompasses a range of configuration options related to the Unreal Editor, the Level Editor Viewport, and the behavior of your game. It provides flexibility and control over your editing environment and project execution.

Level Viewport [3]

The **Level Viewport** is a critical component of the Unreal Editor interface, serving as the canvas where the contents of the currently open level are displayed and edited. It provides a dynamic visual representation of your level, enabling you to interact with and manipulate the various elements that comprise your project.

In *Figure 1.7*, we can see the Level Viewport. Additionally, it's possible to observe that within its workspace, there are other tools and functionalities.

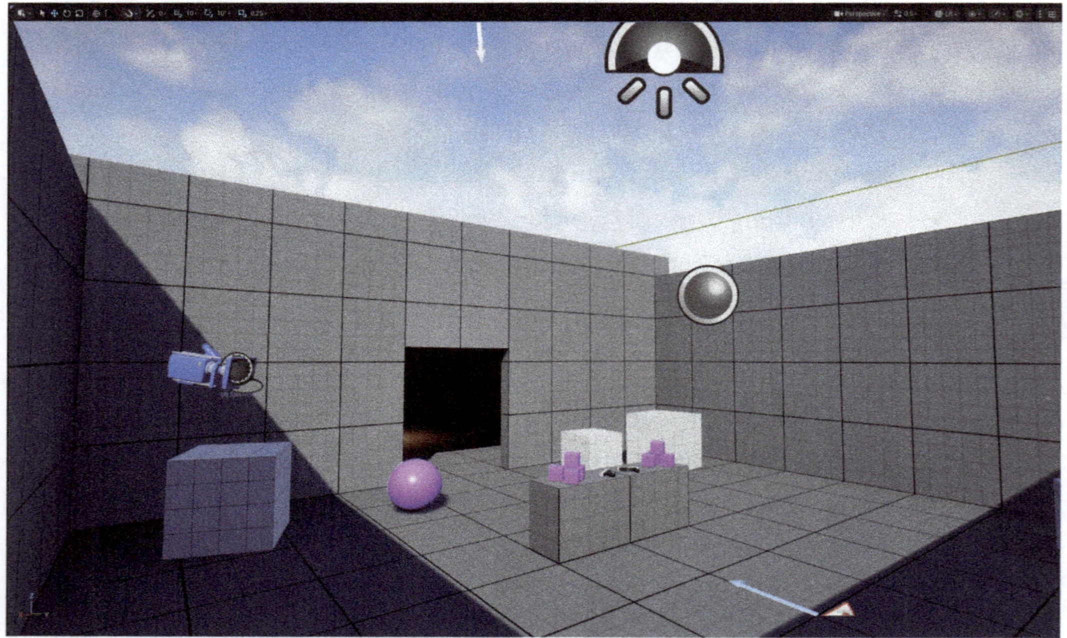

Figure 1.7 – Level Viewport

Understanding the functionalities available within this key interface can greatly enhance your development workflow:

- **View modes**: The Level Viewport offers two primary ways to display the contents of your level:
  - **Perspective view**: This view provides a 3D perspective, allowing you to navigate and explore your level from different angles. It offers a lifelike representation of your environment, making it ideal for assessing the visual aesthetics and spatial relationships of your assets.
  - **Orthographic view**: In contrast, this view offers a 2D representation by looking directly down one of the main axes (*X*, *Y*, or *Z*). This view mode simplifies the visualization of your level in a more structured and planar manner, making it well-suited for precise alignment and adjustments.
- **Viewport controls**: Within the Level Viewport window, you'll notice a set of buttons located in the upper-left corner:

Figure 1.8 – The Viewport controls

In *Figure 1.8*, from left to right, these buttons include the following:

- **Viewport options**: Clicking this button reveals a menu with various Viewport-related options, enabling you to customize your viewing experience according to your specific needs.
- **Perspective**: Toggles between the **Perspective** and **Orthographic** view modes, allowing you to seamlessly switch between 3D exploration and 2D precision as required.
- **View Mode**: The **View Mode** drop-down list within the Level Viewport of Unreal Editor offers an array of versatile viewing modes to enhance the user's experience during project development. These modes serve various purposes, from assessing the visual quality of a level with **Lit Mode** to simplifying the view with **Unlit Mode** for precision alignment. These modes empower users to tailor their level's visual representation to their specific tasks, enhancing productivity within Unreal Editor. For example, here is what each of these modes does:
  - **Detail Lighting Mode** spotlights intricate lighting details
  - **Lighting Complexity Mode** helps identify resource-intensive lighting areas

    - **Shader Complexity Mode** pinpoints shader-heavy regions
    - **Wireframe Mode** simplifies geometry inspection
    - **Collision Mode** reveals collision geometry
    - **Lightmap Density Mode** visualizes the lightmap resolution distribution
    - **Quad Overdraw Mode** identifies rendering inefficiencies
    - **Level of Detail (LOD) Mode** allows previewing object detail levels
    - **Buffer Visualization** provides access to rendering buffers for in-depth analysis
- **Show**: Clicking this button reveals additional display options, providing control over what elements are visible within the Viewport, aiding in efficient content editing.
- **Scalability**: In this panel, you can control the quality balance of different rendering groups, such as **View Distance**, **Anti-Aliasing**, **Shadow**, **Global Illumination**, **Effects**, or **Foliage**.
- **Translation and snappings:** Translation options provide control over object movement, including freeform translation for unrestricted placement and switching your gizmo between local and world coordinate systems. You can also control grid snapping for precise alignment to a grid, angle, or scale values. You can also control your camera speed.

Content Browser [4]

The Unreal Engine **Content Browser** is a central and indispensable tool for managing and organizing assets within your project. It serves as a comprehensive hub for importing, creating, browsing, and manipulating various types of assets, including 3D models, textures, audio files, materials, Blueprints, and more.

Figure 1.9 – The Content Browser

Among its possibilities, the **Content Browser** helps us with the following:

- **Asset management**: It enables users to efficiently organize, search, and categorize assets. You can create folders, subfolders, and collections to structure your assets logically, making it easy to locate and access what you need.
- **Asset creation**: Users can create new assets directly within the **Content Browser**. Whether it's a new material, Blueprint, or other asset type, this feature streamlines the asset creation process.
- **Import and export**: Importing assets into your project is straightforward with the **Content Browser**. Supported file formats include FBX, OBJ, WAV, PNG, and many others. You can also export assets for use in other applications.
- **Preview and thumbnail generation**: It generates thumbnails for assets, providing visual previews that aid in identifying assets quickly. This feature is particularly helpful when working with large asset libraries.
- **Asset information**: Detailed information about each asset is readily accessible. You can view properties, such as file size, import settings, and references, helping you manage assets more effectively.
- **Asset interactions**: Drag-and-drop functionality simplifies asset placement within your level or Blueprint graphs. You can easily reference and link assets to other parts of your project, fostering efficient asset integration.
- **Filtering and sorting**: Robust filtering and sorting options enable users to refine their asset searches based on various criteria, such as asset type, date modified, or keywords, streamlining asset retrieval.

Bottom toolbar [5]

The bottom toolbar serves as a valuable resource within the Unreal Editor interface, offering convenient shortcuts to essential tools and features while also providing important status information.

The bottom toolbar can be found at the bottom of the editor window in Unreal Engine and looks like this:

Figure 1.10 – The bottom toolbar

The bottom toolbar is divided into distinct sections, each contributing to an efficient workflow:

- **Output Log**: Positioned as a debugging tool, **Output Log** serves as a critical resource for developers. It provides real-time feedback by displaying useful information, warnings, errors, and debugging messages. This feature aids in identifying and resolving issues during the development process, ensuring the smooth functioning of your project.
- **Command Console**: The Command Console, functioning akin to a traditional command-line interface, empowers users to trigger specific editor behaviors through the input of console commands. This direct interaction with the editor allows for rapid execution of various actions, streamlining the editing process.
- **Derived Data**: This section offers access to **Derived Data** functionality. **Derived Data** encompasses preprocessed and optimized assets, including textures and shaders, that enhance the efficiency of your project. It is an integral part of Unreal Engine's asset management system, ensuring that assets are readily available in the desired format, contributing to optimal runtime performance.
- **Source Control Status**: This area provides critical information about the source control status of your project, particularly if your project is connected to a source control system such as SVN, Git, or Perforce. It serves as a visual indicator, displaying the current source control status. If the project is not connected to source control, it will indicate **Revision Control is disabled**.

Outliner [6]

The **Outliner** panel is a powerful organizational tool within Unreal Editor, offering a hierarchical view of all the content present in your level. Typically situated in the upper-right corner of the Unreal Editor window by default, it provides a visual representation of the assets and objects that populate your project.

You can see an example of its representation in the following figure:

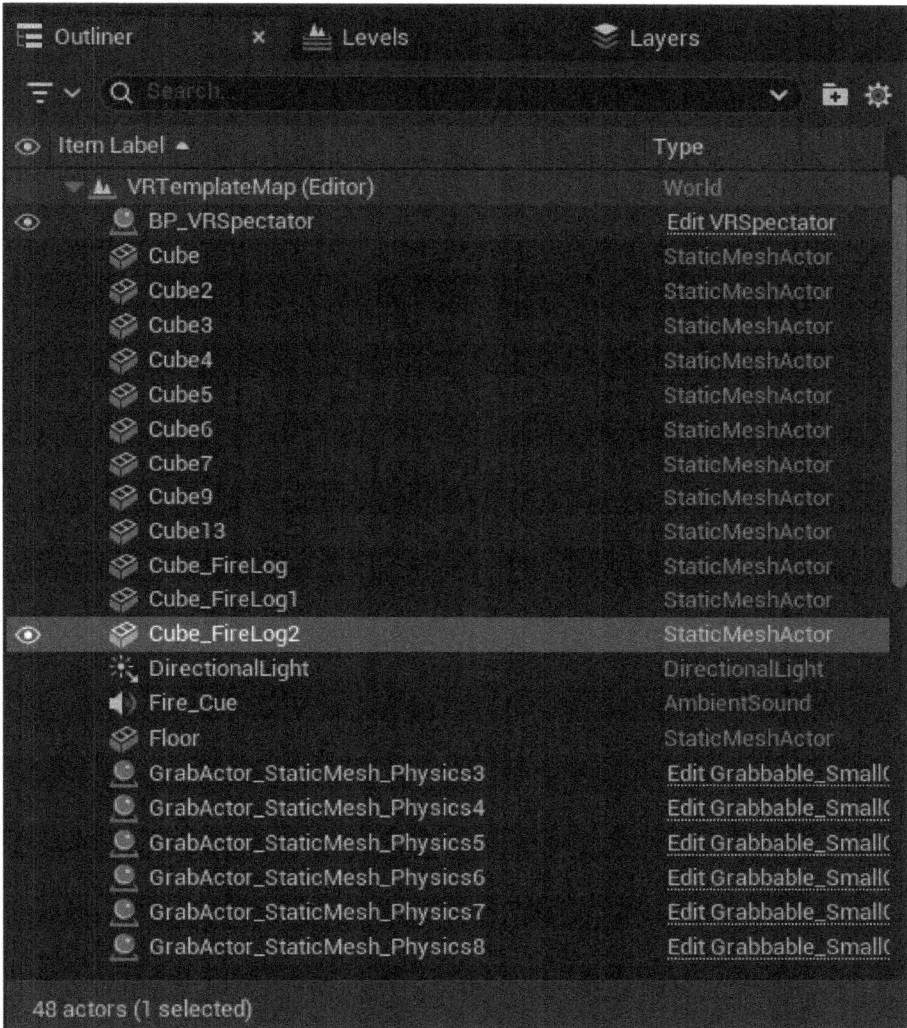

Figure 1.11 – The Outliner panel

Beyond its fundamental role as a content hierarchy viewer, the **Outliner** panel offers several valuable functionalities:

- **Visibility control**: You can efficiently manage the visibility of Actors within your level by interacting with the associated **eye** button in **Outliner**. This allows you to instantly toggle the visibility of specific Actors on or off, enhancing your control over the visual representation of your scene.

Important note

Be aware that hiding the Actors in the level with the **eye** button will not hide them while in **Play Mode** or **Runtime**. If you play, simulate, or render your cinematic, you must disable its visibility or enable **Actor Hidden in Game** from the **Details** panel.

- **Contextual interaction**: *Right-clicking* on an Actor in the **Outliner** panel opens an Actor-specific context menu. This menu grants you access to a range of additional operations and settings that pertain to the selected Actor. It provides a convenient means to perform targeted actions on individual assets, streamlining your editing process.
- **Folder management**: The **Outliner** panel extends its capabilities beyond Actors and assets. It also facilitates the creation, movement, and deletion of content folders within your project. This feature aids in maintaining a well-organized project structure, ensuring that assets are logically grouped and easily accessible.

In essence, the **Outliner** panel not only offers an overview of your level's content hierarchy but also provides essential tools for asset visibility control, contextual interaction with individual Actors, and efficient content folder management. By harnessing these capabilities, you can navigate and manage your project with greater ease and precision within Unreal Engine.

Details panel [7]

The **Details** panel is a central component of Unreal Engine 5's user interface, offering a wealth of information and control over the properties and attributes of selected objects or Actors within your project.

You can see an example of its representation in the following figure:

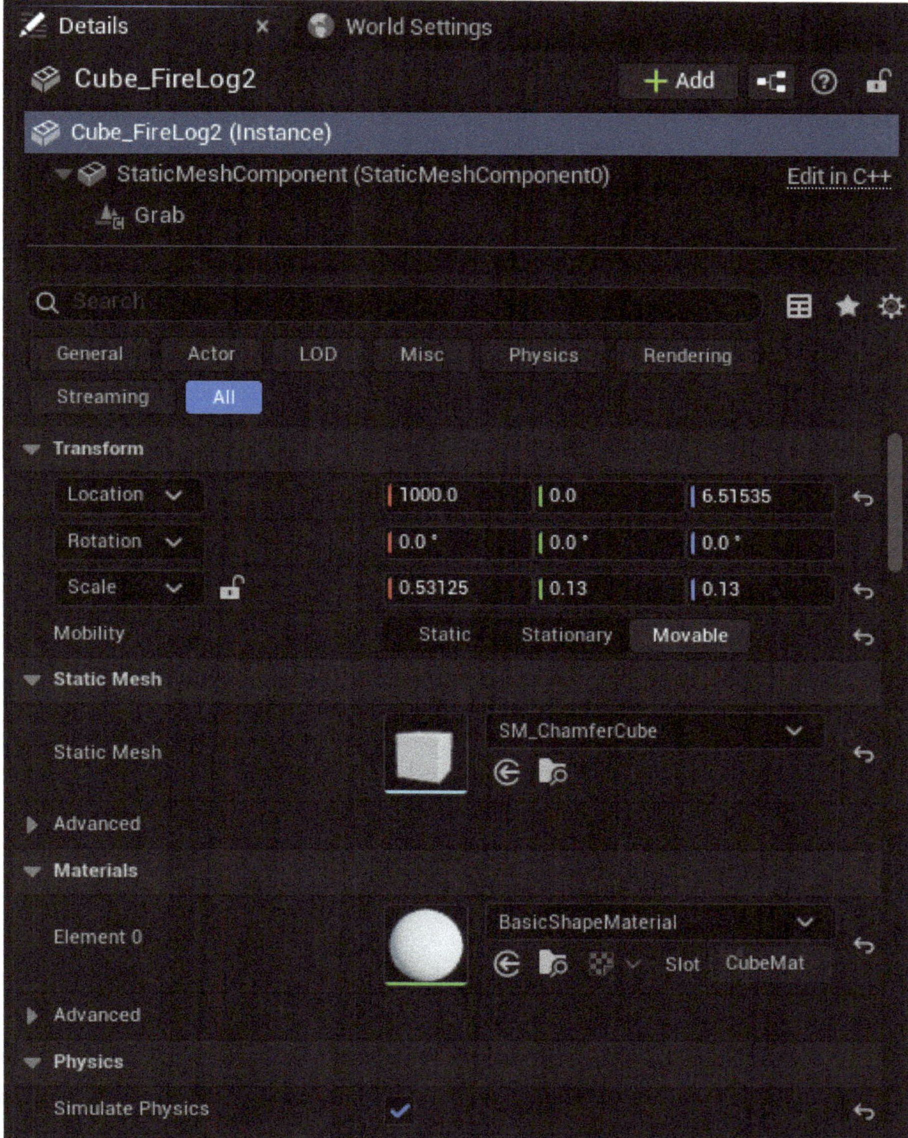

Figure 1.12 – The Details panel

Positioned typically on the right-hand side of the Unreal Editor interface, the **Details** panel provides a comprehensive set of features and functions, and it's grouped normally without tabs such as **Level Details** or **World Settings**, as shown in *Figure 1.12*.

The main functions of the **Details** panel are as follows:

- **Property inspection**: At its core, the **Details** panel serves as a hub for inspecting and managing the properties of selected objects. When you select an Actor, asset, or component in your level, the panel dynamically populates with relevant information, presenting a detailed breakdown of its attributes. This includes essential properties such as transforming data (position, rotation, and scale), mesh references, materials, and more.
- **Customization and editing**: Beyond passive property display, the **Details** panel empowers users to customize and modify these attributes. It provides interactive fields and controls, allowing for direct input and manipulation of object properties. For instance, you can precisely adjust an Actor's position or change its material assignment by interacting with these fields, fostering granular control over your level's elements.
- **Component management**: For complex Actors composed of multiple components (e.g., static meshes, lights, and cameras), the **Details** panel offers a hierarchical view of these components. This hierarchy enables users to navigate and edit the properties of individual components within the context of the larger Actor, streamlining the editing process.
- **Advanced features**: Advanced users can leverage additional features within the **Details** panel, such as Actor tagging, collision settings, replication parameters, and more. These options provide fine-tuned control over object behavior and interactions in your project.

We've covered the basics of the Unreal Engine interface, touching on everything from the menu bar and toolbar to the **Content Browser** and **Details** panel. This overview gives you a good starting point for diving into game and application development with Unreal Engine.

Summary

In this chapter, we began with the installation of the Epic Games Launcher. We ensured that your system met the required hardware specifications, covering both minimum and recommended configurations, to optimize your Unreal Engine experience. Building a strong foundation, we introduced you to key terminology within the Unreal Engine ecosystem, essential for effective communication in the world of game development.

Transitioning into practical application, we focused on project setup and templates, enabling you to create and configure Unreal Engine projects tailored to your vision. From selecting target platforms to fine-tuning ray tracing settings, you gained the skills needed to initiate your projects efficiently. Our exploration concluded with an in-depth tour of the Unreal Engine interface, empowering you with insights into its various components and functions, setting the stage for your creative journey.

In the next chapter, we dive into Quixel Bridge, Megascans, and Fab within Unreal Engine 5. This immersive journey will guide you through asset selection, acquisition, and the process of managing these libraries effectively. With a focus on technical efficiency and creative potential, you'll learn how to seamlessly integrate top-tier assets into your Unreal Engine projects. These tools support a smoother workflow and offer reliable ways to enhance your game development and world-building process.

2

Quixel Bridge, Megascans, and Fab

In this chapter, we will progress deeper into the technicalities of **Unreal Engine 5** (**UE5**), turning our focus to its integral asset management tools and plugins that are essential for project development. Building on the foundational understanding established in the first chapter, this chapter aims to dissect the functionalities of the Fab platform, the technical aspects of the Quixel Bridge plugin, and the ever-growing Megascans library.

After exploring the ecosystem surrounding Unreal Engine and the set of acquisitions by Epic Games, we will talk about **Fab**, the latest marketplace innovation from Epic Games. This section will dissect its role in unifying the digital asset offerings from Quixel, Sketchfab, Unreal Engine Marketplace (now Fab), and ArtStation Marketplace. Emphasis will be placed on navigating its extensive catalog encompassing 3D models, materials, sound effects, VFX, and digital humans, and integrating these assets into a unified workflow within Unreal Engine.

The **Quixel Bridge plugin** is a crucial component of the Unreal Engine ecosystem, providing a user-friendly interface for accessing and managing the Megascans library directly within the **Level Editor**. It enables advanced features such as asset browsing, targeted searches, and seamless integration of assets, including MetaHumans, into Unreal Engine projects.

Following that, we delve into the specifics of the **Megascans library**. As a comprehensive repository of high-fidelity 3D assets, tileable surfaces, and various environmental materials, Megascans offers unparalleled realism and detail, which is pivotal for creating immersive environments. The chapter will cover how Megascans assets are downloaded and imported into Unreal Engine, and how they are organized and configured once added to a project.

Key topics to be covered in this chapter include the following:

- Evolution of the Unreal Engine ecosystem and understanding its acquisitions
- Introducing Fab – one engine, one marketplace
- Introducing Quixel Bridge
- Importing and integrating Megascans assets
- Understanding the imported resources
- Exercise 2.1: Adding a 3D asset from Quixel Bridge to Unreal Engine
- Exercise 2.2: Selecting and applying a material to a Static Mesh
- Why is asset configuration important in Quixel Bridge?

This chapter is designed to provide deep technical insight into these tools, focusing on both the efficiency and quality of asset management and integration in UE5.

Technical requirements

The technical requirements for this chapter follow the same specifications as *Chapter 1*. Please refer to that chapter, but let's remember the recommended hardware for working with UE5 with **Lumen Global Illumination and Reflections** and **Nanite** virtualized geometry:

- **Operating system**: Windows 10 64-bit version 1909 revision .1350 or higher, or versions 2004 and 20H2 revision .789 or higher. Support for DirectX 12 Agility SDK
- **Processor**: Quad-core Intel or AMD, 2.5 GHz or faster
- **Memory**: 8 GB RAM
- **Software Ray Tracing**: This feature may require a video card using DirectX 11 with support for Shader Model 5
- **Hardware Ray Tracing**: This requires Windows 10 build 1909.1350 or newer with DirectX 12 support and specific compatible graphics cards (e.g., NVIDIA RTX-2000 series or newer, AMD RX-6000 series or newer, Intel® Arc™ A-series graphics cards or newer)
- **Internet access**: An internet connection is required to download the plugins and additional content required for this chapter

Evolution of the Unreal Engine ecosystem and understanding its acquisitions

Let's take a small step back to understand the dynamic and ever-expanding universe of the Unreal Engine ecosystem. Its main goal is to be a comprehensive suite of tools and platforms that collectively redefine the landscape of digital creation. While many resources within the ecosystem are free to use, such as Quixel assets when working inside Unreal Engine, other tools and platforms follow their own licensing or marketplace models.

At its core, Unreal Engine provides a powerful and versatile engine for game development, virtual production, and real-time 3D creation. However, the ecosystem extends far beyond the engine itself, encompassing a range of acquisitions and integrations designed to empower creators across various disciplines.

To contextualize the evolution of the Unreal Engine ecosystem, it is crucial to examine its strategic expansions and acquisitions closely. The subsequent subsections covering Unreal Engine Marketplace (now known as Fab), Quixel, ArtStation, and Sketchfab serve as key pillars in understanding how Epic Games has enhanced Unreal Engine's capabilities and offerings. Each platform, with its unique contributions, has been integral to broadening the scope of tools and assets available to creators.

Unreal Engine Marketplace (now Fab)

Launched on September 4, 2014, the **Unreal Engine Marketplace** stood as a cornerstone in digital creation, offering a vast array of art, assets, and tools tailored for Unreal Engine use. It democratized game development and digital art by providing accessible, high-quality resources. The Marketplace fostered a vibrant community and laid the groundwork for what would become **Fab**, Epic Games' unified platform that now integrates Marketplace, Quixel, and other Epic asset libraries into a single ecosystem (see the *Introducing Fab – one engine, one marketplace* section). Its inception marked a significant milestone in Unreal Engine's evolution as a comprehensive tool for real-time 3D creation.

Quixel

On November 12, 2019, a significant announcement was made at the Unreal Engine Academy in London by Epic Games: **Quixel** was to become a part of its expansive ecosystem. This integration marked a pivotal moment for Unreal Engine users, as it meant unrestricted access to the entire Megascans library at no additional cost.

Note

If you'd like to explore more about this integration and its implications, we recommend checking out the following link: `https://www.unrealengine.com/en-US/blog/epic-games-and-quixel-join-forces-to-empower-creators`.

ArtStation

On April 30, 2021, Epic Games announced the acquisition of **ArtStation**, a leading platform in the digital artist community. This significant move integrates ArtStation's extensive network of artists and its rich repository of creative content into the Epic Games ecosystem. The acquisition is aimed at empowering artists across various disciplines, providing them with more resources and tools.

Note

For more detailed information and insights on this acquisition, check out this link: `https://www.epicgames.com/site/en-US/news/artstation-is-now-part-of-epic-games`.

Sketchfab

On July 21, 2021, Epic Games and Sketchfab announced a significant development in the 3D content creation and distribution landscape. **Sketchfab**, known for its extensive web-based service that simplifies the discovery, editing, purchase, and sale of 3D content, joined the Epic Games family. Sketchfab has a robust collection of over 4 million 3D assets and comprehensive technology integrations across major 3D tools and platforms. This move is a strategic step toward expanding the creator ecosystem and advancing the vision of an interconnected metaverse.

Note

For more information about Sketchfab, visit the following link: `https://www.epicgames.com/site/en-US/news/sketchfab-is-now-part-of-epic-games`.

Overall, Unreal Engine is a powerful, flexible platform for digital creation. From the foundational engine to the diverse and strategic integrations and creations, such as the Unreal Engine Marketplace (now Fab), ArtStation, Sketchfab, Twinmotion, and RealityCapture, the ecosystem is crafted to address a wide spectrum of creative needs.

This broader framework also includes advanced technologies for creating photorealistic digital humans, exemplified by the MetaHuman project. This highlights Epic Games' commitment to pushing the frontiers of technology and creativity. This ecosystem not only advances the state of the art in digital tools but also nurtures an ever-growing community of artists, developers, and creators. It stands as a testament to the limitless possibilities of digital innovation, inviting users to explore, create, and redefine the boundaries of digital art and technology.

Transitioning from the overview of the Unreal Engine ecosystem and its notable acquisitions, we'll now focus on a detailed exploration of Fab, Epic Games' unified marketplace platform that consolidates asset sources such as Quixel, Sketchfab, and ArtStation.

Introducing Fab – one Engine, one marketplace

Fab, a groundbreaking open marketplace developed by Epic Games, represents a *significant unification of several key digital asset platforms*. It amalgamates the resources from Sketchfab, Quixel Megascans, MetaHuman, ArtStation, and Unreal Engine Marketplace into a singular, cohesive platform. The integration of Fab within Unreal Engine is set to offer a user experience akin to the current functionality of Bridge, streamlining the process of selecting and integrating content directly into your scene.

The Epic Games team has envisioned Fab as a multiplatform tool, capable of hosting content from all the tools it owns and making it easier for users to work not only in UE5 and **Unreal Editor for Fortnite** (**UEFN**), but also in other DCC tools and applications. The most common way to work with Fab is through its website (`https://www.fab.com/`). That said, it also includes a plugin that integrates directly into Unreal Engine.

In *Figure 2.1*, we can see Fab's main page and its structure:

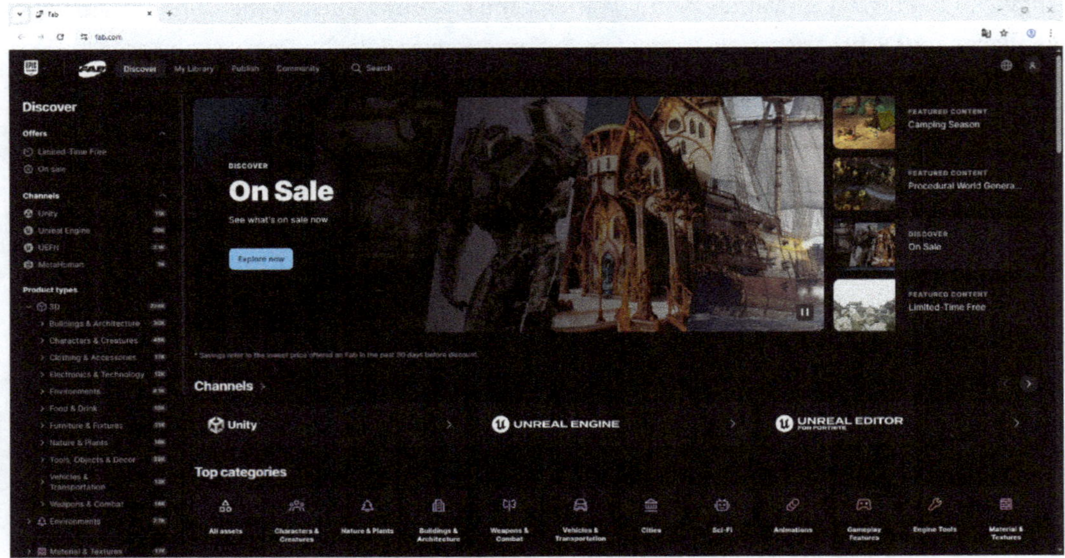

Figure 2.1 – Fab's landing page

At a glance, we can get an idea of the platform's structure. On the left-hand side, there is the **Discover** panel, where resources are organized into **channels**, which group the various platforms currently supported by Fab (such as Quixel, Sketchfab, and ArtStation). In the central area, the content is presented in a simplified way, showcasing the featured content and top categories from the past month.

Searching for assets on Fab

While an Epic Games account is not required to browse the platform and view the available content, it is essential in order to download both free and paid assets.

To sign in or create an account, click the **user** icon in the top-right corner of Fab. For help, see `https://www.epicgames.com/help/en-US/c-202300000001645/c-202300000001752/a202300000018101`. The **search bar** is available on all Fab pages. Clicking it lets you start filtering content. As you type, a popup suggests filters such as game engines, tags, and publishers.

You can refine your search using Boolean operators such as `AND` and `OR` for more accurate results. For deeper filtering, use the side panel and filter menu. The panel updates dynamically with a **Search In** section that includes **Products** and **Publisher**.

Figure 2.2 shows how the search bar and filters work together to display relevant content:

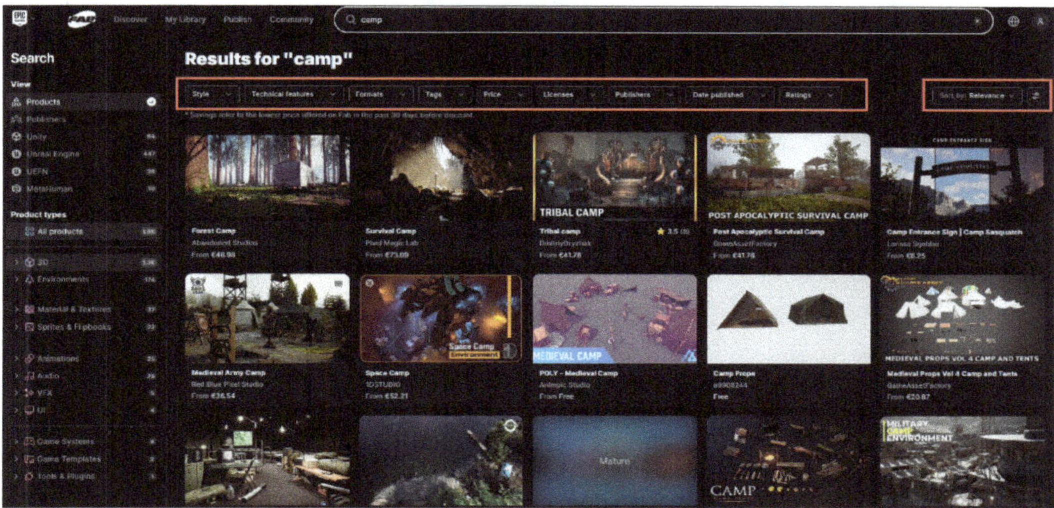

Figure 2.2 – Search and filter menus

We could spend hours browsing assets on Fab, especially with filters by platform, asset type, price, and more. But what exactly can we find on a product page?

Browsing and acquiring assets on Fab

Let's take `POLY - Medieval Camp` by Animpic Studio (`https://www.fab.com/listings/436d467a-6955-4aac-be0d-a05c99966ea2`) as an example. Clicking on it opens the product page.

In the center, there's a gallery with screenshots or videos and a description of the asset. On the right, you'll find a summary with key details, such as publisher, rating, pricing, and licensing, as shown in *Figure 2.3*:

Figure 2.3 – Product page

Fab provides access to both free and paid digital assets through an intuitive interface. From your wishlist, you can hover over any item and click the **cart** icon to select a license. Paid items are added to your cart, while free items can be added directly to your library. To remove a product from your wishlist, simply click the **trash** icon and an undo option will briefly appear.

To purchase a product, open its page, choose a license from the drop-down menu, and click **Buy Now** or **Add to Cart**. If required, you'll be prompted to accept the latest **End User License Agreement** (**EULA**). After reviewing your cart, proceed to checkout and follow the payment steps. Once the order is complete, you'll receive confirmation and be able to download your products from the listing or from **My Library**.

Unreal Engine and UEFN products must be downloaded through the Fab plugin or the Epic Games Launcher.

Free content on Fab is easy to find and claim. You can filter by **Price** | **Free** or explore the **Limited-Time Free** section under **Discover** | **Offers**. Products may also appear under the **Free Content** category or on dedicated promotional pages.

To acquire a free asset, accept the EULA and either download the asset directly or add it to your library.

My Library and Downloads

All acquired products are stored in the **My Library** tab on Fab, which provides a centralized view of your assets. From this section, you can browse your collection, use the search bar, and apply filters to quickly locate specific items.

Note

While downloads can be anonymous, signing in is required to save items to your library for future use. In *Figure 2.4*, you can see all acquired items stored in the **My Library** section.

Figure 2.4 – My Library

While all available formats provided by the creator can be downloaded directly from the Fab website, there are additional methods for accessing and managing content.

Using Fab with Unreal Engine

For assets intended for Unreal Engine, files are also available through the Fab Library in the Epic Games Launcher when using the same Epic Games account. To ensure products appear in the Launcher, you must first add them to your Fab Library. Once added, the assets become accessible within the Launcher's **Library** section, allowing you to easily integrate them into your Unreal Engine projects, as we can see in *Figure 2.5*:

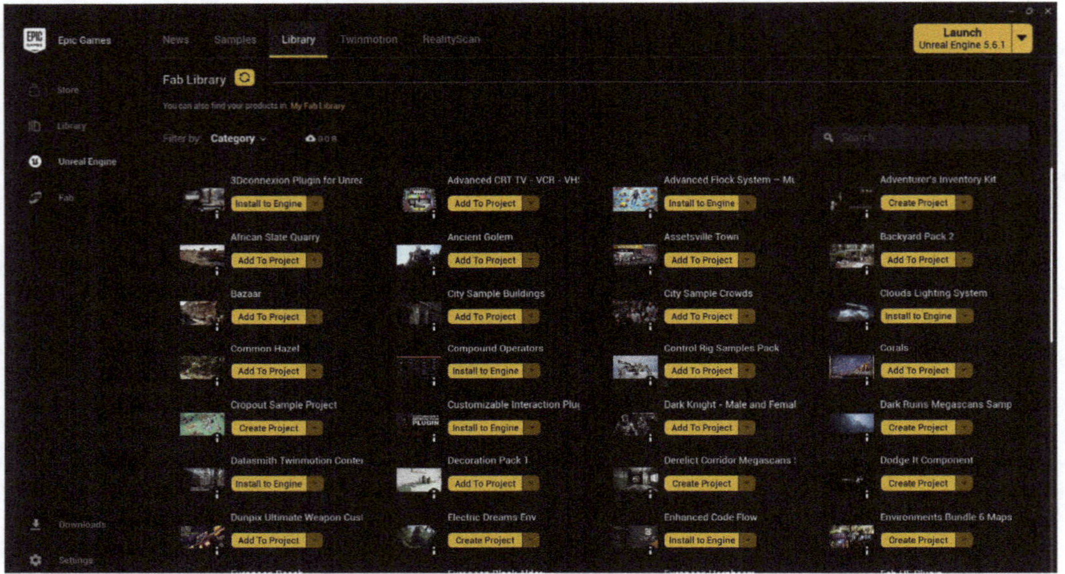

Figure 2.5 – Epic Games Launcher – Fab Library

Note

If you have UE version 5.3 or 5.4 installed, you'll need to download the plugin manually from the Fab Library in the Epic Games Launcher. For new engine installations or updates, the plugin is included automatically.

Once installed, Fab can be accessed within Unreal Engine from the top menu via **Window** | **Fab**, or through the Content Drawer by clicking the **Fab** icon on the toolbar (see *Figure 2.6*). Sample projects require adding the asset to your library and downloading it through the Launcher, while non-project-based content can be imported directly into an open project.

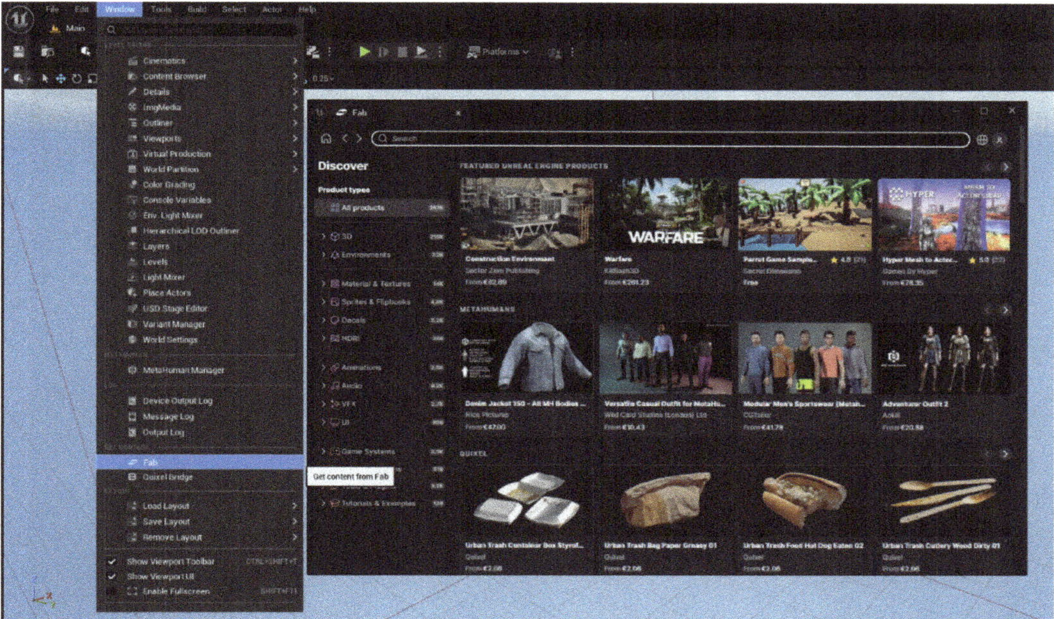

Figure 2.6 – Fab tool location and interface inside Unreal Engine

Fab represents a significant stride in digital asset management and integration, engineered by Epic Games. As a unified marketplace, it brings together an array of assets from different platforms in the Unreal Engine ecosystem. This integration within Unreal Engine mirrors the functionality of Quixel Bridge, providing a streamlined and efficient process for selecting and importing diverse digital assets directly into project scenes. Users can also inspect details such as topology, textures, and animations through the integrated Sketchfab 3D Viewer, ensuring well-informed decisions when selecting content.

With a user-friendly interface and a vast library of high-quality assets, Fab streamlines the workflow for Unreal Engine users. Its integration reflects Epic Games' ongoing commitment to empowering creators and enhancing the Unreal Engine ecosystem.

One of the key technologies behind Fab's ecosystem is Quixel, whose tool, most notably Quixel Bridge, forms a fundamental part of Unreal Engine's real-time world-building pipeline. In the next section, we'll explore how Quixel Bridge powers high-quality asset workflows and plays a central role in environment creation within Unreal Engine.

Introducing Quixel Bridge

In this section, we will shift our focus to practical application, specifically working with **Quixel Bridge** within the Unreal Engine environment. To begin this hands-on exploration, the first step is to open your Unreal Engine project. Quixel Bridge, seamlessly integrated into Unreal Engine, is a powerful portal to an extensive library of high-quality assets. This integration streamlines the process of importing photorealistic 3D assets directly into your project, enhancing both efficiency and the visual quality of your work.

Enabling Quixel Bridge for Unreal Engine

Quixel Bridge is incorporated by default within your installation of UE5. To verify and activate the Quixel Bridge plugin in your Unreal Engine environment, follow these steps:

1. Navigate to **Edit** and then select **Plugins** from the drop-down menu.
2. In the **Plugins** window, utilize the search functionality by typing `Quixel Bridge` into the search bar.
3. Upon locating the Quixel Bridge plugin, ensure its activation by clicking the checkbox next to it, as shown in *Figure 2.7*:

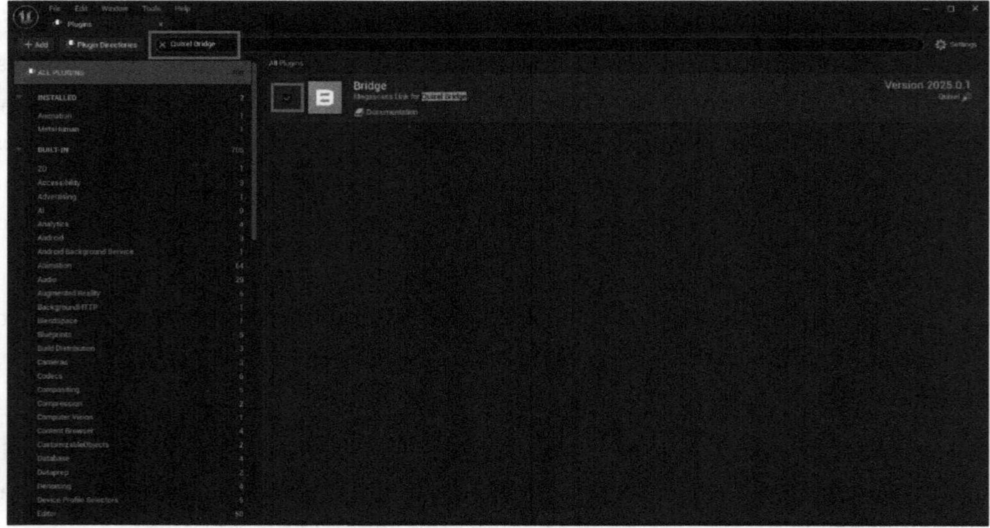

Figure 2.7 – Searching for the Quixel Bridge plugin

4. In instances where the **Quixel Bridge** plugin is not listed in your **Plugins** window, an additional installation step through the Epic Games Launcher may be necessary. To do this, take the following steps:

    1. Open the Epic Games Launcher and navigate to the **Library** section.
    2. Within this area, scroll to the **Fab Library** section and enter `bridge` in the search bar, as seen in *Figure 2.8*.
    3. Upon finding Quixel Bridge in the search results, select **Install to Engine**. This will integrate the plugin with your Unreal Engine.

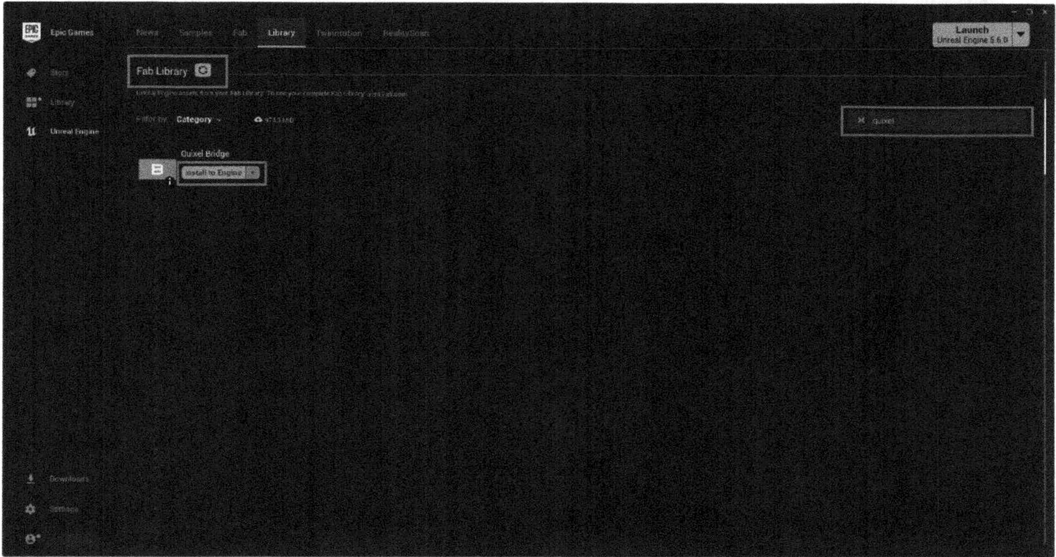

Figure 2.8 – Epic Games Fab Library

After completing the installation, relaunch Unreal Engine to enable the newly installed Quixel Bridge plugin by returning to **Edit** | **Plugins**.

Launching Quixel Bridge in Unreal Engine

Within the Unreal Engine editor, Quixel Bridge is accessible from multiple locations, offering flexibility in how you integrate assets into your projects. Here are the methods to access Quixel Bridge:

- One straightforward method is through the content shortcuts—a quick and efficient entry point.
- Alternatively, you can access Quixel Bridge via the top menu by selecting **Window** and then choosing **Quixel Bridge** from the drop-down options.

- Another convenient pathway is in the **Content Browser**; simply *right-click* on an empty space and navigate to the **Get Content** section to find Quixel Bridge.

We can see here the three different options to access Quixel Bridge:

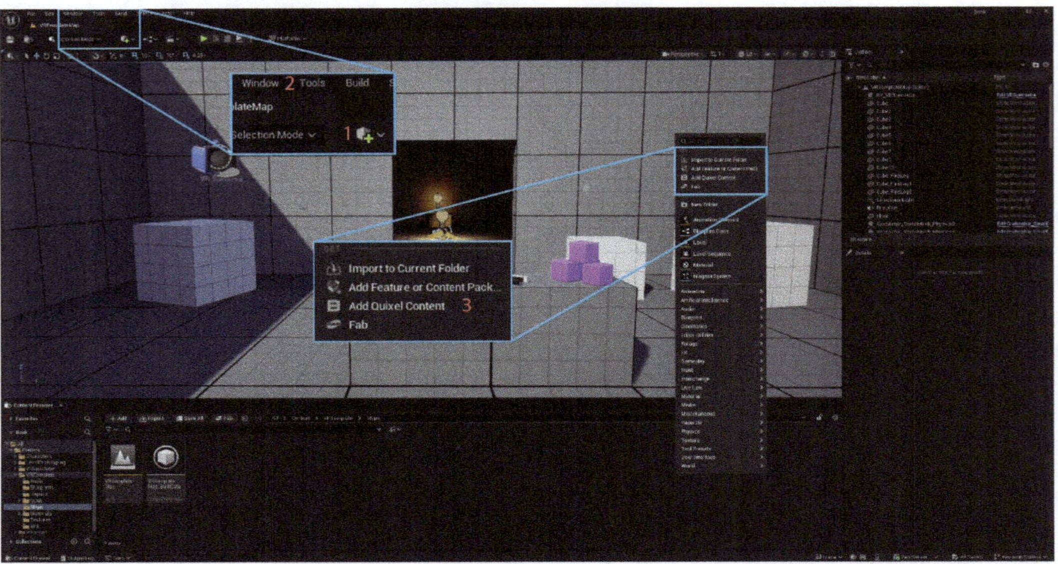

Figure 2.9 – Locations from where Quixel Bridge is accessible

It's recommended to try each of them, as this will allow you to set your preference for the future.

Using Quixel Bridge for Unreal Engine

Quixel Bridge, tailored for integration with Unreal Engine, is designed to be compatible across multiple operating systems, including Windows, macOS, and Linux.

A key operational requirement for Quixel Bridge is an *active internet connection*. This connectivity is essential for both displaying and downloading assets from its online content library. However, Quixel Bridge also accommodates scenarios where an internet connection might not be available. In such instances, you can still access your locally stored content. This is achieved by navigating to the **Local** tab, which is conveniently located in the left navigation pane of Quixel Bridge. Here, you can browse and utilize assets that have been previously downloaded and stored on your disk, ensuring that your workflow remains uninterrupted even when offline.

Browsing the content

Within Unreal Engine, Quixel Bridge operates as a versatile floating window, offering a high degree of adaptability to suit your workflow. Its interface is designed for customization, allowing you to resize and reposition the window according to your convenience and screen layout. We can see the Quixel Bridge interface here as an example:

Figure 2.10 – Quixel Bridge – asset selection and details

At the core of Quixel Bridge's user interface is a search bar, which you can use to swiftly search for specific items across various categories. To further enhance your search, Quixel Bridge incorporates a filter bar, equipped with a range of specific filters, such as asset type, color, biome, state, and size. This filter bar can be easily shown or hidden by clicking the **filter** icon located in the top-right corner.

On the left side of the Quixel Bridge panel, a series of buttons provides access to different tabs, each serving a distinct purpose:

- **Home**: This tab is organized into sections displaying the latest collections, trending assets, and the newest uploads across all categories. It features a structured category tree with multiple levels of subcategories, listing all available asset types. Filtering by category and subcategory is also available here.

- **Collections**: Here, you will find curated content, including references and renders across various biomes, essentials, architectural selections, tutorial assets, and community collections.
- **MetaHuman**: For users engaging with the MetaHuman Creator app (`https://metahuman.unrealengine.com/`), the **My MetaHumans** page under the **MetaHumans** tab in Quixel Bridge offers access to created characters. These can be downloaded and seamlessly integrated into your projects.
- **Favorites**: Any asset within Quixel Bridge can be marked as a favorite for quick and easy future access. To favorite an asset, simply hover over it and click the **heart** icon.
- **Local**: This section displays all assets that have been downloaded and are available on your machine, providing online and offline access to your local repository.

After understanding the main tabs, let's move on to working with Quixel Bridge assets.

Assets

In Quixel Bridge, selecting an asset opens an information panel that provides a detailed overview of its characteristics. This panel helps assess the asset's technical aspects and suitability for your project. Icons offer quick insights, such as file size, important for resource management and whether a texture is tileable, which is key for creating seamless environments.

The panel also shows related assets, aiding in finding visually consistent or complementary options and streamlining selection.

At the bottom of the right panel is a control for selecting the asset's download resolution.

Positioned at the bottom of the asset's right panel is a vital control for selecting the download resolution of the asset, as shown in *Figure 2.11*:

Figure 2.11 – Asset information from selected object in Quixel Bridge

This functionality lets you customize assets to fit your project's needs, offering resolution options that balance visual quality and performance. After selecting a resolution, you can download the asset or add it directly to your project.

Download settings

In the context of asset management within Quixel Bridge for Unreal Engine, it is essential to be aware of the default storage location for downloaded assets. These locations vary depending on the operating system you are using:

- For Windows users, assets are stored in `C:\Users\user\Documents\Megascans Library`
- On macOS, the default path is `~/Documents/Megascans Library`
- For Linux, assets are similarly placed in `~/Documents/Megascans Library`

Understanding asset storage is key, as high-quality downloads can quickly consume disk space. A large library may lead to significant storage use, so it's important to ensure sufficient space to avoid workflow disruptions.

Should you need to alter the default storage path for your assets, Quixel Bridge provides a straightforward method. To modify this setting, click on the **user** icon located in the top-right corner of the Quixel Bridge window and select **Preferences**:

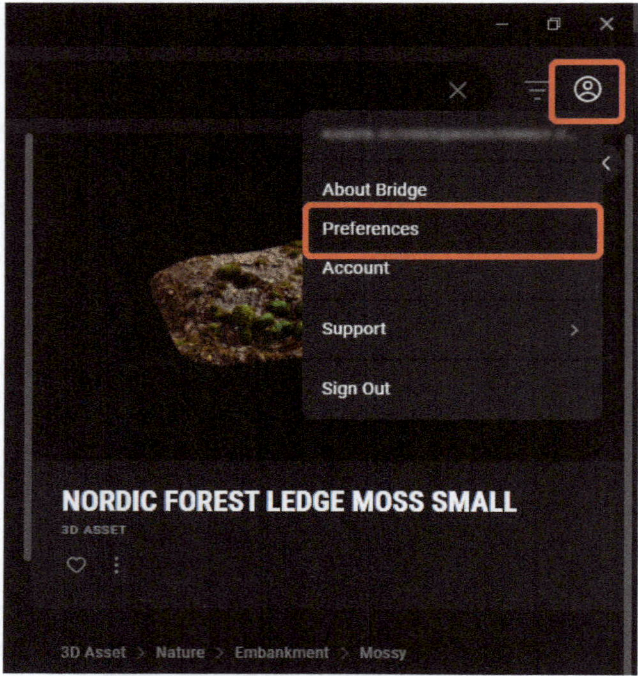

Figure 2.12 – Quixel Bridge Preferences

In the **Preferences** dialog, you will find an option to enter a new library path. Here, it specifies the desired destination for saving your future assets. After entering the new path, confirm the change by clicking **Save**. This adjustment allows you to customize the storage location of your assets, ensuring it aligns with your project organization and disk space management strategies.

Resolution

In Quixel Bridge, you are equipped with the capability to meticulously select the quality of each asset, be it a surface, decal, or any other type, according to the specific requirements of your project. This feature is fundamental in optimizing the balance between visual fidelity and performance efficiency in your projects.

All 3D assets within Quixel Bridge are made available in the UAsset format, a native Unreal Engine asset format that ensures seamless integration and compatibility. These 3D assets are offered in a range of resolutions to cater to diverse project needs. The available resolutions include Nanite, high, medium, and low. The Nanite resolution represents the cutting-edge of Unreal Engine's rendering technology, enabling highly detailed and complex geometries with minimal performance impact. The choice between high, medium, and low resolutions provides further flexibility, allowing you to choose an optimal balance of asset detail and resource allocation based on your project's scope and hardware capabilities.

Similarly, other asset types available in Quixel Bridge, such as surfaces, 3D plants, decals, and imperfections, are also accessible in multiple resolutions. These include the highest, high, medium, and low options, providing a spectrum of quality levels to align with various artistic visions and technical constraints. The highest resolution offers unparalleled detail and texture depth, ideal for close-up shots or high-resolution renders. On the other hand, lower resolutions are more suited for background elements or performance-intensive scenarios.

This granular control over asset resolution in Quixel Bridge empowers creators to tailor their asset choices precisely, ensuring that each element within their Unreal Engine project is optimized for both visual quality and performance efficiency.

Export settings

In Quixel Bridge, each asset's specific export settings are accessible via the asset's information panel, providing you with precise control over how assets are exported or integrated into your Unreal Engine project.

To access these settings, click on the export settings button between the quality selector and the **Download** button. This opens the **Export Settings** dialog box.

Figure 2.13 – Export quality setting

It is imperative to configure these settings prior to adding an asset to your scene to ensure optimal integration and alignment with your project requirements. The key features within the **Export Settings** dialog box include the following:

- **Auto-Populate Foliage Painter**: When enabled, this option automatically updates the foliage editor's asset list in your project with the latest imported assets. This feature is particularly useful for scatter and plant assets, streamlining the process of adding natural elements to your scene. It is essential to activate this setting before exporting these types of assets.
- **Apply to Selection**: Activating this setting applies the exported material directly to objects currently selected in your scene. This is a convenient tool for quickly assigning new materials to specific elements within your project.
- **Master Material Overrides**: This section grants the flexibility to substitute the default master materials provided by the plugin with custom master materials of your choice. It offers a higher degree of customization, allowing for more personalized and unique asset appearances in your project.
- **Material Blend Settings**: Here, you can blend materials using those already imported into your **Content Browser**. The Quixel Bridge plugin includes a vertex blend shader, which is utilized for this material blending process. This functionality is instrumental in achieving complex material effects, such as transitions between different terrain types or the integration of various surface textures, enhancing the realism and visual depth of your project.

At this point, we've learned how to move around the Quixel Bridge interface. Now we'll understand how to import the library assets into our Unreal Engine project.

Importing and integrating Megascans assets

Importing Megascans assets into Unreal Engine is different from importing other 3D models, materials, and textures, but it is not complicated.

Let's look at two methods of bringing Megascans resources into our scene:

- **Method 1 – direct drag and drop**: This approach involves *directly dragging an asset* from Quixel Bridge into your Unreal Engine scene. This method is intuitive and efficient, particularly when working in a dynamic design process. If the asset has not been previously downloaded, Quixel Bridge facilitates an *automatic download*, adhering to the resolution specified in the asset's information panel.

- **Method 2 – download and add to Content Browser**: For more controlled asset management, you can opt to download and then add assets to your scene as separate steps. To download an asset, select it in the grid view within Quixel Bridge and click the *green* **Download** button. Upon completion of the download, you can then add the asset to your scene by clicking the **Add** button. This is shown in *Figure 2.14*:

Figure 2.14 – Download and add to the project

The downloaded content will then appear in the `Megascans` folder inside the **Content Browser**, ready for use in your project.

Each of these methods provides a tailored approach to asset integration, ensuring that whether you require immediate drag-and-drop functionality or prefer organized, step-by-step asset addition, Quixel Bridge accommodates your workflow in Unreal Engine.

Important note

During the asset download process, a placeholder or a lower version of the asset is initially visible in Unreal Engine. Once the final high-resolution asset is fully downloaded, it automatically replaces the placeholder in your scene. This mechanism ensures a continuous workflow, allowing you to position and scale assets while their final versions are being retrieved.

When you download an asset for the first time from Quixel Bridge to Unreal Engine, Bridge automatically creates specific folders in your **Content Browser**:

- `Megascans` **folder**: This folder acts as the primary storage location for all assets downloaded from Quixel Bridge, organizing them within your Unreal Engine project.
- `MSPresets` **folder**: This contains all the template master materials necessary for rendering the downloaded assets in your scene. These preset materials are important for ensuring that the assets display correctly with their intended textures and shading.

So far, we have worked directly with Quixel Megascans resources, which are by default correctly structured, named, and organized into folders. This organizational scheme serves as a good example of how to structure assets for future projects. Let's take a closer look at how this folder structure works.

Understanding the imported resources

When an asset is downloaded from Quixel Bridge into Unreal Engine, it is systematically organized within the `Megascans` folder in the **Content Browser**. This folder serves as a centralized repository for all downloaded assets, ensuring efficient asset management and accessibility. Within the `Megascans` folder, each asset is stored in its respective subfolder, maintaining a structured and navigable hierarchy.

For 3D assets, each subfolder typically contains several key components:

- **Static Mesh**: This is the 3D model of the asset, representing its geometric structure.
- **Material Instance**: Accompanying the Static Mesh is a Material Instance, which is a variant of the master material, adjusted and optimized for the specific asset.
- **Textures**: These are the image files that define the surface appearance of the asset, such as its color, reflectivity, and surface detail.

We'll understand these in more detail later in this section.

The following figure shows the standard file structure you get once your 3D asset is downloaded: a 3D Static Mesh, a Material Instance, and specific textures. The **Material Instance** parent material will be based on a Megascans material defined by you, or the default one.

Figure 2.15 – Quixel Bridge 3D asset in the Content Browser

Important note

Depending on the method of download, a `Preview` folder might be generated. This folder temporarily houses lower-quality versions of the assets while their high-resolution counterparts are being downloaded. This feature is particularly useful for maintaining workflow continuity, allowing for the preliminary placement and adjustment of assets in the scene before their final versions are fully integrated.

It is necessary to ensure that downloaded assets from Quixel Bridge are ready to use, with their materials and textures pre-assigned. This automatic setup contrasts with the process for externally imported or self-created assets, where additional steps are required. For such assets, you must manually add any additional content, including textures, and create the necessary material or Material Instance.

Following the introduction of assets from Quixel Bridge into your Unreal Engine project, here we will delve into the specifics of working with these different asset types. This exploration will provide a deeper understanding of the asset integration process and how to effectively utilize the comprehensive content provided by Quixel Bridge in your projects.

Static Mesh

The **Static Mesh Actor** in Unreal Engine is a basic form of Actor used to display 3D meshes within a Level. The term *static* implies that the mesh's geometry is unchanging, not that the Actor is immobile. However, in reality, Static Mesh Actors can be moved or otherwise modified during gameplay.

They are commonly employed to construct game environments and worlds. Unreal Engine includes some default Static Mesh Actors, but additional meshes can be downloaded from Quixel Bridge or imported from other 3D applications.

Any time you open or double-click a Static Mesh, the Static Mesh Editor will open, showing the selected Static Mesh:

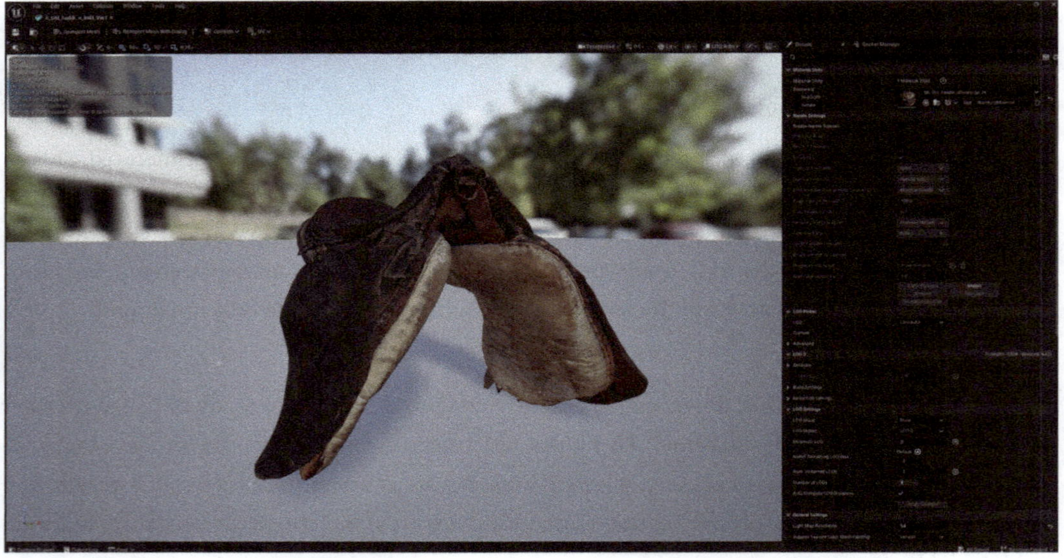

Figure 2.16 – Static Mesh view from a Megascans downloaded horse saddle

In the Static Mesh Editor, you can view parameters like Level of Detail (LOD), collision, and lightmap settings under the **Details** panel. Adjusting these helps optimize performance and lighting accuracy.

Material and Material Instance

Understanding the concepts of material and Material Instance is crucial for effective asset creation and management in Unreal Engine. Although we will dive deeper into these concepts in *Chapter 8*, it's important to have a basic understanding of them now.

Materials

A **material** in Unreal Engine fundamentally determines the surface properties of objects in your scene. Conceptually, think of a material as the "paint" that gives a mesh its visual appearance.

More technically, materials instruct the render engine on how the surface should interact with light, encompassing aspects such as color, reflectivity, texture, bumpiness, and transparency. These properties are calculated using a combination of input data from textures and node-based material expressions, alongside inherent material properties.

Figure 2.17 shows the Material preview and connected texture nodes:

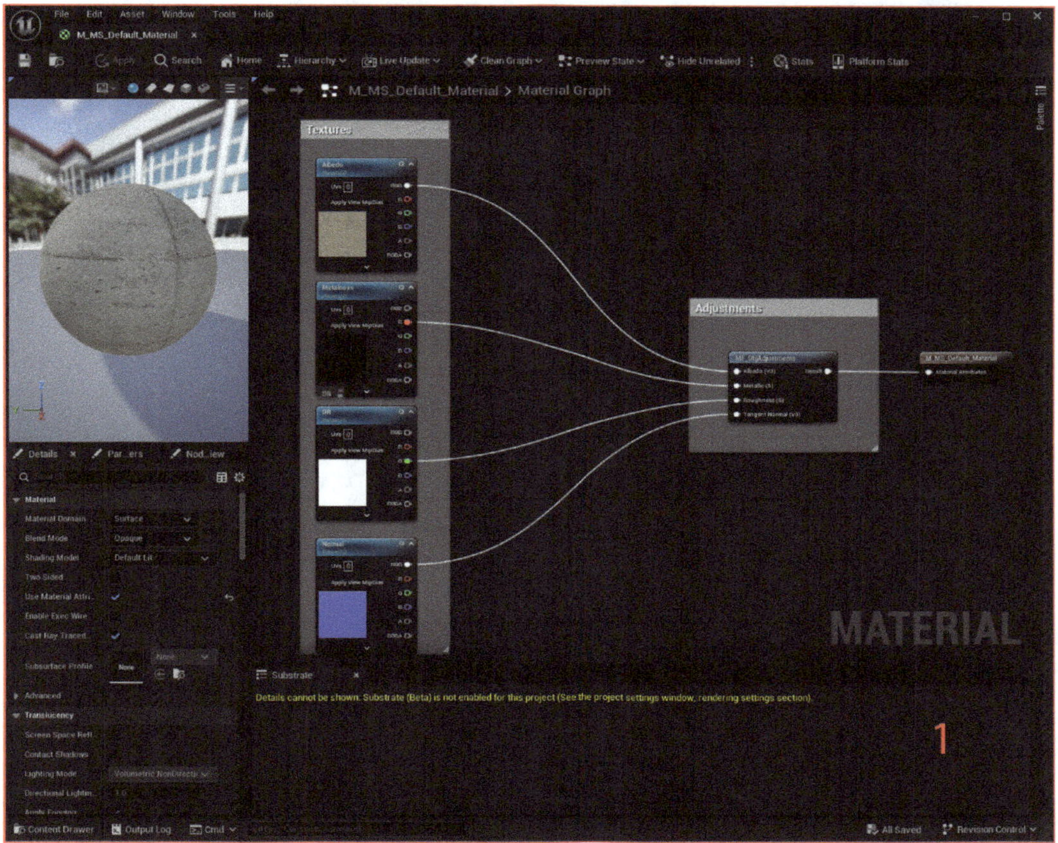

Figure 2.17 – Material and Material Instance view

We can see the preview of the material in the top left, and in the graph, the different textures that will be connected to the **material attributes**.

Material instancing

Material instancing, on the other hand, offers a method to alter a material's appearance without the need for expensive recompilation. Unlike a standard material, which requires recompiling for any change (a process that must be completed before gameplay), a parameterized material can be edited through an instance, bypassing the need for recompilation. This approach not only enhances the workflow but also can contribute to improved material performance.

In *Figure 2.18*, we can see the structure of exposed parameters that allow real-time adjustments to the Material Instance:

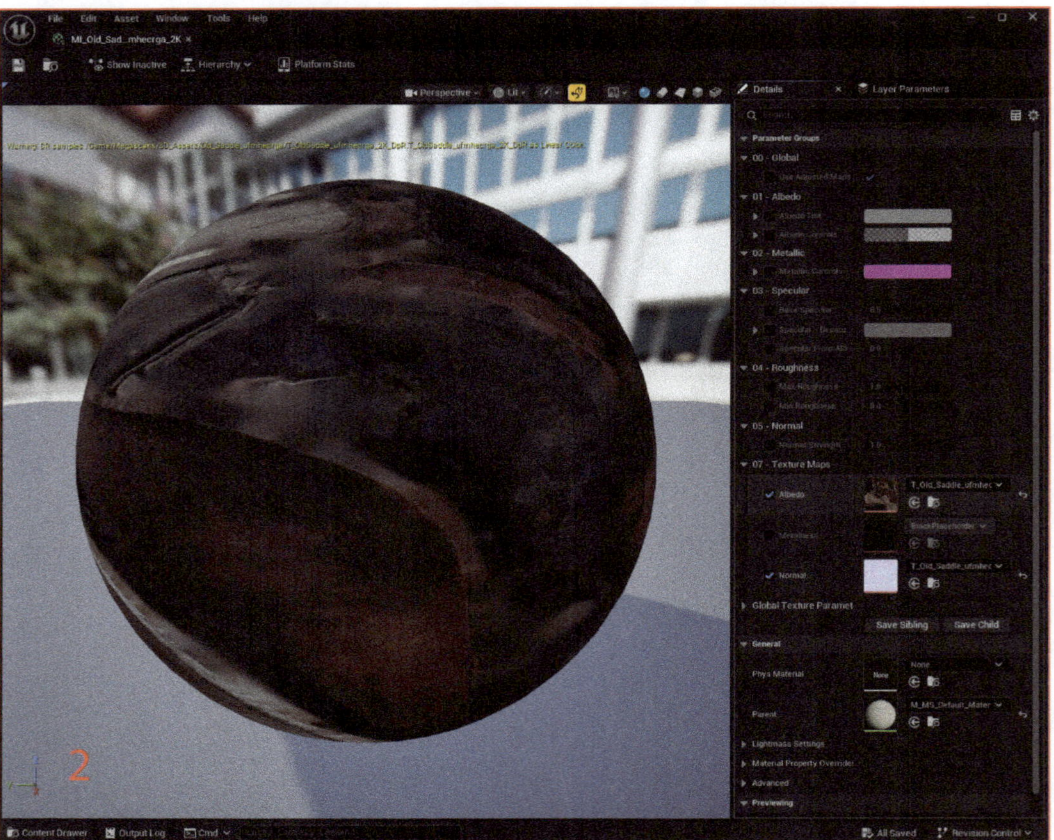

Figure 2.18 – Material and Material Instance view

Textures

Textures in Unreal Engine serve as image assets used predominantly in materials, but they can also be applied in other contexts, such as in a **heads-up display** (**HUD**).

Within materials, textures are mapped to surfaces to which the material is applied. They can be used directly for inputs such as **Base Color**, **Normal Map**, or **Opacity Mask**, employed as masks, or utilized in other calculations using their RGBA values.

A single material may incorporate multiple textures, each serving a different function. For example, a basic material might include a **Base Color** texture, a **Specular** texture, and a **Normal Map** texture. Additionally, it might feature maps for **Emissive** and **Roughness** packed within the alpha channels of these textures. This practice of packing multiple values into a single texture optimizes performance by saving on draw calls and reducing disk space requirements, while still providing a wide range of visual effects.

In the following figure, we can see a **Base** texture opened with the **Texture Properties Editor**:

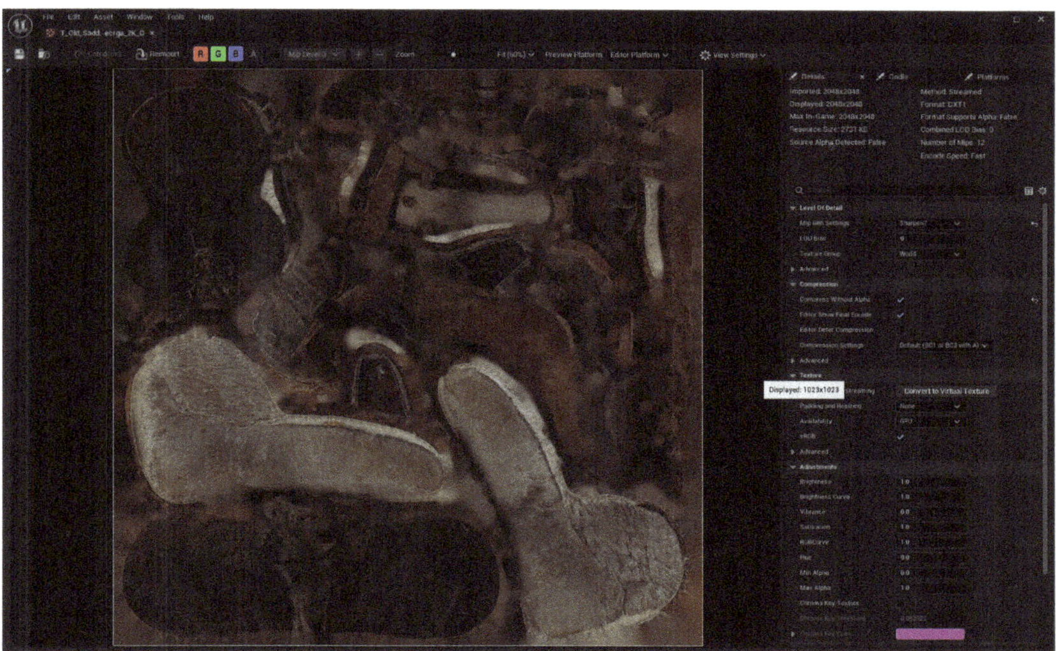

Figure 2.19 – Texture view

In conclusion, the understanding and application of Static Meshes, materials and Material Instances, and textures in Unreal Engine are pivotal in the creation of engaging and realistic 3D environments.

Let's have a quick recap of the terms we discussed in this section:

- **Static Meshes**: Core 3D building blocks in Unreal Engine that provide stable geometry and flexibility for manipulation within the game world, essential for creating detailed and immersive scenes.
- **Materials and Material Instances**: Define visual and interactive surface properties. Materials add realism to meshes, while Material Instances allow for efficient, non-destructive edits and quick adjustments without recompilation, optimizing both workflow and performance.
- **Textures**: Add layers of detail and realism to materials, enhancing visual effects and supporting complex calculations. This is essential for achieving high-quality visuals and contributing to the project's aesthetic impact.

By integrating Quixel Bridge into Unreal Engine, creators gain access to high-quality 3D assets that can be imported seamlessly for game development, architectural visualization, or cinematic storytelling. This asset pipeline enables the quick implementation of photorealistic models, textures, and materials, helping to build more immersive environments. However, it's essential to manage assets carefully to avoid issues such as disorganized file structures or mismatched resolutions that could impact performance and visual consistency. Ensuring assets are properly categorized within the **Content Browser** and optimizing resolutions for specific use cases is crucial for maintaining a balance between performance and visual fidelity. Mastering the import process and efficient asset management will streamline your workflow and improve the overall quality of your Unreal Engine projects.

In the next section, we'll complete a practical exercise to apply what we've learned about Quixel Bridge and asset import workflows.

Note

For more in-depth guidance on asset management, refer to *Chapter 4*.

Exercise 2.1: Adding a 3D asset from Quixel Bridge to Unreal Engine

Let's engage in a practical exercise to consolidate our understanding of working with Quixel Bridge and Unreal Engine. We will download a 3D asset from Quixel Bridge and position it within the main template map:

1. Start by launching Quixel Bridge. This is where you'll browse and select the asset you wish to add to your Unreal Engine project.
2. In the left menu of Quixel Bridge, follow this path – **3D Assets** | **Interior** | **Decoration** | **Statuette**. This will direct you to a specific category of assets.
3. From the displayed options in the library grid, select **Female Bust**, as shown in the following figure:

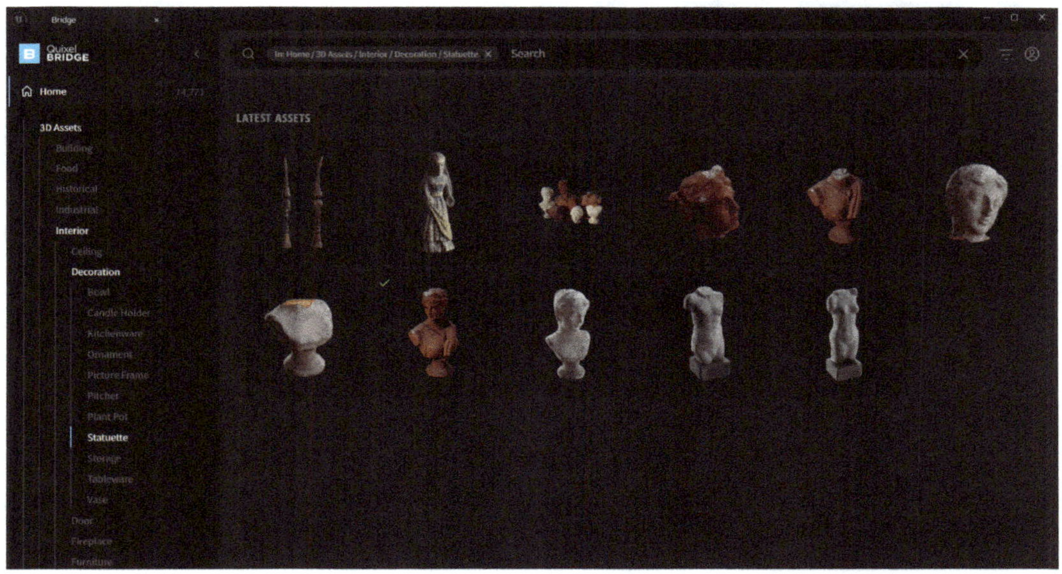

Figure 2.20 – Exercise 01 – Quixel Bridge 3D asset import

4. You have two methods to add the asset to your Unreal Engine project:
    1. **Method 1 (drag and drop)**: Directly drag and drop the asset from Quixel Bridge into your Unreal Engine scene (read *step 5* for placement suggestions). If the asset has not been downloaded previously, it will automatically download in the resolution selected in the asset information panel.

   2. **Method 2 (download then add)**: Download the asset by clicking the **Download** button on the asset's **Details** panel. Once downloaded, add it to your scene from the **Content Browser**.

5. Once the asset is in your Unreal Engine scene, you can place it at a location of your choice. Two suggested placements are provided for guidance in *Figure 2.21*, but feel free to position it as per your creative preference.

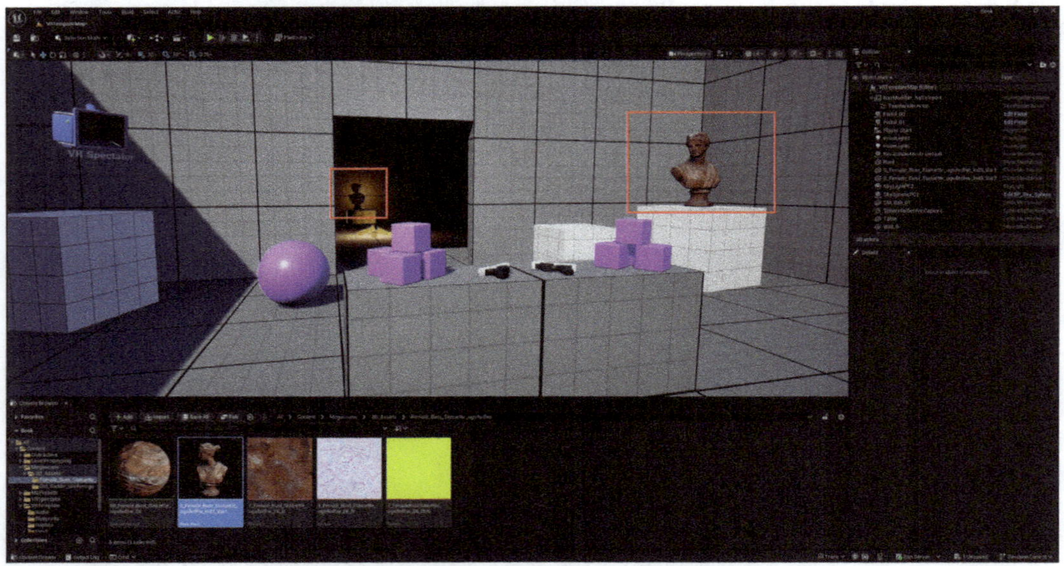

Figure 2.21 – Exercise 01 – Placement suggestions

6. After downloading, navigate to the **Content Browser** in Unreal Engine. Here, under **Megascans | 3D_Assets | Female_Bust_Statuette_[Bridge Code]**, you will find the Static Mesh, Textures, and Material Instance associated with the **Female Bust** asset you just added.
7. Compare your scene with the example provided in *Figure 2.21* to ensure that the asset has been correctly integrated into your Unreal Engine project.

This exercise demonstrates the seamless process of integrating high-quality 3D assets from Quixel Bridge into Unreal Engine, enhancing your scene with professionally crafted elements. It also familiarizes you with asset management within the Unreal Engine interface.

Exercise 2.2: Selecting and applying a material to a Static Mesh

In this exercise, we will focus on selecting and applying a material to a Static Mesh within Unreal Engine, using a surface from Quixel Bridge. To do so, follow these steps:

1. Open Quixel Bridge to start browsing for materials.
2. Now, browse for a material:
    1. In the left menu, go to **Collections** | **Environment** | **Historic** | **Roman Empire**.
    2. Use the search bar to refine your search. Type in `surface and floor`.
    3. Select **Roman Brick Floor**, as shown in the following figure:

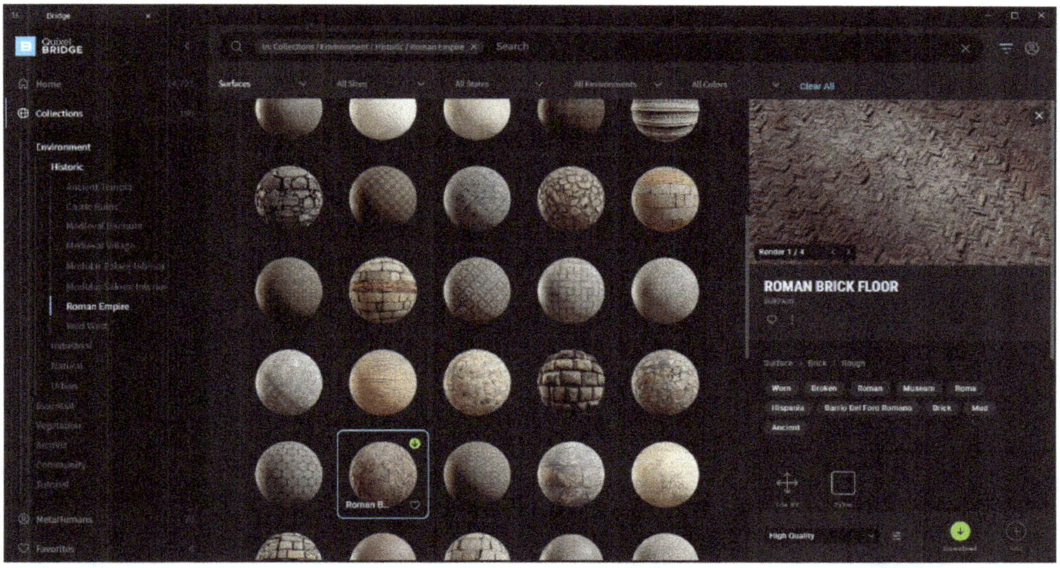

Figure 2.22 – Exercise 02 – Quixel Bridge surface import

3. Download the **Roman Brick Floor** material. Wait until the download is complete before proceeding.
4. Next, locate and create a Material Instance:
    1. In Unreal Engine, navigate to the folder where the material is downloaded.
    2. Locate **MI_Roman_Brick_Floor**.
    3. *Right-click* on its thumbnail and select **Create Material Instance** from the pop-up window.

5. Drag and drop the newly created Material Instance onto the floor of your atrium, or the targeted Static Mesh in your scene.
6. Then, double-click the new Material Instance to open its settings:

    1. Under **00 - Global**, do the following:

        1. Enable **Tiling/Offset**, expand the dropdown, and modify these values:

        - **Tiling X**: 35
        - **Tiling Y**: 17

        2. Optionally, for rotation, check **Rotation Angle** and set it to `0.25` (this rotates the material by 90 degrees)

    2. For normal map adjustment, under **05 – Normal**, check **Normal Strength** and modify the value as desired (it's generally recommended to keep values between 0 and 1 to maintain realism and avoid overly exaggerated textures).

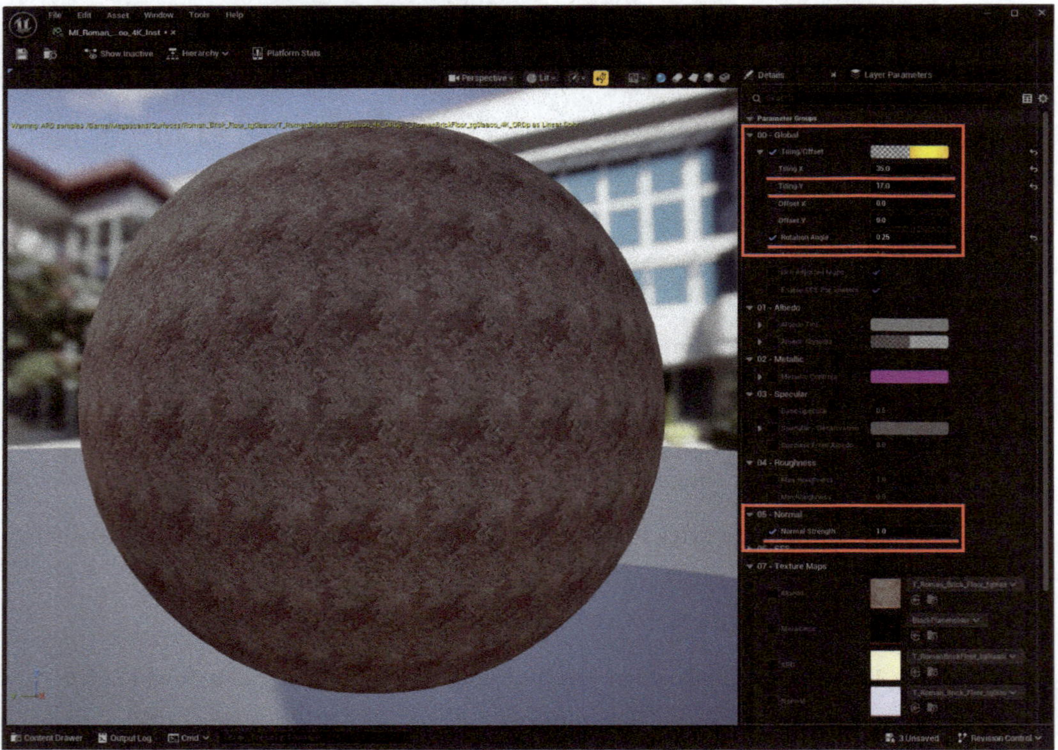

Figure 2.23 – Exercise 02 – Material Instance customization

7. After adjusting the values in the Material Instance, your scene should now align with the desired aesthetic. The material applied to your Static Mesh should enhance the scene's realism and visual appeal.

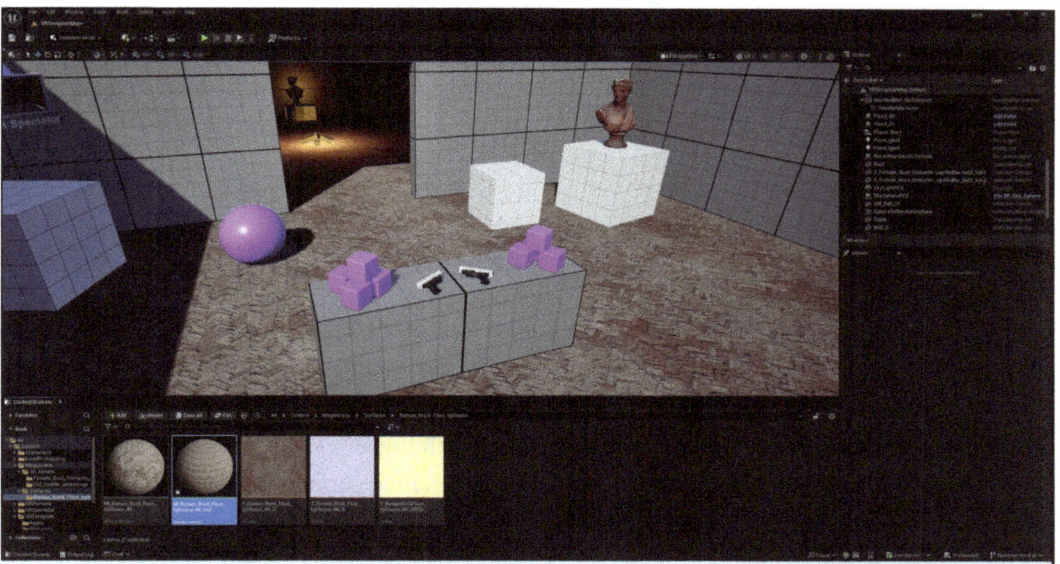

Figure 2.24 – Exercise 02 – New Material Instance and final result

This exercise demonstrates the process of selecting, downloading, and applying a material from Quixel Bridge to a Static Mesh in Unreal Engine. By adjusting the tiling, rotation, and normal strength properties, you can significantly enhance the material's appearance, making it fit seamlessly within your scene. Such adjustments are vital in achieving the desired visual impact and realism in your environment, showcasing the power of material customization in Unreal Engine. As you proceed through the next chapters, these skills will be expanded upon, allowing for even greater control and refinement in your projects. But before we move on, it's worth understanding why proper asset setup in Bridge is so important.

Why is asset configuration important in Quixel Bridge?

Proper asset configuration within Quixel Bridge plays a crucial role in the successful development of real-time projects in Unreal Engine. While it may be tempting to rely on default settings, overlooking specific parameters such as texture resolution, material setup, or mesh quality can lead to the following:

- Performance issues
- Visual inconsistencies
- Wasted development time

One of the first key decisions is choosing the *quality level* of the assets you import. Quixel Bridge allows users to download assets in high, medium, or low quality, affecting not only the resolution of textures but also the complexity of the Static Meshes. This flexibility is especially useful in the early stages of development, where working with lower-resolution assets can speed up iteration and reduce resource consumption. Later, once environments are more finalized, these assets can be reimported at higher resolutions, preserving material setups and scene structure while improving visual fidelity.

Texture resolution, in particular, is a critical factor. Quixel Bridge supports downloads in 2K, 4K, and 8K, allowing developers to tailor assets to the needs of each scene. For instance, large terrain surfaces viewed from afar may only require 2K textures, while focal-point assets such as hero props or cinematic set pieces benefit from 4K or 8K textures. Managing resolution carefully helps optimize memory usage and maintain a smooth frame rate in real-time environments.

Quixel also provides flexibility in *material setup*. Users can choose to import Unreal-compatible materials with automatically configured packed maps or opt for individual texture files when a custom shader pipeline is preferred. This is particularly important for stylized projects, advanced blending workflows, or cinematic rendering, where more control is needed.

In addition to textures and materials, *Static Meshes* downloaded through Quixel Bridge are a vital part of any real-time project. These meshes come with predefined LODs, which allow Unreal Engine to automatically reduce the polygon count based on camera distance, helping maintain performance without sacrificing visual quality. These LODs are generated by Quixel and optimized for real-time use, saving artists and developers the time-consuming process of manually setting them up.

Moreover, for projects targeting high visual fidelity, many Quixel meshes are compatible with **Nanite**, Unreal Engine's virtualized geometry system. When enabled, Nanite allows the engine to render high-poly meshes efficiently, removing the need for LODs altogether. This is ideal for detailed environments where traditional LOD transitions might become noticeable or distracting.

When importing meshes from Quixel Bridge, users can choose whether to enable Nanite per asset, depending on the project's performance targets and platform constraints. This makes it possible to work with cinematic-quality models in real-time applications, while still having the flexibility to optimize where needed.

Summary

In conclusion, this chapter has provided an in-depth exploration of the vast and dynamic ecosystem of Unreal Engine, focusing on the integration and utilization of various asset management tools, such as Quixel Bridge, Fab, and other significant acquisitions by Epic Games. We delved into the functionalities of Quixel Bridge, highlighting its seamless integration with Unreal Engine for accessing and managing the extensive Megascans library. The introduction of Fab, a unified marketplace, marked another significant development, amalgamating assets from diverse platforms such as Sketchfab, Quixel Megascans, MetaHuman, and ArtStation into a singular, cohesive environment.

Throughout the chapter, practical exercises and detailed explanations were provided to enhance your understanding of these tools. These exercises were designed to demonstrate the process of adding 3D assets, materials, and surfaces from Quixel Bridge and Fab to your Unreal Engine projects. By doing so, we covered the essential aspects of asset downloading and placement, and the critical adjustments needed for materials and textures, ensuring their optimal application in a scene.

The upcoming chapter will shift focus from specific asset management tools to the standard ingestion pipeline in Unreal Engine. It will cover core concepts and techniques for handling Static Meshes, materials, and textures within Unreal Engine without relying on external tools such as Quixel Bridge or Fab. Topics include asset organization, optimization for performance, and creating and applying materials and textures for realism and visual appeal. This knowledge is essential for anyone aiming to deepen their Unreal Engine understanding and improve their ability to create immersive and visually stunning environments.

3

Ingestion and Static Meshes

In an open world environment game, thousands of Static Meshes make up cities, vegetation, and props. This chapter focuses on how to ingest and optimize those meshes for performance and visual fidelity in **Unreal Engine 5 (UE5)**.

Static Meshes are central to environmental and object design in game development. The process begins with an in-depth look at importing Static Meshes into Unreal Engine. This step involves more than just file transfer; it requires a strategic approach to ensure that these assets are optimized for performance, meet technical requirements, and are free from common import-related issues.

After addressing the import process, the chapter moves on to optimization techniques. The emphasis here is on balancing performance with visual fidelity, a critical consideration in game development. High-level exploration of **Level of Detail (LOD)** settings, mesh simplification, and efficient UV mapping will provide practical insights into enhancing the performance of these meshes while maintaining their aesthetic quality.

The final section of this chapter covers the application and adjustment of materials to Static Meshes. This part covers the basic application, focusing on techniques to realistically integrate these objects within a virtual environment. Discussions on material assignment will explore how textures, shaders, and lighting work together to create visually compelling assets.

Included in this chapter are practical exercises designed to reinforce the concepts covered and provide hands-on experience. These exercises are crucial for consolidating your understanding and applying theoretical knowledge to real-world scenarios.

As we delve into these topics, it's important to recognize that each aspect of importing and optimizing Static Meshes in Unreal Engine is fundamental to the creation of complex, detailed, and high-performance game environments. The skills and techniques you learn here will be instrumental in your development as a game creator, enabling you to effectively bring your imaginative worlds to life.

Key topics to be covered include the following:

- Understanding different mesh formats and their implications
- Best practices for file preparation before import
- Importing Static Meshes
- Material assignment and adjustments
- Mesh optimization techniques
- Exercise 3.1: Importing our first Static Mesh
- Exercise 3.2: Importing FBX as Skeletal Meshes

Technical requirements

To continue the development of this chapter, it is necessary to have a PC with **Unreal Engine 5.5** (or a later version) installed that meets the recommended requirements by EPIC Games and has internet access: `https://dev.epicgames.com/documentation/en-us/unreal-engine/hardware-and-software-specifications-for-unreal-engine`.

Understanding different mesh formats and their implications

In the intricate process of creating and populating virtual environments in Unreal Engine, one of the initial, crucial steps is selecting the appropriate Static Mesh format. Static Meshes, being the 3D models representing objects and structures in a game environment, come in various file formats. Each of these formats has its own set of characteristics that can significantly influence both the performance of the game and the compatibility of the assets within the Unreal Engine ecosystem.

Commonly used static mesh formats in Unreal Engine

Unreal Engine allows working with a wide variety of formats for 3D models. Understanding these formats is crucial for ensuring compatibility and performance in your projects. We will discuss popular formats such as FBX, OBJ, USD, and GLTF, as well as other supported formats, such as STL and COLLADA. This knowledge will help you make informed decisions when importing and managing 3D assets in Unreal Engine. Let's take a quick look at each of these formats in detail:

- **FBX (Filmbox Format)**: Often the preferred choice for Unreal Engine, FBX is a versatile format that supports a wide range of features, including 3D models, animations, and textures. Its ability to handle complex assets makes it ideal for detailed game environments.
- **OBJ (Object File)**: Known for its simplicity, the OBJ format is widely used for Static Meshes that do not require animation. Its straightforward nature allows for ease of use, though it lacks some of the advanced features found in FBX, such as joints, skinning information, animations, multiple takes of animation in one file, curves, and even embedded texture files
- **USD (Universal Scene Description)**: USD is becoming significant in game development for projects requiring intricate scene management and collaborative workflows. It facilitates seamless asset sharing, non-destructive editing, and layered management, making it valuable for complex asset handling in Unreal Engine. While versatile, its real-time rendering performance should be compared with formats such as FBX or OBJ.
- **GLTF (Graphics Library Transmission Format)**: GLTF is gaining popularity for its lightweight and efficient format, ideal for open world game development. Its compact size and fast loading times are crucial for performance. GLTF supports PBR workflows, aligns well with Unreal Engine's rendering capabilities, and integrates smoothly with popular 3D modeling tools. Its performance in large-scale environments should be assessed to ensure it meets specific project demands. GLTF offers a balance of efficiency, cross-platform compatibility, and modern rendering practices, making it suitable for agile and cross-platform projects.
- **GLB (Binary GLTF)**: GLB is the binary version of the GLTF format, combining all the assets (geometry, materials, and textures) into a single file. It is compact and efficient, reducing the complexity of handling multiple files. GLB maintains the same advantages as GLTF, such as support for PBR workflows and fast loading times, making it ideal for real-time applications in Unreal Engine. Its all-in-one structure simplifies asset management, making it a popular choice for web-based or VR/AR projects that require portability and ease of use.

- **Other formats:** Unreal Engine also supports additional formats such as **STL (Stereolithography)** and **COLLADA (Collaborative Design Activity)**. Each of these has specific use cases, such as STL for 3D printing models and COLLADA as an interchange file format for diverse 3D applications.

As you can see in Unreal Engine, it's possible to work with multiple formats and even have them all within the same project and level. Let's look at some of the advantages to consider when selecting a format for our 3D models.

Importance of format selection

The choice of format can have a direct impact on the development workflow and the final output in several ways:

- **Performance**: Some formats are more efficient than others in terms of how they handle data complexity. For instance, formats such as FBX, OBJ, and GLTF that support LOD can greatly optimize rendering performance in-game.
- **Compatibility**: Certain formats integrate more seamlessly with Unreal Engine, ensuring smoother import processes, better asset management, and fewer compatibility issues. This can be crucial when working with complex scenes or integrating assets from various sources.
- **Feature support**: Depending on the format, specific features such as animations, lighting effects, and texture mappings might be supported to varying degrees. Selecting a format that aligns with the project's needs in terms of these features is critical for achieving the desired visual and interactive effects.
- **Workflow efficiency**: Some formats are more conducive to iterative workflows, allowing for easy updates and modifications – for example, FBX and OBJ can be reimported, maintaining the same properties as the previous file. This can significantly affect development speed and flexibility, especially in larger projects with dynamic requirements.

In summary, understanding the distinctions and implications of each Static Mesh format is essential for any developer working in Unreal Engine. This knowledge not only ensures the efficient and effective integration of 3D models into the game environment but also plays a pivotal role in optimizing performance and maintaining a smooth development process. As we delve deeper into the specifics of importing Static Meshes, keeping these considerations in mind will be key to successful asset integration.

Choosing the right format

When building open world environments in Unreal Engine, selecting the appropriate format for Static Meshes is a decision that significantly impacts both the quality and performance of the game world. The right choice hinges on a balance between the visual fidelity of the assets and the efficiency with which they are rendered, especially in expansive and detail-rich open world settings.

Here's a snapshot of different strategies for choosing the right format:

- **Model complexity**: For highly detailed models, such as main characters, FBX is preferred due to its advanced features, such as animations and complex textures. Simpler assets can be efficiently handled by formats such as OBJ.
- **Animation**: When animation or rigging is required, FBX remains the go-to format, with **ALEMBIC (ABC)** serving as a useful alternative for complex animations.
- **Open world games**: Managing LOD settings is critical for open world games, with FBX supporting different mesh resolutions to optimize rendering performance, while OBJ requires manual setup.
- **Texture and material compatibility**: Texture and material compatibility are also important, with FBX excelling in embedding these elements and GLTF/GLB emerging as an efficient alternative.
- **Project scale**: For large-scale projects, FBX is favored for its ease of management and widespread acceptance, while simpler projects might use OBJ or COLLADA (exported as `.dae` files).

When working with Static Meshes for environment building in Unreal Engine, selecting the right file format is key to maintaining an efficient pipeline. FBX is the most widely supported and feature-rich format, offering reliable imports of geometry, hierarchy, collision, and custom lightmap UVs, making it the default choice for most Unreal Engine workflows.

When needs differ, consider alternatives by use case. OBJ is a simpler alternative, ideal for static, non-animated meshes where materials are assigned directly in the engine and is useful for lightweight props or quick iterations. GLTF (and GLB) is gaining popularity for real-time or web-based pipelines thanks to its compact size and ability to embed geometry and textures, though material compatibility may vary. USD, developed by Pixar, offers a robust, nondestructive solution for large-scale, collaborative pipelines, especially when multiple DCC tools are involved.

While all these formats can be used to bring Static Meshes into Unreal, your choice should align with the project scope, team workflow, and performance requirements. FBX will serve as your go-to format in most scenarios, but exploring other formats can help tailor your pipeline to specific production needs.

Important note

While we'll list recommendations for Static Mesh formats in Unreal Engine to serve as a general guide, it's *crucial* for developers and artists to assess each project individually. The specific requirements of your project, such as asset complexity and performance goals, should drive the choice of format. Remember, these guidelines are starting points and adapting them to fit the unique needs of your game is essential for achieving the best balance between visual quality and performance.

Best practices for file preparation before import

The transition of 3D models from creation to integration into a game engine is a pivotal stage in game development. This section delves into the critical pre-import processes necessary for ensuring that models are not only visually appealing but also optimized for performance within Unreal Engine. Key areas of focus include optimizing mesh topology, efficient UV unwrapping, and the process of texture baking.

Optimizing mesh topology: ensuring efficient geometry

Mesh topology, the foundational structure of 3D models, is essential for balancing visual quality and performance in a game environment. Optimizing topology involves refining the model's geometry to reduce computational load while maintaining its aesthetic integrity. This process is crucial for ensuring that models not only look good but also perform efficiently, especially in resource-demanding scenarios.

In modern games, optimized mesh topology plays a key role in supporting configuration options such as performance mode (better FPS) and quality mode. By streamlining the mesh's structure, developers enable smoother gameplay on a range of hardware. In performance mode, a well-optimized mesh reduces processing demands, leading to higher frame rates. In quality mode, efficient geometry allows for enhanced visual detail without major performance sacrifices. This flexibility ensures that players can choose between high performance and superior visual fidelity, catering to diverse preferences and hardware capabilities.

UV unwrapping: laying the foundation for texturing

UV unwrapping is the process of mapping a 3D model's surface onto a 2D texture space. This step is crucial for texturing models accurately and efficiently, as it dictates how textures wrap around the 3D geometry.

Texture baking: capturing detail and realism

Texture baking is a powerful technique used to capture the intricate details of high-poly models and imprint them onto textures for use on lower-poly counterparts. This process is a cornerstone in creating detailed and realistic game assets that are performance friendly.

By meticulously adhering to these best practices, developers can ensure that their Static Meshes are not only visually impressive but also optimized for the demanding environment of real-time game rendering in Unreal Engine. This preparation is fundamental to achieving a seamless and efficient gaming experience.

Importing Static Meshes

This process involves transferring 3D models from external software into the engine while ensuring that their properties are maintained and correctly configured for optimal performance and visual fidelity.

Step-by-step guide to importing Static Meshes

Let's take a detailed look at the process of importing assets into Unreal Engine.

1. **Navigating the Content Browser**: You can see it at the bottom of the Unreal Engine interface. If you can't see it, you can go to the **Menu** window and look for **Content Browser** there. You can also try the shortcut *Ctrl + Space bar* with the keyboard.

    1. **Accessing the Content Browser**: Initially, access the **Content Browser** within Unreal Engine. This is the hub for managing all game assets, including Static Meshes.

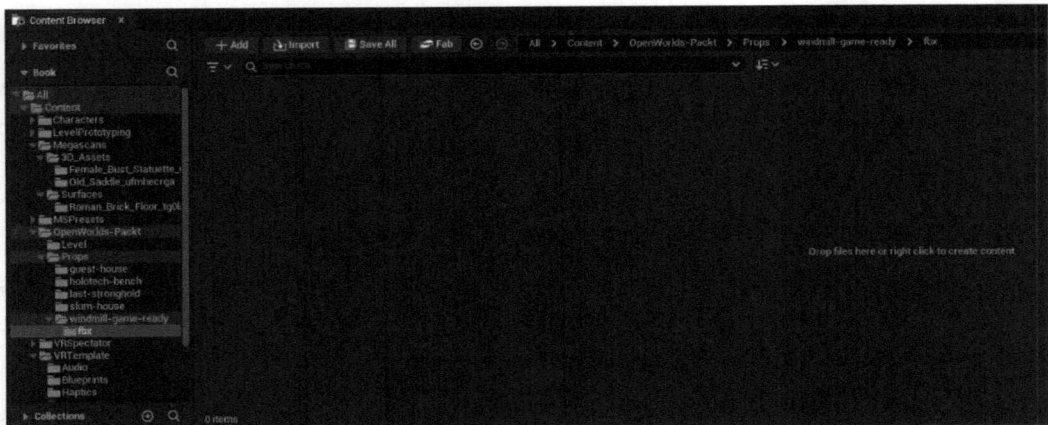

Figure 3.1 – Content Browser

    2. **Creating asset folders**: Before importing, organize your project by creating appropriate folders in the **Content Browser**. This step aids in efficient asset management and avoids clutter.

2. **Importing the mesh**:

    1. **Selecting the file**: There are several options to import your assets:

        1. Use the **Import** button in the **Content Browser** to navigate to the location of your Static Mesh file.

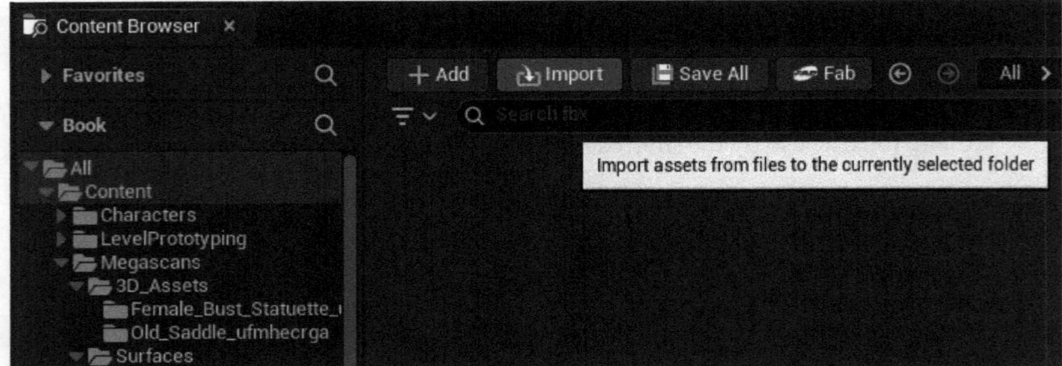

Figure 3.2 – Import option

        2. *Drag and drop* your file directly into the desired folder.

3. Select the **File** tab on the upper editor menu and select **Import Into Level...**.

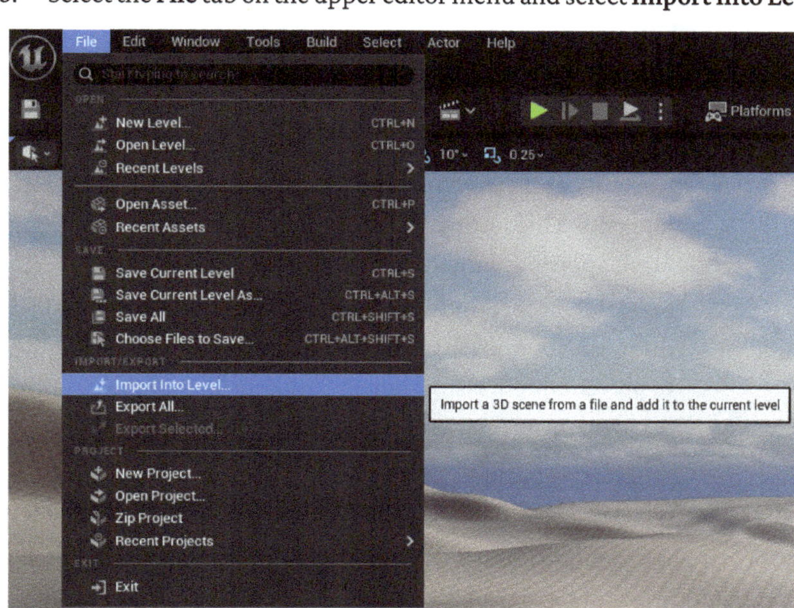

Figure 3.3 – Import option

4. Go to the desired folder on the **Content Browser**, *right-click*, and select **Import to Current Folder**.

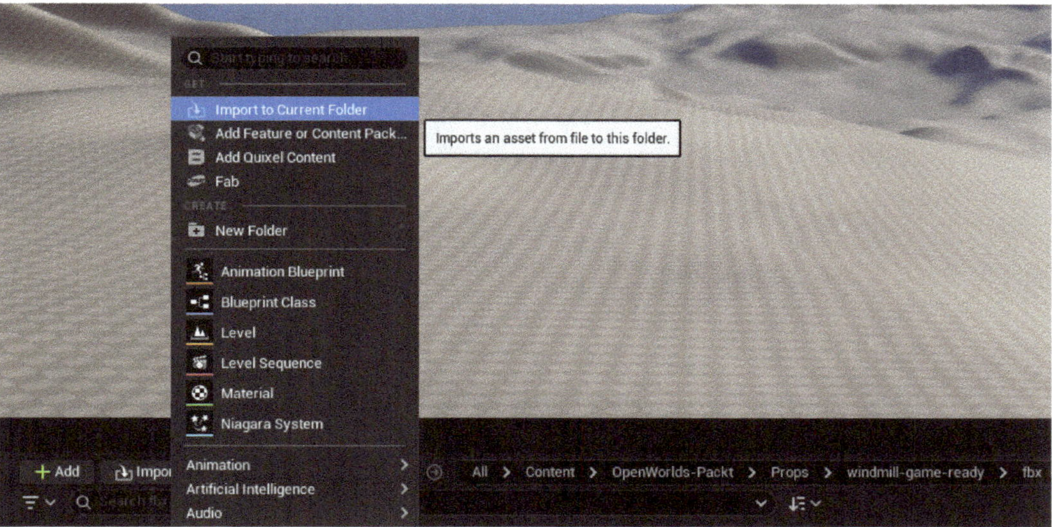

Figure 3.4 – Import option

   2. **Configuring import settings**: A dialog box will appear, presenting various import options. Here, adjust settings such as scale, which must match the scale used in your 3D modeling software to maintain consistency in the game environment.

3. **Adjusting import settings:**

   1. **Normals and tangents:** Configure how Unreal Engine interprets normals and tangents. This setting is crucial for ensuring that the lighting and shading on the mesh appear as intended.

   2. **Material import options**: Decide whether to import materials and textures with the mesh. If the mesh uses materials created in Unreal Engine, deselect this option to prevent duplicate materials.

Let's see how these considerations are applied by importing an FBX file as an example.

Understanding the main parameters from the Import Options

Every format has its unique **Import Options** window or wizard, but we will go through the most used one that corresponds to the FBX format.

Mesh and Transform

Although we won't describe every single option here, it's important to understand the main parameters of each section.

Figure 3.5 shows the import options for the FBX format:

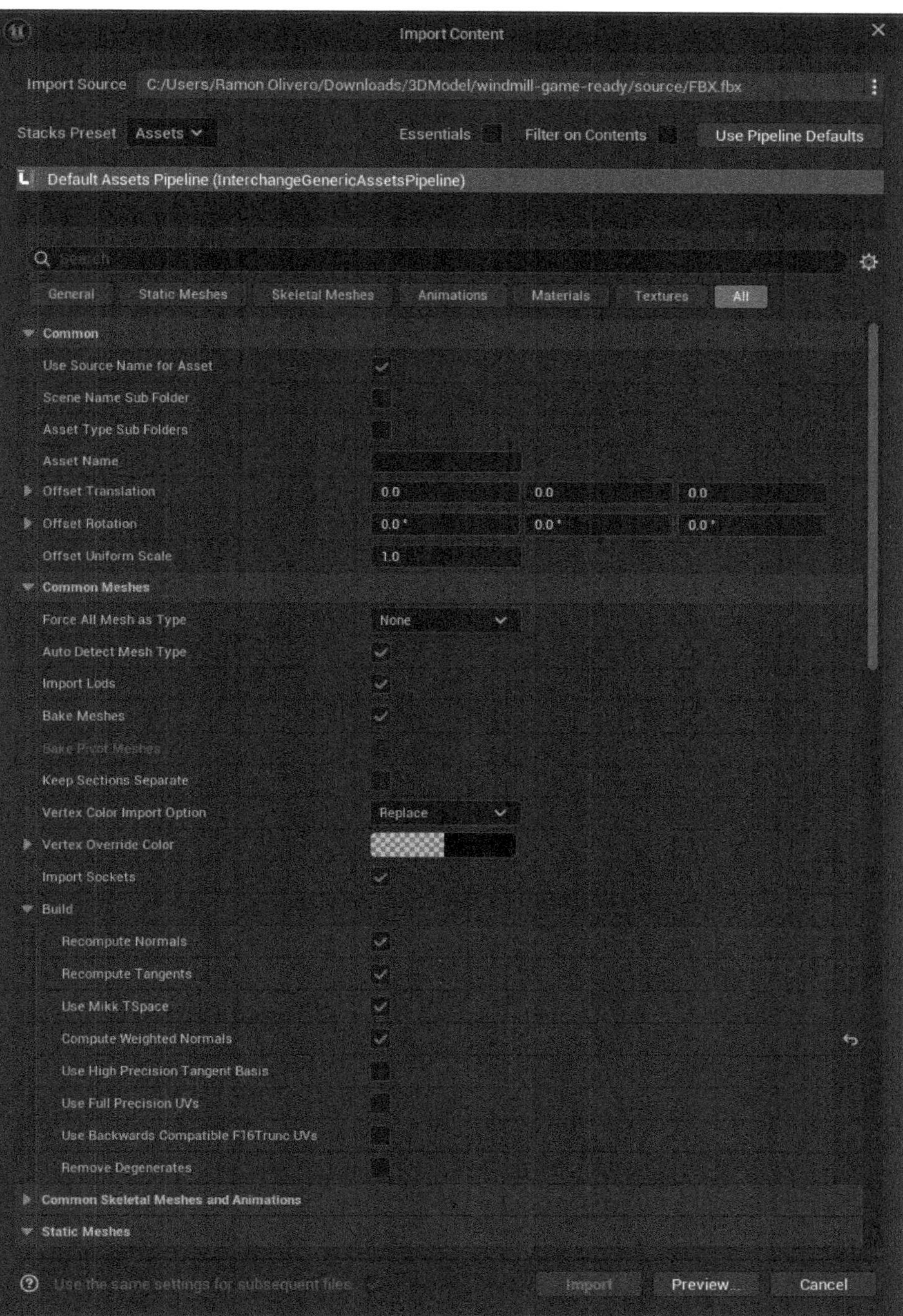

Figure 3.5 – FBX import options

The first time you import any FBX into your project, you will have the default values available. You can modify these values depending on the specific requirements that the FBX you import requires. These values used in the **FBX Import Options** dialog are saved for later use – even when you close Unreal Engine, you can use them the next time you start the engine. Alternatively, you can restore all the default values using the **Reset to Default** button found in the top-right corner.

Static Mesh versus Skeletal Mesh

In case the FBX contains one or more animations, it should also have a skeleton, and therefore, the **Skeletal Mesh** and **Import Mesh** options will be checked. If you don't want to import the skeleton or any animations, you should uncheck the **Skeletal Mesh** checkbox, and you will see how all of the animation-related parameters will disappear, as in *Figure 3.5*.

On the contrary, if you want to import your FBX with animations, keep the **Skeletal Mesh** option checked. In that case, you might find yourself in three situations:

- **Import mesh (or preview mesh), skeleton, and animations**: This is usually the starting point where you want to import the mesh you'll be working with, you don't have previous skeletons useful for this particular mesh, and you also want to import new animations. In this case, you should have the following settings:
    - **Skeletal Mesh**: Checked
    - **Import Mesh**: Checked
    - **Skeleton**: None
    - Under the **Animation** section: **Import Animations** checked
- **Import mesh (or preview mesh) and animations selecting a skeleton from the project**: This is a common situation where you are using common skeletons such as the metahuman skeleton, mannequins, or any other character or prop from your game and you want to import a new skin and new animations for it. The following settings are required:
    - **Skeletal Mesh**: Checked
    - **Import Mesh**: Checked
    - **Skeleton**: Select your character or prop skeleton from the project

- **Import only animation**: Here, you might find yourself in a latter process where you have all the meshes required for your asset as well as its skeleton, and you only need to import new animations. The settings will be the following:
    - **Skeletal Mesh**: Checked
    - **Import Mesh**: Unchecked
    - **Skeleton**: Select your character or prop skeleton from the project
    - Under the **Animation** section: **Import Animations** checked

Note

When importing animations, it is important to indicate to Unreal Engine the initial reference frames for the Skeletal Meshes. This can be done from the **Advanced** drop-down menu of the **FBX Import Options** menu, activating the **Use T0 As Ref Pose** box to avoid warnings after importing the asset, as we can see in *Figure 3.6*.

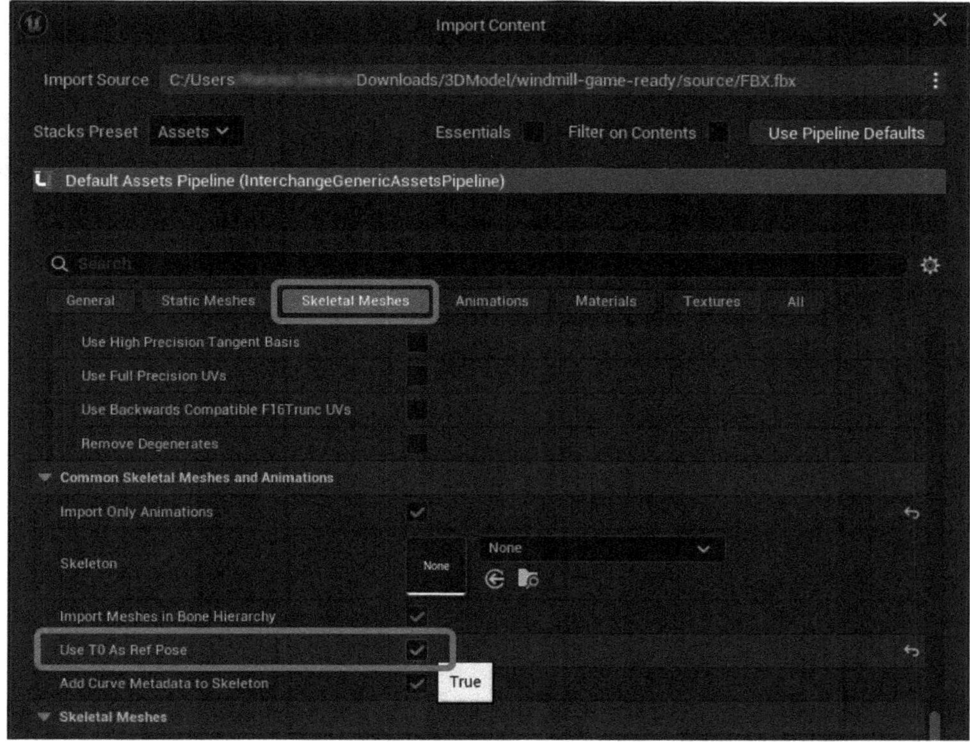

Figure 3.6 – Advanced FBX import options

Note

When importing assets, you may occasionally see a warning in **Message Log** (see *Figure 3.7*). This log appears when the editor detects issues with assets and displays a warning about the affected files. To continue working with your imported asset, simply click the **CLEAR** button at the bottom of the warning window and close it.

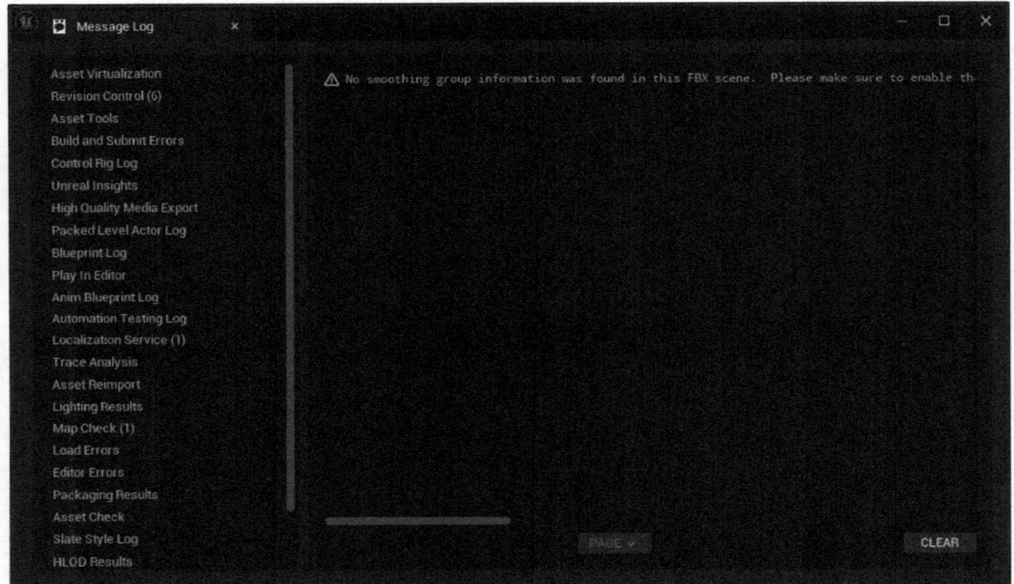

Figure 3.7 – Message Log

Collision

For Static Meshes, as mentioned before, uncheck the **Skeletal Mesh** option. After this, you will need to decide whether you want to select **Build Nanite** for your mesh or **Generate Missing Collision** if the FBX file doesn't contain a collision geometry. In case you want to create your simplified collision geometry in your DCC tool, you will be able to import these collisions while naming the geometries with the following collision-naming syntax, as referred to in the Unreal Engine documentation:

- `UBX_[RenderMeshName]_##`: A box must be created using a standard 3D rectangular object. You cannot move the vertices or deform it in any way that changes it from being a rectangular prism, or it will not function correctly. Do not alter the vertices or shape, as it needs to remain a rectangular prism to work properly.

- `UCP_[RenderMeshName]_##`: A capsule must be a cylindrical object capped with hemispheres. It doesn't need many segments (8 is a good number) because it is converted into a true capsule for collision. Like boxes, you should not move the individual vertices around.
- `USP_[RenderMeshName]_##`: A sphere doesn't need many segments (8 is a good number) because it is converted into a true sphere for collision. Like boxes, you should not move the individual vertices.
- `UCX_[RenderMeshName]_##`: A convex object can be any completely closed convex 3D shape. For example, a box can also be considered a convex object.

Optimization and LODs

We will go into more depth about LODs in the optimization chapters, but it's important for you to understand a few simple steps during the import process. We've already spoken about **Level of Detail** or **LOD**, but if this is your first time in Unreal Engine, it's useful for you to understand how it works in the engine.

LOD in Unreal Engine is a technique used to optimize game performance by adjusting the complexity of 3D models based on their distance from the camera. In essence, it involves creating several versions of a model, each with a different LOD. The most detailed version (LOD0) is used when the object is close to the camera, ensuring the highest visual quality. As the object moves further away, the engine switches to less detailed versions (LOD1, LOD2, etc.), which have fewer polygons and require less processing power to render. This switch happens automatically, based on distance thresholds set within the engine.

This system is particularly beneficial in large, open world games where rendering numerous high-detail objects simultaneously can strain the game's performance. By using simpler models for distant objects (which appear smaller on the screen and therefore don't need as much detail), Unreal Engine can significantly reduce the computational load, leading to smoother gameplay. Additionally, Unreal Engine offers tools for both the manual creation of LODs and automatic LOD generation, giving developers flexibility in how they optimize their models for different viewing distances. LOD, combined with techniques such as texture streaming and mipmaps, ensures that games run efficiently without compromising on the visual experience.

In Unreal Engine, **LOD Groups** are predefined settings that categorize 3D models based on their typical usage and optimize their LOD configurations accordingly. Each **LOD Group**, such as `Character` or `Vehicle`, comes with default settings that determine how many LOD levels a model should have and at what distances these levels should switch. This system simplifies the LOD setup process, allowing developers to quickly apply appropriate LOD settings to different types of objects. By using **LOD Groups**, developers can ensure consistent and optimal LOD behavior across various models in the game, enhancing performance while maintaining visual fidelity.

As you will be able to see, in the **FBX Import Options** window, there is a drop list named **Static Mesh LOD Group**, where you can select the desired **LOD Group** for your asset. You can also check the **Import Mesh LODs** option if you don't want Unreal Engine to generate LODs automatically.

Other commonly used settings under Mesh

Most of the time, parameters and options have a very descriptive name, and you usually also have a longer description if you hover for one or two seconds over them. Anyway, we can talk briefly about the most commonly used ones:

- **Generate Lightmap UVs**: In most cases, your mesh will have a UV generated for its textures and material creation. Speaking in a general case scenario, this UV will be assigned in Unreal Engine as `Channel 0`. For static light baking, very useful in games targeting mobile or XR, Static Meshes will require a new UV for its lightmap. If you enable this option, Unreal Engine will get the UV islands from `Channel 0` and will repack them in `Channel 1`, optimizing them for behaving as a lightmap.
- **Combine Meshes**: This is *not* as simple as it seems. As you may know, FBX files might contain more than one mesh, and Unreal Engine, if this option is unchecked, will import each mesh as a separate Static Mesh. If checked, only one Static Mesh will be generated, and material IDs will be reassigned. This can be good for optimization and organization purposes, but undesired if you want to reuse assets or meshes from this FBX for other designs.

Materials

Under the **Materials** section, you will be able to select some basic, critical options for the import process of textures and materials for your assets and files. Under **Search Location**, the texture location of your assets will be selected and searched. The options for **Material Import** will allow you to create materials, Material Instances, or leave your Static Meshes without a material assigned to set it up at a later stage.

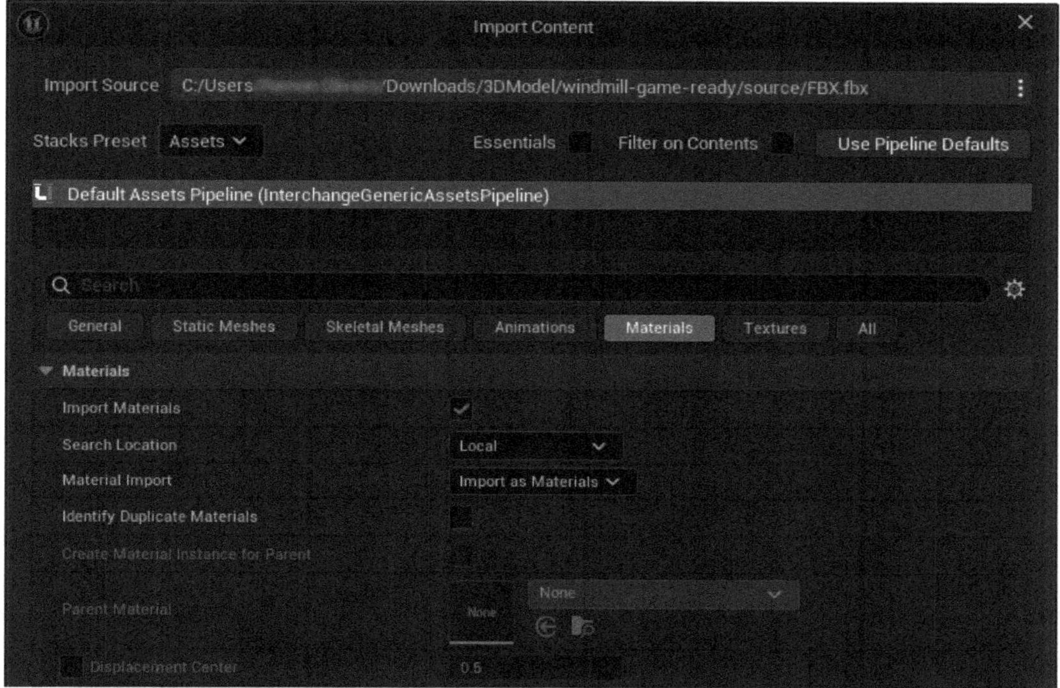

Figure 3.8 – Material import options

Finishing the import process

Finally, select **Import** if you want to bulk import and modify your settings for the different files you're importing, or **Import All** if the settings you've set up are the desired ones for all the bulk import selected files.

Troubleshooting common import issues

Even with careful preparation, certain issues can arise during the import process. Being able to identify and resolve these issues is essential for maintaining workflow efficiency and asset quality.

- **Scaling errors:**
    - *Problem identification*: If a mesh appears too large or too small, it indicates a mismatch in scale units between the 3D modeling software and Unreal Engine.
    - *Solution*: Adjust the scale factor in the import settings. Ensure that the units of measurement in your 3D modeling software align with those in Unreal Engine (e.g., centimeters).

- **Missing textures**:
  - *Problem identification*: Textures may fail to import, leading to meshes appearing untextured or with incorrect materials.
  - *Solution*: Ensure that texture paths are correctly set up and that textures are located in the same directory as the mesh file. *If textures are still missing, manually reassign them in the Material Editor*.
- **Shading issues**:
  - *Problem Identification*: Improper shading, such as black spots or unexpected shadows, can occur due to incorrect normals or smoothing groups.
  - *Solution*: Verify the normals and smoothing groups in the original 3D model. In Unreal Engine, experiment with the **Compute Normals** and **Compute Tangents** options in the import settings to correct these issues.
- **Mesh orientation**:
  - *Problem identification*: The mesh might appear rotated or flipped because different 3D software packages use different axis orientations.
  - *Solution*: Adjust the axis orientation in your 3D modeling software to match Unreal Engine's coordinate system (*X* forward, *Z* up). Alternatively, correct the orientation during the import process by adjusting the rotation values.
- **Mesh flickering**:
  - *Problem identification*: Z-fighting occurs when two surfaces are very close or overlapping, causing rendering issues where the surfaces flicker.
  - *Solution*: Ensure that overlapping geometry is avoided in your 3D model. You may also need to adjust the distance between surfaces in your modeling software or optimize the mesh to remove duplicate faces.
- **Importing time**:
  - *Problem identification*: High-poly meshes or overly complex geometry can cause performance issues during import and real-time rendering.
  - *Solution*: Optimize the mesh by reducing the polygon count, merging smaller components, and simplifying unnecessary details. You can also adjust LOD settings in Unreal Engine to improve performance.

Although the import process within Unreal Engine is quite straightforward, it's important to understand the interface and potential issues that may arise during the process. Now that we have our 3D mesh, let's look at how the material assignment system works.

Material assignment and adjustments

In 3D game development, **material assignment** is a critical process that significantly enhances the visual appeal of models. This section delves into the technical aspects of how materials are assigned and modified within a game engine, such as Unreal Engine.

Assigning materials

The material assignment process involves applying texture maps and defining material properties to 3D models. The process starts in the Material Editor, where developers can create material instances, defining various parameters such as color, reflectivity, and texture maps.

It is possible to see the materials applied to the material IDs of the Static Meshes from the **Details** panel in Unreal Engine, as shown in *Figure 3.9*:

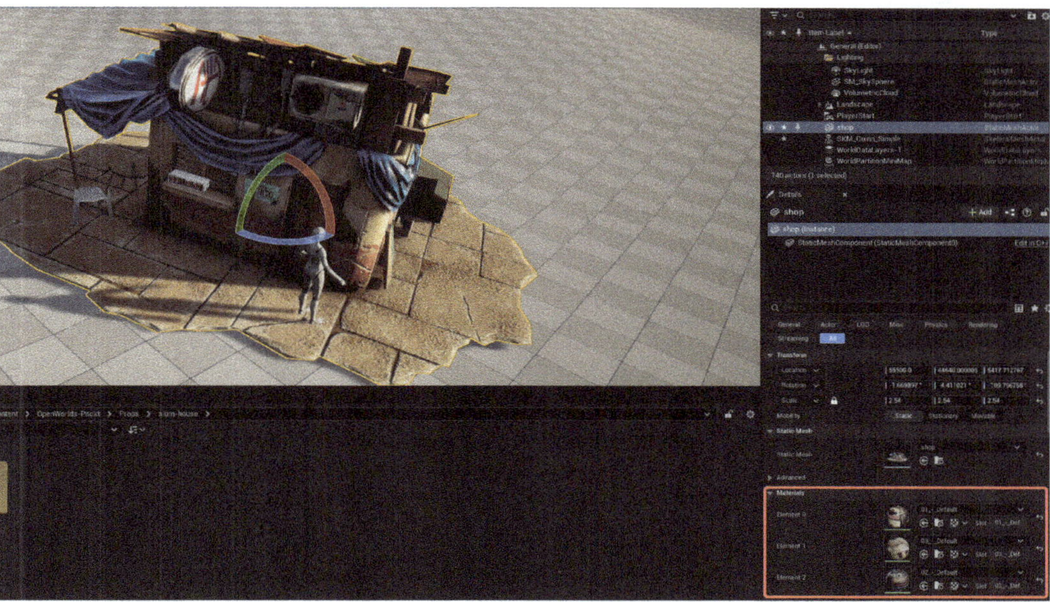

Figure 3.9 – Materials in the Details panel

In the **Details** panel, we can see the materials applied to the instance within the level. If we enter the Static Mesh Editor, we can see the material IDs applied to the asset, as well as to its future instances.

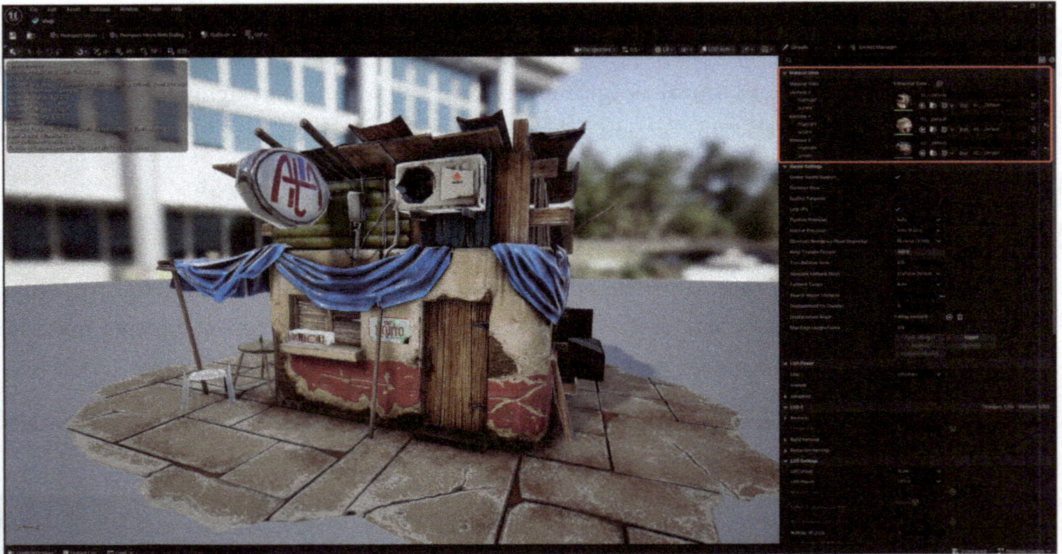

Figure 3.10 – Materials in the Static Mesh Editor

The main advantage of these two workspaces for changing materials comes from the ability to create variations in Static Meshes simply by modifying the material instances.

Modifying materials

Material modification entails adjusting properties to achieve the desired visual effect. This could include tweaking diffuse colors, adjusting specular highlights, or altering normal maps for enhanced surface detail. In real-time applications, such as games, materials also need to be optimized for performance, which may involve simplifying shaders or reducing texture resolution.

Within the material construction system in Unreal Engine, we have parent materials and Material Instances. Material Instances help us fine-tune the final look of our materials. Their interface is simple and includes various sliders.

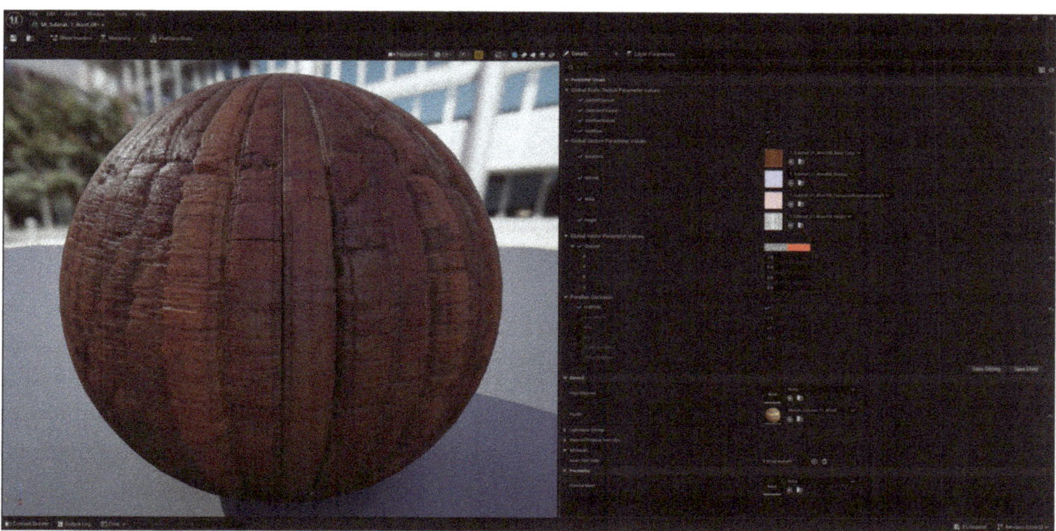

Figure 3.11 – Material Instance

Parent materials define the architecture of our main material, including its nodes and primary properties. Their construction is based on nodes and mathematical operations.

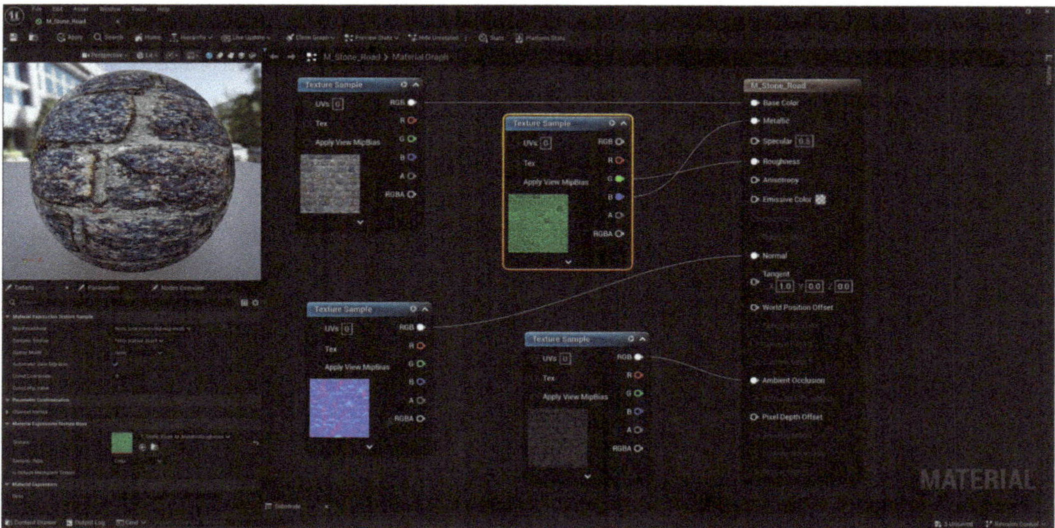

Figure 3.12 – Parent Material

This duality allows us to create parent materials from which Material Instances are generated, keeping the performance cost relatively low.

Performance and aesthetics

Balancing the visual quality of materials with the performance of the game is a nuanced task that requires a deep understanding of both artistic and technical aspects. We'll now get a high-level overview of the most important aspects.

Balancing visual quality with performance

The key is to achieve the highest possible visual fidelity without overburdening the GPU and CPU. This involves optimizing texture resolutions, utilizing efficient shader algorithms, and employing techniques such as LOD for textures. Developers must carefully consider the impact of material complexity on frame rates and loading times.

Material adjustments for environmental conditions

Materials in a game often need to react dynamically to environmental conditions. This could include changes in lighting, weather effects, or interactions with other in-game elements. For instance, materials might need to appear wet during rain or change texture when a character moves through different environments. Implementing such dynamic material adjustments involves scripting interactions within the game engine and may require advanced techniques such as **shader morphing** or **dynamic texture blending**.

In this section, we have covered the main concepts related to material assignment for Static Meshes and the importance of the initial configuration of the asset and its subsequent instances. We also discussed parent materials and Material Instances (which we will explore in more depth in *Chapter 8*). Finally, we addressed some considerations regarding the performance of materials and textures. In the next section, we will focus on optimization specifically for Static Meshes.

Mesh optimization techniques

The optimization of a project begins from the outset. Every element onscreen has a performance cost, so it is essential to be aware of this to ensure that the optimization process starts early in the development of any project.

Why optimize?

In 3D game development, **mesh optimization** is a process of modifying and fine-tuning the mesh to ensure that it meets the performance requirements of a game engine, such as Unreal Engine, without compromising visual quality.

Optimized meshes directly contribute to the game's overall performance. Lower polygon counts reduce the rendering load on the GPU, enabling smoother frame rates and faster rendering times. This is especially crucial in open world games where numerous assets need to be rendered simultaneously. Additionally, optimized meshes consume less memory, which is a vital consideration for platforms with limited resources.

Optimization strategies

This subsection delves into the various techniques and methodologies employed to optimize meshes effectively. Each strategy is aimed at reducing the computational burden while maintaining the aesthetic essence of the asset.

- **Reduction techniques**: This technique involves strategically removing superfluous vertices, which streamlines the mesh without significantly impacting its appearance. Effective polygon reduction can dramatically decrease render times and improve overall game performance.
- **LOD implementation**: LOD systems involve creating several versions of a model, each with different complexity levels. The game engine dynamically selects the most appropriate version based on the camera's proximity, optimizing resource use without compromising visual quality. This will also include **Hierarchical LOD (HLOD)**, where several Static Meshes will be merged or combined to improve performance.
- **Optimization for draw call reduction**: Combining multiple small textures into a single larger texture (**texture atlasing**) and grouping several small meshes to be rendered together (**mesh batching**) can significantly reduce draw calls. This technique is especially effective for environments with repetitive elements, such as landscapes or architectural interiors.

- **Nanite**: Of course, talking about Unreal Engine, we can't forget Nanite, which allows rendering extremely high-detail assets with a vast number of polygons, far beyond what traditional methods can handle. It's a virtualized geometry technology developed by Epic Games that reduces or even eliminates performance issues typically associated with high polygon counts. Nanite achieves this by efficiently streaming and processing only the visible detail needed at any given time.

We've learned how mesh optimization is essential in 3D game development to ensure high performance without compromising visual quality. Optimized meshes lead to smoother frame rates, faster rendering times, and efficient memory use, which are crucial for open world games. Key optimization strategies are critical to your project, and we will always try to take advantage of Nanite if our project is suited for it.

Now, we will perform exercises on importing a Static Mesh and a Skeletal Mesh, demonstrating the import process in Unreal Engine.

Exercise 3.1: Importing our first Static Mesh

Let's engage in a new practical exercise, importing an FBX Static Mesh into Unreal Engine. We will use a model uploaded to **Sketchfab** by Francis Lamoureux named **Windmill** (Lamoureux 2022).

Downloading an FBX file from Sketchfab

1. Go to `https://sketchfab.com/`.
2. Register or log in to Sketchfab.
3. Go to the asset link in Sketchfab: `https://skfb.ly/osGzx`.
4. Click on the **Download 3D Model** button.

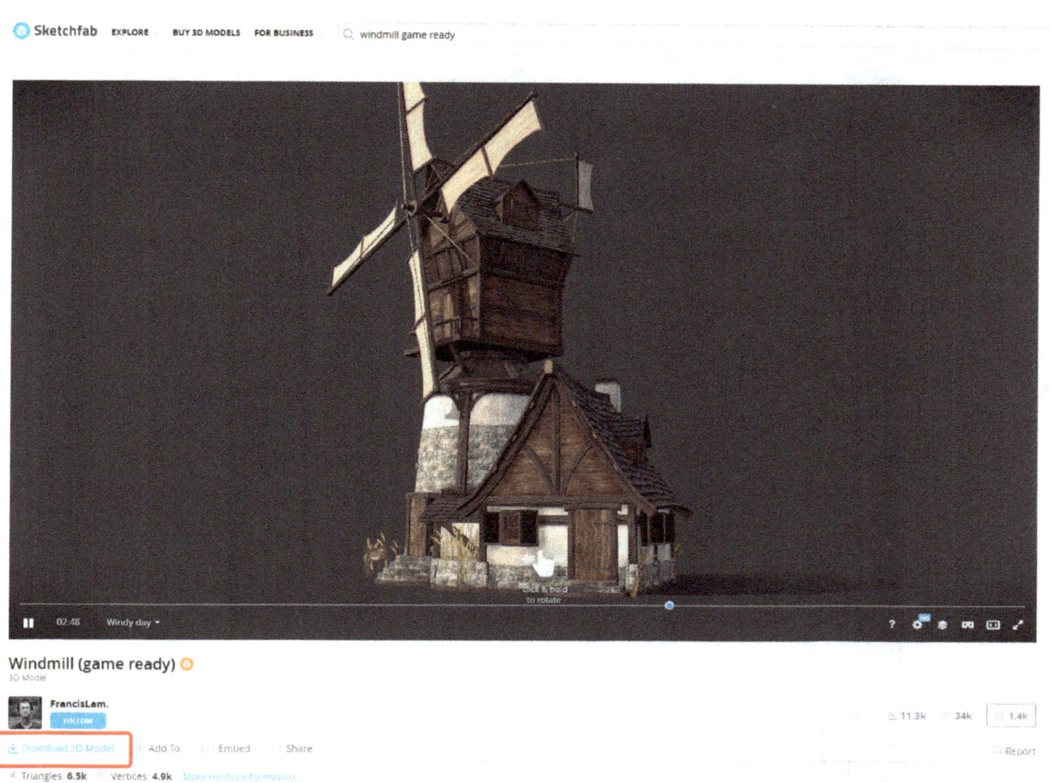

Figure 3.13 – Download 3D model from Sketchfab

5. Download the FBX file.

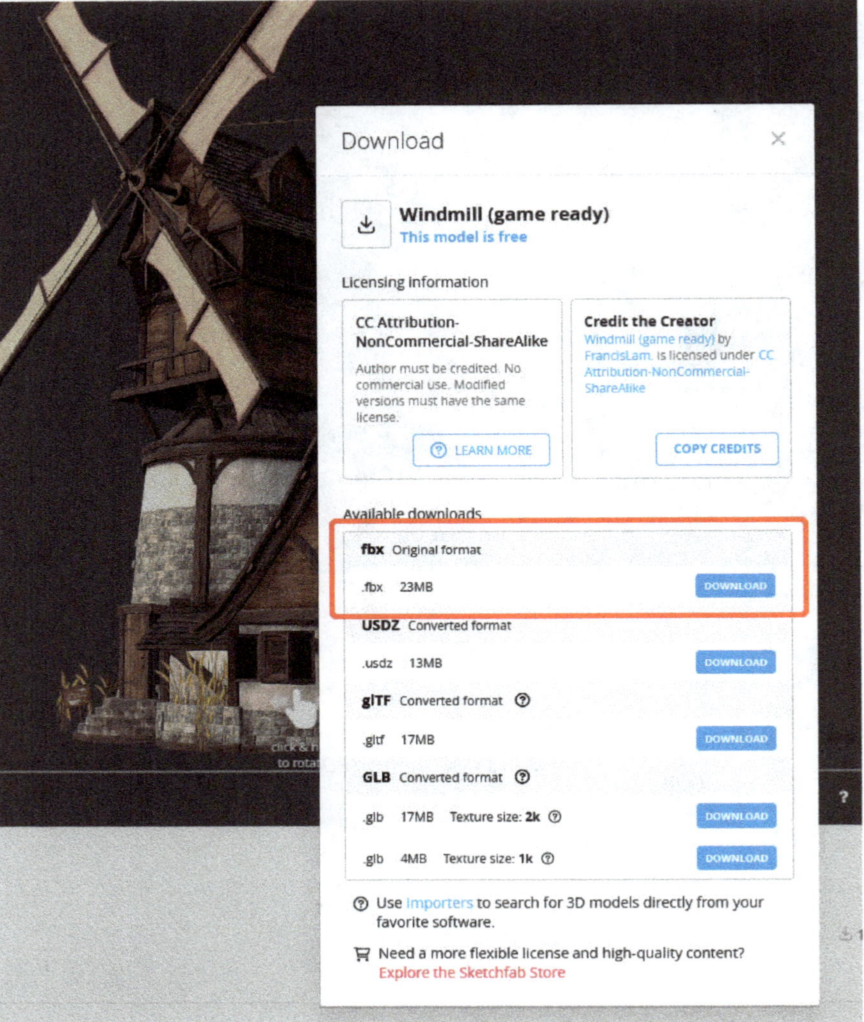

Figure 3.14 – Download Windmill FBX

6. Save the file at the desired location and unzip it.

Importing an FBX file into Unreal Engine

Now that we have our model downloaded on our PC, let's open a new project in Unreal Engine.

1. In the Unreal Engine Editor, locate the **Content Browser** at the bottom of the screen.
2. *Right-click* in the **Content Browser** and select **New Folder** to create a folder where you will import your FBX file (e.g., name it `Windmill` under `Props` and `OpenWorlds-Packt`). The path would be as follows: `Content | OpenWorlds-Packt | Props | Windmill`.
3. Use any of the techniques written in *Importing Static Meshes* section on how to import the file from the `source` folder. For example, *drag and drop* the file into the **Content Browser**.
4. You will get the **FBX Import Options** window.
    1. Set **Offset Uniform Scale** to `300` if you want to achieve a scale relative to the UE Mannequin (this adjustment is necessary because the Static Mesh was not authored at real-world scale and needs to be resized appropriately during import).
    2. Select **Static Mesh** from the **Force All Mesh as Type** drop-down menu.
    3. Uncheck the **Import Only Animations** checkbox.
    4. Enable **Combine Static Meshes.**
    5. Assign **LevelArchitecture** as **Static Mesh LODGroup**.
    6. Enable the **Generate Lightmap UVs** checkbox.

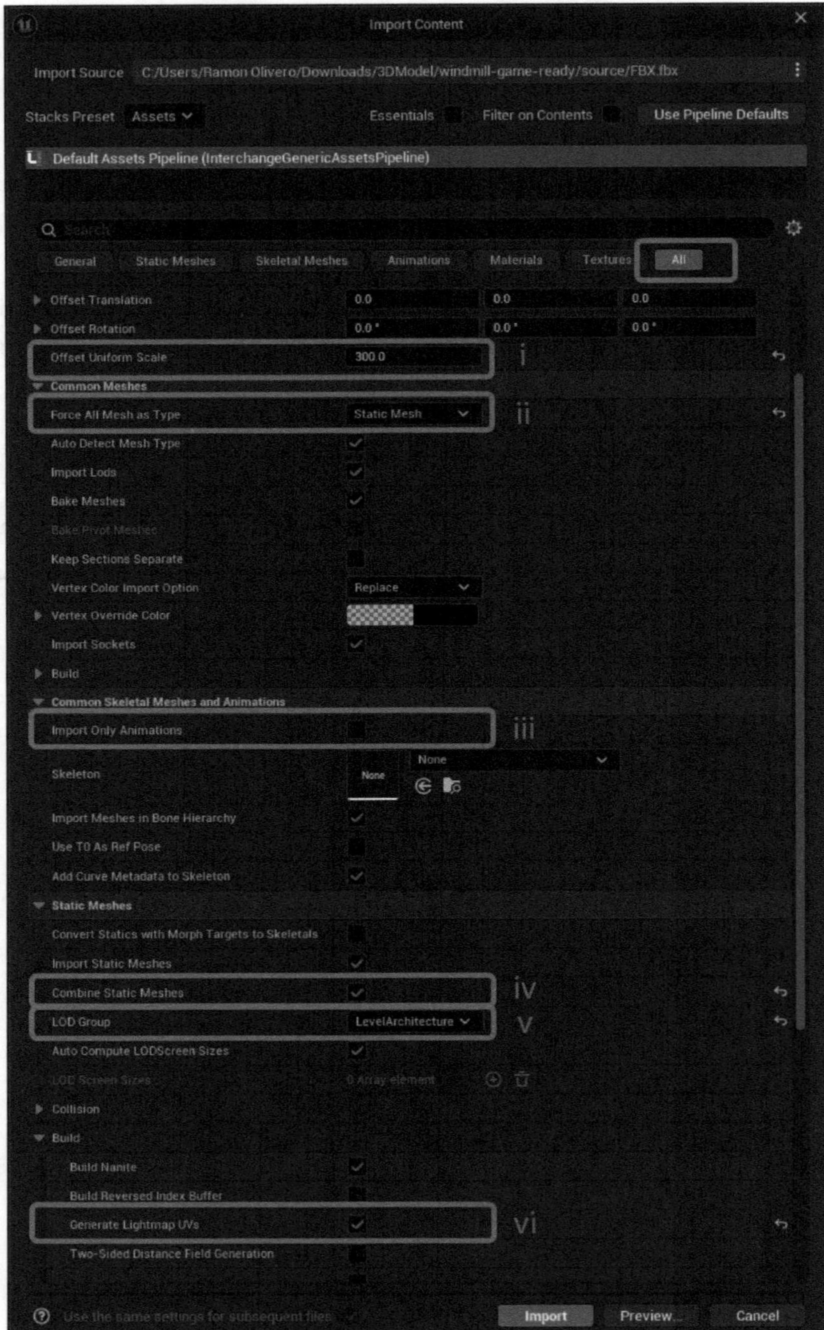

Figure 3.15 – Import options Static Mesh FBX

7. Now we can click the **Import** button at the end of the **FBX Import Options** window.
8. You will now see a Static Mesh called **FBX** and a material called **standardSurface1**.

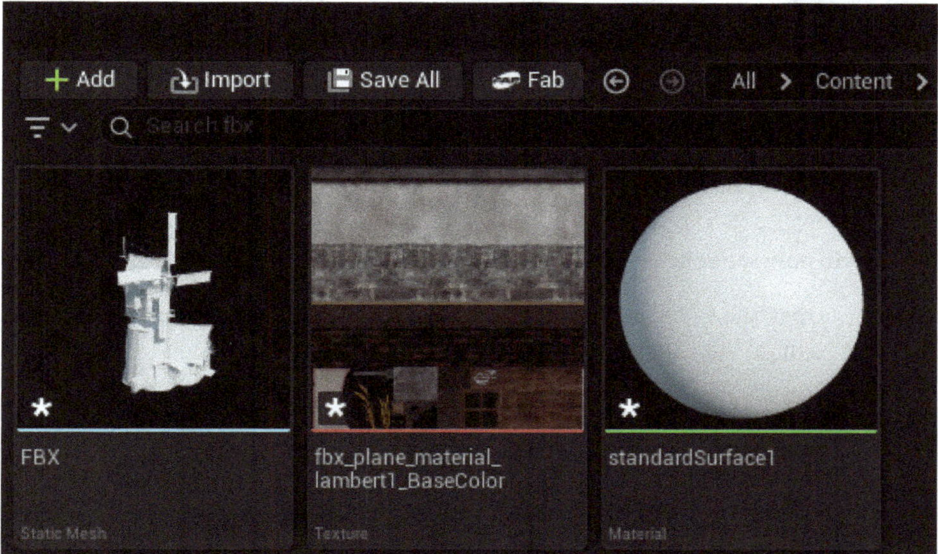

Figure 3.16 – Imported Static Mesh FBX

9. Import the textures from the `textures` folder.

Important note

It doesn't happen often, but sometimes, textures can be damaged or corrupted and will be rejected by Unreal Engine. If that's the case, you can always open the image with your preferred image editor software and resave the image. Try reimporting after that. Long names and paths can also generate an import conflict. If that's the case, try shortening the name of the file and reimporting.

In the following screenshot, we can see the Static Mesh, materials, and textures from the import process.

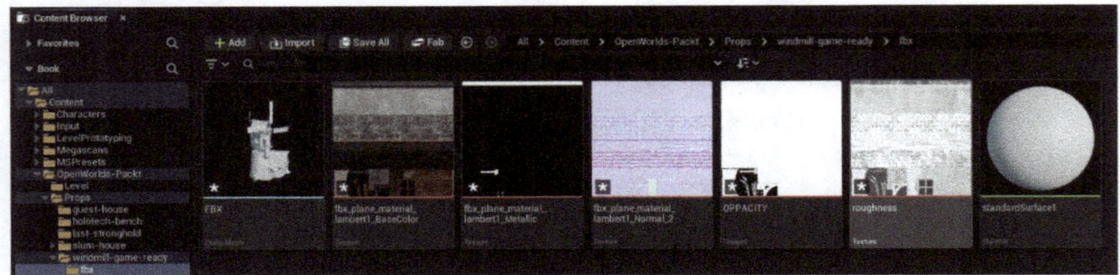

Figure 3.17 – Imported textures, Static Mesh FBX

5. You will now see your textures in the **Content Browser**.

    1. Open the `standardSurface1` material with a double-click on the thumbnail. You will see two nodes:

        - `Param`
        - `Standardsurface1`

    2. Delete the `Param` node, *drag and drop* the textures in the Material Graph Editor, and connect them, following *Figure 3.18*:

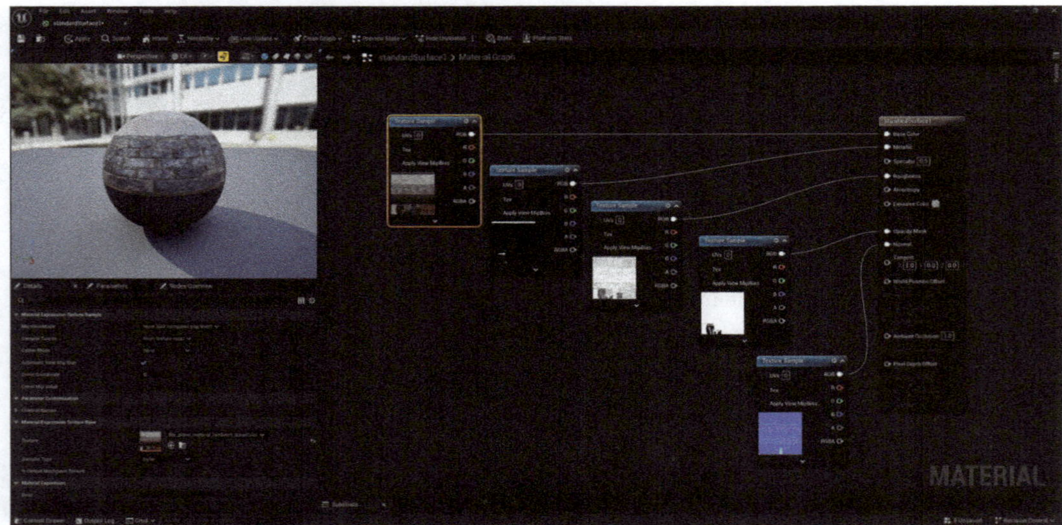

Figure 3.18 – Materials, Static Mesh FBX

3. Pay attention to the highlighted node and connection string. After connecting it to the **Opacity Mask**, it will remain grayed out.
4. Select the `standardSurface1` node on the right, or unselect everything, and you will see the **Material** detail panel.
5. Under **Blend Mode**, select **Masked**.
6. Click **Apply** in the top toolbar next to the **Search** button.

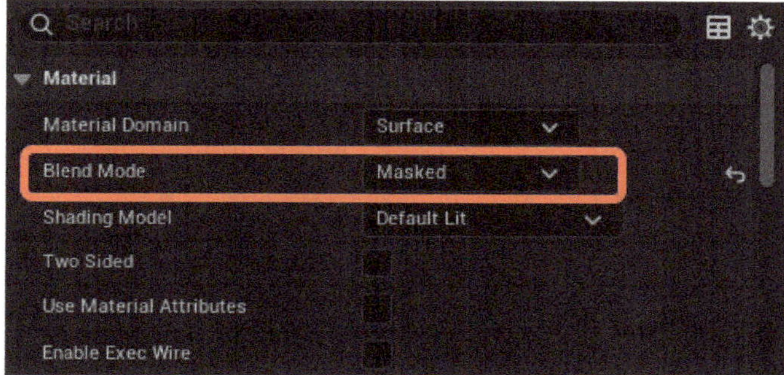

Figure 3.19 – Masked Material, Static Mesh FBX

See how your Static Mesh Material preview has already changed. You can now drop your FBX Static Mesh into your level as many times as you want.

Figure 3.20 – Masked Material, Static Mesh FBX

With our first Static Mesh imported, we're now ready to move on to importing FBX files as Skeletal Meshes.

Exercise 3.2: Importing FBX as Skeletal Meshes

In this new exercise, we will learn how to import a Skeletal Mesh. Our goal is to import a 3D model with associated animations. For this purpose, we will use the **Windmill FBX**.

Important note

This chapter was captured in Unreal Engine 5.3. Although 5.3 includes the **Content Drawer**, we use the standard **Content Browser** terminology to keep one consistent, workflow (especially for readers coming from earlier versions). The steps work in UE5.3 or later; expect only minor UI/name differences in newer releases.

1. In the Unreal Engine Editor, locate the **Content Browser** at the bottom of the screen.
2. *Right-click* in the **Content Browser** and select **New Folder** to create a folder where you will import your FBX file (e.g., name it `Windmill-SK` under `Props` and `OpenWorlds-Packt`). The path would be as follows: `Content | OpenWorlds-Packt | Props | Windmill-SK`.
3. Use any of the techniques written in *Importing Static Meshes* section on how to import files from the `source` folder. For example, *drag and drop* the file into the **Content Browser**.
4. You will get the **FBX Import Options** window:
    1. Click **Use Pipeline Defaults** to reset any changes made previously.
    2. Set **Offset Uniform Scale** to `300`.
    3. Select **Skeletal Mesh** from the dropdown in **Force All Mesh as Type**.
    4. Deselect **Import Only Animations.**
    5. Uncheck **Import Material**, and in **Search Location**, pick **Do not Search.**
    6. Click on **Import**.

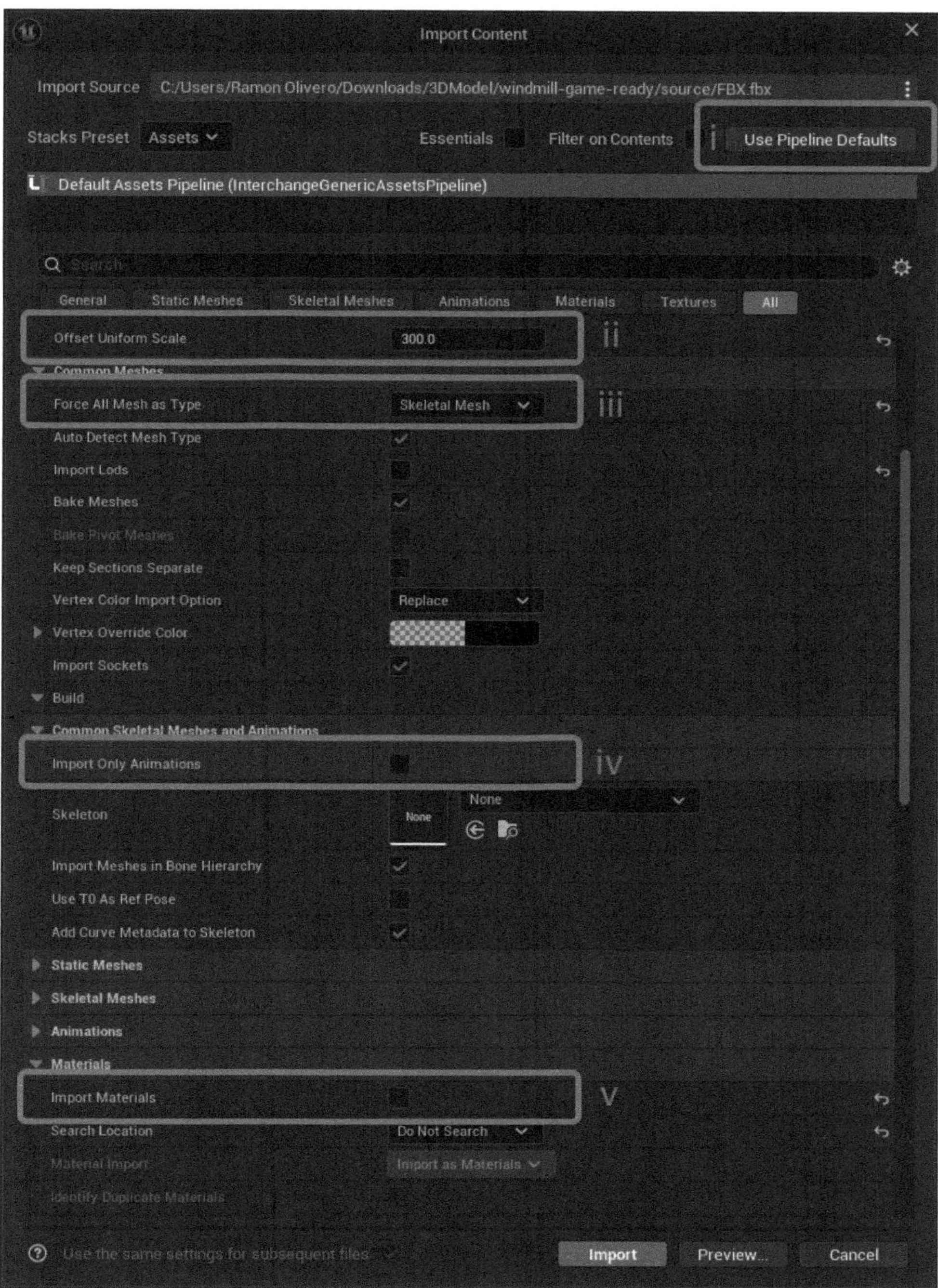

Figure 3.21 – Import, Skeletal Mesh FBX

After importing the asset, you will see a window called **Message Log** displaying the warning **Could not find the bind pose** (sometimes shown twice). This is *not* an error, just a warning related to skeletal data that is not relevant for Static Meshes. You can safely ignore it by closing the window or clicking **CLEAR**, as shown in *Figure 3.22*:

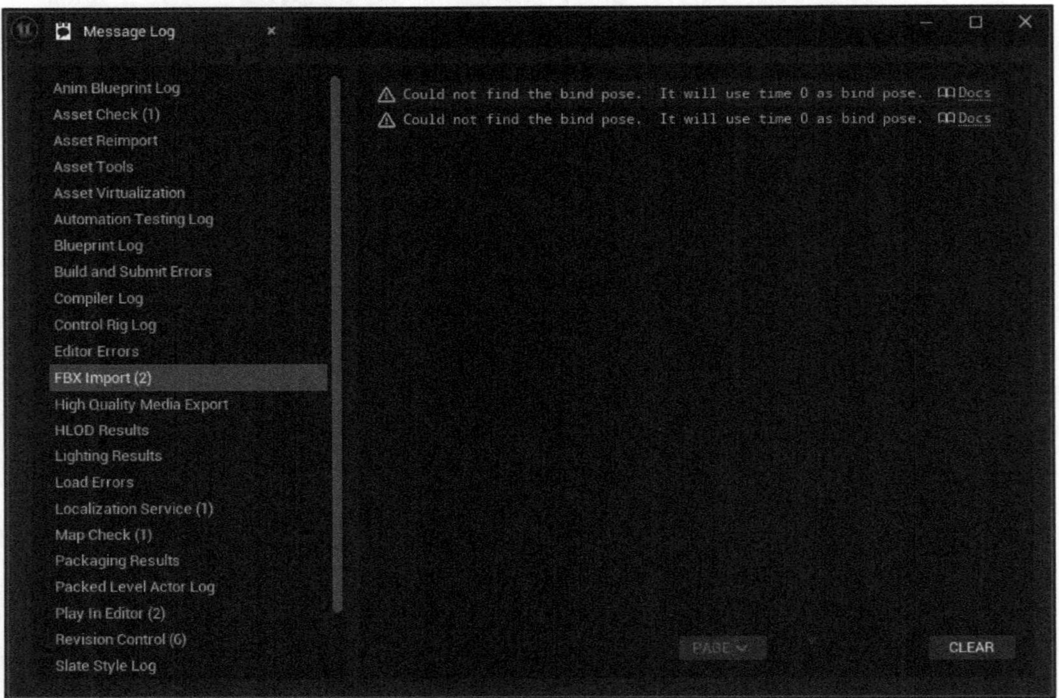

Figure 3.22 – Import, Message Log

5. As we imported and modified the material in the preceding exercise, the material might be assigned directly to the Skeletal Mesh. If this is not the case for you, assign the material created for the Static Mesh to the Skeletal Mesh. You can assign it in the Skeletal Mesh Editor, as shown in *Figure 3.21*, or directly on the level instance. In order to open the Skeletal Mesh Editor, open any of the assets created in the folder where you can see the windmill, as shown in *Figure 3.23*, and select the Skeletal Mesh Editor in the top right of the window (see *Figure 3.24*):

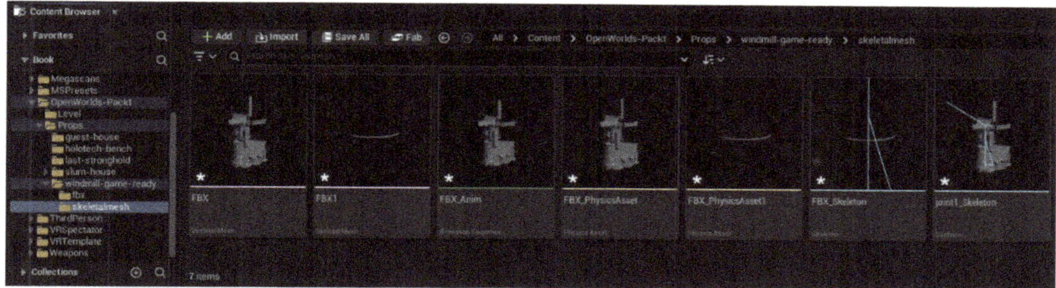

Figure 3.23 – Animation sequence asset, Skeletal Mesh FBX

In *Figure 3.23*, we can see the assets imported into our project, with a focus on those related to the Skeletal Mesh. We can observe the Skeleton, Physical Assets, and Animation Sequence.

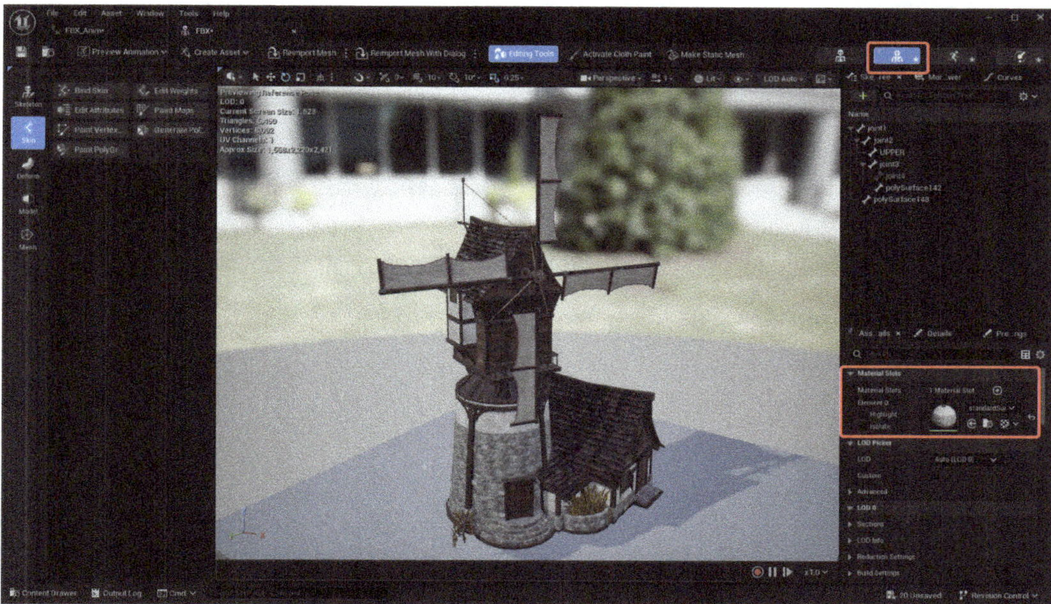

Figure 3.24 – Skeletal Mesh Editor, Material Slots, Skeletal Mesh FBX

6. Place the asset on the level.
7. If the scale is not as desired, please keep in mind that you can modify the scale of the imported assets in both Skeletal Mesh Editor and **Animation Sequence Editor**, as shown in *Figures 3.25* and *3.26*. After choosing the desired scale, select **Reimport Mesh With Dialog**. This is also highlighted in the following screenshots:

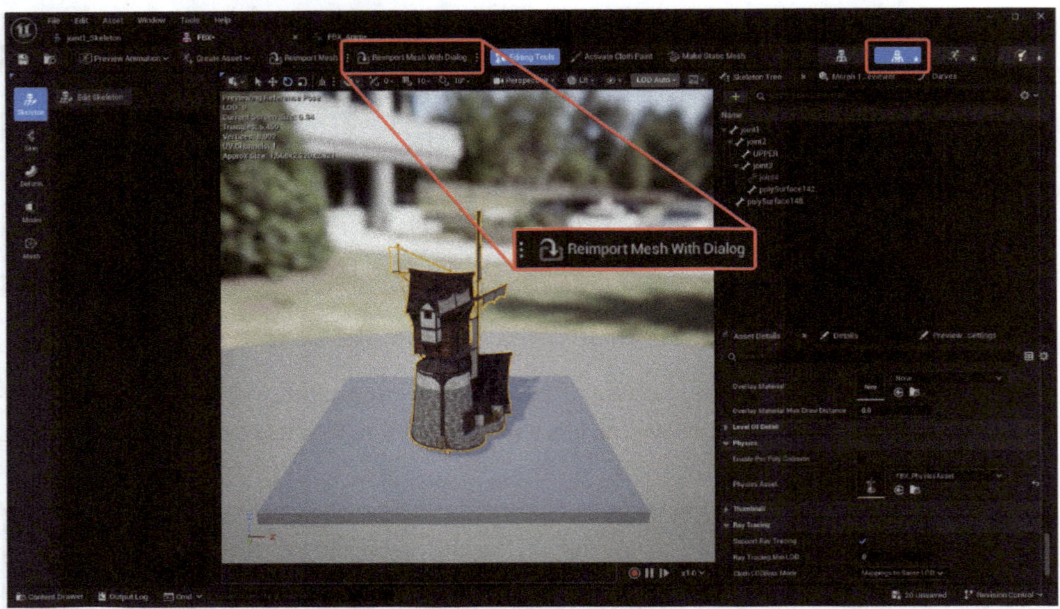

Figure 3.25 – Import scale, reimport base mesh, Skeletal Mesh FBX

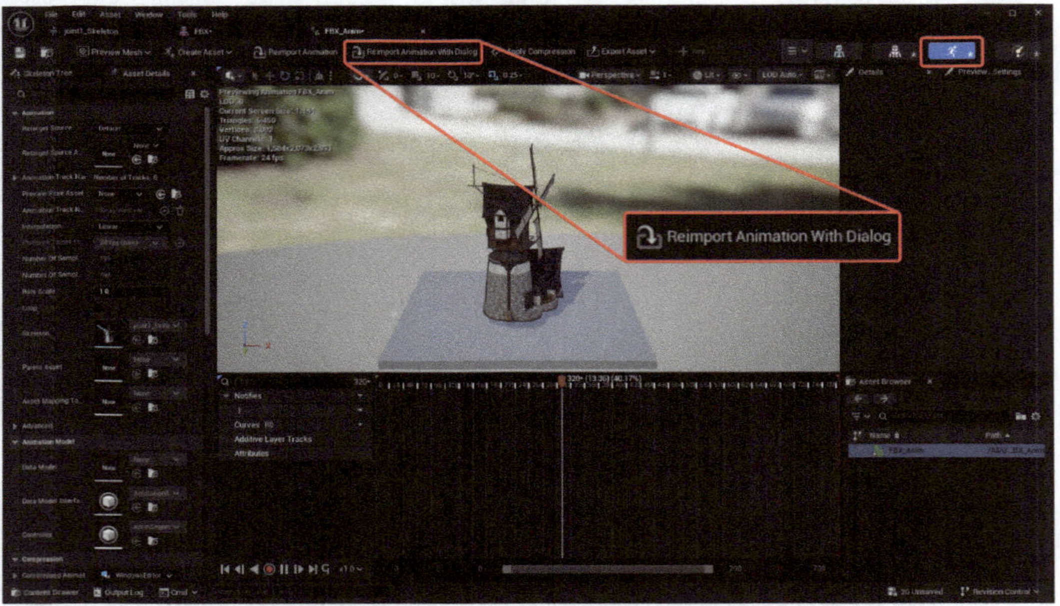

Figure 3.26 – Import scale, reimport animation, Skeletal Mesh FBX

8. If you've modified the import scale and reimported the asset, you'll see the modification directly in the instance of the asset in the level.
9. In order to see the animation playing, click the **Simulate** button on the top toolbar. Double-check that your asset is correctly set up. Your Skeletal Mesh placed in the level should have the following settings in the **Animation** section:

Figure 3.27 – Setting and simulation, Skeletal Mesh FBX

1. **Animation Mode: Use Animation Asset**
2. **Anim to Play: Desired animation** (e.g., `FBX_Anim`)
3. **Looping**: Checked
4. **Playing**: Checked

Skeletal Meshes are a straightforward way to bring animated objects (or objects ready for animation) into our projects, allowing us to bring life to our scenes with moving elements.

Summary

The first part of this chapter focused on the concept of asset ingestion in Unreal Engine, an essential process for integrating external assets into game projects. We delved into the detailed steps of importing Static Meshes, particularly in FBX format, into Unreal Engine. This included preparing the **Content Browser**, configuring import settings to suit the project's requirements, and troubleshooting common issues that might arise during the import process. By guiding you through the practical exercise of importing an FBX file, the chapter aimed to equip you with a fundamental understanding of how to efficiently bring external 3D models into your Unreal Engine projects, setting the stage for further manipulation and integration within the game environment.

The second part of the chapter dealt extensively with optimization techniques, crucial for enhancing game performance while maintaining high visual quality. We explored the implementation of **Level of Detail (LOD)** strategies, explaining how different LODs are used to manage the complexity of models based on their proximity to the camera. The chapter also covered optimization strategies for materials, emphasizing the balance between aesthetics and performance and the importance of adjustments in response to environmental conditions.

The next chapter will shift our focus to the foundational elements of project structure and naming conventions in Unreal Engine. This crucial aspect of game development ensures efficient management and organization of assets, which is especially important in complex projects with numerous elements.

References

- Design Bureau. 2020. "Slum house - Download Free 3D model by DESIGN BUREAU (@designbureau)." Sketchfab. `https://sketchfab.com/3d-models/slum-house-e902e0af80804d01924387da6af8eecf`.
- Farinha, Diego. 2023. "Implementing USD for Game Development Pipelines: An Interview with Polyphony Digital | NVIDIA Technical Blog." NVIDIA Developer. `https://developer.nvidia.com/blog/implementing-usd-for-game-development-pipelines-an-interview-with-polyphony-digital/`.
- Lamoureux, Francis. 2022. "Windmill (game ready) - Download Free 3D model by FrancisLam. (@francislam)." Sketchfab. `https://sketchfab.com/3d-models/windmill-game-ready-6a006afce57a447baa60c7a6791f0086`.

Subscribe to Game Dev Assembly Newsletter!

We are excited to introduce **Game Dev Assembly**, our brand-new newsletter dedicated to everything game development. Whether you're a programmer, designer, artist, animator, or studio lead, you'll get exclusive insights, industry trends, and expert tips to help you build better games and grow your skills. Sign up today and become part of a growing community of creators, innovators, and game changers.

`https://packt.link/gamedev-newsletter`

Scan the QR code to join instantly!

Get This Book's PDF Version and Exclusive Extras

UNLOCK NOW

Scan the QR code (or go to `packtpub.com/unlock`). Search for this book by name, confirm the edition, and then follow the steps on the page.

Note: *Keep your invoice handy. Purchases made directly from Packt don't require an invoice.*

Subscribe to Game Dev Assembly Newsletter!

4

Project Structure and Naming Conventions

Picture this: an Unreal project devoid of folders, where all assets are haphazardly scattered throughout the root directory with random names. This chaotic setup would be a developer's nightmare, rendering asset retrieval a time-consuming ordeal.

Now, envision the same project meticulously organized, with assets grouped logically within a folder hierarchy and named descriptively to clarify their purpose and relationships. Moreover, imagine all departments adhering to the same organizational structure and naming conventions. In this scenario, locating required assets becomes effortless, maximizing developer efficiency and productivity.

This chapter stresses the importance of establishing and maintaining a structured project layout and naming convention in Unreal Engine. This applies not only to project elements such as assets and code but also to scene actors and the project repository.

Maintaining a clear and consistent project structure is especially vital when building open world landscapes, where multiple assets, levels, and systems must work together seamlessly. While these practices may not directly impact engine performance or graphical fidelity, they are essential for the success of any project, particularly those involving numerous assets or collaborators.

In the upcoming sections, we'll delve into the specifics of the Allar Style Guide, offering it as both an example and a guide for crafting project structures and naming conventions. Additionally, we'll discuss strategies for safeguarding our work and facilitating collaborative efforts among team members. This will involve utilizing repositories and revision control tools such as SVN, Git, Plastic, or Perforce.

Key topics to be covered include the following:

- Advantages of a correct project structure and naming convention
- Examples of project structure and naming conventions
- Revision control tools for Unreal Engine
- Exercise 4.1: Applying a project structure and naming convention protocols
- Exercise 4.2: Using revision control tools for Unreal Engine

This chapter is designed to provide deep technical insight into these tools, enhancing both the efficiency and quality of asset management and integration in Unreal Engine 5.

Technical requirements

To proceed with this chapter, you will need a PC with **Unreal Engine 5.5 (or a later version)** installed, meeting the recommended system requirements provided by Epic Games, along with internet access.

You can find the hardware and software specifications for Unreal Engine here:

`https://dev.epicgames.com/documentation/en-us/unreal-engine/hardware-and-software-specifications-for-unreal-engine`

Additionally, you will need to have both **GitHub Desktop** and **Sourcetree** installed on your machine:

- To download GitHub Desktop, visit `https://github.com/apps/desktop`
- To download Sourcetree, visit `https://www.sourcetreeapp.com/`

Advantages of a correct project structure and naming convention

This section provides detailed technical insights into effective project structure and naming conventions. By implementing these practices, you can significantly enhance the efficiency and quality of asset management and integration in Unreal Engine 5 (UE5). Additionally, maintaining order and clarity in your project files helps improve collaboration among team members and facilitates the scalability of your projects as they grow in complexity.

Let's explore these tools and techniques in detail and discover how they can streamline your development process.

Maintaining order and clarity

Achieving a well-structured and organized project is essential for efficient development in Unreal Engine 5. By adhering to these guidelines, you can enhance collaboration, streamline debugging, and facilitate the scalability of your projects:

- **Project structure**:
    - **Folder hierarchy**: Establishing a clear hierarchy of folders is crucial for a well-defined project structure, as it separates assets, code, and other resources in an organized manner. This structured approach facilitates efficient collaboration among team members by making it easier to locate, manage, and update project files.
    - **Content organization**: Categorizing assets into folders based on their type (textures, meshes, Blueprints, etc.) simplifies asset retrieval and modification.
- **Folder organization**:
    - **Asset management**: Storing assets within the `Content` directory in an organized manner streamlines asset management. Subfolders categorized by asset type simplify navigation and aid in the digital construction and debugging process.
    - **Asset identification**: While Unreal's interface visually identifies asset types through icons, external programs such as Git and Windows Explorer rely solely on asset names and directory paths.
    - **Source code**: Dedicating specific folders to C++ or Blueprint Classes facilitates version control and fosters modular and object-oriented coding practices.

In *Figure 4.1*, we can see a screenshot of the Unreal Engine **Content Browser**, where color-coded stripes define the category of the stored asset.

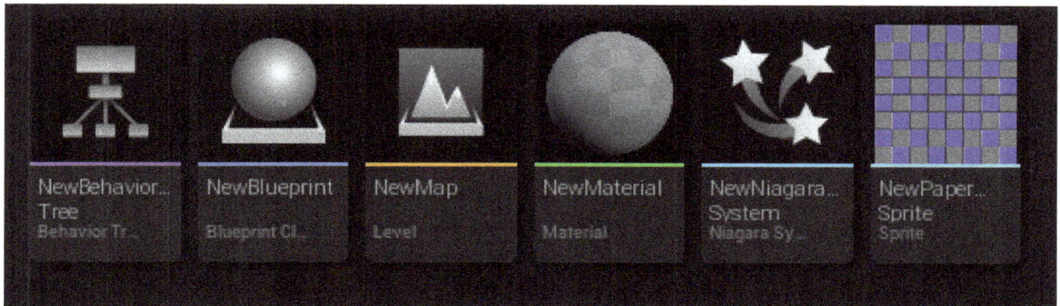

Figure 4.1 – Different assets and their icons in Unreal's interface

On the other hand, in *Figure 4.2*, we can see from the filesystem manager that all the previously viewed assets have the same `.uasset` extension, except for maps, which have a `.umap` extension:

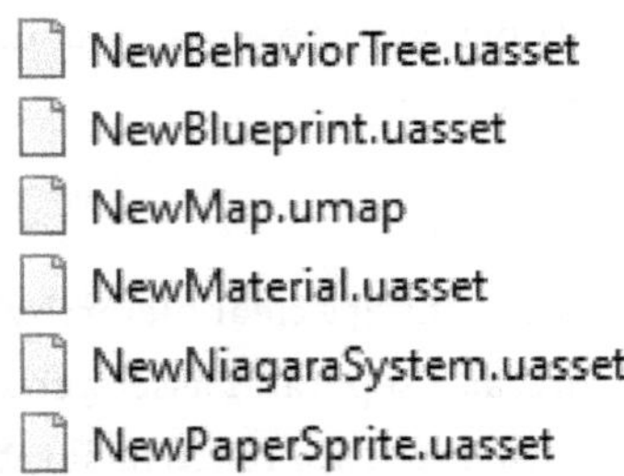

Figure 4.2 – Different assets in the filesystem manager

When storing assets in Unreal Engine, they are converted into a format that allows the engine to interpret and apply them in real time to our projects. This underscores the importance of categorizing them correctly into folders based on the type of asset being used.

Enhancing collaboration

Effective collaboration in UE5 relies on clear communication and consistent workflows. Establishing shared standards for language, naming conventions, and version control helps teams work together efficiently across different stages of development. These practices ensure that every contributor can navigate, modify, and expand the project with confidence. The following guidelines will help you maintain coordinated teamwork throughout your project:

- **Language**: Opting for a common language, typically English, ensures effective communication and facilitates sharing with diverse stakeholders.
- **Consistent naming conventions**:
    - **Assets identification**: Employing a consistent naming convention for assets enhances understanding and streamlines collaboration, particularly in multi-department projects
    - **Blueprints and classes**: Clear and indicative naming conventions for Blueprints and classes aid in communication and prevent errors or duplication of work during collaboration

- **Version control**:
    - **Branch naming**: Establishing a convention for branch names in **version control systems (VCSs)** aids in identifying branch purpose and scope, promoting seamless collaboration
    - **Commit messages**: Standardized commit messages enable team members to easily comprehend changes and make informed decisions, fostering efficient collaboration and issue tracking
- **Outsourcing**: Language selection, project structure, and naming conventions are crucial when collaborating with external teams.

Maintaining a clear project structure and consistent naming conventions not only improves current workflows but also sets a solid foundation for future growth.

Facilitating scalability and maintenance

In the world of game development, Unreal Engine 5 is a versatile tool for realizing creative visions. Yet, its full potential emerges when developers prioritize a well-structured project. This organization is key for scalability and maintenance, enabling easier adaptation, efficient debugging, and futureproofing.

Here's how effective project management can ensure adaptability to growth:

- **Modularity**: A structured project easily accommodates new requirements or design changes. Modularity in both code and assets facilitates scalability, simplifying the integration of new features or expansion of the game world.
- **Futureproofing**: Investing time in establishing a robust project structure and adhering to naming conventions preemptively addresses potential issues as the project grows in complexity.
- **Debugging and troubleshooting**: A well-organized project structure expedites issue identification and resolution. Developers can pinpoint problems efficiently, minimizing downtime and improving the development process.

Hence, to fully leverage the capabilities of UE5, developers must recognize the pivotal role of project structure and naming conventions. A meticulously organized project not only fosters collaboration and enhances daily efficiency but also lays the groundwork for scalable and maintainable game development.

Examples of project structure and name conventions

Before looking at specific naming conventions, it's essential to understand why the `Content` folder in Unreal Engine holds such importance in project structure. This folder serves as the central hub for all assets used in a project—whether they are 3D models, materials, textures, or Blueprints.

A well-organized `Content` folder not only ensures that team members can easily find and manage assets but also prevents issues such as duplicate files, lost references, and inconsistent asset use, which can lead to unnecessary complications in large-scale projects.

This organization becomes especially *critical* in open world environments or projects that involve multiple teams, where efficient collaboration depends on a unified structure. It's for these reasons that adhering to a proper project structure within the `Content` folder is considered an industry best practice.

To illustrate how these principles can be applied effectively, we will reference the Allar Style Guide: a widely adopted industry standard that provides concrete examples of how to structure and name assets in day-to-day workflows. The guide outlines practices that not only promote consistency across projects but also improve scalability and performance, making it an essential tool for any studio or development team.

Exploring the Allar Style Guide

One of the most renowned conventions in the Unreal Engine community is the **Allar Style Guide**, named after its creator, Michael Allar. Widely embraced by developers, this guide serves as a cornerstone for Unreal Engine projects. For detailed insights, the complete guide is available at the GitHub repository: `https://github.com/Allar/ue5-style-guide`.

In the subsequent sections, we'll outline the key principles of Allar's project structure and naming conventions.

Allowed characters

Any identifier should strive to only have the following characters when possible: *A–Z*, *a–z*, *0–9*, *_*.

Naming assets

Any asset within this logical group should adhere to the standard `Prefix_BaseAssetName_Variant_Suffix`, as follows:

- `Prefix` and `Suffix` are to be determined by the asset type, following the asset name modifier tables, as we can see in the following figure. For additional assets, please refer to the Allar Style Guide documentation: `https://github.com/Allar/ue5-style-guide`.

  In the following table from the Allar Style Guide, we can see the suffixes and prefixes used for the most common assets in Unreal Engine and their variations.

Asset Type	Prefix	Suffix	Notes
Level / Map			Should be in a folder called Maps.
Level (Persistent)		_P	
Level (Audio)		_Audio	
Level (Lighting)		_Lighting	
Level (Geometry)		_Geo	
Level (Gameplay)		_Gameplay	
Blueprint	BP_		
Material	M_		
Static Mesh	S_		Many use SM_. We use S_.
Skeletal Mesh	SK_		
Texture	T_	_?	See Textures
Particle System	PS_		
Widget Blueprint	WBP_		

Figure 4.3 – Allar Style Guide asset name modifier table (Credit: `https://github.com/Allar/ue5-style-guide?tab=readme-ov-file#asset-name-modifiers`*)*

It is also important to categorize the naming conventions for textures and material-related resources, as this will aid in their subsequent use. *Figure 4.4* illustrates this:

Asset Type	Prefix	Suffix	Notes
Texture	T_		
Texture (Diffuse/Albedo/Base Color)	T_	_D	
Texture (Normal)	T_	_N	
Texture (Roughness)	T_	_R	
Texture (Alpha/Opacity)	T_	_A	
Texture (Ambient Occlusion)	T_	_O	
Texture (Bump)	T_	_B	
Texture (Emissive)	T_	_E	
Texture (Mask)	T_	_M	
Texture (Specular)	T_	_S	
Texture (Metallic)	T_	_M	
Texture (Packed)	T_	_*	See notes below about packing.
Texture Cube	TC_		
Media Texture	MT_		
Render Target	RT_		
Cube Render Target	RTC_		
Texture Light Profile	TLP		

Figure 4.4 – Allar Style Guide asset name modifier table (Credit: `https://github.com/Allar/ue5-style-guide?tab=readme-ov-file#126-textures`*)*

- `BaseAssetName` should be a concise and easily identifiable name that pertains to a group of assets. For instance, if all assets are related to a character named Bob, `Bob` would serve as `BaseAssetName`.
- `Variant` represents specific variations of an asset and is also short and recognizable. It groups subsets of the base asset. For instance, Bob's different skins would be named `Bob_Evil` for an evil skin and `Bob_Retro` for a retro skin.

  For unique but generic asset variations, `Variant` is designated by a two-digit number starting from 01. For instance, rocks created by an environment artist would be named `Rock_01`, `Rock_02`, `Rock_03`, and so on.

Let's examine a specific case of a complete asset within Unreal Engine, considering the Skeletal Mesh, materials, and textures:

Asset Type	Asset Name
Skeletal Mesh	SK_Bob
Material	M_Bob
Texture (Diffuse/Albedo)	T_Bob_D
Texture (Normal)	T_Bob_N
Texture (Evil Diffuse)	T_Bob_Evil_D

Figure 4.5 – Bob's asset naming example (Credit: `https://github.com/Allar/ue5-style-guide?tab=readme-ov-file#11e1-bob`*)*

Let's also look at what we encounter when dealing with assets that have different variants.

Asset Type	Asset Name
Static Mesh (01)	S_Rock_01
Static Mesh (02)	S_Rock_02
Static Mesh (03)	S_Rock_03
Material	M_Rock
Material Instance (Snow)	MI_Rock_Snow

Figure 4.6 – Rock variants asset naming example (Credit: `https://github.com/Allar/ue5-style-guide?tab=readme-ov-file#11e2-rocks`*)*

As you can see, the structure is simple and scalable, but that doesn't mean it's rigid. You can adapt it to the specific needs of your project, if it maintains an internal logic that allows everyone involved in the project to understand and work with it effectively.

Content directory structure

Allar uses the Unreal **Content Browser**'s filtering and search features to find specific types of assets, rather than organizing assets into folders by type. Since asset names already indicate their type, there's no need for extra folders such as `Asset` or `AssetType`. This approach avoids redundancy and takes advantage of the **Content Browser**'s filtering system. For instance, to view only Static Meshes in the `Environment/Rocks/` directory, just activate the **Static Mesh** filter.

Examples of an open world project structure can be found in *Figure 4.7*:

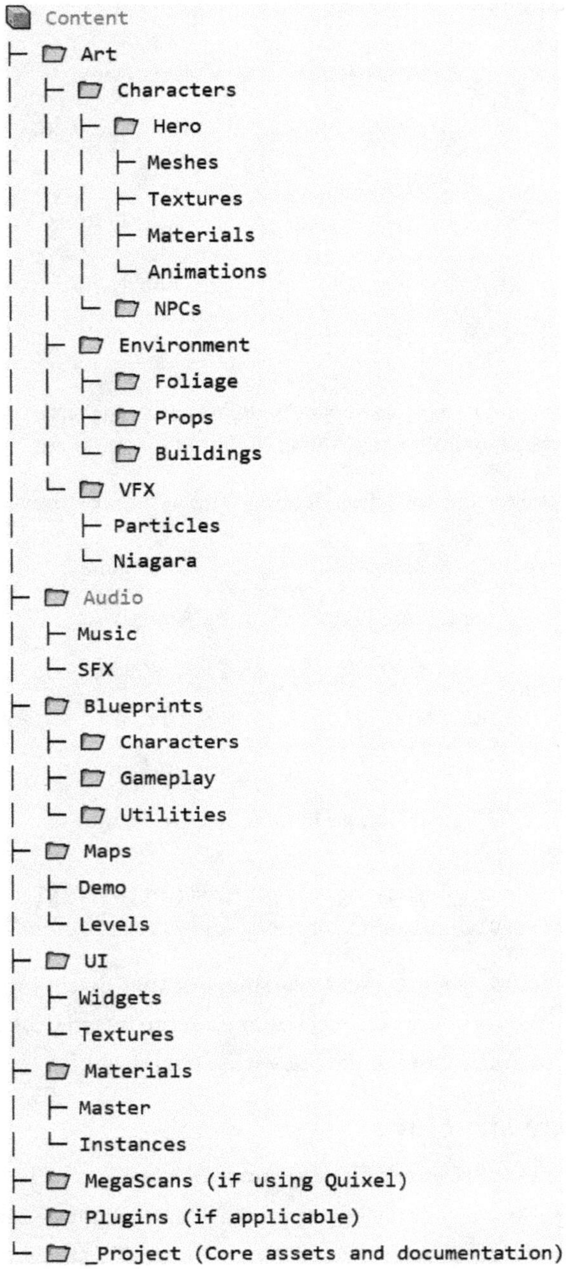

```
Content
├─ Art
│  ├─ Characters
│  │  ├─ Hero
│  │  │  ├─ Meshes
│  │  │  ├─ Textures
│  │  │  ├─ Materials
│  │  │  └─ Animations
│  │  └─ NPCs
│  ├─ Environment
│  │  ├─ Foliage
│  │  ├─ Props
│  │  └─ Buildings
│  └─ VFX
│     ├─ Particles
│     └─ Niagara
├─ Audio
│  ├─ Music
│  └─ SFX
├─ Blueprints
│  ├─ Characters
│  ├─ Gameplay
│  └─ Utilities
├─ Maps
│  ├─ Demo
│  └─ Levels
├─ UI
│  ├─ Widgets
│  └─ Textures
├─ Materials
│  ├─ Master
│  └─ Instances
├─ MegaScans (if using Quixel)
├─ Plugins (if applicable)
└─ _Project (Core assets and documentation)
```

```
|-- Content
    |-- GenericShooter
        |-- Art
        |   |-- Industrial
        |   |   |-- Ambient
        |   |   |-- Machinery
        |   |   |-- Pipes
        |   |-- Nature
        |   |   |-- Ambient
        |   |   |-- Foliage
        |   |   |-- Rocks
        |   |   |-- Trees
        |   |-- Office
        |-- Characters
        |   |-- Bob
        |   |-- Common
        |   |   |-- Animations
        |   |   |-- Audio
        |   |-- Jack
        |   |-- Steve
        |   |-- Zoe
        |-- Core
        |   |-- Characters
        |   |-- Engine
        |   |-- GameModes
        |   |-- Interactables
        |   |-- Pickups
        |   |-- Weapons
        |-- Effects
        |   |-- Electrical
        |   |-- Fire
        |   |-- Weather
        |-- Maps
        |   |-- Campaign1
        |   |-- Campaign2
        |-- MaterialLibrary
        |   |-- Debug
        |   |-- Metal
        |   |-- Paint
        |   |-- Utility
        |   |-- Weathering
        |-- Placeables
        |   |-- Pickups
        |-- Weapons
            |-- Common
            |-- Pistols
            |   |-- DesertEagle
            |   |-- RocketPistol
            |-- Rifles
```

Figure 4.7 – Project structure example

Next, let's look at some considerations when working with organizational structures based on folders:

- **Folder names:** Start folder names with a capital letter, followed by subsequent words, all in capitals and no spaces, using the *A–Z, a–z, 0–9* characters only.
- **Use a top-level folder for project-specific assets:** Keep all project assets in a folder named after the project to avoid conflicts and maintain organization.
- **Use the Developers folder for local testing:** Use the `Developers` folder for local testing to create a safe environment for experimentation.
- **All map files belong in a folder called Maps:** Place all map files in a `Maps` folder within `/Content/Project` for easy access and organization.
- **Use a Core folder for critical assets and Blueprints:** Store fundamental assets in the `/Content/Project/Core` folder and avoid direct modifications.
- **Very large asset sets get their own folder layout:** Use specialized folder layouts for large asset sets such as animations and audio.

  For example, animations shared across multiple characters should be placed in `Characters/Common/Animations` and may be further organized into subfolders such as `Locomotion` or `Cinematic`. This approach does not apply to assets such as textures and materials.
- **Materials library:** Store reusable materials or textures in `Content/Project/MaterialLibrary` for easy access and consistency.
- **No empty folders:** There shouldn't be any empty folders as they clutter the **Content Browser**.

Following the correct project structure and naming conventions is equally important for assets and resources that we create and import into the engine, whether they are 3D models or textures. However, it's important to note that these rules are not set in stone. They are a set of guidelines aimed at keeping the workspace organized, facilitating the workflow across different teams, and ensuring consistency throughout the project.

As development progresses, it's common for teams to adapt these guidelines to better suit their specific needs. This flexibility is entirely normal, as long as any changes are well documented and communicated clearly to everyone involved in the project. Proper documentation ensures that all team members stay on the same page, preventing confusion or disruptions in the workflow, even as the project evolves.

Let's now review these conventions and explore how they can be applied effectively.

Guidelines for assets and resources created and imported into Unreal Engine

Whenever we consider importing assets into Unreal Engine, whether they are 3D models, textures, or assets being migrated between projects, it is crucial to conduct an initial check to ensure that the assets meet our final requirements. If they do not, we need to understand their initial state and apply corrective measures within the engine. Let's explore what these considerations are:

- **Static Meshes**:
    - **Static Mesh UV channels should be correctly configured**: Specifically, **UV Channel 0** should be set up for textures, and **UV Channel 1** should be used for Lightmaps. In the Lightmap UV channel, UV islands should not overlap to ensure accurate lighting calculations.
    - **Levels of detail (LODs) should be set up correctly**: This check is project-specific, but generally, any mesh visible at different distances should have proper LOD. LODs reduce the complexity of a 3D model as it gets farther from the viewer, improving rendering efficiency by lessening the graphics pipeline's workload.
    - **All meshes must have collision**: This aids the engine with tasks such as bounds calculations, occlusion, and lighting. Additionally, the collision should be accurately aligned with the asset.
    - **All meshes should be scaled correctly**: Level designers or Blueprint authors should not have to tweak the scale of meshes. Scaling meshes in the engine should be treated as a scale override, not a scale correction.
- **Niagara**:
    - **There should be no spaces**: All names should begin with a capital letter, followed by subsequent words also starting with capital letters, without using spaces. Only the *A–Z*, *a–z*, *0–9*, and _ characters should be used to avoid unexpected issues when working with HLSL or other scripting systems.
- **Textures**:
    - **Texture dimensions should be powers of 2 (2, 4, 8, 16, 32, or 64 pixels)**: While square textures are commonly used in the engine, rectangular textures are also acceptable as long as they adhere to this power-of-2 rule. This ensures that mipmaps can be generated for the textures, which helps the engine operate more efficiently. This rule does not apply to UI textures, which can have any size as needed.

- **Texture density should be uniform**: All textures should be of a size appropriate for their standard use case. Appropriate texture density varies from project to project, but all textures within that project should have a consistent density. For example, if a project's texture density is 8 pixels per 1 unit, a texture that is meant to be applied to a 100x100 unit cube should be 1,024x1,024, as that is the closest power of 2 that matches the project's texture density.
- **Textures shouldn't be huge**: No texture should have a dimension that exceeds 8,192 in size, unless you have a very explicit reason to do so.
- **Textures should be grouped correctly**: Every texture has a **Texture Group** property used for LOD, and this should be set correctly based on its use. For example, all UI textures should belong in the UI texture group.

- **Content directory structure**:
    - **World Composition**: For large open world projects or Levels with extensive environments, Unreal Engine's **World Composition** feature allows you to split a vast world into smaller, more manageable sublevels. Each sublevel can be edited independently, reducing the likelihood of errors or conflicts between team members. This is especially useful in collaborative environments, as different team members can work on separate parts of the project simultaneously.
    - **Subprojects and asset segmentation**: For projects with multiple distinct gameplay systems or environments, consider segmenting large asset sets into subprojects.
    - **Modularity in code and assets**: Structuring your code and assets in a modular way ensures that individual elements can be reused, replaced, or modified without affecting other parts of the project.
    - **Overcomplicated folder hierarchy**: While it may seem intuitive to create deeply nested folder structures for highly specific assets, this can actually lead to confusion. Instead, aim for a simple and flat folder structure, relying on Unreal Engine's powerful filtering tools in the **Content Browser**.
    - **Lack of early naming conventions**: Without clear and consistent naming conventions from the outset, asset duplication and confusion can arise, especially in collaborative projects.
    - **Redundant folders**: It's common for teams to create excessive folders or duplicate folder structures due to poor communication or organization. Redundant folders slow down project navigation and clutter the **Content Browser**.

All the previously discussed points are essential initial considerations for formatting and structuring the resources we develop. Maintaining consistency is key, as it is reassuring to know that, even when migrating information from one project to another, all resources adhere to the same format and structure, eliminating the need for adjustments in this regard.

Revision control tools for Unreal Engine

In the dynamic world of game development, where collaboration, code changes, and asset management are constant, revision control tools play a vital role in maintaining order and efficiency.

Revision control (also known as **source control** or **version control**) is an online system that tracks changes to the project's source code and related assets over time. Changes are usually identified by a unique number or letter code, referred to as the *revision number*, *revision level*, or simply *revision*. Each revision is associated with a timestamp and the developer who made the change, facilitating effective remote collaboration.

The tool provides the following features:

- Tracking of the project modifications
- Project changes and history versions safeguarding
- Project versions comparison
- Restoration or rolling back to previous versions
- Conflict avoidance (when more than one developer is modifying the same file at the same time)
- With some types of files (mostly code or text), automatically or manually merges the changes
- Efficient collaboration in both small and large development teams/projects

Let's delve a bit deeper into the revision control options available within Unreal Engine.

Revision control options for Unreal Engine

Revision control is the backbone of collaborative software development. It enables multiple developers to work on a project simultaneously, keeps track of changes made to the source code and assets, and provides a safety net by allowing you to roll back to previous versions if something goes wrong.

In order to enable revision control features directly in Unreal Engine, you can click the **Revision Control** button on the very bottom right of the Editor. After clicking **Connect to Revision Control...**, you will be able to select your desired VCS and configure it.

In *Figure 4.8*, we can see the login window for Unreal Engine's revision control system, where you can select from various services compatible with the engine:

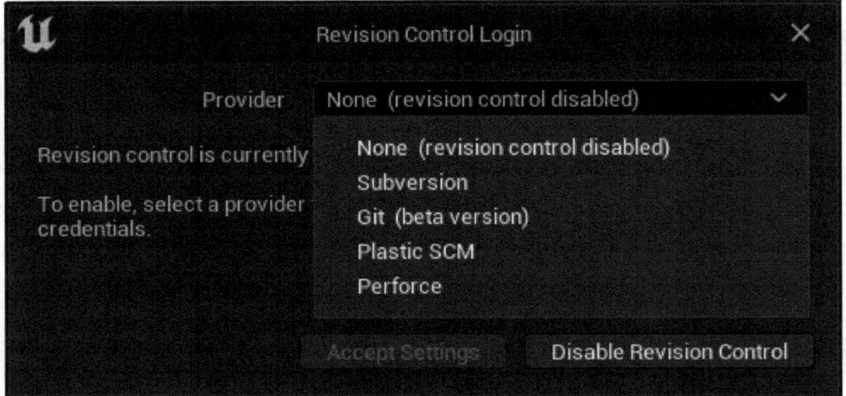

Figure 4.8 – Unreal revision control window

There are a variety of tools for achieving source control for Unreal Engine, such as the following:

- **Subversion (SVN)** is a centralized VCS similar to Perforce. While it's not as common in game development, Unreal Engine does provide support for SVN.

  Its pros are the following:

  - Centralized repository simplifies management
  - Easier learning curve compared to Git
  - Suitable for smaller projects with simpler requirements
  - Better support for binary files compared to Git

  Its cons are the following:

  - Lack of advanced branching and merging features
  - Centralized models may lead to bottlenecks

- **Git** is a **distributed version control system** (**DVCS**) widely used in the software development industry. Unreal Engine has built-in support for Git, making it easy to integrate into your workflow.

  Its pros are as follows:

  - Widely used and well supported in the industry
  - Decentralized, allowing for easy branching and merging
  - Efficient handling of text-based files
  - Large and active community

  Its cons are as follows:

  - Handling of large binary files can be challenging. It's a steeper learning curve for beginners.

- **Plastic SCM** is a DVCS that focuses on branching and merging capabilities. While not as widely known as Git or Perforce, it offers robust features for version control.

  The following are its pros:

  - Visual representation of branches for better understanding
  - Efficient handling of branching and merging
  - Good support for large binary assets
  - Distributed architecture provides flexibility

  Here are its cons:

  - Smaller community compared to Git and Perforce
  - Less widespread adoption in the industry

- **Perforce**, also known as **Helix Core**, is a centralized VCS commonly used in larger projects or enterprises. Unreal Engine provides robust Perforce integration for teams that prefer this system.

  Here are its pros:

  - Excellent support for large binary assets
  - Robust locking mechanism to prevent conflicts
  - Efficient handling of large projects and assets
  - Advanced branching and merging capabilities

The following are its cons:

- Centralized models may lead to bottlenecks
- Licensing costs for large teams

Table 4.1 shows a comparison among all the supported systems for Unreal Engine:

Feature	Subversion (SVN)	Git	Plastic SCM	Perforce
Version control model	Centralized	Distributed	Distributed	Centralized
Locking mechanism	N/A (merge-based)	N/A (merge-based)	N/A (merge-based)	File locking
Scalability	Suitable for small to medium projects	Good for all project sizes	Suitable for all project sizes	Excellent for large projects
Branching and merging	Supports branching and merging	Strong support	Powerful branching and merging	Supported, but less flexible
Integration with UE	Native support	Native support	Native support	Native support
Community support	Active community	Large and active community	Active community	Big and active community

Table 4.1 – VCS features comparison

Choosing the right revision control system depends on the specific needs of your project, team preferences, and the complexity of your development workflow. Consider factors such as project size, asset types, collaboration requirements, and individual developer preferences when making your decision.

In the next section, we will discuss best practices to follow when working in a VCS environment.

Best practices for source control in Unreal Engine

Working in a VCS environment provides the reassurance that the work done by us and our teammates is secure and backed up. However, it is important to keep in mind some key considerations to make the most of this system:

- **Commit regularly**: Regular commits help maintain a clear history of changes and make it easier to identify and revert problematic updates.
- **Use name conventions**: Apply your team's name conventions for commits and branches.
- **Use meaningful commit messages**: Write descriptive commit messages to provide context and make it easier for team members to understand the purpose of each change. Since we are discussing folder standardization, filenaming conventions, and version control management, it's important to introduce at least one widely accepted commit message standard.

  A recommended approach is to follow the **Conventional Commits** specification, which provides a structured format for commit messages that makes them easier to understand and automate. This format uses specific prefixes such as fix, feat, or chore to indicate the nature of the commit. For more detailed guidelines, refer to the Conventional Commits specification.

- **Branch strategically**: Plan your branching strategy based on your project's needs. Feature branches, release branches, and hotfix branches are common in game development.
- **Periodic code reviews**: Regular code reviews help catch issues early, ensure code quality, and facilitate knowledge sharing among team members.
- **Back up before major changes**: Before making significant changes, create a backup or snapshot of your project to safeguard against unforeseen issues.

Effective source control is a critical aspect of game development, and Unreal Engine provides seamless integration with popular tools such as Git and Perforce. Whether you're working on a small indie project or a large-scale production, adopting best practices for source control will contribute to a smoother development process, improved collaboration, and a more reliable codebase. Choose the source control system that best fits your project's needs and enjoy the benefits of version control in your development journey.

Exercise 4.1: Applying a project structure and name convention protocols

Let's engage in a practical exercise to consolidate our understanding of applying a project structure and name convention protocol. Let's create a new project and organize some assets!

Let's begin:

1. **Create a new Unreal Engine project**: Start by launching Unreal Engine and creating a new project. Name it according to these characteristics: it will be a 3D third-person character view multiplayer online coop PVE medieval fantasy RPG.
2. **Create the folder's main structure and include some assets**: We are going to include some different assets in the project:
    - The following maps:
        - Swamp
        - Village
    - The following assets for the maps:
        - Swamp trees and rocks
        - Village houses and street market stalls
    - Our three characters:
        - Our main character
        - An orc enemy
        - A vendor NPC
    - The following base Blueprints for controlling characters and environment:
        - Character movement
        - Character attacks
        - Sun controller
        - Music controller
        - Scene controller
    - A VFX for an attack

- The following materials to use freely in the project:
    - Polished metal
    - Cedar wood
    - Dark gray rock
    - Grass (this one is in the testing process)

Remember to name the assets properly, using Allar naming conventions.

The result of your organization should look similar to the structure shown in *Figure 4.9*:

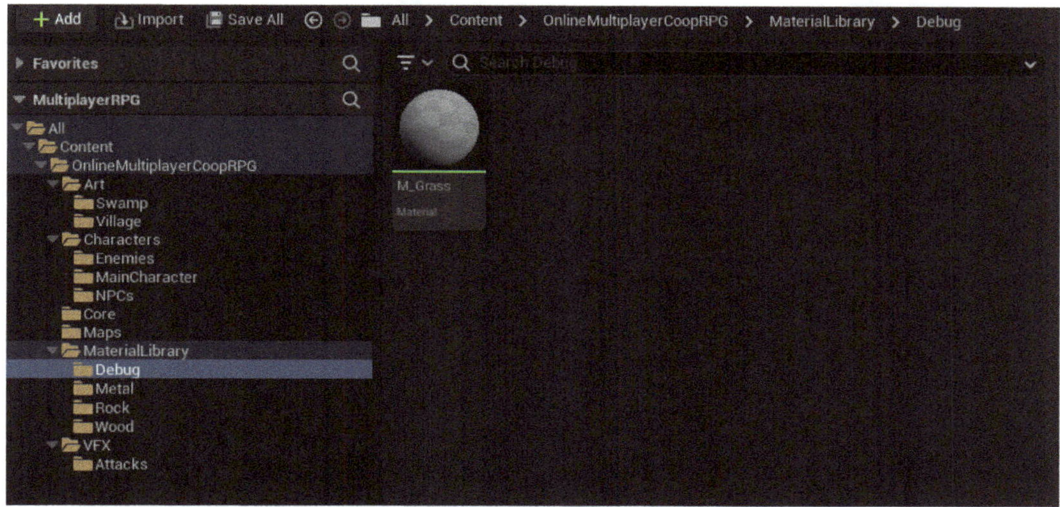

Figure 4.9 – Exercise 01 – project structure

Let's look at our next exercise.

Exercise 4.2: Using revision control tools for Unreal Engine

For our second exercise, we'll propose the practice of using a revision control tool for Unreal Engine.

You can choose any revision control tool for this exercise, though the step-by-step walk-through uses Git:

1. Create a (free personal) GitHub account. GitHub will store our project in their repositories. You could also investigate other platforms, such as AWS CodeCommit, GitLab, or Azure DevOps, and their characteristics and pricing.

2. Open or create your Unreal Engine account and connect GitHub to it. You will find the **Apps and Accounts** tab in the sidebar:

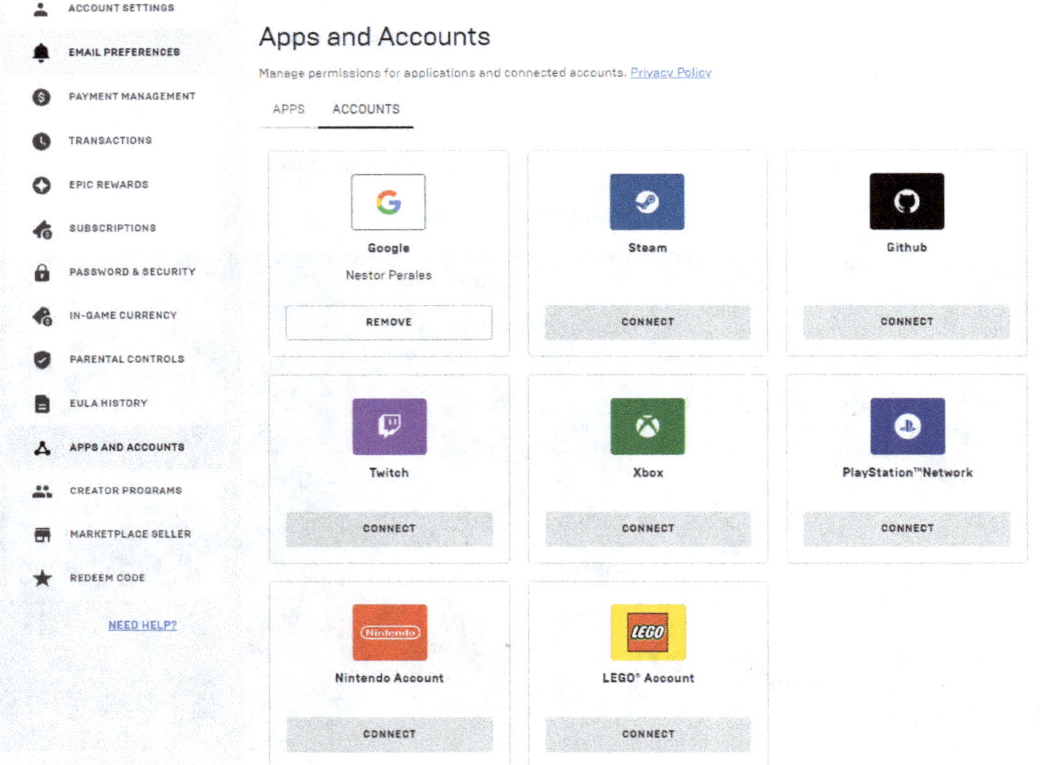

Figure 4.10 – Exercise 02 – GitHub connection to Unreal account

3. You will receive an email from GitHub with a **Join@EpicGames** button you must press to complete the linking process.
4. Download a Git GUI app, such as one of the following:
   - **GitHub Desktop app**: `https://desktop.github.com/`
   - **Sourcetree**: `https://www.sourcetreeapp.com/` (you will need a free Atlassian account; we will use this for this exercise)
5. Open the Sourcetree app and connect the GitHub account to it by clicking on the **Remote** option in the upper navigation bar and then the **Add an account...** button. Select GitHub for **Hosting Service** and click on the **Refresh OAuth Token** button.

6. Once we have connected both services, we can create a new repository. Click on the **Create** button in the upper navigation bar. Select the path for your local copy of the repository (a folder where you will create or copy the Unreal Engine project), then click on **Create Repository on Account** and set up the GitHub account.

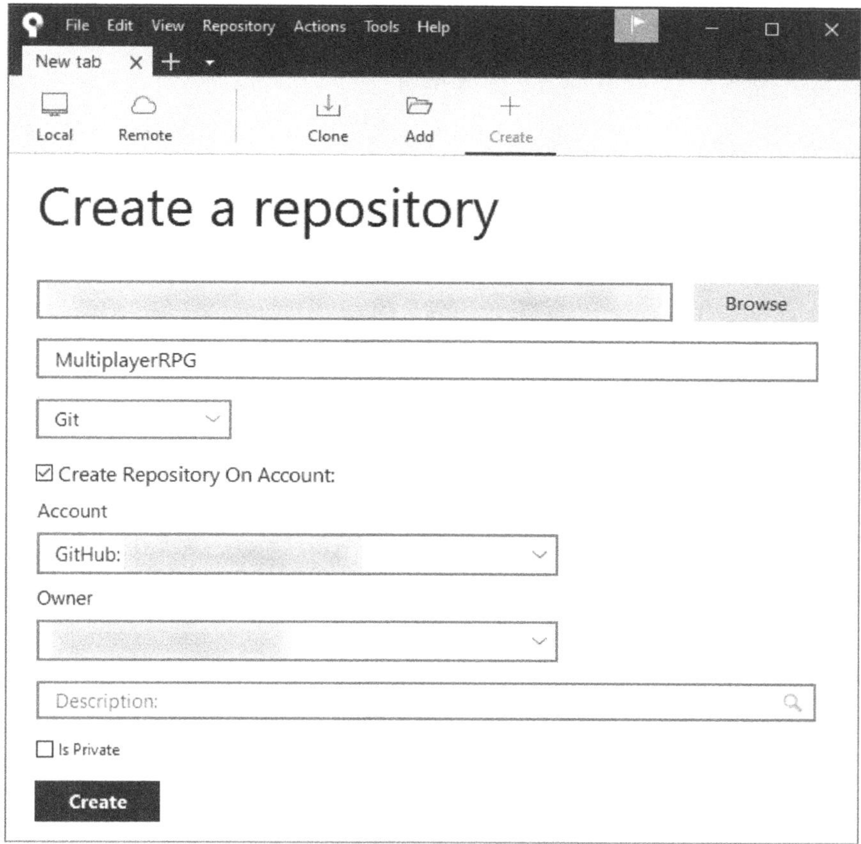

Figure 4.11 – Exercise 03 – Bitbucket repository creation on GitHub

7. Now we are ready to commit and push any changes to the repository. Create or copy an Unreal Engine project in the folder, and new changes will appear in the Sourcetree window.

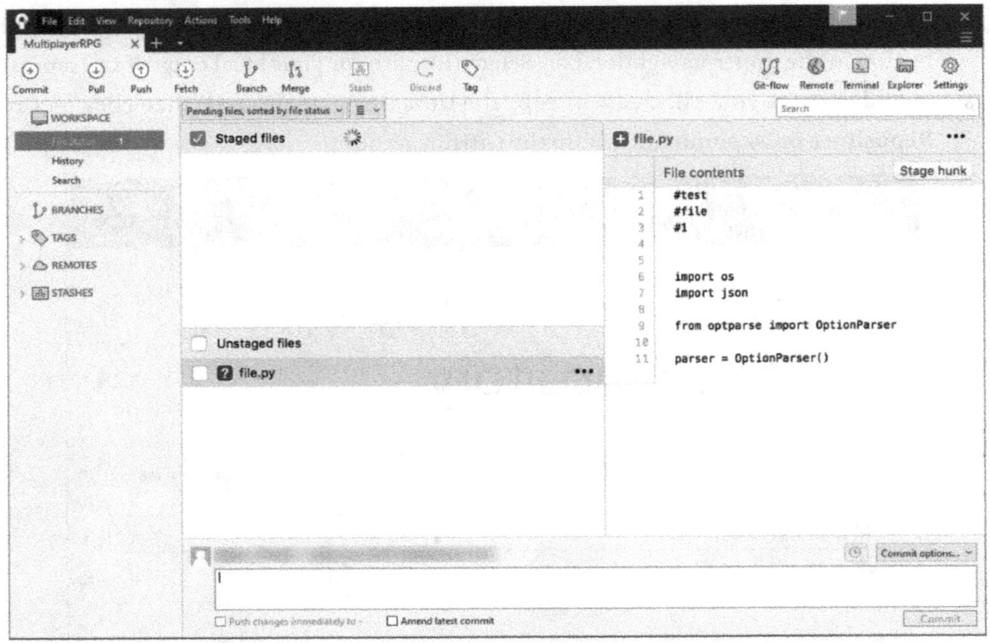

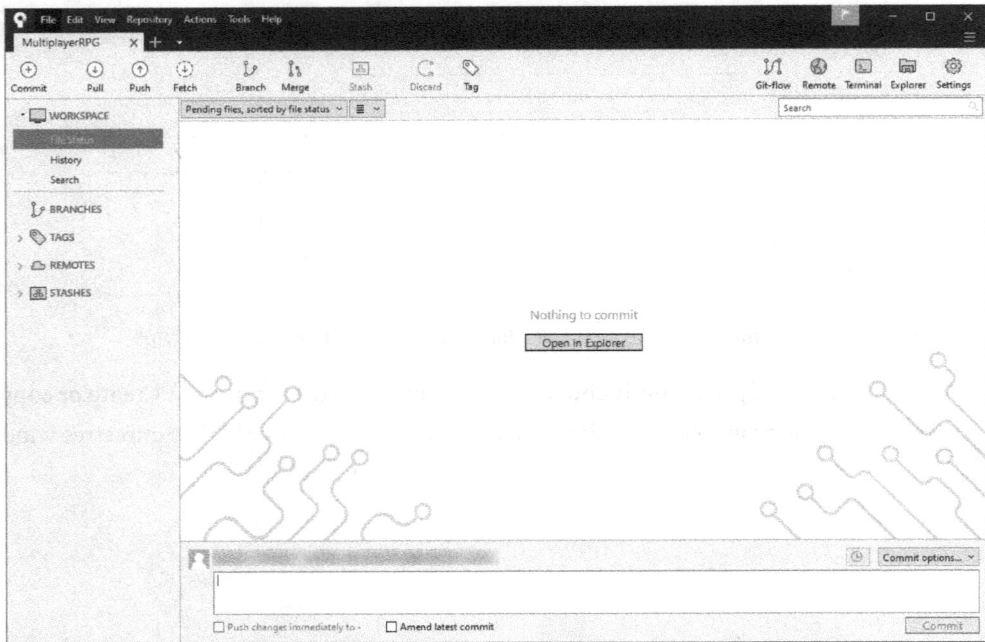

Figure 4.12 – Exercise 04 – Sourcetree project interface

Using a revision control tool such as Git is essential for efficient project management, especially in collaborative environments. Version control allows you to track changes, collaborate with other developers, and revert to previous versions if needed, ensuring that the project remains organized and manageable.

As your project grows, proper version control helps prevent data loss and facilitates smoother teamwork, making it an invaluable tool in any development pipeline.

If you encounter any issues while using Sourcetree or GitHub Desktop, the following help pages can assist you:

- **Sourcetree help**: `https://confluence.atlassian.com/get-started-with-sourcetree`
- **GitHub Desktop help**: `https://docs.github.com/en/desktop`

This brings us to the end of the exercise.

Summary

In this chapter, we explored the critical importance of project structure and naming conventions in Unreal Engine. Key points covered include establishing a well-defined project hierarchy and using clear, consistent naming conventions to facilitate asset management and collaboration. We discussed the Allar Style Guide, emphasizing the principles for project organization, such as using a top-level folder for project-specific assets and a developer's folder for local testing, properly organizing map files, core assets, and large asset sets, and creating a centralized Materials Library for reusable assets.

Additionally, we covered best practices for asset management, including ensuring proper LOD setup for meshes, maintaining uniform texture density, and avoiding empty folders and player-visible Z-fighting. The chapter also addressed the role of source control tools in tracking changes, safeguarding project versions, and facilitating efficient collaboration, with a focus on integrating Unreal Engine with popular source control systems such as Git and Perforce. By implementing these guidelines and utilizing the right tools, developers can enhance project organization, streamline workflows, and improve collaboration, leading to more efficient and successful game development.

In the next chapter, we will discuss levels within Unreal Engine, focusing on traditional levels versus **World Partition**. We will apply the concepts of organization and structure covered in this chapter to understand how to efficiently manage and organize game levels.

Part 2

Creating and Detailing Your Open World

In this part, you'll be introduced to the practical process of constructing and refining environments in Unreal Engine. It begins with an overview of how levels and layers are managed, enabling better control and scalability across large worlds. You'll then move into terrain creation using the **Landscape** and **Sculpt** tools, learning how to shape and modify natural surfaces. The following chapters guide you through adding vegetation using the **Foliage** system and creating materials that define the look and realism of surfaces.

Together, these chapters establish the key techniques for producing detailed, believable environments ready for lighting and rendering.

This part of the book includes the following chapters:

- *Chapter 5, Managing Levels and Layers*
- *Chapter 6, Building Your Landscape*
- *Chapter 7, Populating Your World with Foliage*
- *Chapter 8, Introduction to Materials*

5

Managing Levels and Layers

When working with Unreal Engine, understanding the organization of your game world within levels is crucial. Levels shape the game's environment, narrative, and performance optimization.

Building on this, consider the two primary approaches to structuring environments. Unreal Engine offers two distinct approaches to managing game environments: the traditional method using levels, sublevels, and layers, and the modern **World Partition** system. Both these approaches ultimately share the same structural foundation. Their primary difference lies in how they handle the loading and unloading of information, especially during runtime. Understanding how each system works is essential for developing interactive, cinematic, and gamified projects efficiently and at scale.

In the traditional workflow, this hierarchy can be extended further through sublevels, nested inside a *persistent level*. Each sublevel can have its own layers and sets of Actors. This method supports collaborative workflows by letting teams divide work across different levels without causing file conflicts. It's also widely used in games and cinematics, where transitioning between environments can be scripted or triggered in real time.

The **World Partition** system, on the other hand, has revolutionized environment-building by offering a streamlined and optimized approach. This system supports expansive open worlds and enhances performance management, facilitating collaboration by dividing a level into regions. This allows multiple team members to work simultaneously without conflict.

Choosing between traditional level/sublevel organization and the **World Partition** system is critical during pre-production. This decision impacts the project's development pipeline and workflow. While projects that start with a conventional hierarchy can transition to **World Partition**, reverting is not feasible once the **World Partition** method is adopted. This chapter explores these concepts, providing a clear understanding of their differences and impact on game development.

Key topics to be covered include the following:

- Working with levels
- Exploring lighting scenarios
- Using layers
- Understanding **World Partition**
- Exercise 5.1: Setup and configuration of the level systems
- Choosing the right approach to level management

Let's now take a closer look at each system and how it can be used in practice.

Important note

As this is a theoretical reference chapter, the result is not expected to be visually expressive. Rather, the focus is on familiarizing you with the corresponding tools.

Technical requirements

To continue the development of this chapter, it is necessary to have a PC with **Unreal Engine 5.5** (or a later version) installed that meets the recommended requirements by Epic Games and has internet access: `https://dev.epicgames.com/documentation/en-us/unreal-engine/hardware-and-software-specifications-for-unreal-engine`.

Working with levels

Levels are the cornerstone of your game's world in Unreal Engine, encompassing every asset, environment, character, and interactive object. At its simplest, the organizational hierarchy starts with levels, which can contain multiple layers. Each layer organizes Actors within the level and helps maintain a clean and modular structure inside the **Content Browser**. Therefore, the design and organization of levels are crucial for both narrative progression and gameplay experience.

In the next section, we will see the aspects related to the creation, storage, organization, management, and interactions between levels through sublevels and persistent levels.

Important note

This section is aimed at new users and will cover the basics of level creation in Unreal Engine (i.e., creating, saving, and opening levels). If you're already comfortable with these concepts, I'd recommend skipping ahead to the *Managing levels* section.

Creating levels

Levels can be created in multiple ways within Unreal Engine:

- **Via the main menu**: Navigate to **File** | **New Level...** to initiate the creation of a new level.

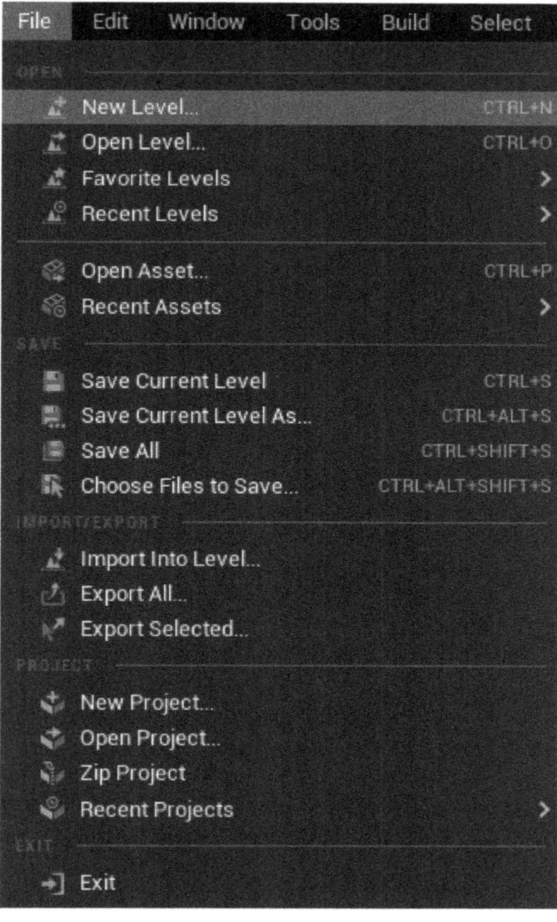

Figure 5.1 – File | New Level...

This action presents various templates to kickstart your level design, including **Open World**, **Empty Open World**, **Basic**, and **Empty Level**.

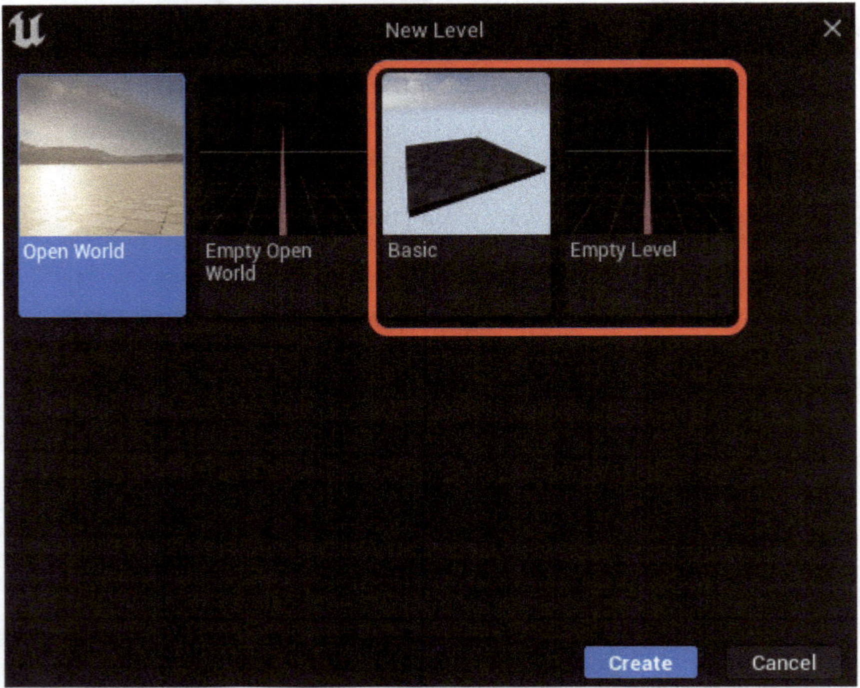

Figure 5.2 – New Level templates

Each template caters to different project needs.

- **Open World:** A level featuring sample content that utilizes the **World Partition** feature to construct a vast, streamable open world
- **Empty Open World:** A level employing **World Partition** without any content included
- **Basic:** A level equipped with a floor plan, lighting, atmosphere, and exponential fog
- **Empty Level:** A level completely devoid of content

To create a new standard level, choose either **Basic** or **Empty Level**. Once you've made your selection, press **Create**, and a new level will be loaded for you to start working on.

- **Through the Content Browser**: *Right-click* and select **Create Basic Asset** | **Level**. This method doesn't grant access to Unreal Engine's predefined level templates and creates an empty level, being a more straightforward approach if you understand your needs.

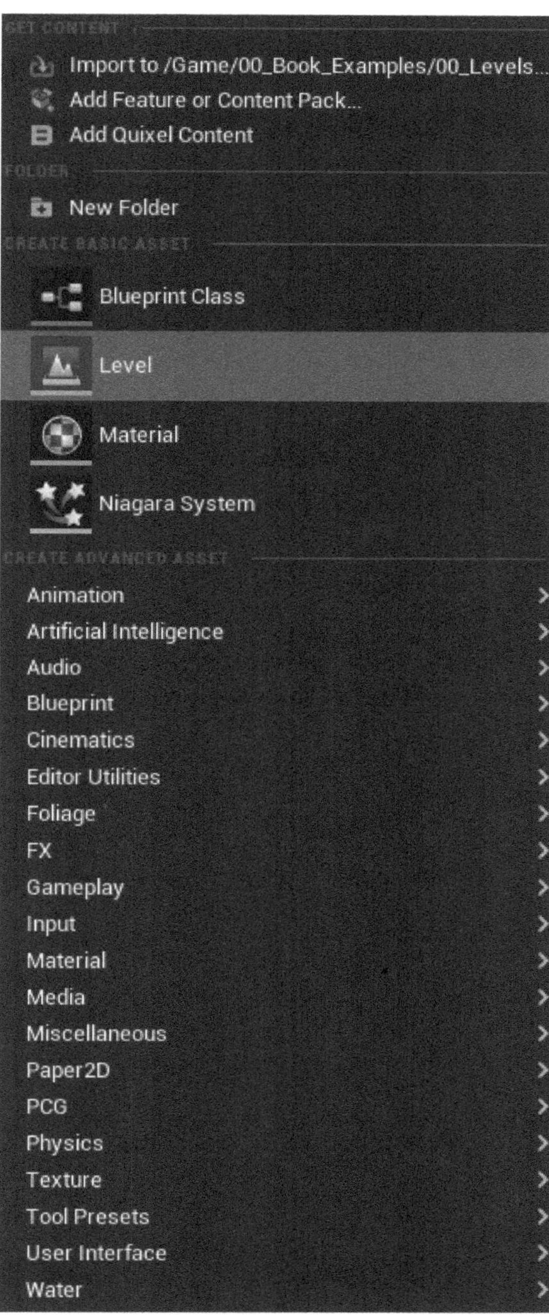

Figure 5.3 – Content Browser | Level

Saving levels

Similar to other assets, you need to save a level to preserve your changes when you close Unreal Engine or switch to another level. You can save your level using one of the following methods:

- From the main menu, go to **File**, then select **Save Current Level**
- Use the *Ctrl* + *S* (Windows) or *Cmd* + *S* (Mac) keyboard shortcut

If this is the first time you are saving the level, specify the location and name for **Level Asset**.

Opening levels

Levels can be accessed in the following ways:

- Locating them within the **Content Browser** and double-clicking
- Navigating to **File** | **Open Level** and then selecting the desired level from your project's assets

Managing levels

The **Levels** window is the hub for managing your project's hierarchical level structure, including the persistent level and any sublevels. This window can be accessed via **Window** | **Levels**:

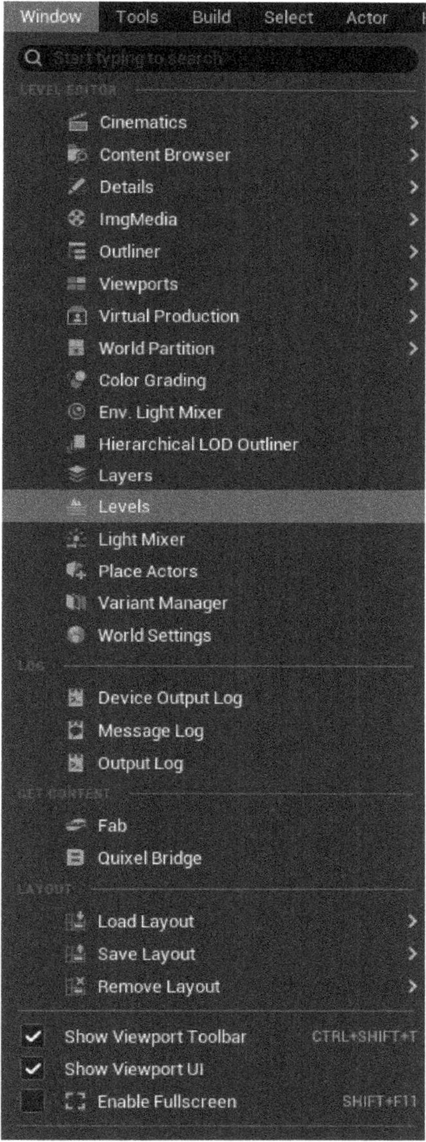

Figure 5.4 – Levels tab

This interface allows for the addition, organization, and visibility management of levels, streamlining the development process, especially when working with complex environments or large development teams.

Persistent level and sublevels

The **Persistent Level** acts as the master level.

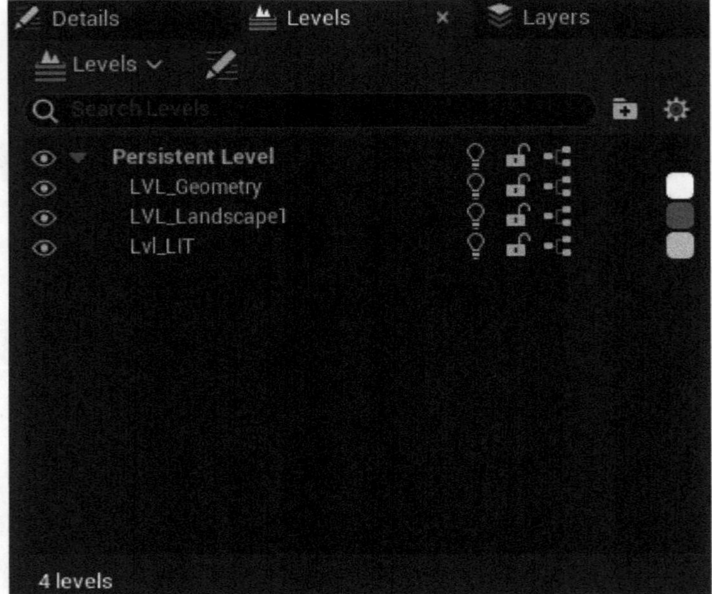

Figure 5.5 – Persistent Level

Meanwhile, sublevels can be dynamically loaded through various methods such as **Level Streaming Volumes**, **Blueprints**, or **C++ code**. This enables a modular approach to level design.

Visibility and operations

You can choose from different operations by *right-clicking* on any of the levels/sublevels in the **Levels** tab.

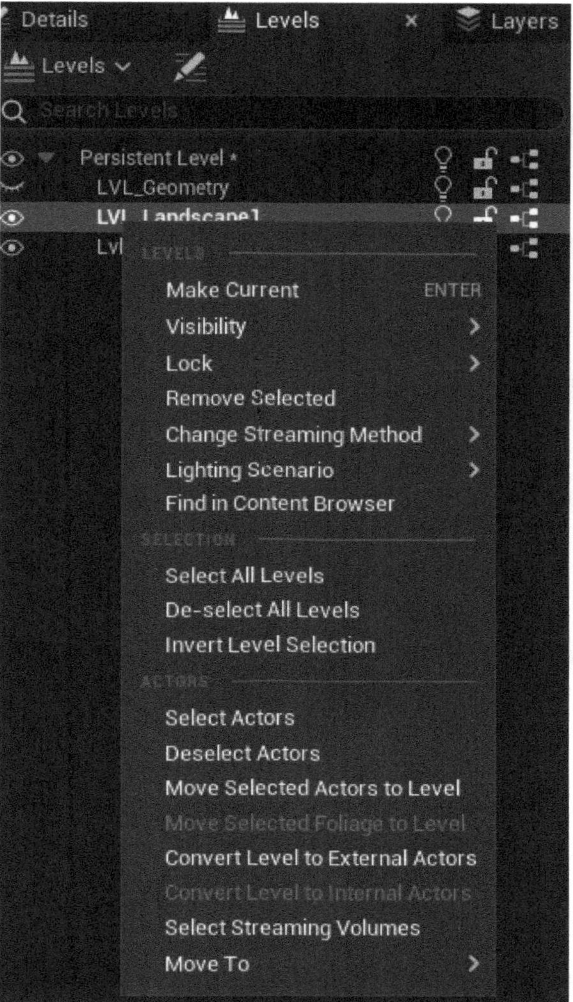

Figure 5.6 – Level operations

You can also toggle the visibility of a given level on or off by clicking on the **eye** icon that you can find on the left of the name of the level.

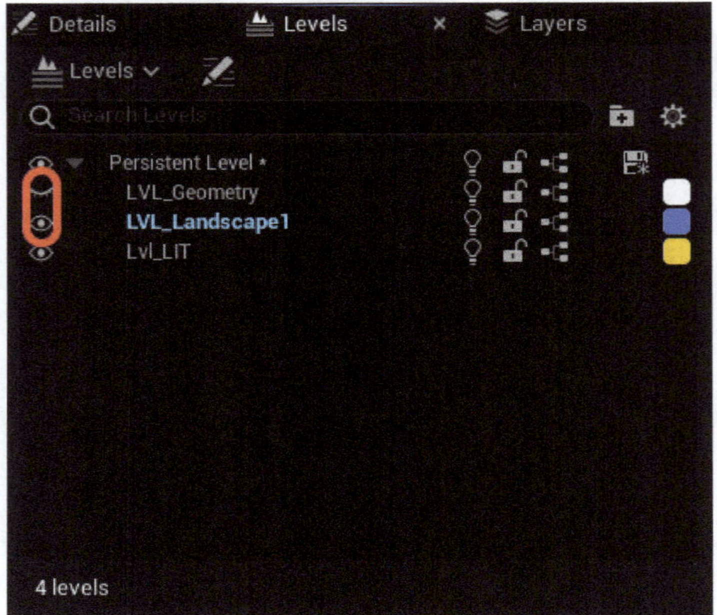

Figure 5.7 – Visibility

Adjusting a level's visibility is solely for viewing purposes and does not influence whether the level will stream into the game during execution. However, if a level is not visible here, it will remain unaffected during a rebuild, potentially saving significant time with complex levels.

If, by any chance, you already have a sublevel created and nested with the persistent level, you can move any of the Actors from one level to another by following these steps:

1. Select the level you want your Actors to be migrated to.
2. Go to the **Outliner** and choose all the Actors you want to migrate.
3. *Right-click* on them and select **Move Selected Actors to Level**.

Level Details

The **Level Details** button, shown by a **pencil** icon in the **Levels** window, gives extra information about your current levels. Persistent levels show no additional details, but you can switch to another level using the drop-down menu. For sublevels, you can adjust parameters such as position, rotation, streaming volumes, and debug color. Advanced settings, such as minimum unload request time for better performance, are also available.

Level streaming

Level streaming involves asynchronously loading and unloading levels during gameplay to reduce memory usage and create seamless worlds. This process enables us to load and unload map files into memory and toggle their visibility during gameplay. By breaking worlds into smaller pieces, only the necessary parts are rendered and take up resources when needed.

Level streaming options

In Unreal Engine, streaming options control how levels and content are loaded and displayed during gameplay. These options are key for optimizing performance and ensuring a seamless player experience, especially in level streaming scenarios. Let's take an overview of the common streaming options in the subsequent sections.

Always Loaded

Levels marked with this option are always loaded into memory when the game starts and remain loaded throughout the game session. This is typically used for essential content required at all times, such as core gameplay mechanics or persistent environments.

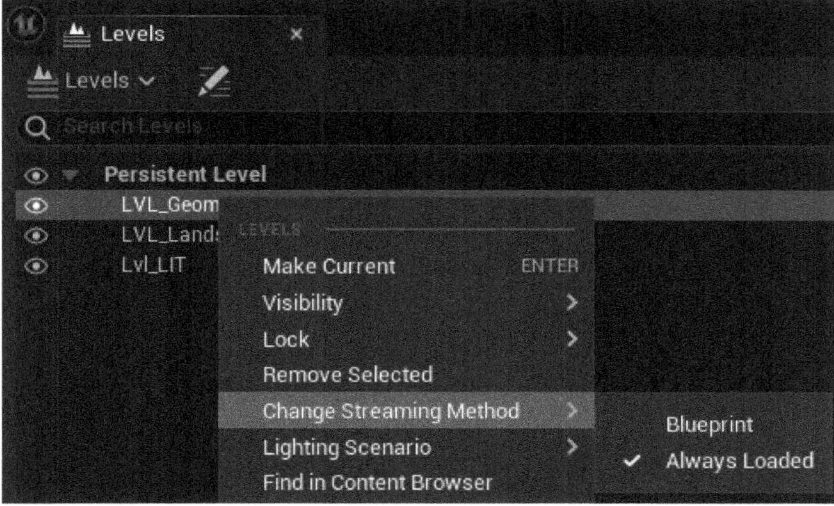

Figure 5.8 – Streaming methods

Blueprint

This option enables levels to be loaded or unloaded based on conditions or events defined in Blueprints, offering developers precise control for dynamic content loading in response to player actions, game state changes, or other gameplay events.

Level Streaming Volumes

In Unreal Engine, **Level Streaming Volumes** control streaming levels based on the player's position. These volumes determine when levels should load or unload, simplifying level management. Volume-based streaming is easier to use than scripted methods and can be adjusted by resizing volumes as needed, ensuring smooth level transitions as the game evolves.

There are two primary intentions to utilize Level Streaming Volumes:

- **In-game behavior**: When the player's viewpoint enters a Level Streaming Volume, the associated level loads into the game environment, becoming active and interactable. When the player exits the volume, the level unloads, removing it from active memory. This method ensures that only relevant parts of the game world are loaded, optimizing resource usage and performance.
- **Editor previews**: In Unreal Editor, Level Streaming Volumes simulate in-game level loading and unloading behavior. This allows developers to preview how levels will appear and function based on the camera's position within the editor, streamlining the level design and testing process.

Another feature of managing level streaming is the ability to change the time of day in our projects in cases where it is not otherwise possible (such as with precomputed lighting). This is where lighting scenarios come into play.

Exploring lighting scenarios

Unreal Engine supports precomputed lighting scenarios, allowing multiple lighting setups in one level. This combines real-time lighting with efficient precomputed lighting, enabling developers to switch between lighting configurations such as day and night cycles without real-time computations, preserving performance and enhancing visuals.

You can find these options in the **Levels** window by *right-clicking* on the level you want to modify, as shown in the following screenshot:

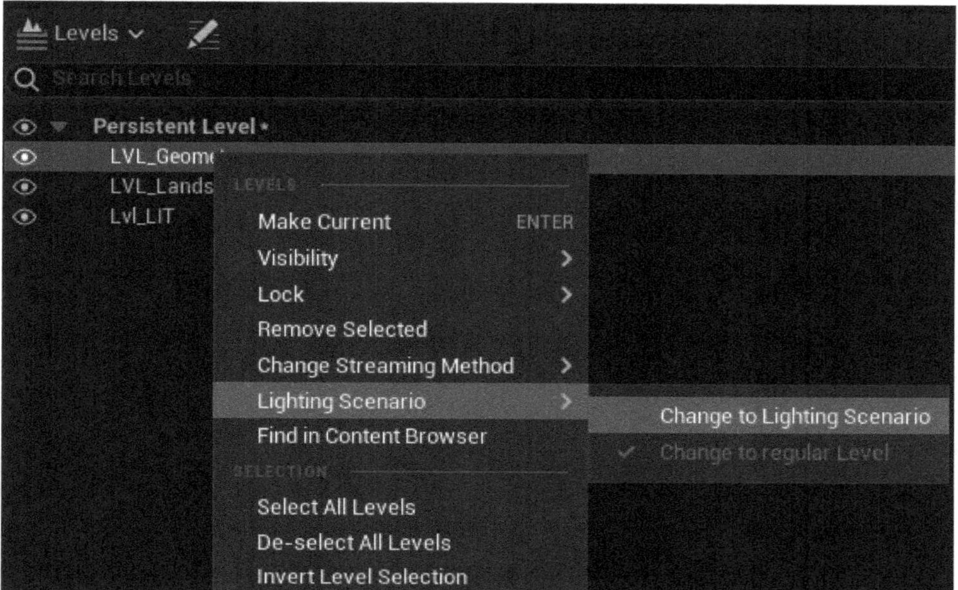

Figure 5.9 – Lighting Scenario

Let's now take a look at the key aspects of precomputed lighting scenarios:

- **Flexibility and visual quality**: Precomputed lighting scenarios simulate dynamic lighting environments within a level, offering the visual richness of real-time lighting. This method is advantageous in games with changing atmospheres and moods, providing an immersive experience for players.
- **Efficiency**: Because the lighting is precomputed, the game utilizes highly optimized lightmap data, reducing computational load during gameplay significantly. This efficiency allows for high-quality lighting effects on various hardware, from high-end PCs to mobile devices.

When configuring lighting scenarios, we can separate information related to the level's lighting and shadows. This approach is a simple and efficient way to manage hardware resources, allowing the engine to load and apply only the build data for each level as needed.

If you need to further separate or organize information about Actors within the same level, there are other strategies available, such as layers, which we will discuss next.

Using layers

The **Layers** panel in Unreal Engine organizes Actors within levels, making it easier to navigate and edit complex scenes. Actors can be in multiple layers at once, allowing flexible categorization. Using a well-structured layer system from the start improves efficiency and organization. In summary, the **Layers** panel is essential for managing large levels, ensuring control over the game's environment, and a smooth development process.

The process of creating and managing Layers is quite similar to other 3D design or Digital Content Creation (DCC) programs. You need to access the **Layers** menu to create and manage them. Let's see how to do this.

Creating layers

To access the **Layers** panel in Unreal Engine, go to **Window** | **Layers** in the menu bar. This panel is crucial for managing the visibility and organization of Actors within your levels.

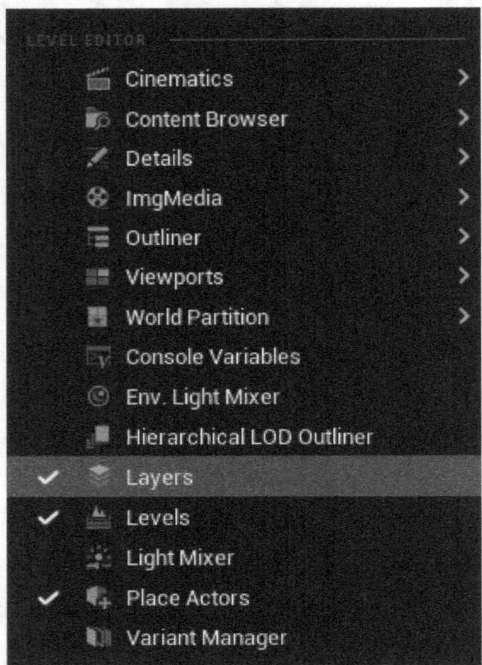

Figure 5.10 – Layers tab

In the **Layers** panel, you can create new layers from scratch or by grouping selected Actors from the **Outliner**, helping organize complex environments. To rename a layer, *right-click* on it and select the **Rename** option. This simplifies layer management, especially in projects with many categorized elements.

Right-clicking on a layer also reveals a context menu packed with additional options for layer management, including but not limited to the following:

- **Add Selected Actors to Selected Layers**: This option quickly assigns the currently selected Actors in the Viewport or **Outliner** to the chosen layers, facilitating rapid organization.
- **Select Actors**: This option makes it easy to select all Actors within a layer at once, simplifying processes such as mass editing or inspection.

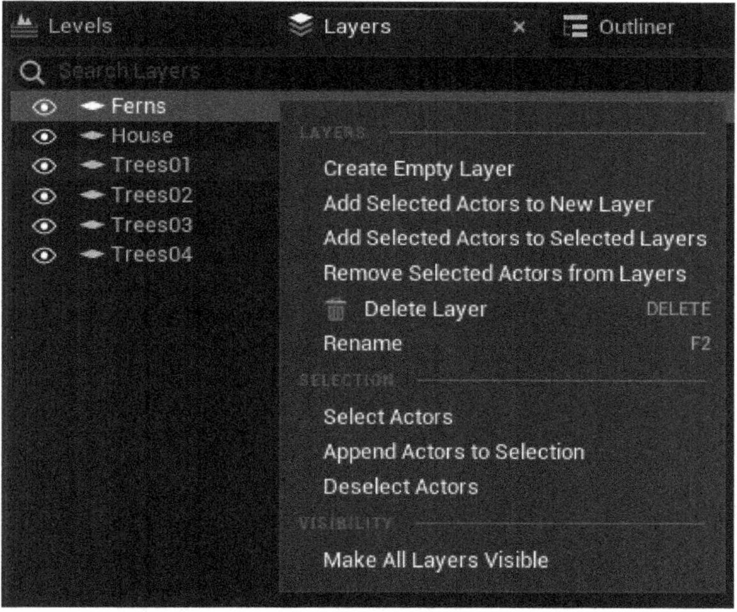

Figure 5.11 – Layer operations

Working with layers

The **Layers** panel in Unreal Engine organizes scene Actors and offers detailed views of each layer's contents, including Actors' names and additional details. This control extends to individual layer management, with visibility toggles for focusing on specific aspects of the scene.

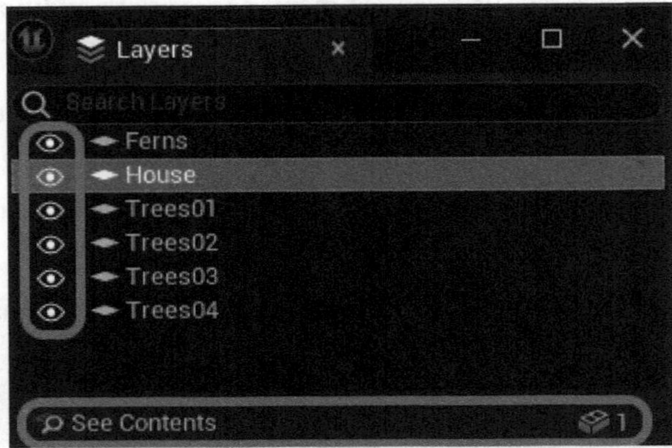

Figure 5.12 – Visibility and layers content

The **See Contents** button allows deeper examination and management of layer Actors, facilitating organization and workflow efficiency.

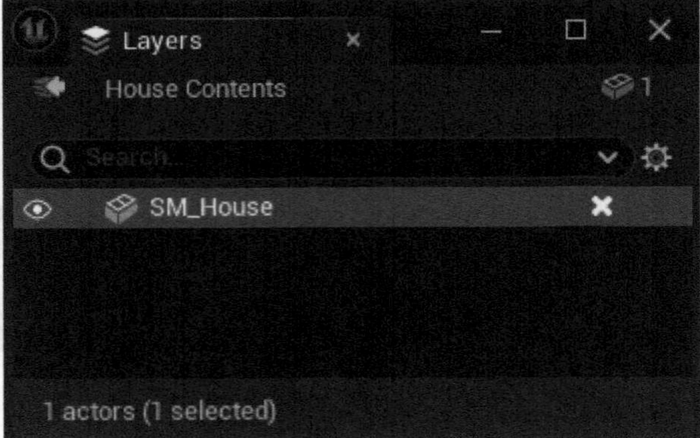

Figure 5.13 – Content in Layers

The **Layers** panel provides essential tools for managing Unreal Engine projects, whether fine-tuning scene elements or restructuring the game world.

In this way, we can also manage the Actors within each layer, making the organization process as detailed as needed. This allows for macro-level organization through layers and micro-level organization through individual Actors.

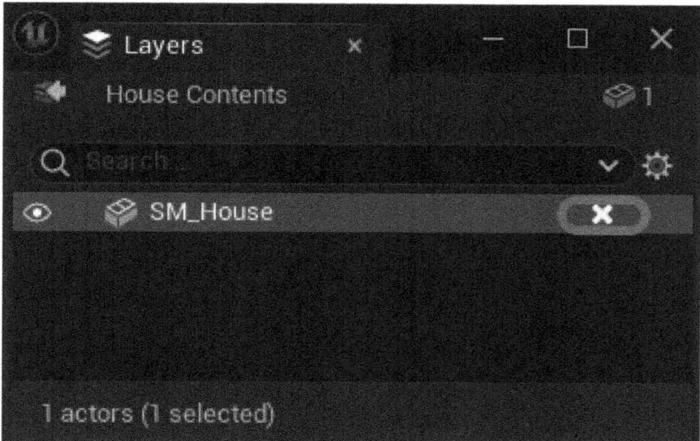

Figure 5.14 – Removing content

So far, we have discussed levels as foundational tools for structuring and organizing projects, along with layers to compartmentalize Actors within the **Outliner**. However, these are not the only tools available. Starting with Unreal Engine 5, a more flexible and scalable system was introduced: **World Partition**.

Don't worry, despite following a different philosophy, **World Partition** operates in a way that is conceptually familiar. The main difference lies in its powerful support for region-based level streaming and the introduction of **One File Per Actor** (**OFPA**). This allows developers to work within a single unified level while still maintaining structure and control using Data Layers. These new concepts preserve many of the benefits of the traditional sublevel workflow, while offering improved performance, collaboration, and scalability.

In the next section, we'll take a closer look at how **World Partition** works and how it compares to previous methods.

Understanding World Partition

World Partition in Unreal Engine transforms how expansive game worlds are managed. It treats the entire world as a single, persistent level divided into grid cells. These cells are dynamically loaded and unloaded based on distance, optimizing performance and memory usage for a seamless player experience.

Let's start by learning how to work with **World Partition**.

Working with World Partition

The **World Partition** system in Unreal Engine provides developers with an extensive toolkit, including streaming sources, runtime grid settings, and **World Partition Editor**, for constructing and navigating vast, dynamic game environments efficiently and precisely.

Let's dive deeper into the system, starting by learning how to enable it.

Enabling World Partition

Activating **World Partition** in Unreal Engine enhances the management of large game worlds. It can be enabled using three methods:

- **Creating a new project from a template in the Games category**: Choose a template supporting **World Partition** from the **Games** category to set up the project with this system from the start, ideal for open world games.
- **Creating a new level using the Open World template**: For existing projects, or when adding new levels, utilize the **Open World** template designed for **World Partition**. It streamlines the integration of **World Partition** features into specific areas of the game.

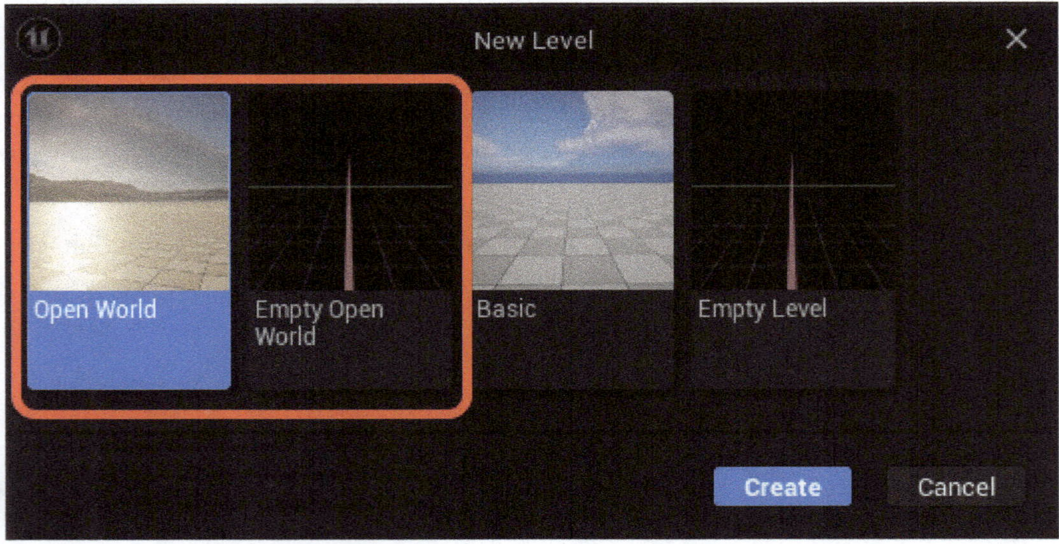

Figure 5.15 – Open World New Level template

- **Converting existing levels to use World Partition**: Developers can convert existing levels to support **World Partition**, enhancing performance and management of large-scale environments. This involves modifying level settings to fit within the grid cell framework and retroactively applying the benefits of **World Partition** to previously designed game areas.

Each method offers a way to utilize **World Partition**, whether starting a new project, expanding an existing game, or optimizing current levels. Enabling **World Partition** allows developers to leverage Unreal Engine's capabilities for creating immersive, vast game worlds with efficient resource management and a smoother player experience.

Using World Partition

The **World Partition** system in Unreal Engine condenses large game worlds into a single persistent level file, divided into streamable grid cells. It enhances performance by loading only cells near streaming sources such as the player, minimizing resource usage by dynamically loading relevant parts of the world.

In the **World Partition** system, Actors' management is based on their **Is Spatially Loaded** setting, found in the Actor's **Details** panel. When enabled, Actors load into memory within the streaming source range, ensuring that dynamic elements are loaded for player immersion. Disabled Actors remain loaded regardless of proximity to streaming sources, ensuring that essential elements are always available.

World Partition in Unreal Engine dynamically loads and unloads grid cells at runtime, influenced by **streaming sources** and **runtime grid settings**.

Streaming sources

Streaming sources, such as the player's location or designated points in the world, dictate loading behavior, ensuring a seamless gaming experience. These sources are typically enabled by default, ensuring smooth operation of the **World Partition** system.

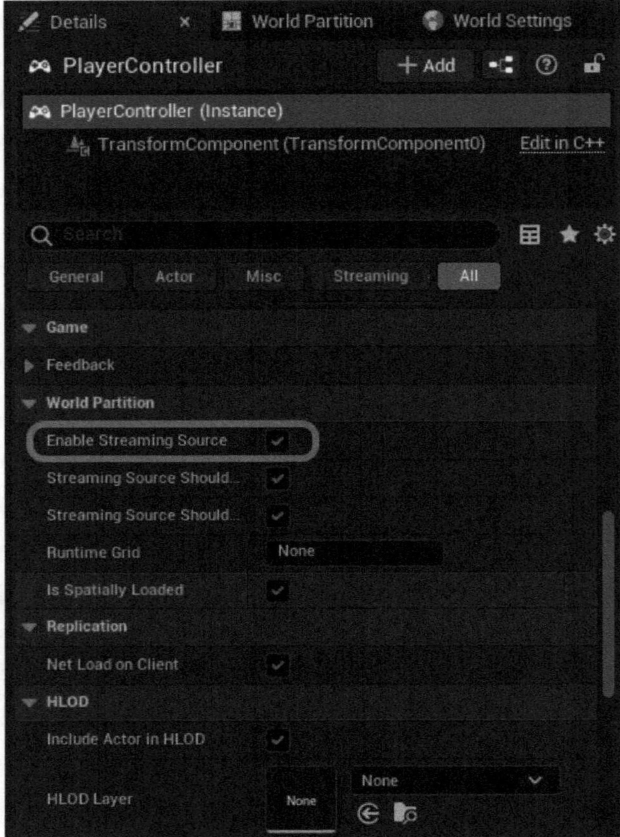

Figure 5.16 – Enable Streaming Source

Runtime grid settings

The runtime grid in the **World Partition** system is controlled by settings in the **World Settings** panel, specifically in the **World Partition Setup** section. These settings decide how grid regions load initially and interact with streaming sources. In developing large worlds, grid regions start unloaded, except for Actors marked as **Always Loaded**, ensuring that vital elements such as environmental backdrops are ready when the level begins.

Developers have the flexibility to manually manage the loading state of grid regions through the **World Partition** tab, offering precise control over which parts of the world are active at any given time.

Loading and unloading regions in the World Partition Editor

The **World Partition Editor**, accessible via the **Window | World Partition | World Partition Editor** menu, provides a graphical interface for managing the streaming of grid cells directly within the Unreal Editor.

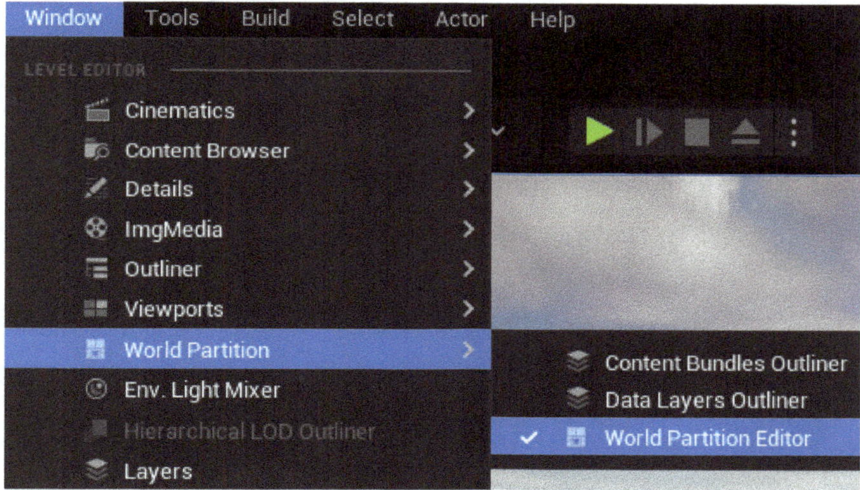

Figure 5.17 – How to get the World Partition Editor

This tool is essential for the following:

- **Manually loading and unloading regions**: Developers can *right-click* on the grid in **World Partition Editor** to load or unload specific regions, facilitating detailed control over the game world's structure and optimization.

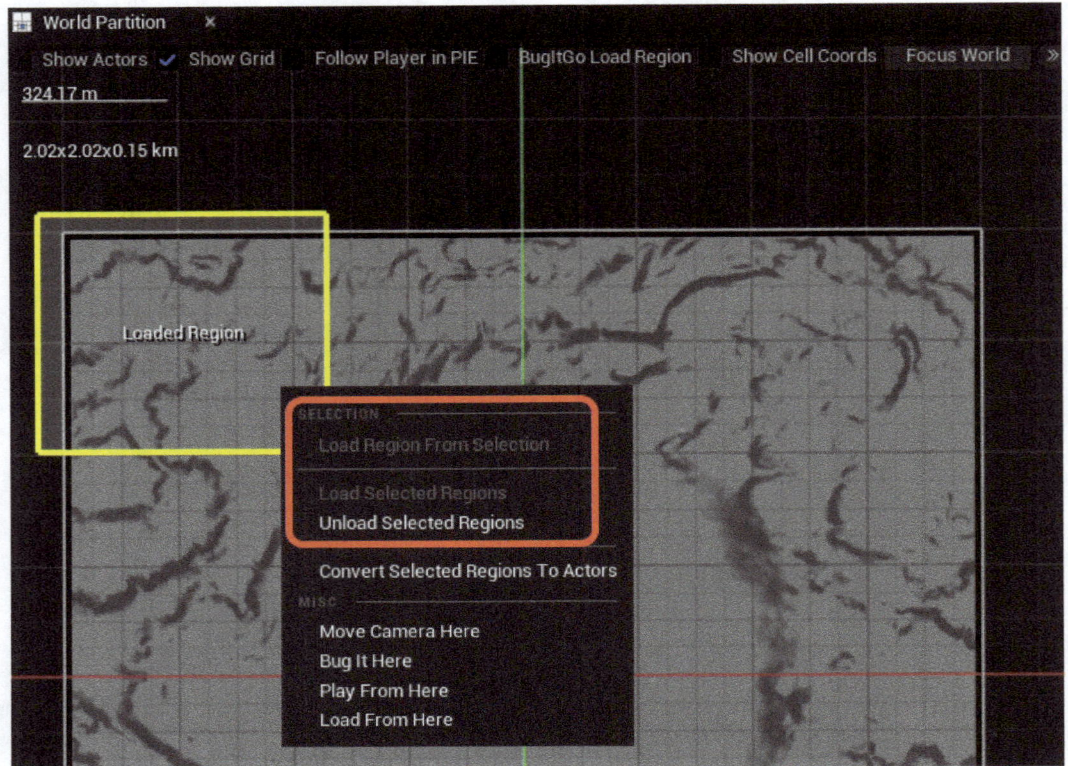

Figure 5.18 – Loading/unloading regions

- **Generating a Minimap**: You can create a Minimap in the **World Partition** window for easier navigation by using the **Build Minimap** option in the **Build** menu's **World Partition** section or the **World Partition Minimap Builder** commandlet. This generates an image of your **World Partition** world and displays it within the **World Partition** window. This Minimap simplifies the overview of the entire game world, aiding in grid cell management.

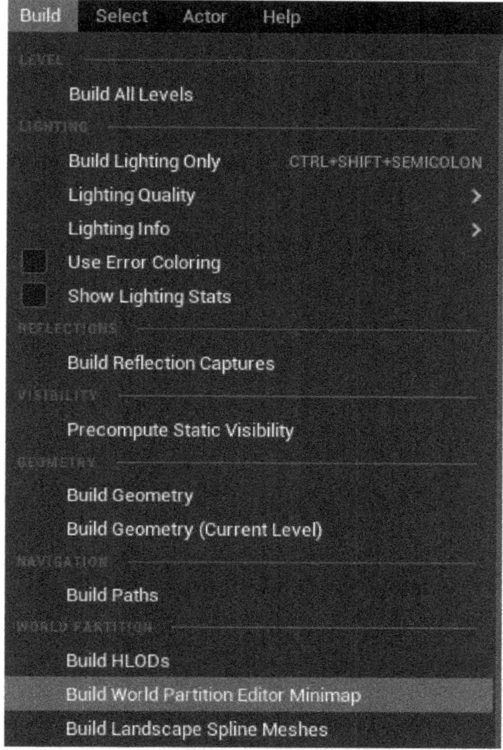

Figure 5.19 – Building Minimaps

Creating and managing a Minimap can be resource-intensive, highlighting the scale and complexity of worlds achievable with Unreal Engine's **World Partition** system.

With the knowledge of working with **World Partition** under our belt, let's now learn about its components and functionalities.

Components and functionalities of World Partition

World Partition in Unreal Engine simplifies the management and streaming of vast game worlds by integrating components such as:

- Data Layers
- Level Instancing
- Hierarchical Level of Detail (HLOD)
- One File Per Actor (OFPA)

This enhances the quality and performance of the final game, providing players with an immersive and uninterrupted experience as they explore. This section delves deeper into these components and functionalities of **World Partition**, shedding light on how it enhances game development workflows. Let's look at them one by one.

Data Layers

Data Layers in Unreal Engine's World Partition system represent a sophisticated framework designed for organizing and managing Actors within your game world. This system facilitates the separation of Actors into distinct layers, which can be individually loaded or unloaded, thereby streamlining the handling of complex environments. Data Layers enhance the development workflow by allowing dynamic control over the game's assets directly within the Level Editor and through gameplay logic implemented via Blueprints.

In the **Content Browser**, *right-click* and navigate to the **Miscellaneous** category, which has the **Data Layer** option.

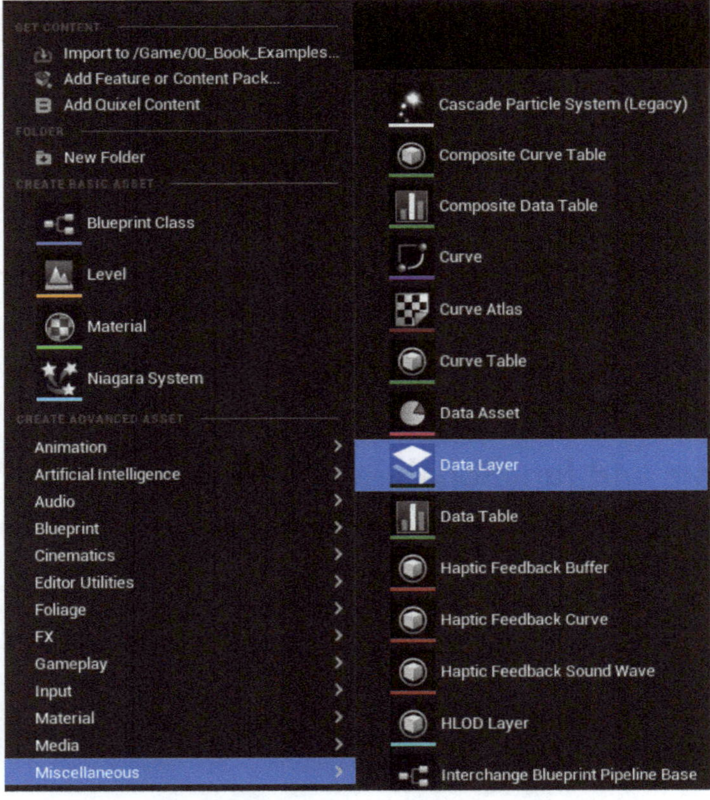

Figure 5.20 – Data Layer in the Content Browser

You can create a new Data Layer by *right-clicking* on the **Content Browser**, selecting **Miscellaneous**, and then choosing **Data Layer** in the menu:

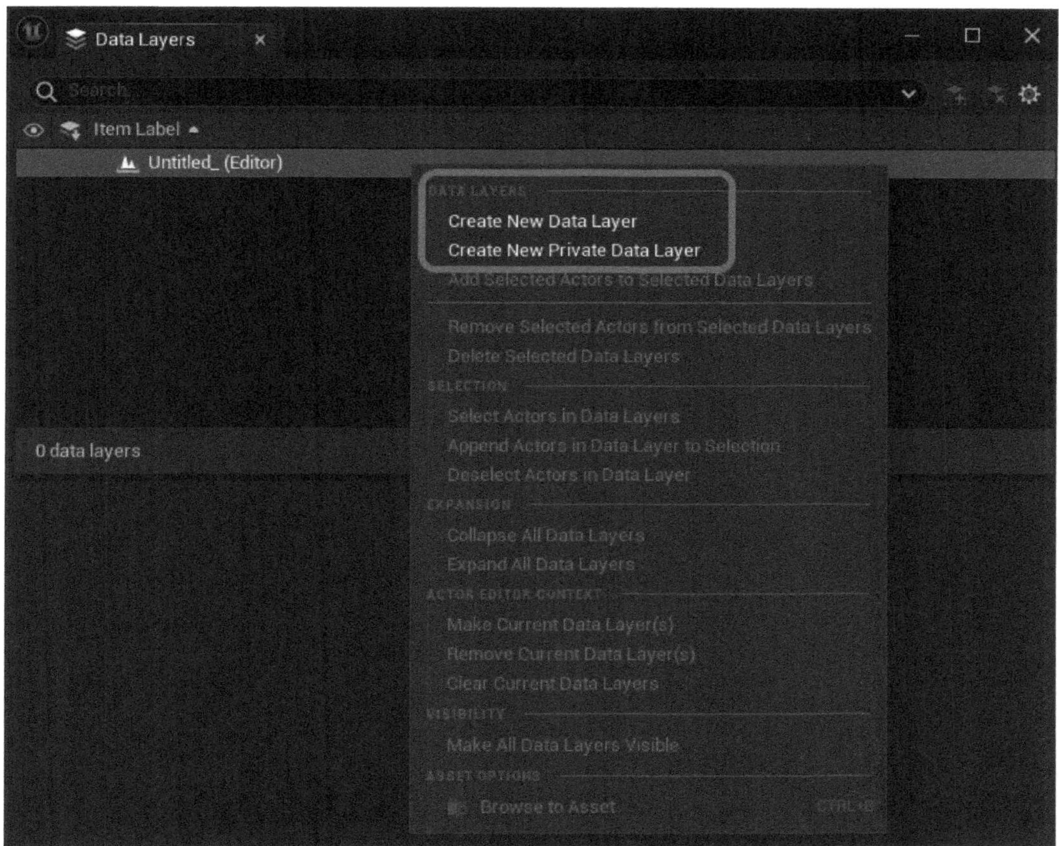

Figure 5.21 – Creating Data Layers

This newly created asset needs to be linked with the **Data Layer Outliner**, which can be found in the menu under **Window | World Partition | Data Layer Outliner**. This will bring up the following screen:

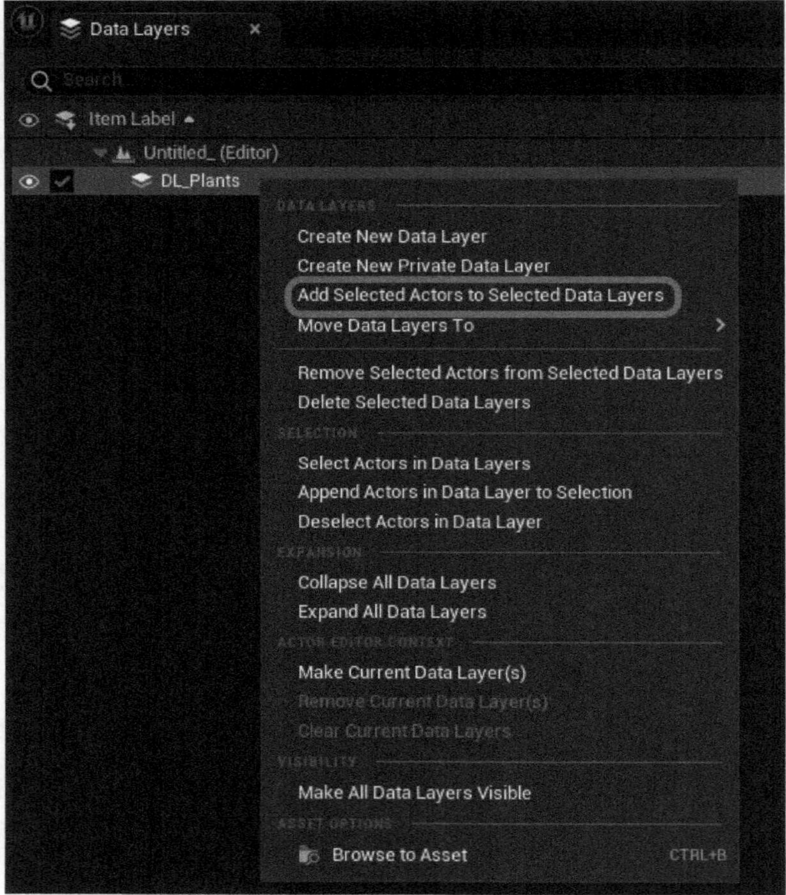

Figure 5.22 – How to add Actors to Data Layers and all of its options

Data Layers simplify collaboration and asset management, minimizing version control issues and conflicts in large-scale projects.

Data Layers streamline *collaboration* by reducing the need to check out critical files, enabling concurrent work without conflicts. They offer *dynamic control* over Actors' association with layers, simplifying scene composition and asset management. Additionally, Data Layers *simplify maintenance* by automatically managing the cleanup of associated Actors when layers are deleted. Overall, Data Layers enhance development efficiency and game design flexibility, empowering developers to create dynamic and immersive gaming experiences.

Level Instancing

Level Instancing is a workflow designed to enhance and streamline the level editing experience, allowing you to use one or more Actors to create Level Instances that can be placed and repeated across your world. This workflow offers benefits such as in-context editing, which lets you see the immediate impact of your changes on your world, with changes made to one instance being propagated to all instances when saved. It also enables efficient copying, allowing you to quickly create templates of any static mesh arrangement, including points of interest, buildings, and gameplay setups. I present it in the same way the engine does.

HLOD system

The **HLOD system** is an integral component of Unreal Engine's **World Partition** system, designed to optimize performance in large open world games. It achieves this by dynamically managing the detail levels of distant, non-interactive objects such as mountains, trees, and cliffs, ensuring that they remain visible without significantly impacting performance.

Implementing HLOD in World Partition

In **World Partition**, the HLOD system organizes many Static Mesh Actors into custom layers. These layers create a single proxy mesh and material for groups of objects, visually representing unloaded grid cells. This reduces draw calls per frame, essential for performance in large game environments.

It's important to note that certain world components, such as landscapes and water, are not compatible with HLOD Actors due to their dynamic nature or complexity.

Creating HLOD layers

To use the HLOD system, developers need to create a new **HLOD layer asset** in the **Content Browser** under **Miscellaneous**. Once named, this asset helps manage and optimize Static Mesh Actors.

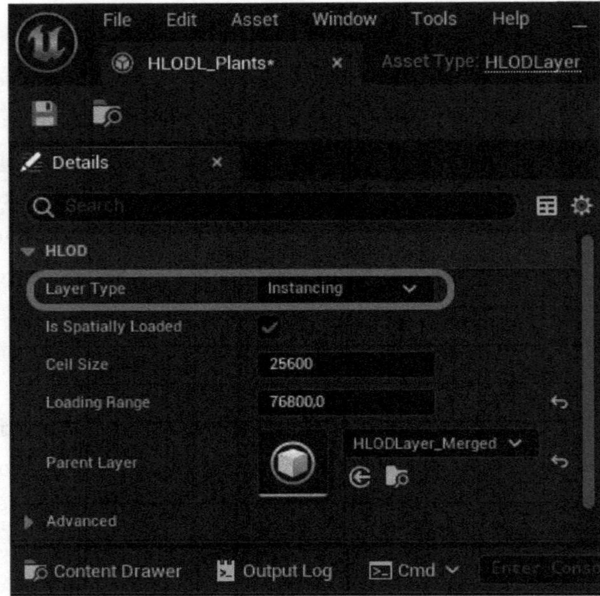

Figure 5.23 – HLOD layer

These are the types of HLOD layers:

- **Instancing**: This method converts Static Mesh assets into **Instanced Static Mesh** (**ISM**) components using their lowest **Level of Detail** (**LOD**) settings. It's perfect for efficiently creating impostor meshes representing objects such as trees and foliage.
- **Merged Mesh**: In this layer type, several Static Mesh assets are merged into a single proxy mesh, simplifying rendering.
- **Simplified Mesh**: Similar to the **Merged Mesh** layer, this one combines Static Mesh assets into a single proxy mesh. However, it also simplifies the mesh to reduce complexity and enhance performance.

Working with HLOD layers

To create HLOD proxy meshes, assign Static Mesh Actors to an HLOD layer by selecting them and specifying the layer. This simplifies managing detailed worlds. After the assignment, execute a commandlet to generate proxy geometry, reducing rendering load for distant objects. This is crucial for large-scale environments, ensuring that distant areas are represented without overloading the system.

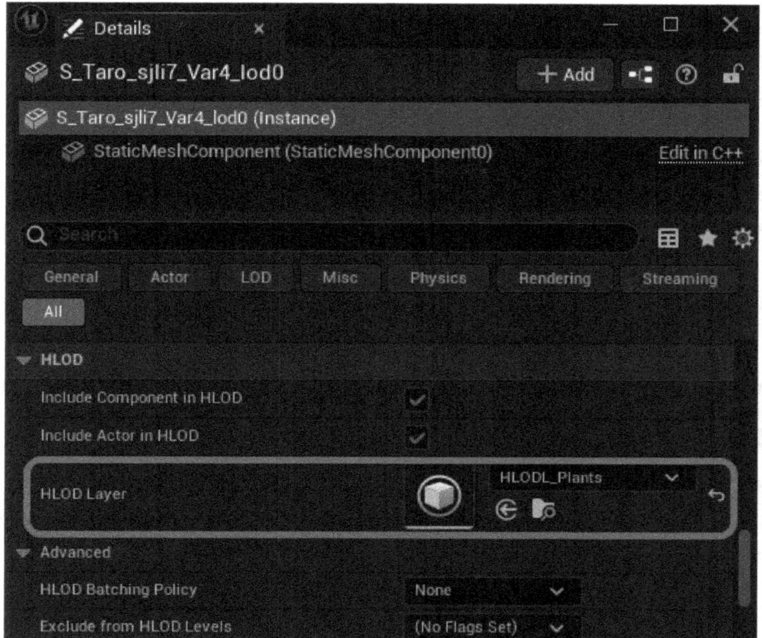

Figure 5.24 – Actor Details for HLOD Layer

By leveraging **HLOD Layer** within the **World Partition** system, developers can significantly enhance the performance of their Unreal Engine projects, especially those that encompass vast, open worlds. This system not only optimizes how distant objects are rendered but also streamlines the development process by providing a clear framework for managing LODs across various game components.

One File Per Actor strategy

The OFPA strategy in Unreal Engine simplifies large-scale level management and collaboration by assigning each Actor to its own file. This reduces complexity and conflicts when multiple users work on the same level. OFPA streamlines development and improves efficiency with source control systems.

Here are some benefits of the OFPA strategy:

- **Reduced overlap in collaboration**: OFPA minimizes merge conflicts in source control by isolating changes to individual Actor files. This allows simultaneous work on different parts of the level without overwriting each other's work.
- **Enhanced source control efficiency**: Isolating Actor changes makes source control operations more manageable, especially in large projects with numerous contributors.

- **Streamlined level modification**: Modifications to Actors don't require resaving the entire level, speeding up the iteration process and facilitating testing and refinement of gameplay elements.

World Partition makes managing large environments in Unreal Engine easier by automating streaming and partitioning. It removes the need for manual sublevels, boosting performance and development efficiency. This allows developers to concentrate on design and gameplay. Whether starting new projects, converting levels, or adjusting settings, **World Partition** provides the tools needed to streamline workflows and improve game world scalability and performance.

Exercise 5.1: Setup and configuration of the level systems

In this exercise, we will create a level system from scratch. We will go through the steps to add new levels using Streaming Volume, to facilitate loading and unloading them based on the character's position. Let's see how to achieve this.

Setting up levels and sublevels

Before starting, it is important to have a root folder in your project where we will create our upcoming levels:

1. For this exercise, let's create two new levels: one using the **Basic** template and another using the **Empty Level** template. This will ensure basic lighting conditions for both levels.
2. Drop any assets you want into the second level. Remember to add your sublevel in the **Levels** tab and ensure that everything you're dropping in is done while the level is *blue*, indicating it's at the correct level. You can check this by *right-clicking* on the **World Outliner** and enabling the **Level** column to see which level assets are placed in.
3. After placing assets in our sandbox, ensure that you have **GameMode** set up for testing. Go to **World Settings** and select **GameMode** under **GameMode Override** in the **Game Mode** section.

Loading and unloading Levels with Level Streaming Volumes

In order to enable the Level Streaming Volume, you will need to follow these steps:

1. Select the persistent level with a *double click*. It will be highlighted in *blue*.
2. Then, add the Level Streaming Volume into the level covering the whole area that is going to be loaded.

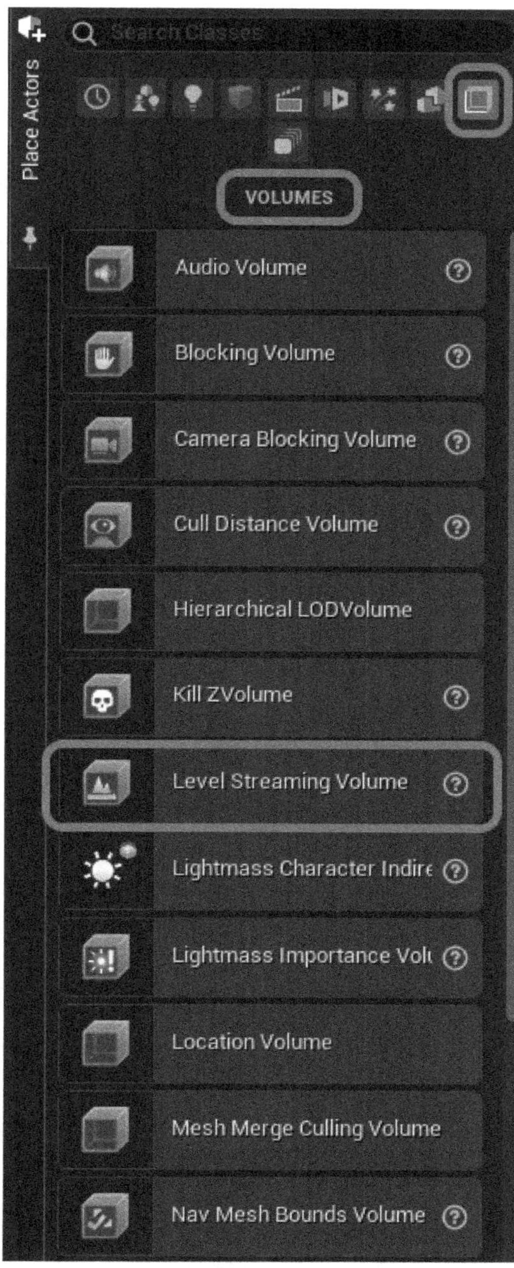

Figure 5.25 – Level Streaming Volume

3. When added to the level, it should look like this:

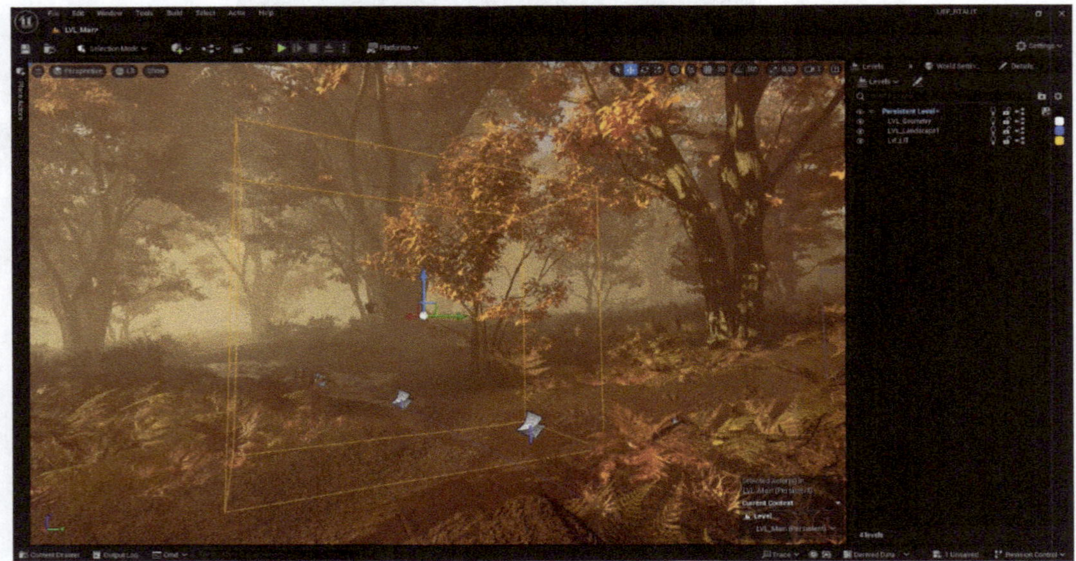

Figure 5.26 – Level Streaming Volume in Level Editor

4. Next, access the level details by selecting the desired sublevel from the **Levels** tab.

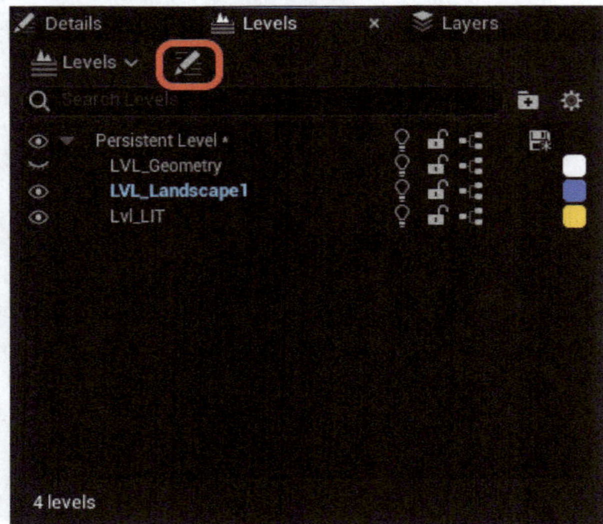

Figure 5.27 – Loading the level details

5. Then, add a new array into the Streaming Volume and select the actual **Level Streaming Volume (LSV)** that will be used:

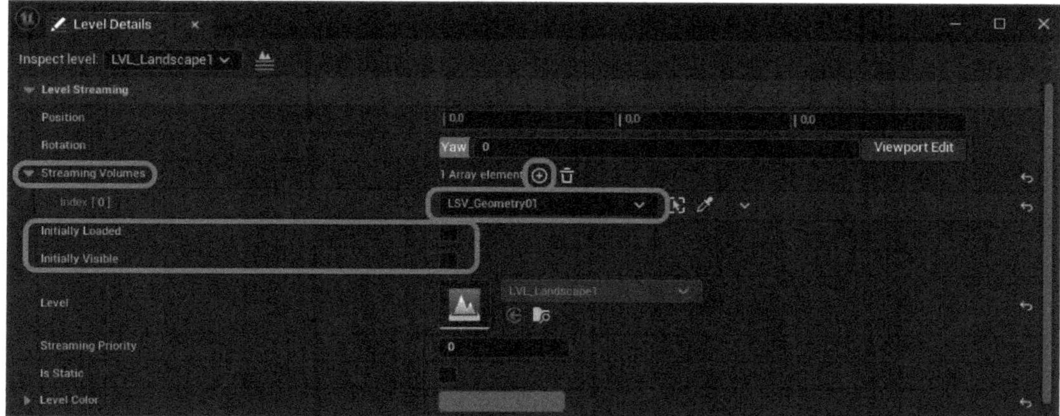

Figure 5.28 – Choosing the LSV

6. Make sure that the boxes from **Initially Loaded** and **Initially Visible** are unchecked.
7. Once this is done, go back to the Viewport and select **Level Streaming Volume**. In the **Details** panel, set the following properties of the volume:

    - **Editor Pre Vis Only**: Unchecked
    - **Disabled**: Unchecked
    - **Streaming Usage: SVB Visibility Blocking on Load**

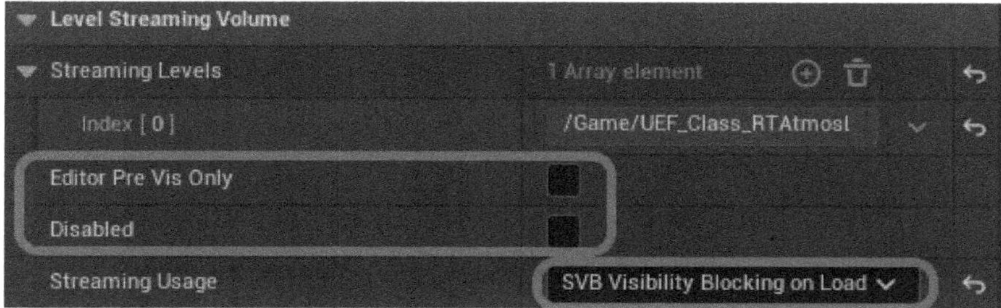

Figure 5.29 – Level Streaming Volume details

8. Ensure that the Level Streaming Volume is triggered when the viewpoint is inside it. Adjust the volume's distance accordingly if the character's camera is far away. This ensures timely level streaming based on the character's position relative to the volume.
9. Try and modify **Streaming Usage** to **SVB Loading not Visible**. Check the difference.

With this simple exercise, we have created a level loading and unloading system within Unreal Engine. These systems help reduce computational load in our projects and can even be used as temporary tools during the development or level design phases.

Choosing the right approach to level management

All the systems and tools introduced in this chapter must be used in alignment with the specific goals of your project, your development workflow, and the size and structure of your team.

Whether you're building immersive worlds or enabling collaboration across disciplines, having a clear understanding of how levels, sublevels, and layers work together is essential to any production. A well-defined structure not only improves organization and performance but also ensures smoother collaboration and scalability.

Core systems of level management

To help visualize how these systems interconnect, the following conceptual mind map outlines the three core layers of level management in Unreal Engine:

- **Levels (base structure)**:
    - Organize your world into persistent and sublevels
    - Enable lighting scenarios for dynamic conditions
- **Layers (Actor organization)**:
    - Group, filter, and manage Actors within a level
    - Separate logic, visuals, and interactivity
- **World Partition (dynamic streaming system)**:
    - Automate loading based on distance and rules
    - Use Data Layers to manage runtime and editor loading
    - Stream content such as AI, audio, and physics efficiently

This layered conceptual view shows a natural progression: from structural foundations (*levels*), to editorial and logical grouping (*layers*), to performance-focused runtime management (**World Partition**).

A common point of confusion is the difference between *layers* and *Data Layers*. While both are used to group Actors, their purpose and behavior are quite different. Layers are purely organizational and exist only within the editor. They help you manage visibility and structure during level design but have no effect at runtime. Data Layers, on the other hand, are part of the **World Partition** system and allow you to dynamically load and unload Actors during gameplay or editor sessions. This makes Data Layers essential for performance optimization and large-scale collaboration, especially in open world projects.

Selecting the most suitable workflow

When determining which system to use for managing levels in Unreal Engine, the size and complexity of your project play a significant role. For large-scale, open world projects, **World Partition** is generally the best choice due to its dynamic loading capabilities and efficient handling of large amounts of assets. This system allows for seamless streaming of world sections, which is crucial in games such as *Fortnite* (first released in 2017) and *Hogwarts Legacy* (first released in 2023), where the player continuously moves through vast environments without hitting performance bottlenecks.

On the other hand, the traditional level and sublevel system is more suitable for smaller, linear games or projects where modularity and separation of levels are key. For instance, a game such as *Inside* (first released in 2016) uses this method effectively, allowing for isolated and highly controlled environments, ideal for narrative-driven gameplay.

Additionally, tools such as OFPA can significantly streamline workflows in both small and large projects, enabling multiple team members to work on the same level simultaneously without conflicts. This is especially beneficial in large-scale games such as *Gears of War 4* (first released in 2016), where collaborative world-building is essential to meet project deadlines.

Summary

This chapter introduced Unreal Engine's systems for structuring and managing environments: levels, layers, and **World Partition**. You learned how to organize projects using persistent and sublevels, manage Actors through layers, and optimize large open worlds via **World Partition** tools such as Data Layers, HLOD, and OFPA.

The chapter also guided you through a practical setup with Level Streaming Volumes and provided criteria for choosing between traditional and modern workflows. By mastering these systems, you can build scalable, performant worlds suitable for both linear and open world projects.

The next chapter will guide you through crafting immersive environments in Unreal Engine. It introduces landscape tools for creating realistic outdoor scenes, covering terrain generation.

6

Building Your Landscape

In previous chapters, we discussed how to import external assets into the engine, such as 3D models and textures, and explored the use of the **Quixel Megascans** library. We also analyzed the structure and different types of levels available in the engine, including both legacy options and the new tools provided by **World Partition**.

Creating an environment from scratch may seem like a daunting task at first, which is completely normal. However, by breaking it down into smaller tasks, it becomes much more manageable than one might think. While it is crucial to consider various aspects of level development, we must also consider the different assets and the final look we are aiming for.

Therefore, in this chapter, we will begin by exploring a series of techniques that can help us translate our ideas into the project, along with tools that will allow us to validate whether we are moving in the right direction.

Subsequently, we will delve into the set of tools specifically designed by Unreal Engine for the creation of natural environments.

Key topics and exercises to be covered include the following:

- Introduction to level design
- Scene development: Inspiration and references
- Environment creation
- Project creation and template selection
- Using Unreal Engine's **Landscape** tools
- Using Unreal Engine's **Sculpt** tools

- Exercise 6.1: Creating a terrain from heightmaps
- Exercise 6.2: Creating a custom landscape
- Exercise 6.3: Sculpting a new terrain

Technical requirements

To continue the development of this chapter, it is necessary to have a PC with **Unreal Engine 5.5** (or a later version) installed that meets the recommended requirements by Epic Games and has internet access: `https://dev.epicgames.com/documentation/en-us/unreal-engine/hardware-and-software-specifications-for-unreal-engine`.

Introduction to level design

Level design for open worlds in Unreal Engine presents unique opportunities and challenges, requiring a blend of creativity, technical skill, and strategic planning. Unlike linear and confined levels, open worlds offer expansive environments that allow players to explore freely and interact with a diverse range of elements. This freedom demands a meticulous approach to design to ensure that the world feels immersive, coherent, and engaging.

Scene development: Inspiration and references

Undoubtedly, one of the most important tasks before starting any creative project that involves building a scene is to have a solid concept art or storyboard (in the case of cinematics) to understand firsthand the scene we are about to develop, and, of course, a set of references to guide us along the way. This is important for several reasons:

- **Visual guidance**: Concepts and references provide a clear visual guide for designers and artists. These can help establish the desired tone, style, and atmosphere for the open world being created.
- **Consistency**: Having visual references ensures aesthetic consistency throughout the world. This is crucial for maintaining visual cohesion and player immersion in the game environment.
- **Inspiration and creativity**: References and concepts can inspire new ideas and creative approaches.
- **Efficiency in development**: Having a clear visual direction from the beginning reduces the likelihood of extensive iterations and revisions later in the development process.

Once the corresponding references have been gathered and the desired look and type of environment have been decided upon, the next step is environment creation.

Environment creation

Within level design, there are typically two approaches. On one hand, artists work with prebuilt models and structures, providing a clear and immediate perception of the level's intentions. On the other hand, the iterative design approach starts with simple shapes and geometries, gradually shaping and refining the level.

Let's explore how each method works.

Selecting the environment creation method

Currently, there are two techniques that are most frequently used in the industry to create an environment:

- Fully modeled environment
- **Landscape** tools

Each method has a series of requirements to consider, such as the materials to be used, non-destructive workflow options, and flexibility in making changes. Let's look at each one in detail.

Fully modeled environment

The **fully modeled environment**, also known as **environment modeling**, is a common technique in video games where every surface and contour, whether natural or artificial, is created within a modeling tool such as 3ds Max, Maya, Blender, and Houdini. This approach allows for complete control over terrain resolution, polygon count, scale, and other details. Subsequently, materials and textures can be added to enhance the realism and visual appeal of the environment. This method is often favored when precise control over every aspect of the environment's design is desired, and when specific artistic or technical requirements need to be met.

Important note

The following examples cited in the case scenarios below reference online visual sources. You can view them at the provided links for context.

You can see how artist *Nikolay Usov* has used a set of prebuilt assets to create a scene that closely resembles real-world expectations here (in the *Blockout* bullet): `https://blog.csdn.net/shebao3333/article/details/128938792`.

The same can be said for *Edgar Martinez*, who, based on level and space design conceptualization, developed a level for *Uncharted 4* (first released in 2016). You can view his work (*sixth image from the top*) here: `https://www.artstation.com/artwork/5gJ8A`.

Landscape tools

Unreal Engine 5 (UE5) offers a comprehensive set of tools specifically designed for building, designing, and customizing landscapes. These **Landscape** tools cater to the essential needs of level design artists.

The primary advantage of using **Landscape** tools within the engine is the immediate feedback loop they provide. Changes made to the landscape are instantly reflected in the scene, including interactions with the environment, lighting, materials, and other assets. This facilitates rapid iteration and adjustments to achieve the desired environmental aesthetics.

Beyond real-time visualization, UE5's **Landscape** tools boast a wide array of features. These include precise terrain sculpting, realistic textures and materials, creation of water bodies such as rivers and lakes, and efficient vegetation generation through foliage systems.

Additionally, these tools seamlessly integrate with other systems and tools within UE5, ensuring cohesive and detailed world creation. They are designed to be intuitive and user-friendly, empowering level design artists to focus on creativity and vision without grappling with technical complexities.

In the *Rebirth* project, the importance of blocking by the landscape to define scale and environment readability is quite evident, as the building is composed of simple geometric shapes. You can view the image here: `https://cdn2.unrealengine.com/Unreal+Engine%2Fspotlights%2Fquixel-creates-real-time-photoreal-cinematic-rebirth-in-ue4%2Fblog_body_archviz2_img-1640x882-14fa65b6847e00527eea412ebdee56892b86e1d6.jpg`

Regardless of the method employed, one of the most crucial phases in environment creation is blockout, which we'll explore in the next section.

Understanding the blockout process

Also known as the **graybox level, blockout** is a rapid draft of a level created using simple 3D models, devoid of final details such as textures or materials. Its primary objective is to prototype the level, test fundamental elements, scales, and references.

During this phase of development, the focus is on spatial experimentation, without getting bogged down by intricate details. Thus, it serves as a valuable tool in the early design stages, helping to establish the level's structure and achieve a balanced design, scale, and metrics. While this technique might seem basic, it is much more powerful than it appears. Many games replace the geometric shapes with final assets only in the later stages of development, allowing for iterative improvements in gameplay without the overhead of detailed assets early on.

Blockout is critical in the level design process for the following reasons:

- It provides a robust foundation for refining the game environment
- It enables designers and artists to explore various ideas and solutions without committing to unnecessary details early on
- It saves time and resources by prioritizing the establishment of a solid structure and gameplay flow before progressing to the detailed phase

We can see how *Brian Lesiangi* has created a 3D environment using boxes and cylinders here (in the *Blockout* section): `https://www.unrealengine.com/en-US/tech-blog/balinese-temple-telling-a-powerful-story-through-ue4-environments`.

Here's how the process works:

1. When starting the blockout phase, our primary tools will be those provided by the engine itself, such as **Landscape**, **BSP**, or **basic geometric models**. The key is to focus on functionality over details and experiment with different primitives by **moving**, **rotating**, and **scaling** them to achieve the desired outcome. Using color codes can also be helpful to visualize the scene's overall appearance based on future material colors.
2. As we progress to more advanced stages, we can incorporate 3D objects, which are crucial for scene decoration (**set dressing**) to enhance realism. Quixel Megascans currently offers a wide variety of materials and 3D objects, both open and closed, which can be used to enhance our landscape.

We can see a clear example of set dressing, where *Pasquale Scionti* enhances the scene using Unreal's landscape along with meshes and resources from Megascans, here: `https://cdnb.artstation.com/p/assets/images/images/038/615/101/large/pasquale-scionti-new2.jpg?1623594223`

.

As we have already seen in *Chapter 2*, Megascans is a resource and asset library integrated into Unreal Engine that accelerates the creation of landscapes with its collections focused on natural environments.

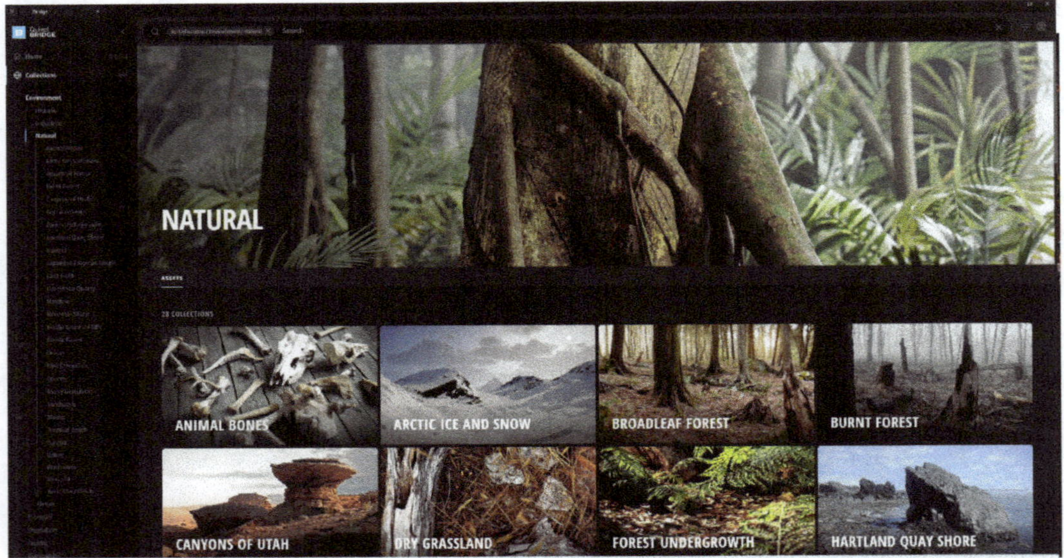

Figure 6.1 – Quixel Bridge – Natural collection

When starting any project, we must recognize that we are working with a blank canvas. It is essential to determine which method of work best suits our project and to align our efforts accordingly.

Project creation and template selection

As previously mentioned, when starting a project, we face a blank canvas. It is crucial to understand the type of project we are developing and choose a template within Unreal Engine that initially includes the elements we need.

Creating a blank project

To begin developing our environment in Unreal Engine, we'll start by creating a new blank project. In my case, I'm using version 5.3 of the engine and selecting the **Third Person** template from the **Games** category in the Launcher:

Figure 6.2 – Epic Games – Template selection

The next step is to create a folder (we'll call it `OpenWorldLevel`) where we can add our own assets specific to our project.

This is a good practice to consolidate all project-related information in one location. If we need to migrate to a new project in the future, redirecting asset locations will be quicker, and all project-related information will be in one place.

Within this folder, we'll add a new level. To do this, we go to the **File** menu and select the **New Level...** option (*Ctrl* + *N* on the keyboard):

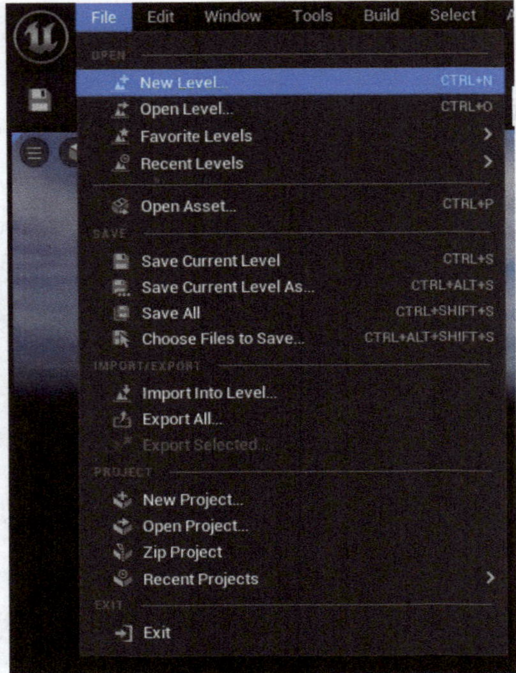

Figure 6.3 – File menu | New Level…

Finally, we can choose from different default levels to select. We will choose the **Open World** option:

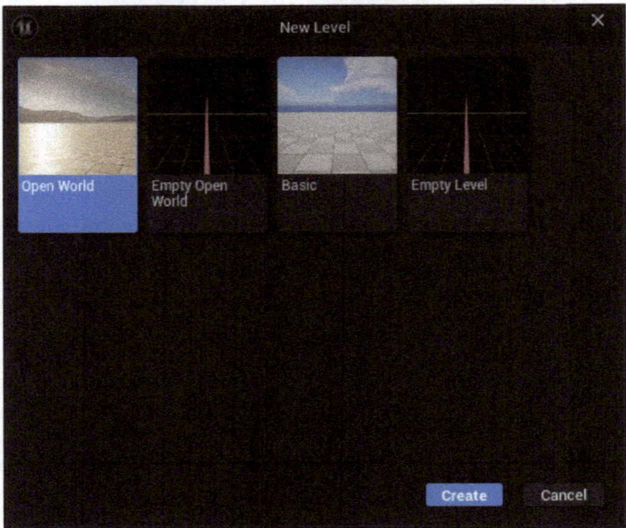

Figure 6.4 – New Level creation

After creating our level, it's a good time to save it in the `OpenWorldLevel` folder created in the previous step before starting to work on any modifications:

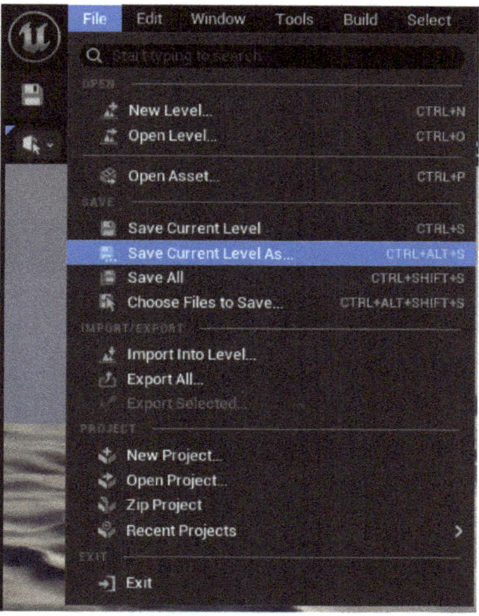

Figure 6.5 – Save new Level

If we take a moment to consider what we have, we should currently have a **World Partition Level** created, with default lighting and a landscape already set up:

Figure 6.6 – Reference Level

Deleting the existing landscape

The next step is to delete the existing landscape so we can generate our own. Simply follow these steps:

1. Select the landscape in the **Outliner** of Unreal Engine.
2. Expand the drop-down menu and select all components.
3. Delete them by pressing the *Delete* key on the keyboard.

Figure 6.7 – Select Landscape Components

4. Finally, select the container (**Landscape**) and delete it in the same manner.

Figure 6.8 – Deleted landscape

At this point, we can begin using the **Landscape** tools.

Using Unreal Engine's Landscape tools

For the **Landscape** tools in Unreal Engine, we first need to switch the current engine mode (**Selection Mode**) to **Landscape Mode**:

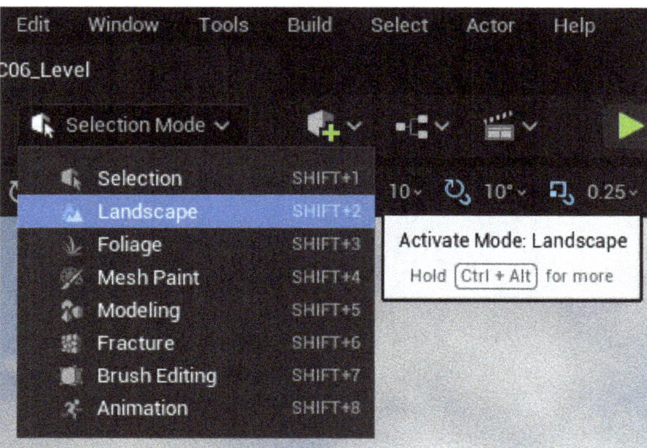

Figure 6.9 – Landscape Mode

We will be greeted by the following menu:

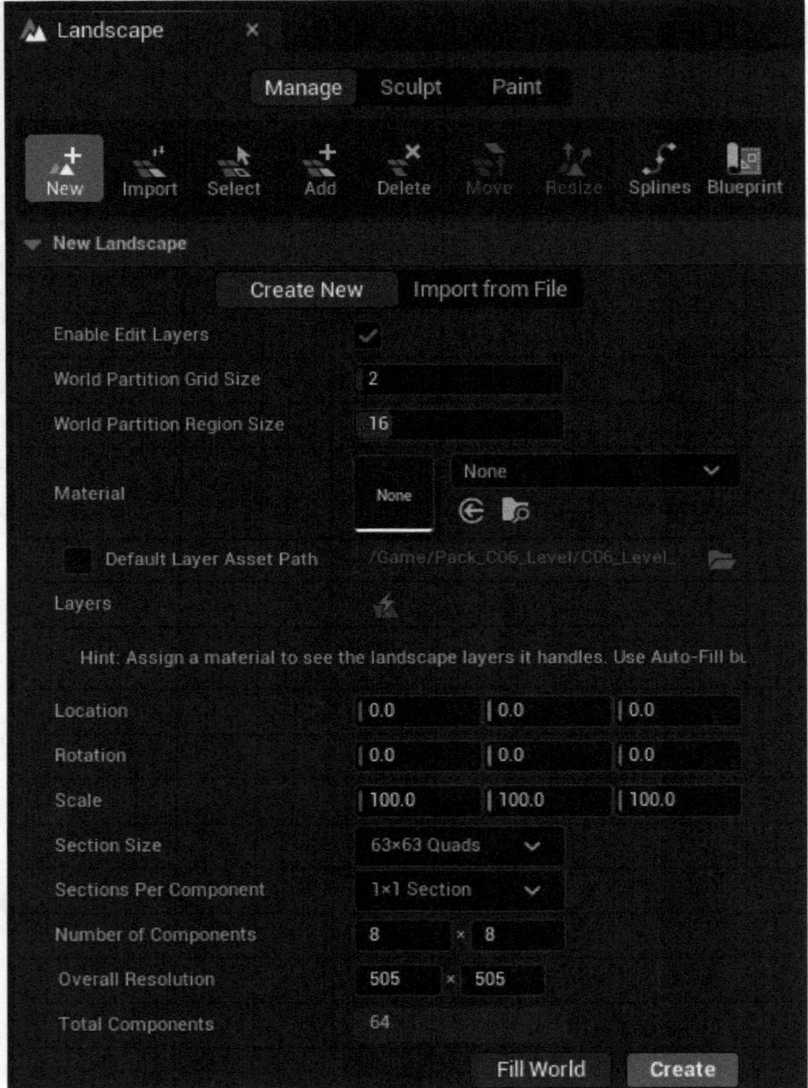

Figure 6.10 – Landscape menu

With the tools in **Landscape Mode**, you can create custom environments by modifying the existing terrain or building new terrain from scratch.

There are three stages to working with **Landscape**:

- **Manage**: Creates a new landscape, adjusts its size, and manages its properties
- **Sculpt**: Edits the heightmap to shape the terrain
- **Paint**: Edits the weight maps to blend between different material layers

Let us learn about each stage in detail.

Manage tools

The **Manage** section includes tools for the landscape as a whole, such as **New** and **Import**, as well as tools for managing its tiles or components: **Select**, **Add**, and **Delete**. It also provides controls for managing additional splines associated with the landscape splines.

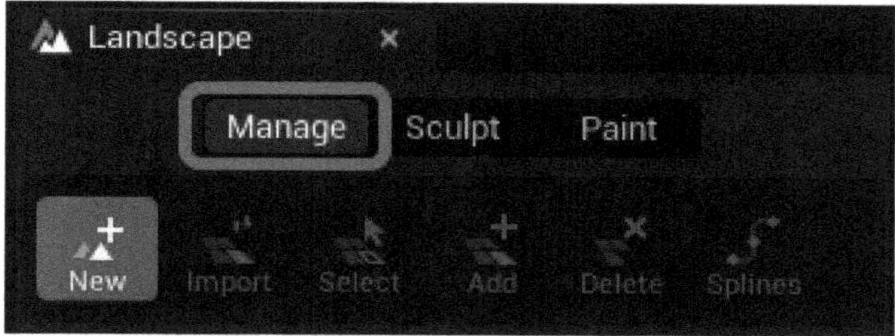

Figure 6.11 – Manage tools

Here's a summary of the use of each tool:

- **New**: Creates a new landscape
- **Import**: Imports a landscape from a file created in a third-party application such as Houdini or Gaea or allows the use of real-world satellite data
- **Select**: Selects components to modify their properties
- **Add**: Adds additional components to the landscape
- **Delete**: Removes components from the landscape
- **Splines**: Creates splines for roads, pathways, or other meshes that need to follow the terrain

You can create a new landscape from scratch in the **Create New** section of the new tool panel.

Here's an overview of the tools used to create our terrain:

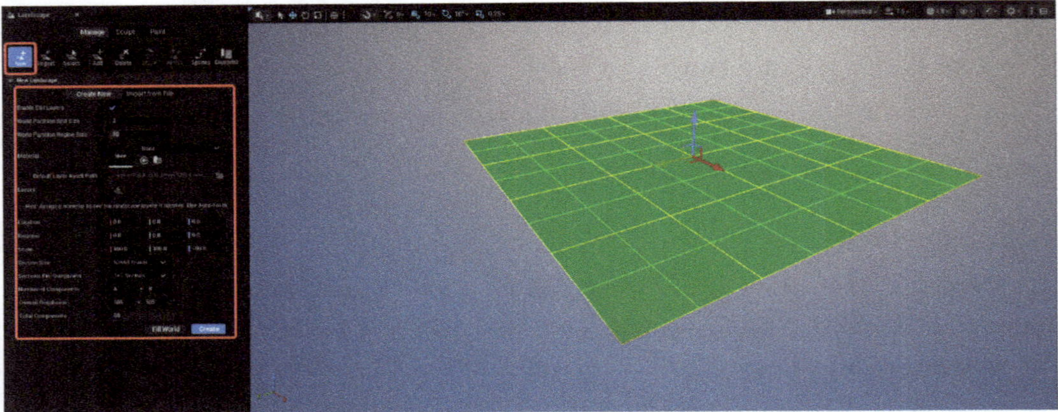

Figure 6.12 – Overview of Landscape creation details panel

We'll delve into the functions of the options annotated in *Figure 6.12* and, later, in *Figure 6.16* in the next section.

Landscape details panel

Let's look at each of the options in detail and what they allow us to do:

- **Create New**: Creates a new landscape in your level.
- **Import from File**: Imports a landscape heightmap created in an external program.
- **World Partition Grid Size**: Gives the number of components per landscape streaming proxies per axis.
- **Material**: Assigns a material to your landscape.
- **Location**: Gives the location of the new landscape.
- **Rotation**: Gives the rotation of the new landscape.
- **Scale**: Gives the scale of the new landscape. This determines the size of each quad in the landscape, defaulting to 100 units.
- **Section Size**: Gives the number of quads in a single component section. Each section is rendered independently, providing control over the LOD transitions within a component.
- **Sections Per Component**: Gives the number of sections in a single component. This, combined with the section size, determines the size of each component. A component is the basic unit for organizing landscape data.
- **Number of Components**: Gives the number of components in the *X* and *Y* directions, determining the overall size of the landscape.

- **Overall Resolution**: Gives the overall resolution of the new landscape in vertices, excluding overlapping vertices between neighboring components.
- **Total Components**: Gives the total number of components that will be created for this landscape.
- **Fill World**: Makes your landscape as large as possible.
- **Create**: Creates your landscape in the world using the specified settings.

Everything related to the initial creation of our terrain—composition, area, structure, and geometric detail—is defined in the landscape details panel. Understanding it is crucial for generating the appropriate landscape for the project we need.

Landscape Components

Although the information we've covered is relatively straightforward, it's important to grasp the internal structure of landscapes and their role in meeting project resolution requirements.

Landscapes are divided into multiple **Landscape Components**, which are the core elements in Unreal Engine for rendering, visibility calculations, and collision. Each Landscape Component is uniform in size and always square. The size of these components is set during the creation of the landscape and is based on the overall size and LOD required.

Figure 6.13 depicts a simple landscape (outlined in *green*) consisting of four Landscape Components. Each component is composed of a single quad, and one has been separated to demonstrate how vertices are duplicated at the boundaries where Landscape Components meet.

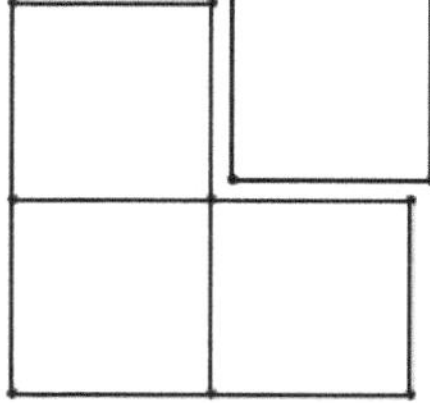

Figure 6.13 – Landscape Components composition

Components can optionally be subdivided into either one or four (2x2) subsections to increase landscape resolution. These subsections are the basic unit for Landscape LOD calculation.

Using four (2x2) subsections provides the same size heightmap as using four times as many Landscape Components with only one subsection each, but using fewer Landscape Components improves performance.

Each section's size (in number of vertices) must be a power of 2 value (up to 256x256) to allow different LOD Levels to be stored in the texture's mipmaps. This determines the number of quads in a Landscape Component: either a power of 2 value minus 1 (for one section per Landscape Component) or a power of 2 value minus 2 (for four sections per Landscape Component).

The following example in *Figure 6.14* shows an individual Landscape Component (outlined in green) containing four sections. Each section consists of nine (3x3) quads. Once again, you can observe that vertices are duplicated where the sections meet:

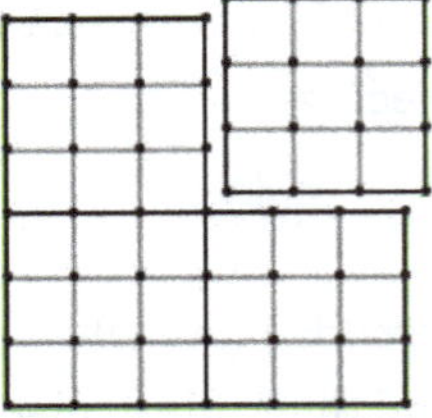

Figure 6.14 – Landscape component subsections

A Landscape Actor is color-coded to simplify the identification of each type of Landscape Component. The edges of the landscape are highlighted in *yellow*; each component edge is in *light green*, section edges are in *medium green*, and individual landscape quads are in *dark green*:

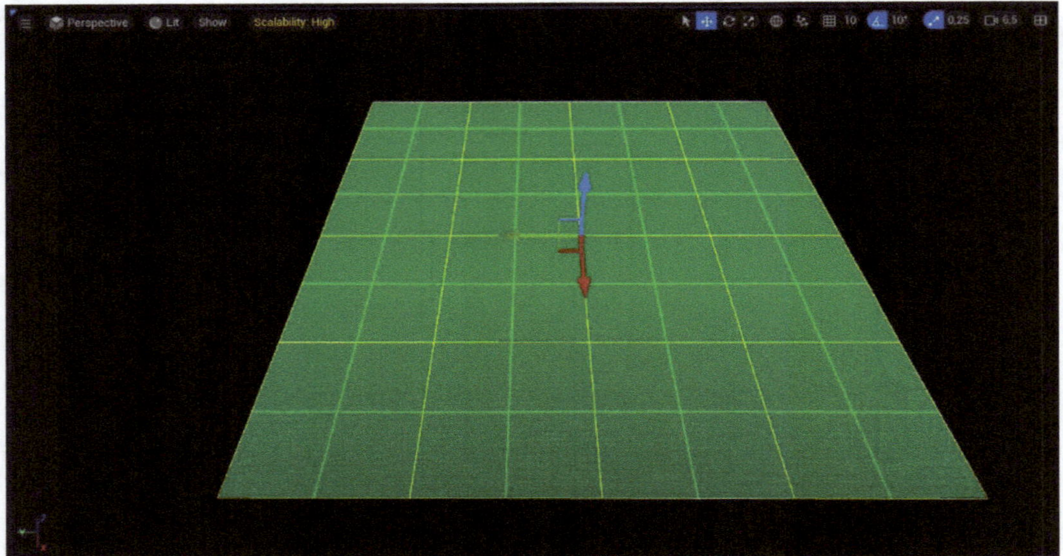

Figure 6.15 – Landscape configuration readout

In *Figure 6.16*, we can see the default configuration for creating landscapes in Unreal Engine.

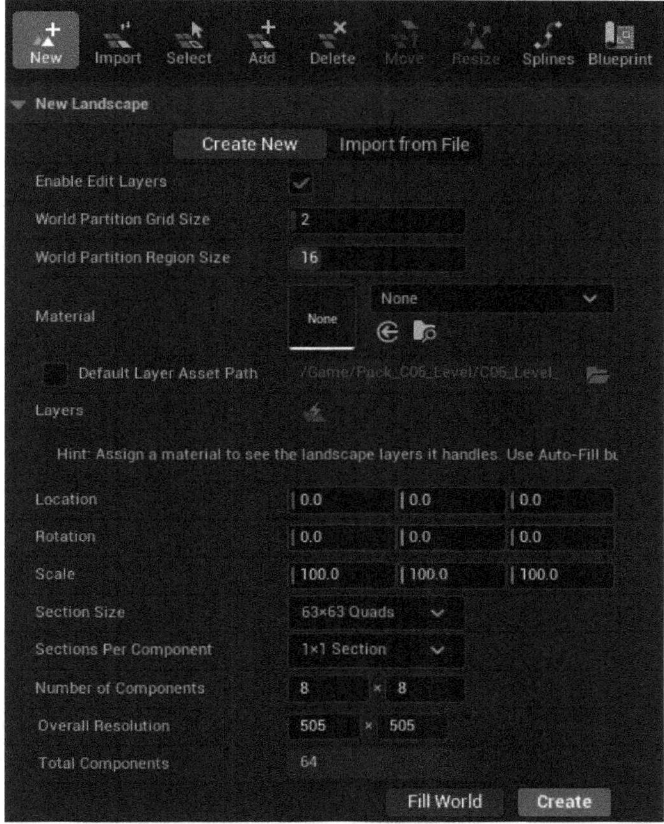

Figure 6.16 – Default Landscape settings

One of the most notable aspects of the default settings is understanding that by keeping the scale at 100%, we can determine the size and area of our terrain. Each section size consists of modules of 1x1 meters. Therefore, with the default section size of 63x63, each Landscape Component measures 63 meters x 63 meters. If we multiply this by the number of components in the initial setup (63x8), we get an area of 504x504 meters, which we can confirm in the **Overall Resolution** setting.

Important note

The **Overall Resolution** setting in any Unreal Engine landscape shows the number of vertices, so the result will always be *one vertex higher* than the product of **Section Size** x **Number of Components.**

Once satisfied with the initial configuration of our landscape, we can click the **Create** button to finalize the landscape. From this point onward, we will have access to the second working tab, called **Sculpt**.

Using Unreal Engine's Sculpt tools

Now that we have a **Landscape surface** to work with, we can use the **Sculpt tools** to adjust the terrain's height and create valleys, hills, mountains, and other features. Different layers can be used to isolate areas or distinguish between broad sculpting changes and finer details. To create a new layer or configure existing ones, *right-click* in the **Edit Layers** section:

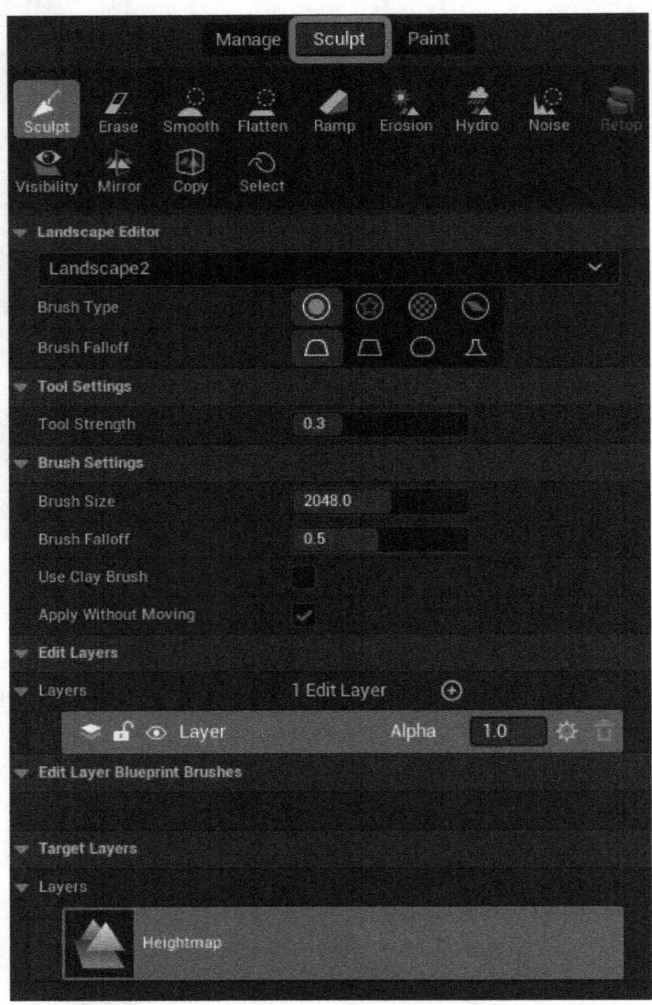

Figure 6.17 – Landscape Sculpt tools

Let's explore the tools available in this working mode:

- **Sculpt**: Raise the terrain by *left-clicking* and moving the mouse within the selected layer. Hold *Shift* while clicking to lower the terrain.
- **Erase**: Reset sculpting changes within the selected layer.
- **Smooth**: Smooth out sculpting changes within the selected layer. Depending on the brush falloff settings, terrain edges will flatten around the brush edges.
- **Flatten**: Flatten the terrain in the selected layer based on the height of the initial *left-click* position.
- **Ramp**: Select two points on the terrain and press **Add Ramp** in the tool settings to create a ramp within the selected layer.
- **Erosion**: Simulate erosion caused by soil movement within the selected layer.
- **Hydro**: Simulate erosion caused by rainfall within the selected layer.
- **Noise**: Add noise within the selected layer to randomly raise and lower the terrain, creating a more natural look.
- **Visibility**: Mask out individual quads in the landscape to create holes, which is useful for making caves or entrances to underground or hidden areas.
- **Mirror**: Copy one side of the selected layer to the other side, facilitating the creation of mirrored terrain.
- **Copy**: Copy and paste areas of terrain. You can also import and export copied terrain areas to or from disk.
- **Select**: Choose a region of the landscape to use as a mask for other tools, such as **Copy** or **Mirror**.

The use of these tools is mostly self-explanatory in many cases. Clicking on each tool reveals that several of them share common options, even with landscape painting tools.

Let's look at the most common and frequently used brush options.

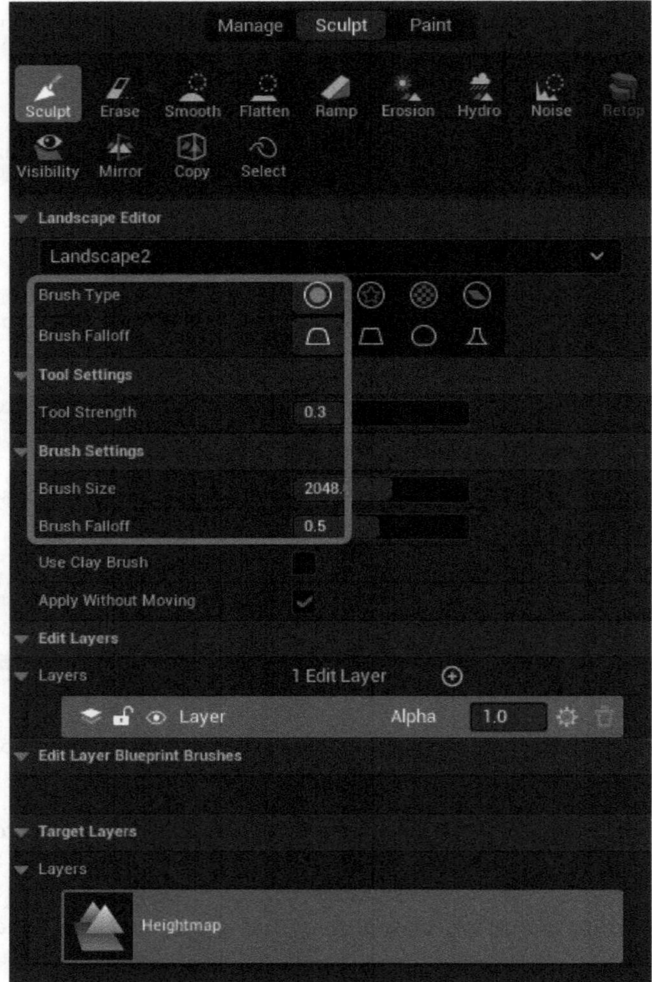

Figure 6.18 – Landscape Sculpt brush options

Let's explore what each of the available options allows us to do:

- **Brush Type**: The different types of brushes available.
- **Brush Falloff**: Determines the falloff behavior of the brush. It defines how quickly the effect of the brush diminishes toward the edge.
- **Tool Strength**: Adjusts the strength or intensity of the brush effect on the terrain.
- **Brush Size**: Sets the radius or size of the brush.

- **Brush Falloff:** Specifies the amount of falloff at the edge of the brush, expressed as a fraction of the brush's size. A value of `0` means no falloff, while a value of `1` means maximum falloff across the entire brush radius.

All these properties affect the final look of the terrain. For the brush properties, there are additional options to fine-tune the brush behavior:

Figure 6.19 – Landscape Sculpt Type / Falloff Options

Let's see where they are located and their description, reading from *left to right*:

- **Brush Type:**
  - **Circular Brush Type:** Creates a circular, rounded terrain effect
  - **Alpha Brush Type:** Applies a mask image to orient the brush stroke
  - **Pattern Brush Type:** Patterns a tile mask across the terrain
  - **Component Brush Type:** Applies changes to the entire Landscape Component
- **Brush Falloff:**
  - **Smooth Brush Falloff:** Provides a smooth transition along the edges of the brush
  - **Sharp Brush Falloff:** Results in a sharp transition at the edges of the brush
  - **Spherical Brush Falloff:** Offers a smooth transition from the center to the edges of the brush
  - **Tip Brush Falloff:** Provides an inverted smooth transition along the edges of the brush

Important note

Experiment with the sculpt brush settings to find the right balance of falloff, strength, and brush size for creating mountains, hills, paths, and more. Try using small semi-circular motions to add variation to your terrain.

Now that we have explored the main tools for both landscape creation and editing, let's proceed to work on our first custom landscape.

Exercise 6.1: Creating a terrain from heightmaps

Throughout this chapter, we have discussed different approaches to creating landscapes and the tools available to modify them. In this exercise, we will explore one of Unreal Engine's strongest features for building large-scale terrains: the ability to import external data through heightmaps.

Heightmaps are grayscale images that represent elevation data. Darker tones correspond to lower areas of the terrain, while lighter tones represent higher points. This method is extremely flexible, as many DCC tools (such as Gaea, World Machine, or Houdini) use heightmaps to transfer terrain information between programs.

Let's see how this process works inside Unreal Engine:

Note

Make sure your heightmap is a 16-bit grayscale file (PNG or RAW16). Avoid using 8-bit images, as they will produce visible banding artifacts.

1. In the Unreal Engine Editor, switch to **Landscape Mode**, located at the top left of the screen.
2. In the **Manage** section, select **Import from File**.
3. In the **Heightmap File** field, click the three dots (**...**) and select the heightmap. You can use a heightmap you created in a terrain tool or download a free heightmap available online.
4. Unreal will generate a preview, display the **Overall Resolution** value, and propose a component layout. Your values may differ from the example shown in *Figure 6.20*, and this is normal; simply confirm that Unreal has recognized your heightmap correctly.

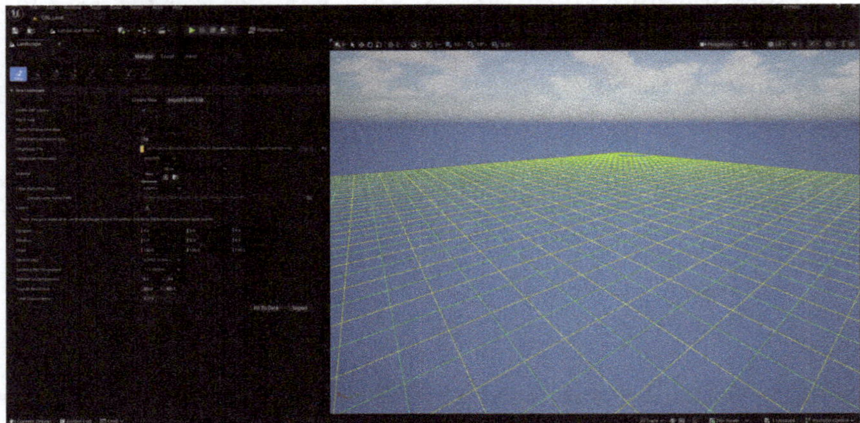

Figure 6.20 – Exercise final configuration

5. Click **Import** to generate the terrain. This process can take a while because Unreal not only interprets the heightmap image but also slices it into components so that **World Partition** can manage and stream it efficiently.

Figure 6.21 highlights the main controls used in this process (*steps 2* to *5*):

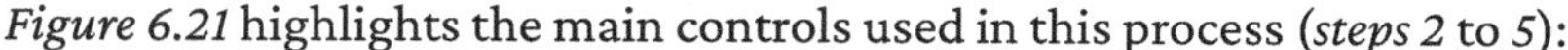

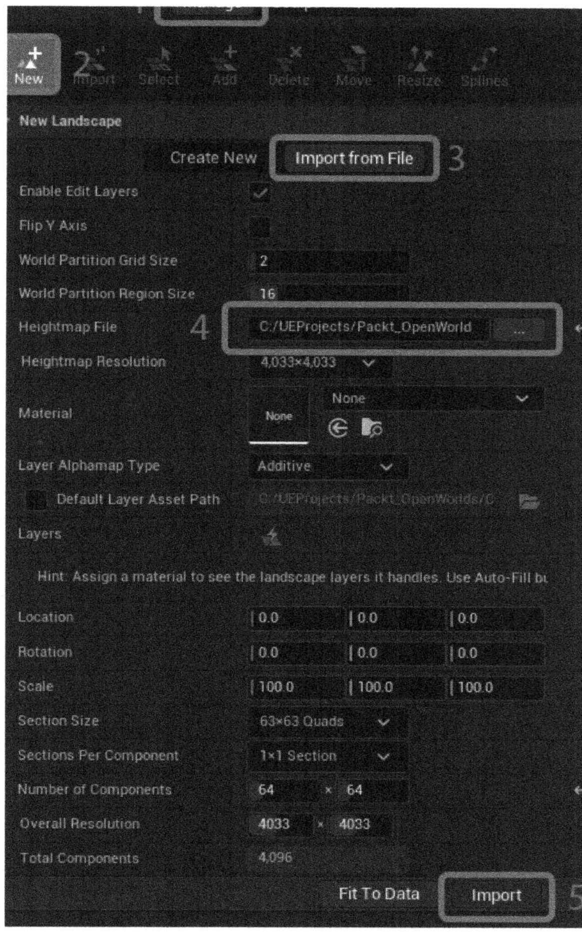

Figure 6.21 – Import from File Landscape process

Note

If your chosen heightmap is too large and causes performance issues, consider using a lower-resolution version. Most free heightmap libraries offer multiple sizes (for example, 1K, 2K, and 4K). Using a lower resolution will make the import process faster and lighter on your system.

Once the process is complete, the resulting landscape should look as in *Figure 6.22*:

Figure 6.22 – Import from File result

Troubleshooting

Sometimes, after the import process, the scene may appear empty except for a few cubes, as shown in *Figure 6.23*:

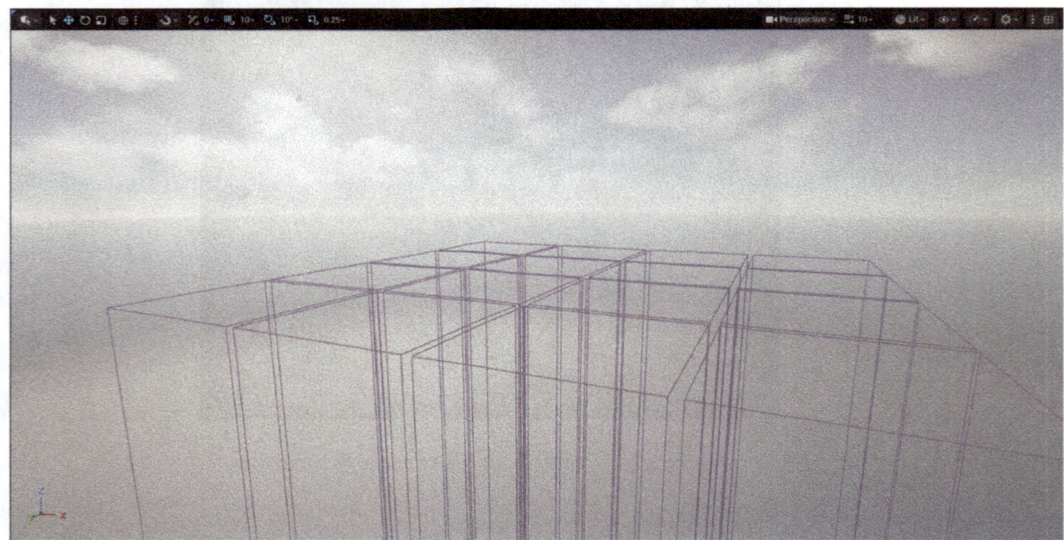

Figure 6.23 – Empty import from file

To fix this issue, do the following:

1. Go to **Window** | **World Partition** and enable **World Partition Editor** (if it is not already active).
2. In the **World Partition** window, you will see a representation of the map.
3. Drag a selection area in the grid, *right-click*, and choose **Load Region From Selection**, as shown in *Figure 6.24*:

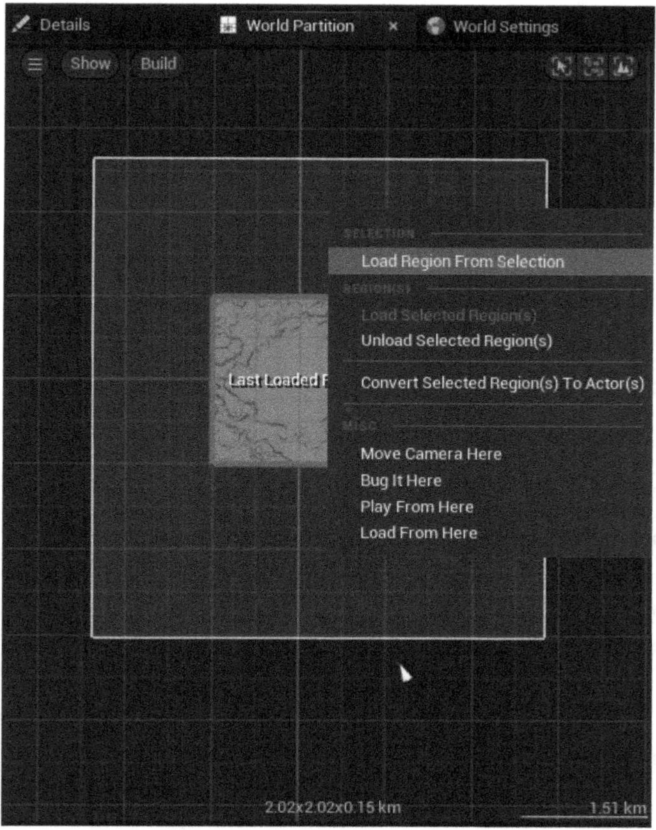

Figure 6.24 – Load Region From Selection

This will load the portion of the landscape into the Viewport.

Importing terrains through heightmaps is a powerful workflow in professional environments. In addition to elevation data, you can also import masks to drive material blending and achieve more natural results.

Note

For supplementary guidance and technical details, consult the Epic Games documentation on landscape heightmaps: `https://dev.epicgames.com/documentation/en-us/unreal-engine/importing-and-exporting-landscape-heightmaps-in-unreal-engine`.

Exercise 6.2: Creating a custom landscape

Now that we understand the tools of our landscape, let's create a custom surface:

1. In the Unreal Engine Editor, switch to **Landscape Mode**, located at the top left of the screen.
2. In the **Manage** section, create a new landscape.
3. Check the **Enable Edit Layers** checkbox.
4. Set **World Partition Grid Size** to `2` and **World Partition Region Size** to `16` accordingly.
5. Reset the **Location** value of the landscape to start at (`0`, `0`, `0`).
6. Adjust the **Scale** on the **X** and **Y** axes to `50%`.
7. Set **Section Size** to `127x127` quads.
8. Set **Sections Per Component** to `2x2` sections.
9. Click **Create** to generate the landscape.

As a verification method, we can change the **Viewport** view (top-left corner) to the **Top** view of our project and measure the surface area of the generated terrain. It should measure approximately `1015` meters. This is because we have adjusted the scale, making the terrain surface smaller but increasing its vertex resolution for better sculpting results.

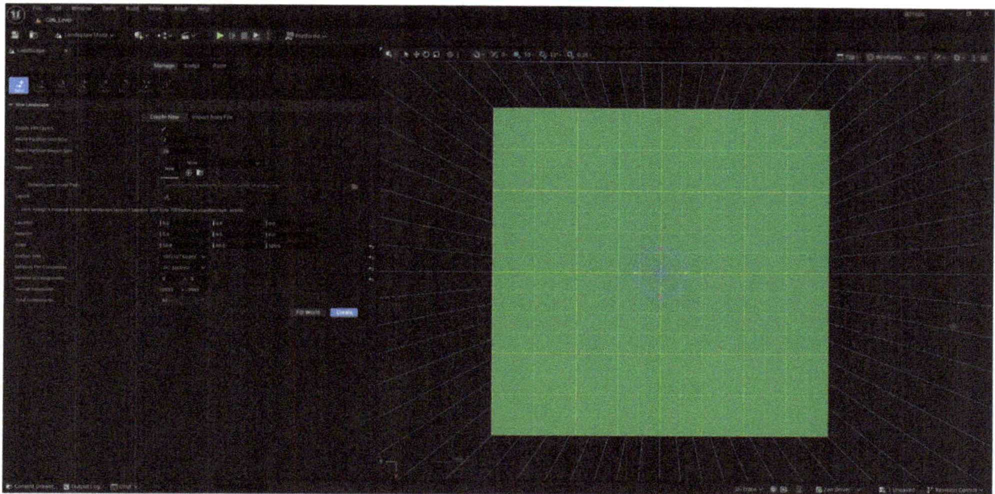

Figure 6.25 – Exercise final configuration

Important note

In this first part, we scaled the terrain down to 50% (*step 6*) with the intention of achieving higher resolution in the resulting landscape geometry. To compensate for the scale difference, we increased **Set Sections Per Component** to 2x2 (*step 8*). These steps are optional because while they provide better resolution for the landscape, they come at a higher performance cost.

Exercise 6.3: Sculpting a new terrain

Now that we have a custom landscape, let's sculpt the shape of our terrain on it:

1. In the **Sculpt** section, select the **Sculpt** tool.
2. Set **Tool Strength** to `0.2` and **Brush Size** to 8192 to begin sculpting the landscape block out (refer to the references mentioned at the beginning of the chapter).
3. In the **Edit Layers** section, select the current layer (usually the only one available) and click the + sign to add a new one:

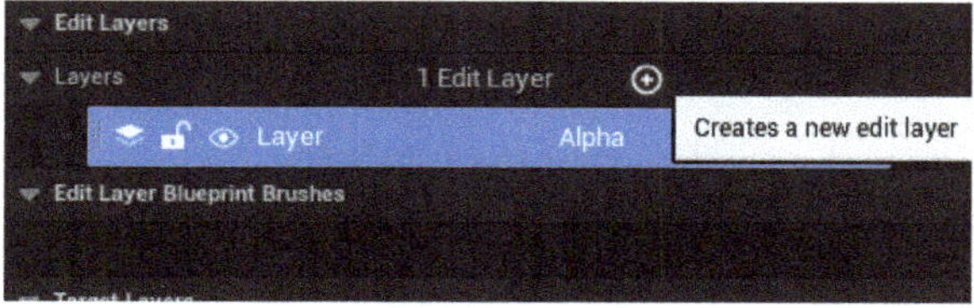

Figure 6.26 – Add new sculpt layer

4. The **Pick Landscape Edit Layer Class** window will appear. Pick **Landscape Edit Layer** and hit **Select**:

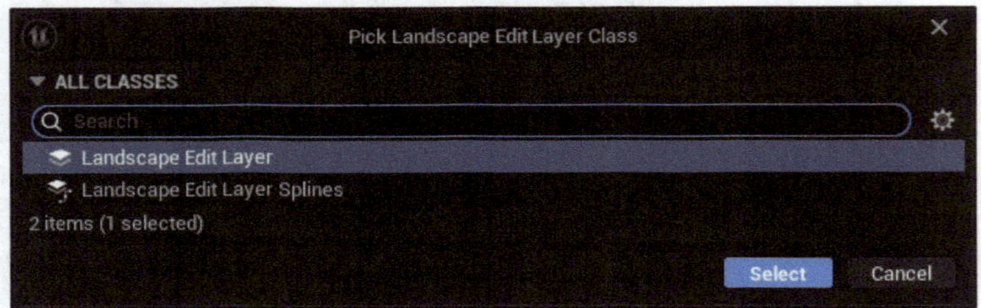

Figure 6.27 – Pick Landscape Edit Layer Class window

5. Rename the new layer to `Blocking`.
6. Using the **Sculpt** brush, begin shaping the terrain, focusing on its overall form.
7. Once you are satisfied with the result, you should have something like this:

Figure 6.28 – Landscape blocking stage

8. To begin the detailing phase, create a new layer, similar to what we did in *step 3* of this exercise, and name it `Details`.
9. Using the **Smooth** tool with a strength value of `0.7`, smooth out the initial iterations of the terrain.

10. Next, use the **Erosion** and **Hydro** tools to simulate weathering effects caused by wind and rain. Feel free to experiment with the tool parameters to achieve different effects. I ended up with this:

Figure 6.29 – Landscape first details stage

11. For the final details, continue using the **Sculpt** tool, but this time, choose the **Alpha Brush** option under **Brush Type**. Experiment with different textures and use a low intensity (between `0.2` and `0.35`) to add the necessary deformations.

Figure 6.30 – Landscape blocking versus details layer

12. Finally, use the **Smooth** tool again to improve the transition and blend the new terrain deformations seamlessly.

Figure 6.31 – Final Landscape result

13. Once finished, you can switch back to **Selection Mode**. If you have the third-person character set up, you can play the level and experience firsthand the result of your landscape. This allows you to interact with and explore the environment you've created.

Figure 6.32 – Your first landscape done

Developing levels and open worlds requires not only creative iteration but also significant amounts of technical research and testing. Achieving accuracy in scale, readability, and gameplay flow takes time and careful planning, as every design choice can affect the player experience.

Additional resource

To complement what you have learned in this chapter, you may also find it useful to explore this resource from Epic Games' Education team: `https://dev.epicgames.com/community/learning/talks-and-demos/KBd/building-natural-environments-in-unreal-engine`. It demonstrates similar techniques in practice.

Summary

In this chapter, we examined the detailed process of creating landscapes in Unreal Engine, highlighting the importance of each step in the development workflow. We started by discussing the role of visual references, such as concept art and storyboards, which are crucial for maintaining consistency, sparking creativity, and enhancing efficiency. These references offer a clear visual guide, ensuring that the game's tone, style, and atmosphere remain cohesive and immersive.

We then explored two main methods for environment creation: building a fully modeled environment and using Unreal Engine's **Landscape** tools. The blockout process was emphasized as a key phase for prototyping the level's structure with simple models, providing a foundation for further development.

Practical application was reinforced through exercises that guided the creation of a custom landscape with specific grid, region, and scale settings. We also practiced sculpting terrain using various tools and layers to achieve desired features. These exercises highlighted the importance of iterative design and real-time adjustments, fostering a dynamic and flexible workflow.

In the next chapter, we will explore the foliage tools to help populate our terrain with various types of vegetation.

7

Populating Your World with Foliage

The use of vegetation in our environment not only adds an aesthetically pleasing and visually attractive component, but it can also deepen the narrative, convey emotions, and create a unique atmosphere. From dense forests to vast fields of grass, on-screen vegetation can play a crucial role in setting the scene and characterizing the depicted environment. In this chapter, we will explore how the strategic use of vegetation can enrich the cinematics of a setting, in terms of both narrative and cinematic aesthetics.

To achieve this, Unreal Engine offers a set of tools that, much like a paintbrush with all its inherent features, allows us to quickly add or remove clusters of geometries. With **Foliage Mode**, it's possible to populate a large area in a short amount of time. It's important to note that this mode is designed to be used as a detailed element within a scene, enabling us to place vegetation wherever we need it. Additionally, Unreal Engine already includes tools that allow us to procedurally add vegetation to cover vast stretches of terrain.

Topics to be covered include the following:

- Understanding the terminology
- Using **Foliage Mode**
- Static Mesh Foliage optimization

Technical requirements

The technical requirements for this chapter follow the same specifications as *Chapter 1* and the rest of the chapters that follow; please refer to that section.

That said, let's remember the recommended hardware for working with Unreal Engine 5 (version 5.5 or later) with **Lumen Global Illumination** and **Reflections** and **Nanite** virtualized geometry:

- **Operating system**: Windows 10 64-bit version 1909 revision .1350 or higher, or versions 2004 and 20H2 revision .789 or higher. Support for DirectX 12 Agility SDK.
- **Processor**: Quad-core Intel or AMD, 2.5 GHz or faster.
- **Memory**: 8 GB RAM.
- **Software Ray Tracing**: This feature may require a video card using DirectX 11 with support for Shader Model 5.
- **Hardware Ray Tracing**: Requires Windows 10 build 1909.1350 or newer with DirectX 12 support and specific compatible graphics cards (e.g., NVIDIA RTX-2000 series or newer, AMD RX-6000 series or newer, Intel® Arc™ A-Series graphics cards or newer).
- **Internet access**: An internet connection is required to download the plugins and additional content required for this chapter.

Understanding the terminology

Here's a list of terminology used in the chapter:

- **Actor Foliage**: This refers to a vegetation asset that can be assigned a Blueprint containing instances of the Actor within the scene. This type of Actor offers much more flexibility and interactivity but can have a higher performance cost due to its dynamic nature.
- **Static Mesh Foliage**: This type of vegetation uses instanced meshes, designed to work through a brush directly on the landscape. It is better suited for a non-destructive vegetation workflow.
- **Brush**: A tool in the form of a brush that, through size, strength, fade, and density properties, allows us to paint vegetation onto the scene.
- **Density**: This refers to the number of vegetation instances painted in the scene per 10 square meters.
- **Cull Distance**: This is the drawing distance for vegetation beyond which it is no longer rendered on screen. This parameter can be modified for specific types of vegetation. By default, this distance is set, and initially, all vegetation is rendered.

Now that we have a broad understanding of the most important concepts, let's see how to access **Foliage Mode**.

Using Foliage Mode

Just like with the **Landscape** tools, everything related to foliage takes place in a specific mode within the editor. Let's see how to access it.

Enabling Foliage Mode

After creating an environment, as discussed in *Chapter 6*, we now have the space needed to place our vegetation. To do this, we need to access the editing modes. We can do this in the **Level Editor Toolbar**: open the **Modes** dropdown, just as we did when creating our landscape. In this case, we select **Foliage** (*Shift* + *3*) to open the tool that allows us to paint vegetation into the scene.

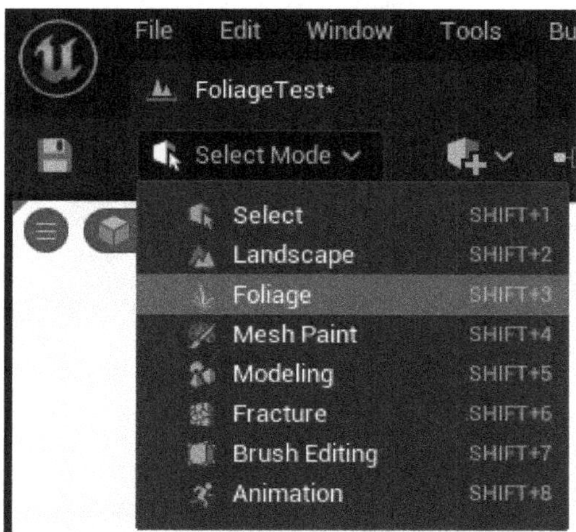

Figure 7.1 – Foliage Mode

It is worth mentioning that **Foliage Mode** generates instances to reduce draw calls, as the number of elements in the scene can be considerable. Once **Foliage Mode** is opened, we will see a panel with two clearly differentiated areas:

- **Tool Palette**: Located at the top, this area contains the main tools used in creating foliage in our projects, such as **Select**, **All**, **Deselect**, **Invalid**, **Lasso**, **Paint**, **Reapply**, **Single**, **Fill**, **Erase**, **Remove**, and **Move**.

- **Foliage Palette:** Located at the bottom, this is where we can add foliage either by clicking the **+ Foliage** button or by dragging our Static Meshes and/or Static Mesh Foliage directly from the **Content Browser**.

Figure 7.2 – Tool Palette (1) and Foliage Palette (2) areas

Since we have not yet specified the type of vegetation we want to paint, there is no data available to work with. To proceed, we need to assign various Static Meshes to the palette area. In this area, we will select the different meshes that we will paint into the scene.

We will use Megascans vegetation, which can be downloaded via Quixel Bridge. `Wild Grass` is a good example to start working with.

Recommendation

Working with low-quality settings allows us to download low-poly meshes and, most importantly, the textures will be 1024 resolution, which is sufficient for low vegetation. In the *Static Mesh Foliage optimization* section of this chapter, we will review measures to improve performance. These assets already have Static Mesh Foliage created in the **Foliage** folder, so simply dragging them into the palette will be sufficient without needing to recreate them.

Figure 7.3 – Wild Grass

When importing Megascans vegetation into the **Content Browser**, a **Foliage** folder is created with Static Mesh Foliage assets. These assets are ready to be dragged into the palette to start working. If we drag Static Meshes directly, Unreal will create the Static Mesh Foliage and prompt for a path to save them.

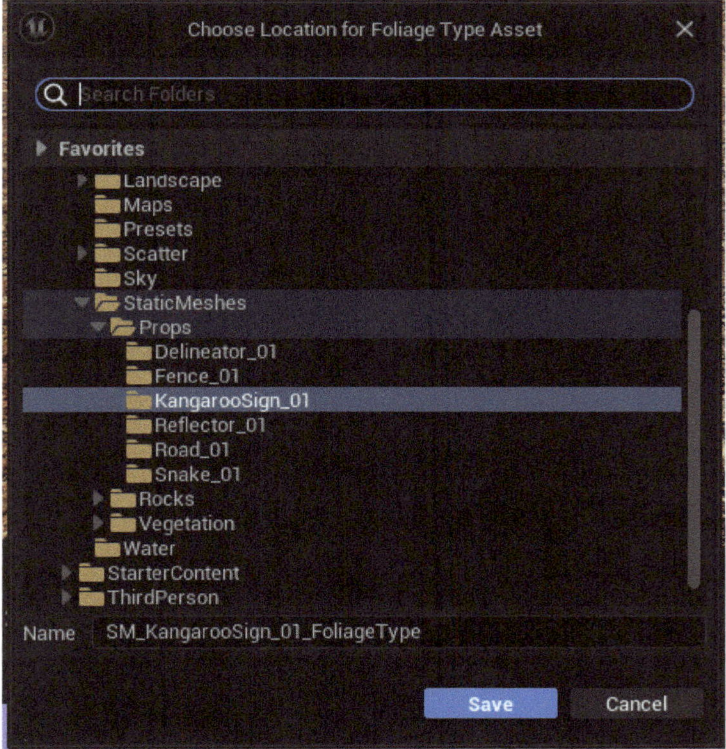

Figure 7.4 – Static Mesh Foliage organization structure

Once the various types of vegetation are assigned to the palette, the first thing we notice are small thumbnails of the models. In the upper-left corner, a *blue* checkmark indicates that the item is selected and will be painted. If it is not selected, the thumbnail appears dark.

In the upper-right corner, a **disk** icon allows us to save the Static Mesh Foliage created when dragging the Static Mesh. In the lower-right corner, the number **0** indicates the number of elements being drawn.

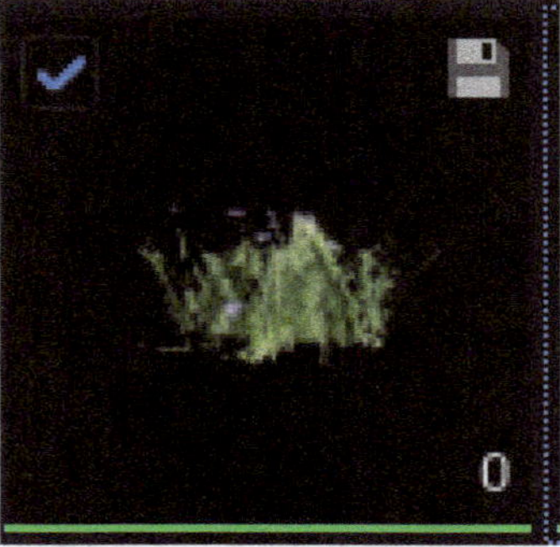

Figure 7.5 – Static Mesh Foliage on palette

Additionally, we will notice that our cursor has changed to a *blue* semi-sphere, indicating the brush size we will use to paint in the scene. We will delve into how to paint vegetation shortly, focusing first on understanding how to effectively use the **Paint** tool.

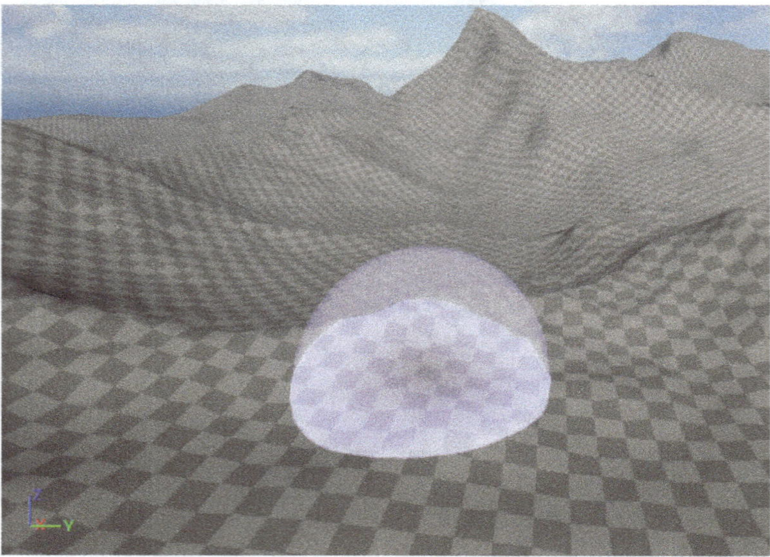

Figure 7.6 – Foliage brush

When selecting any type of vegetation, a menu unfolds displaying a series of details that influence how vegetation is painted in the scene.

Figure 7.7 – Foliage details menu: Mesh (1), Painting (2), Placement (3), and Instance Settings (4)

This menu includes numerous features, but we will focus on the key ones:

- **Mesh**: Here, we have our Static Mesh and the class used for generating instances.
- **Painting**: This feature allows us to modify how the mesh is painted in the scene. We can adjust the density of instances per 10 square meters (**Density**), the spacing between instances to avoid overlap (**Radius**), and even the scale to introduce variability in size (**Scaling**).
- **Placement**: In this section, we adjust how instances should be positioned in the scene. We can set a height offset for placement (**Z Offset**), determine whether instances should align perpendicular to the surface (**Align to Normal**), introduce random rotation around the *Z* axis (**Random Yaw**), adjust the slope angle for placement (**Ground Slope Angle**), and specify the height (**Height**).

- **Instance Settings:** This section adjusts various options, such as the ability to generate shadows and collisions and control how instances receive lighting from different types of lights using **Lighting Channels**.

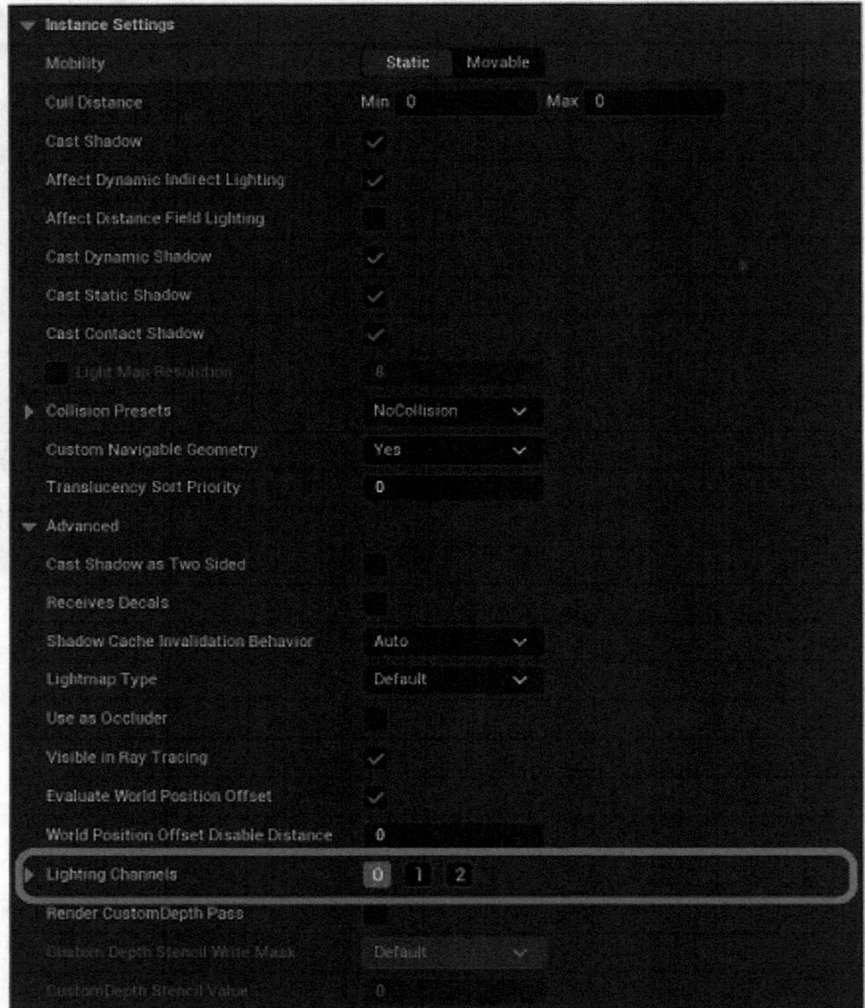

Figure 7.8 – Foliage details menu: Lighting channels

- **Cull Distance:** An important property related to optimization is **Cull Distance**, which by default is set to **0** for both **Min** and **Max** values, meaning it is disabled. This distance varies between the **Min** and **Max** values to ensure that assets fade out gradually rather than disappearing abruptly.

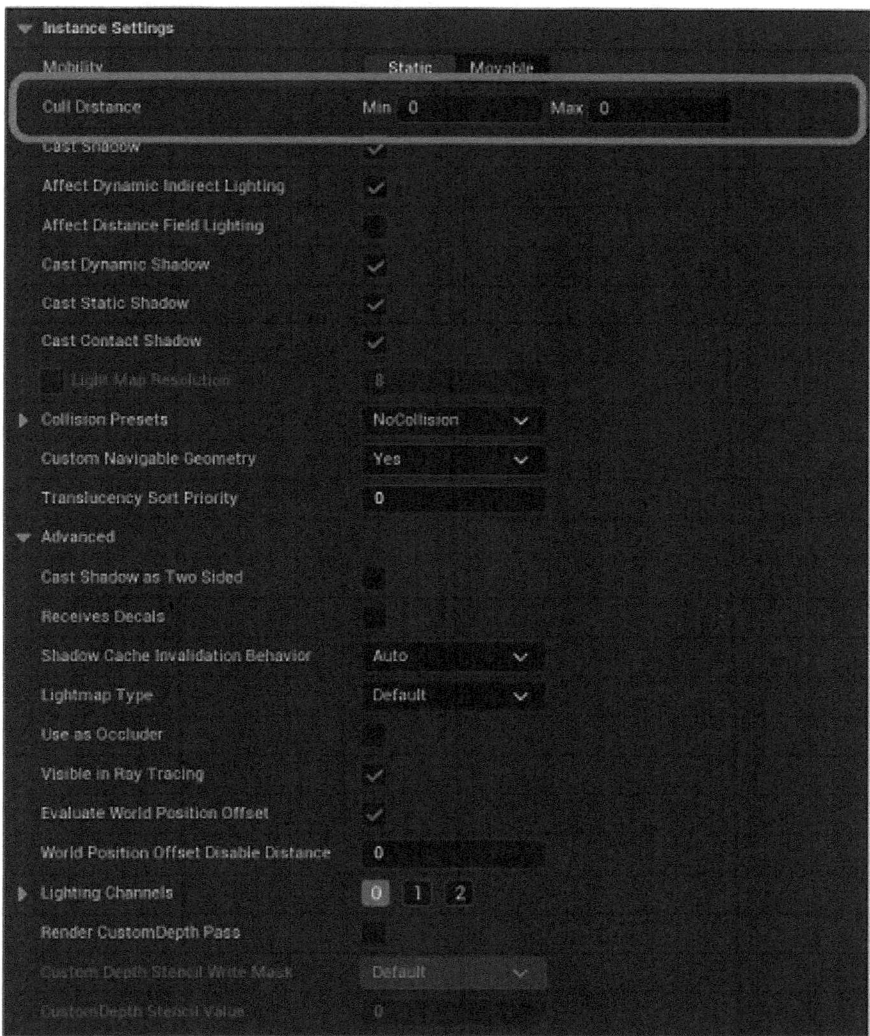

Figure 7.9 – Foliage details menu: Cull Distance

- **Scalability**: Activating this option allows for real-time control over vegetation density.

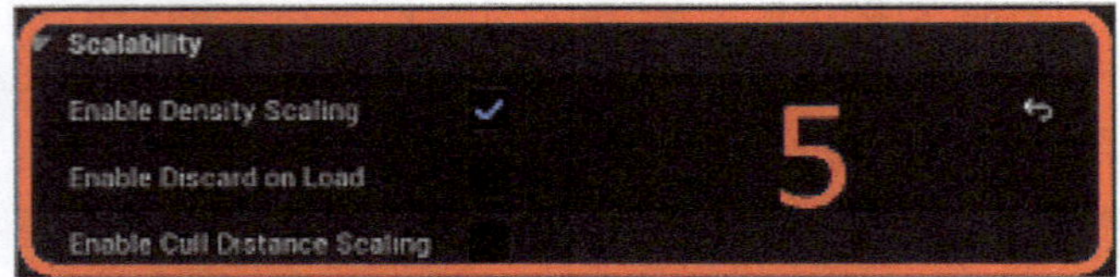

Figure 7.10 – Foliage details menu: Scalability

You can enable it using the `foliage.DensityScale` command with values ranging from `0.1` to `1.0`.

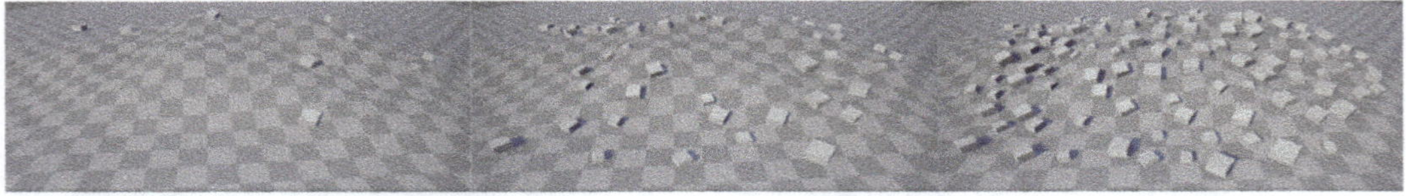

Figure 7.11 – Runtime scalability (values from left to right: 0.1, 0.5, 1.0)

Once our vegetation is configured, it's time to start painting!

Using the Foliage tools

From this point on, the **Foliage** Tool Palette, which we saw at the beginning of the chapter, becomes crucial once again.

Figure 7.12 – Foliage tools

Let's take a look at these tools one by one.

Paint

As we use the various tools, options will open up primarily in the form of brushes to adjust how we paint vegetation. Naturally, to begin painting, we should select the **Paint** option.

With this tool, we can modify the brush size (**Brush Size**) and density of painting (**Paint Density**), as well as erase the density (**Erase Density**). These densities act as multipliers for the vegetation densities. Before making the first stroke, it's crucial to pay attention to filters, as you can paint on the landscape objects such as Binary Space Partition (BSP), Static Meshes, translucent objects, or more vegetation.

Important note

As a very important recommendation, if you are working with levels, you must ensure that you are working at the correct level. Make sure the **Place in Current Level** option (see *Figure 7.13*) is active to ensure that vegetation is placed in the correct level.

Figure 7.13 – Foliage tools: Paint

Working in this manner, all the information, including the position of the vegetation in the scene and the palette we used for painting, will be saved within this Foliage Actor.

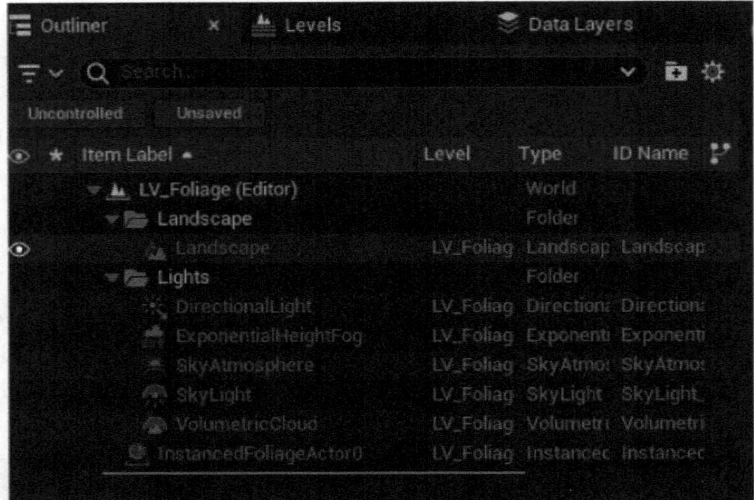

Figure 7.14 – Outliner showing Foliage Actor and instances

As mentioned earlier, **Foliage Mode** is useful for detailed decoration of specific areas because its tools allow for more precise placement compared to other methods within Unreal Engine.

Now we are ready to start painting! To do this, we'll use the *left mouse button* to drag over the scene and paint vegetation on the Actors selected in the filters section mentioned earlier. To erase our strokes or parts of them, we can use *Shift + left mouse button*.

At this point, two scenarios occur depending on the level management system chosen: traditional levels or **World Partition**. In traditional workflows, when we drag Static Mesh Foliage into the palette, the **InstanceFoliageActor** class is created in the **Outliner**, which gathers all the information about the instances of our vegetation. Conversely, if we are working with the automatic data management and level streaming system based on distance (**World Partition**), **InstanceFoliageActor** is created when we perform the first stroke (as we drag).

Figure 7.15 demonstrates how painting and erasing vegetation appear in the Viewport, helping visualize the process described above:

Figure 7.15 – Paint and erase

Erase

Similarly to the **Paint** tool, the same options will appear when using the **Erase** tool (see *Figure 7.16*). In this case, however, our objective will be to remove vegetation. We can accomplish this by holding down the *Shift* key and using the *left mouse button*, just as when painting.

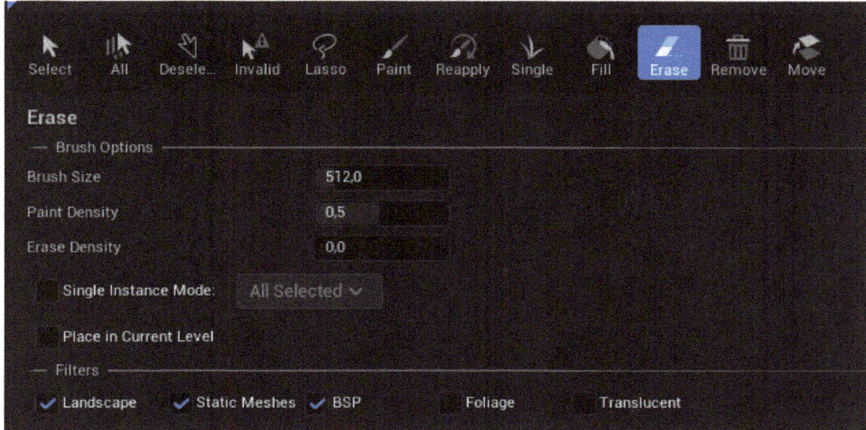

Figure 7.16 – Foliage tools: Erase

Lasso

This tool allows for the selection of instances using a brush, similar to working with **Paint** or **Erase**.

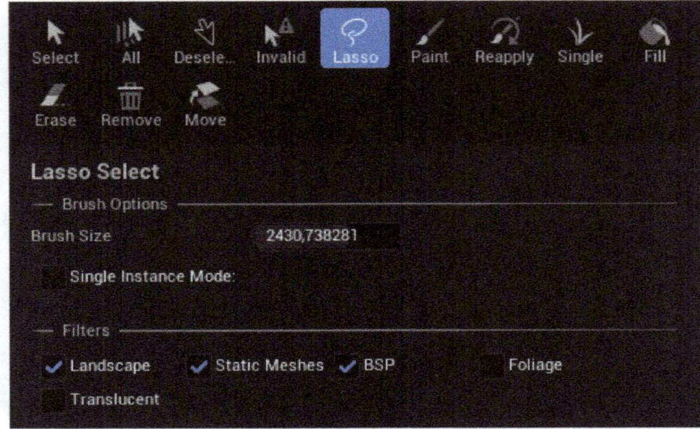

Figure 7.17 – Foliage tools: Lasso

In this case, you can only adjust the brush size and use filters to specify where the selection will apply. To deselect instances while dragging the brush, use *Shift + left mouse button*.

Figure 7.18 – Foliage tools: Lasso (result)

Deselect

With this tool, we deselect all the instances that were previously selected using the **Lasso** tool.

Figure 7.19 – Foliage tools: Deselect

Remove

With this tool, we remove all the instances that were previously selected using the **Lasso** tool.

Figure 7.20 – Foliage tools: Remove

Select

After painting vegetation with the **Paint** tool, we can individually select instances to subsequently delete them or even perform transformations such as move, rotate, and scale.

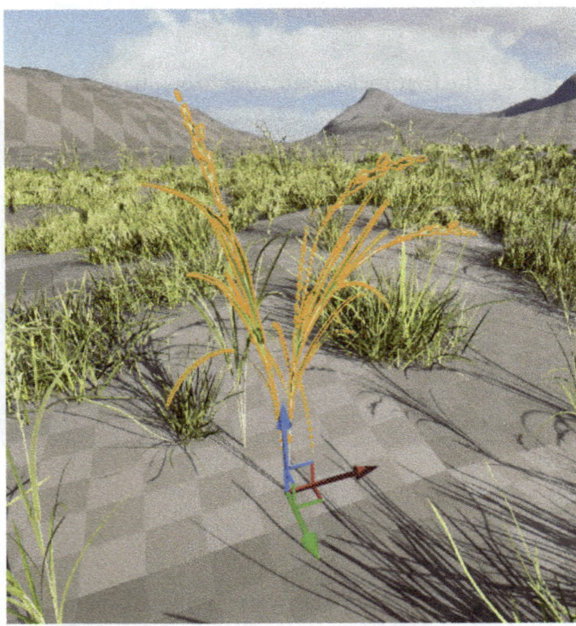

Figure 7.21 – Foliage tools: Select

All

With this tool, you can select all instances with a single click. Once selected, you can delete them using **Remove** or move them to the current level using **Move**.

Figure 7.22 – Foliage tools: Remove and Move

Single

This tool allows you to place vegetation with each mouse click. Each time you click, it randomly paints one type of vegetation from those selected in the palette.

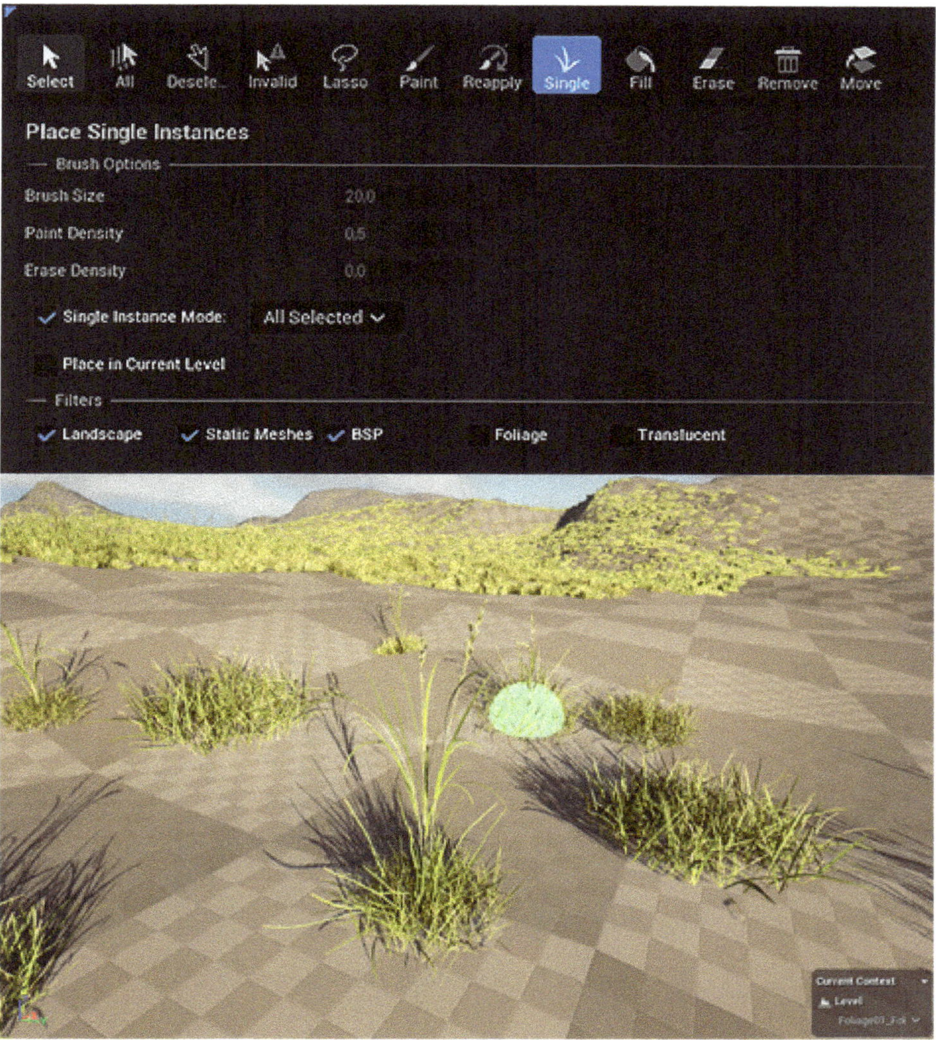

Figure 7.23 – Foliage tools: Single

Fill

This tool allows us to fill any type of Actor in the scene with vegetation that we have selected in the filters.

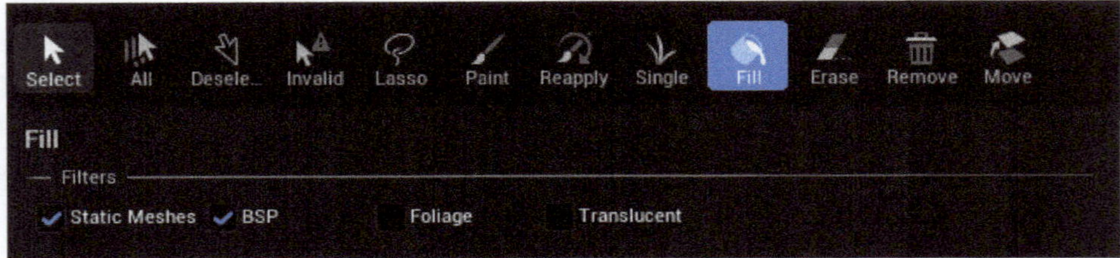

Figure 7.24 – Foliage tools: Fill

As you can see, there is no option to select **Landscape** because it covers a large area and could significantly impact project performance. If we use a plane, sphere, or box as an example, each *left-click* will populate them with vegetation based on the configuration we have set for those instances.

Figure 7.25 – Foliage tools: Fill meshes

Reapply

Once the vegetation is painted, you can change certain parameters of the instances.

Figure 7.26 – Foliage tools: Reapply

The procedure is as follows:

1. **Selecting vegetation types**: Use the **Reapply** tool to select the types of vegetation from your palette to which you want to apply changes.
2. **Adjusting details**: In the vegetation **Details** section, make the desired changes.
3. **Applying changes**: Paint the changes onto the instances in the level.

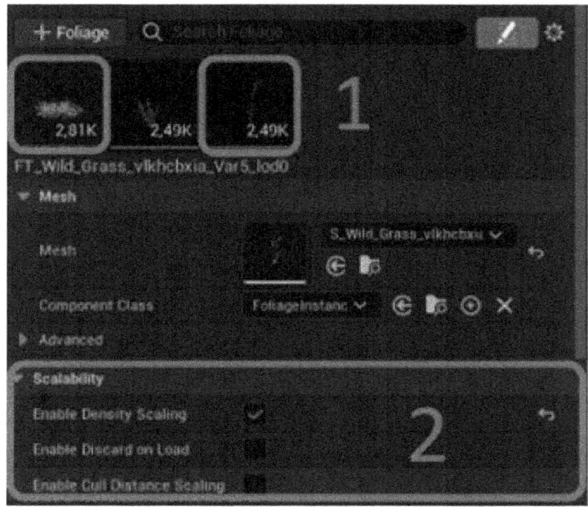

Figure 7.27 – Applying changes with Reapply tool

Important note

It could be a good exercise to select and change the scalability by activating **Density Scaling**:

1. **Select the Reapply tool:** Choose the **Reapply** tool and select the vegetation you want to modify.
2. **Adjust scalability in Details:** In the **Details** panel, under **Scalability**, activate **Density Scaling**.
3. **Apply changes:** Paint the changes onto the instances in the scenes.
4. **Exit Foliage Mode:** Exit **Foliage Mode** once changes are applied.

As discussed, in **Foliage Mode**, under the **Scalability** section in the console, you can input the `foliage DensityScale` command (from 0.1 to 1.0) to observe density changes.

Figure 7.28 – Foliage tools: Reapply/density scale

Now that we understand how to configure our vegetation, we can continue detailing our scene by populating it with grass, trees, and shrubs. The **Foliage** tool is not limited to working only with vegetation; it allows painting of any type of Static Mesh, including paper, cans, bricks, and chairs, as shown in *Figure 7.29*:

Figure 7.29 – Props via Foliage

If we need to download any other assets, we have the option to use high-quality scanned assets accessible through Quixel Bridge, as seen in *Chapter 2*.

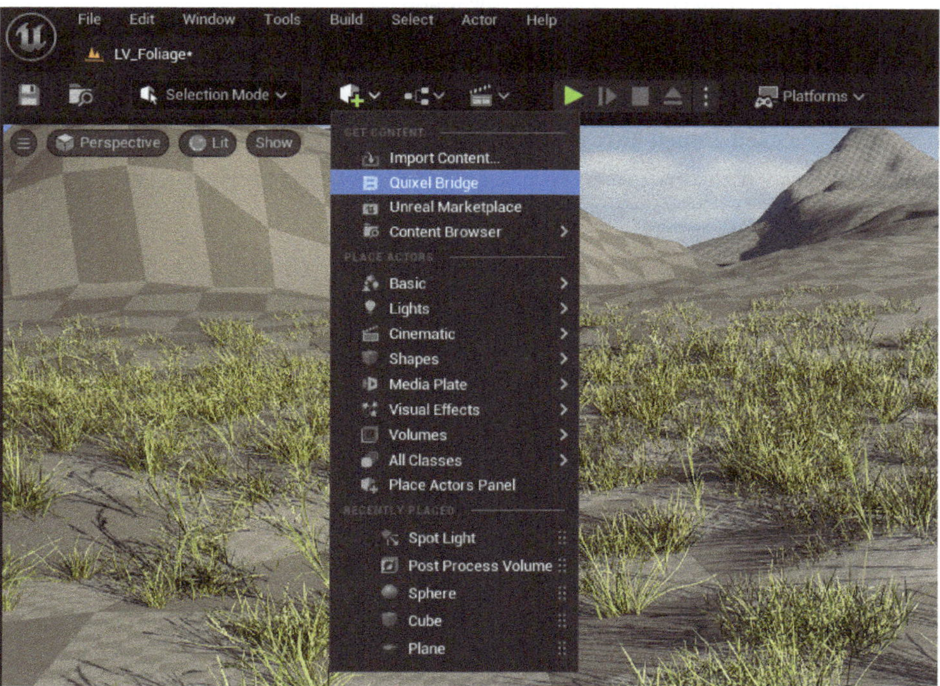

Figure 7.30 – Megascans quick access

When working with vegetation, it's easy to get carried away by both quantity and quality. Creating a forest, jungle, or hillside completely covered with grass or crops requires a large number of instances to make the scene believable. However, this also entails a significant number of calculations and resources that the engine needs to render correctly in real time. Therefore, optimizing your project becomes crucial not only for maintaining smooth performance but also for ensuring that your scenes are both visually impressive and efficiently rendered.

Static Mesh Foliage optimization

The process of optimizing a project, especially those related to open worlds and involving the use of a large number of assets related to foliage that must be instantiated many times, is a crucial task that we must keep in mind at all times. Given that the raw material of our foliage is Static Meshes, here are some considerations to keep in mind.

Firstly, the **polygon count** in vegetation meshes is crucial. The fewer polygons our grass has, the more instances we can have in the scene simultaneously.

Using a well-balanced LOD system, as discussed in *Chapter 3*, ensures that higher LODs (such as LOD0) with more detail are displayed near the camera. At greater distances, lower LODs such as LOD4 or LOD5 are used, which have fewer polygons and lower scene rendering costs.

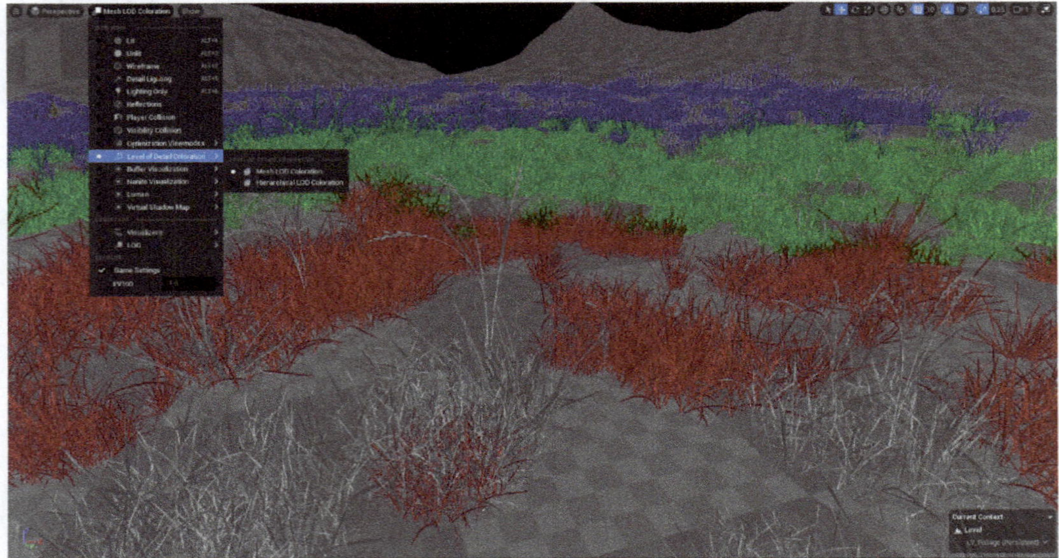

Figure 7.31 – Foliage LODs

Each LOD has a set of properties that can be adjusted individually. Lower LODs (such as LOD3, LOD4, and beyond) are farther from the camera, so their shadows won't be noticeable. Therefore, we will disable shadow generation for these LODs.

Figure 7.32 shows the settings for **LOD 3.** Here, you can view and adjust key options such as shadow casting, collision, and distance field lighting to optimize performance for lower-detail levels:

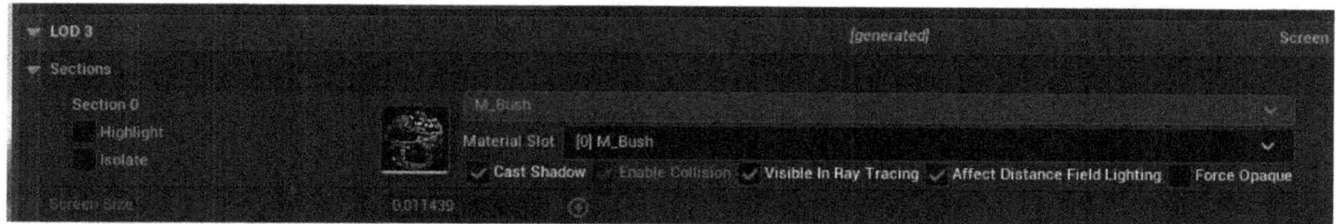

Figure 7.32 – Settings panel for LOD 3, showing optimization options

It's common for vegetation to have movement to simulate wind effects, typically achieved using materials and vertex shaders to modify vertex positions, specifically when working with **World Position Offset**. For vegetation that is far from the camera and where movement is barely perceptible, it need not be animated. In such cases, we can disable this movement using the **World Position Offset Disabled Distance** property in **Static Mesh Foliage**. Setting a distance from the camera (e.g., 2,500 cm) will prevent **World Position Offset** from affecting the vegetation beyond that point. This helps reduce computations, avoid unwanted artifacts, and maintain optimal performance.

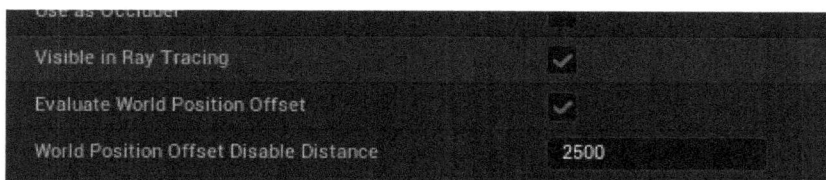

Figure 7.33 – World Position Offset Disable Distance

A more optimal option is to use **Nanite** for vegetation. To activate this geometry virtualization system, go to the Mesh Editor, locate the **Nanite Settings** section, and check **Enable Nanite Support**. Apply the changes and save. If you notice that the vegetation appears flat in the scene, additionally select **Preserve Area** to ensure that when reducing polygon count, it maintains volume (or screen area) effectively.

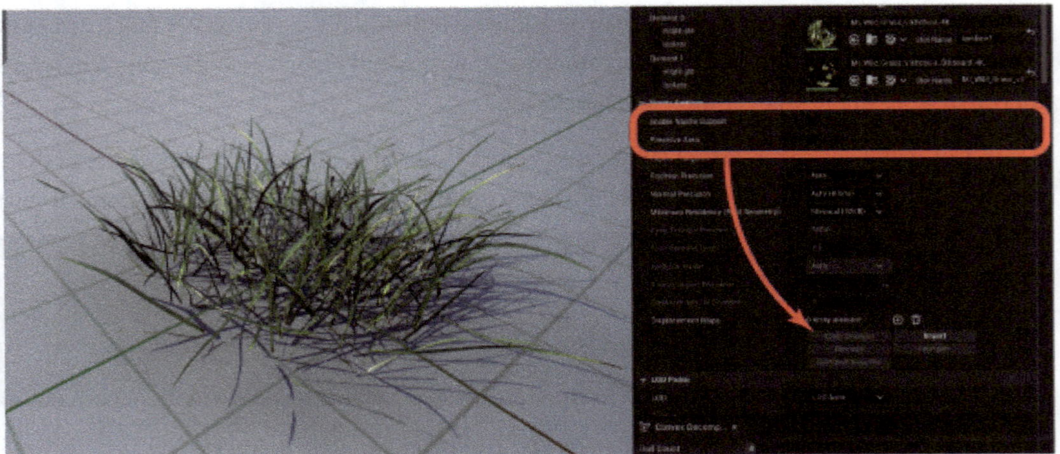

Figure 7.34 – Enable Nanite

Lighting

Unreal's rendering engine, **Lightmass**, generates shadow and light maps individually as needed for each instance. There are several settings in the Static Mesh that must be checked to ensure that precomputed lighting works well with vegetation. Incorrect settings could result in black meshes after building lighting:

- Check that Unreal uses the correct UV channel to generate lightmaps and ensure that the UVs are correctly unwrapped. If they are not, Unreal can generate them quickly, provided the mesh has at least one correct UV channel.
- Lightmap resolution should be small enough to allow all shadow maps from instances within a single group/cluster (default is `100`) to be grouped without exceeding the maximum texture resolution (*4096 x 4096*).

Textures

Another important point when optimizing vegetation is the use of textures, which are often oversized, especially with Megascans vegetation, due to its high quality.

Ideally, creating vegetation from scratch would be most optimal, but when working with Megascans assets, the minimum texture resolution available from Quixel Bridge is *1024 x 1024 px*. However, this doesn't mean you must always work with this resolution. It depends on the type of vegetation and the size of the Static Mesh.

For example, for `Wild Grass`, which has very small stems, textures of 256 x 256 px might be sufficient. On the other hand, for a forest of trees with large trunks, you might need textures of 2048 x 2048 px.

Different types of vegetation require different texture resolutions, so it's essential to configure textures specifically for each case. In the texture editor, under the **Compression** section, adjust **Maximum Texture Size** from its default value of **0** (which means no limit) to a power-of-2 value that maintains detail in the scene while reducing memory load significantly:

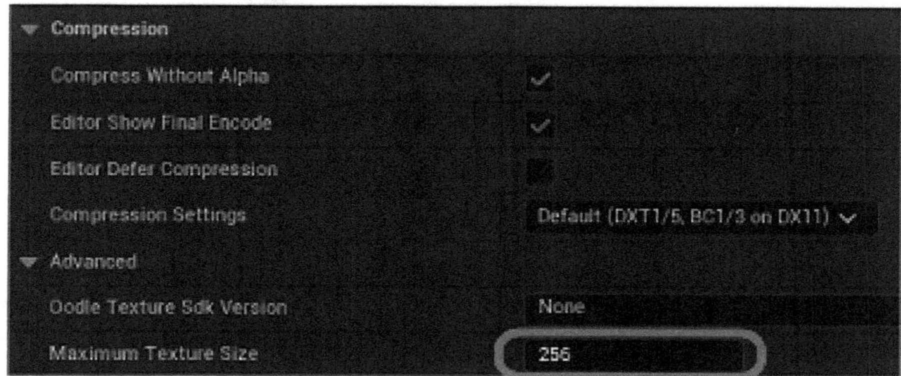

Figure 7.35 – Maximum Texture Size

For a Static Mesh that has a set of textures, you can edit them individually, but considering that the project will likely have many textures, it's more efficient to edit them together. Here's how you can do this:

1. Select all the textures you want to modify simultaneously.
2. *Right-click* to bring up the contextual menu.
3. Navigate to **Asset Actions** and select **Edit Selection in Property Matrix** (or **Bulk Edit in Property Matrix** for versions of Unreal prior to 5.3).

   This action allows you to make bulk edits to properties across multiple selected textures efficiently.

Figure 7.36 – Edit Selection in Property Matrix

4. Now, a window will open displaying all the properties of the textures that can be seen in the texture editor itself. In the tab that appears on the right, **Pinned Columns,** you will find the **Compression** section, where you will again find **Maximum Texture Size** to set the desired resolution.

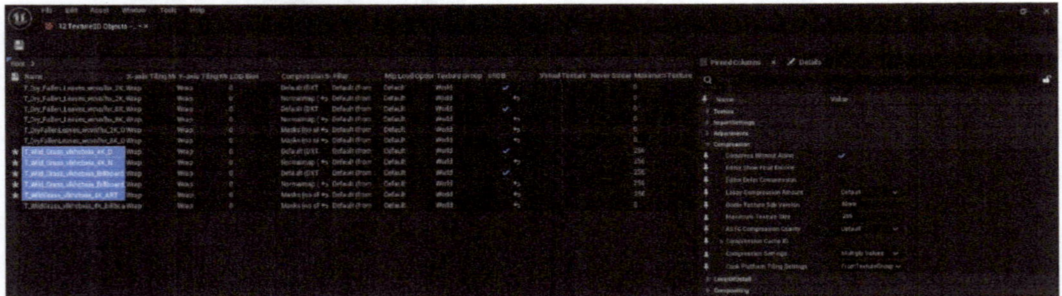

Figure 7.37 – Maximum Texture Size on Edit Selection in Property Matrix

In this section, we have discussed various strategies for auditing the Static Meshes that make up our foliage. These considerations are focused on improving the real-time performance of our projects. Depending on the project's size and the hardware specifications of our PC, we can use them to maintain performance both in the editor and during execution.

Summary

In this chapter, we delved into the use of Unreal Engine's **Foliage Mode** to efficiently populate our environments with vegetation. We learned how to select, configure, and paint various types of foliage using tools such as **Paint**, **Erase**, **Fill**, and **Select**. Additionally, we discussed the importance of optimizing instance density, configuring appropriate LODs, managing foliage movement and lighting, and adjusting textures to enhance performance without sacrificing visual quality.

By gaining proficiency in **Foliage Mode** and applying optimization techniques, we can create more immersive and dynamic worlds in Unreal Engine. It's crucial to strike a balance between visual fidelity and project performance, ensuring that our environments not only look great but also perform well across different hardware configurations. Understanding these tools and techniques empowers developers to craft environments that are both stunning and efficient, enhancing the overall gameplay experience for users.

In the next chapter, we will be working with materials. We will start by understanding basic concepts related to materials, as well as the interface related to material creation. We will study the principles of PBR Materials within Unreal Engine. Finally, we will discuss creating materials from textures and materials for landscapes.

Subscribe to Game Dev Assembly Newsletter!

We are excited to introduce **Game Dev Assembly**, our brand-new newsletter dedicated to everything game development. Whether you're a programmer, designer, artist, animator, or studio lead, you'll get exclusive insights, industry trends, and expert tips to help you build better games and grow your skills. Sign up today and become part of a growing community of creators, innovators, and game changers.

`https://packt.link/gamedev-newsletter`

Scan the QR code to join instantly!

8

Introduction to Materials

In Unreal Engine, **materials** play a critical role in defining the visual characteristics of objects within a scene. Essentially, a material can be viewed as the layer that determines how an object's surface looks and behaves under various lighting conditions. Materials specify how surfaces interact with light, dictating attributes such as color, shine, texture, and opacity. By manipulating these properties, materials help create realistic and visually compelling environments in Unreal Engine.

In this chapter, we will explore how to work with materials, the most common nodes, and the constructions we should follow to achieve the desired look for each type of surface we create.

Topics to be covered include the following:

- Understanding the terminology
- Exploring the Material Editor interface
- Working in the Material Editor
- Overview of PBR materials
- Exercise 8.1: Creating a gold material
- Delving into texture implementation
- Material workflows

Technical requirements

The technical requirements for this chapter follow the same specifications as *Chapter 1* and the rest of the chapters that follow; please refer to the *Technical requirements* section in that chapter.

That said, let's remember the recommended hardware for working with Unreal Engine 5 (recommended version 5.5 or later) with **Lumen Global Illumination** and **Reflections** and **Nanite** virtualized geometry:

- **Operating system**: Windows 10 64-bit version 1909 revision .1350 or higher, or versions 2004 and 20H2 revision .789 or higher. Support for DirectX 12 Agility SDK.
- **Processor**: Quad-core Intel or AMD, 2.5 GHz or faster.
- **Memory**: 8 GB RAM.
- **Software Ray Tracing**: This feature may require a video card using DirectX 11 with support for Shader Model 5.
- **Hardware Ray Tracing**: Requires Windows 10 build 1909.1350 or newer with DirectX 12 support and specific compatible graphics cards (e.g., NVIDIA RTX-2000 series or newer, AMD RX-6000 series or newer, Intel® Arc™ A-Series graphics cards or newer)
- **Internet access**: An internet connection is required to download the plugins and additional content required for this chapter.

Understanding the terminology

Here's a list of the terminology used in the chapter:

- **Shaders and rendering process**: Shaders dictate how vertices and pixels are rendered, written in **High-Level Shading Language** (**HLSL**) for Unreal Engine. In a rendering pipeline, shaders are specialized programs responsible for determining how each vertex or pixel is rendered on screen. This shader code is subsequently translated into a series of assembly language instructions that the GPU hardware can execute, ultimately producing the final pixel colors displayed on your screen.

- **HLSL**: HLSL empowers materials to communicate GPU instructions, enabling artists and programmers to control on-screen visuals.
- **Expressions and functions**: Expressions are individual nodes that perform mathematical operations or provide information to the material. They are combined in the Material Editor and pass the result to the main node. Groups of nodes performing a specific task are called functions.
- **Main node**: The main node of a material is where all nodes converge to determine its appearance. Inputs to this node dictate how the material looks.
- **PBR**: **Physically-Based Rendering** (**PBR**) is a shading and rendering technique that more accurately simulates how light interacts with different materials.

Now that we understand the fundamental concepts of materials in Unreal Engine, let's delve into the Material Editor interface.

Exploring the Material Editor interface

The **Material Editor** in Unreal Engine has its own workspace and related tools. This graphical interface operates using nodes called **Material Expressions**, which are then translated into HLSL code. This approach makes the creation of materials within Unreal Engine a more intuitive process.

To create your first material, open the Material Editor. In Unreal Engine, creating different types of assets, such as materials, blueprints, textures, and others, involves first creating them as assets in a designated folder. To start, *right-click* in an empty area of the **Content Browser** and choose **Material** under **Create Basic Asset**.

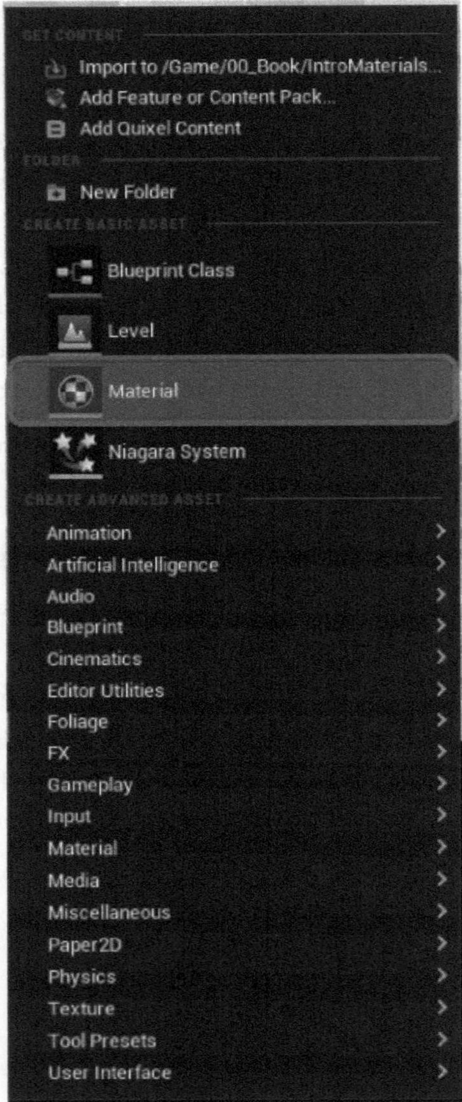

Figure 8.1 – Content Browser

This action will create the asset ready to be renamed. However, not all names are acceptable. In Unreal, maintaining organization is crucial, both at the folder level and in terms of prefixes and suffixes for different assets. It is recommended to follow style guides (mentioned in *Chapter 4*). For materials, use the prefix `M_` followed by the desired name. In this case, since we are reviewing the user interface, the name will be `M_UI`.

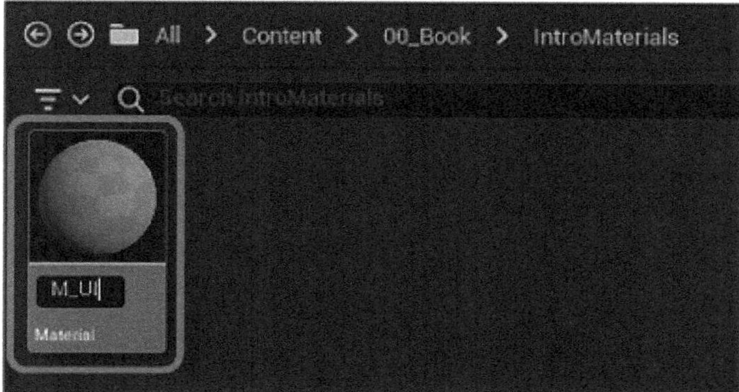

Figure 8.2 – Material asset

Double-clicking the material will open the Material Editor. The interface is divided into several areas, and we will primarily focus on the zones marked in the following figure:

Figure 8.3 – Overview of the Material Editor user interface

Figure 8.3 depicts the following zones of the Material Editor user interface:

1. Graph
2. Palette
3. Viewport
4. Details
5. Toolbar
6. Stats

Let's take a look at each of these zones in detail next.

Graph

When you create a material, a main node with multiple inputs appears. This main node serves as the central hub where you connect expressions and functions to create materials. Here are the controls for performing various operations:

- *Left mouse button*: Select individual nodes; if you click and drag, you can select multiple nodes simultaneously.
- *Right mouse button + drag*: Move or pan across the Graph.
- *Mouse wheel* (or *right mouse button + Alt* key): Zoom in and out.
- *Right mouse button* in the Graph (or *Tab* key): Access the palette, which will be covered later.
- *Left mouse button* (click and *drag* between pins): Make connections between nodes. Connections are always made from the outputs to the inputs, moving from left to right.

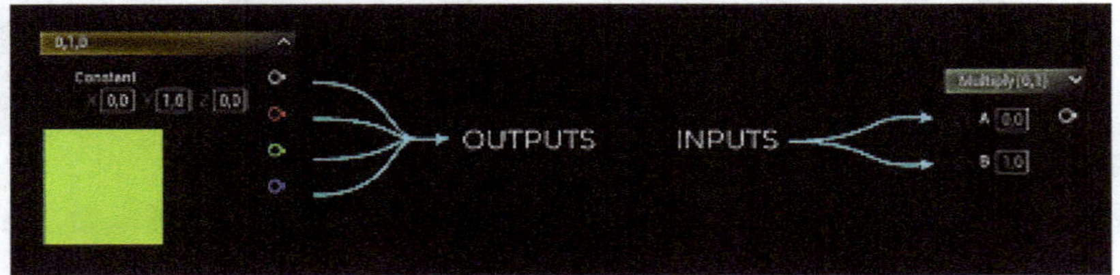

Figure 8.4 – Material Editor user interface: OUTPUTS/INPUTS

- *Left mouse button + Alt* key: Disconnect nodes, both at the inputs/outputs and at the connections themselves.
- *Left mouse button + Ctrl* key: Change connections between inputs or outputs.

Figure 8.5 gives an overview of all these shortcuts:

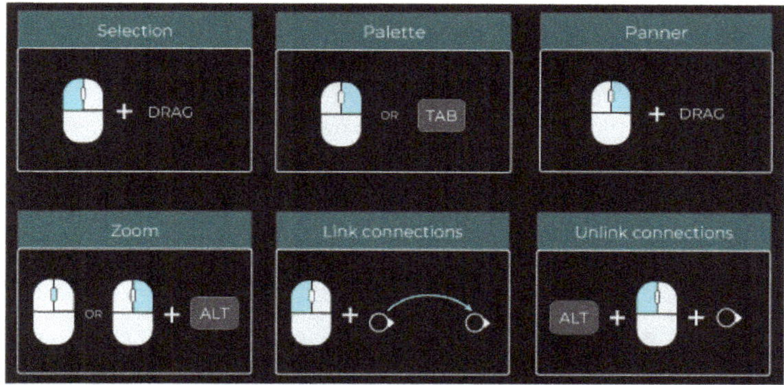

Figure 8.5 – Material Editor user interface: shortcuts

Palette

In this window, you'll find all expressions and functions for composing your material. You can access it by pressing *Tab* or by *right-clicking* in an empty Graph space. Nodes are categorized based on their functionality, such as **Math**, **Textures**, **Utility**, and **Material Functions**, which help organize and streamline the process of building complex materials:

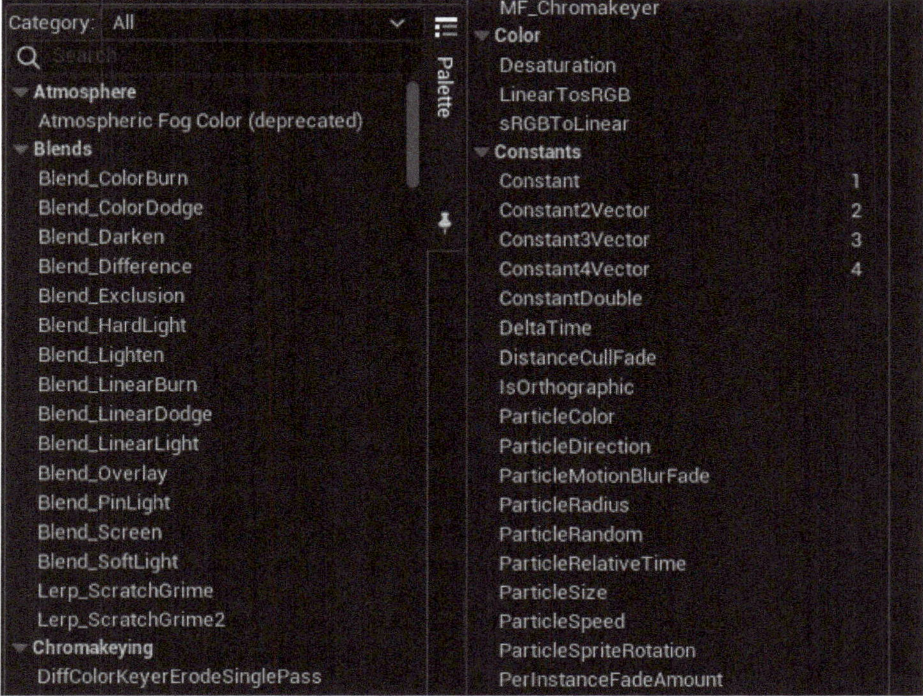

Figure 8.6 – Material Editor user interface: node palette

Viewport

Initially, the Viewport in the Material Editor shares nearly the same menus as the **Scene** Viewport, except for the icons located in the bottom-right corner:

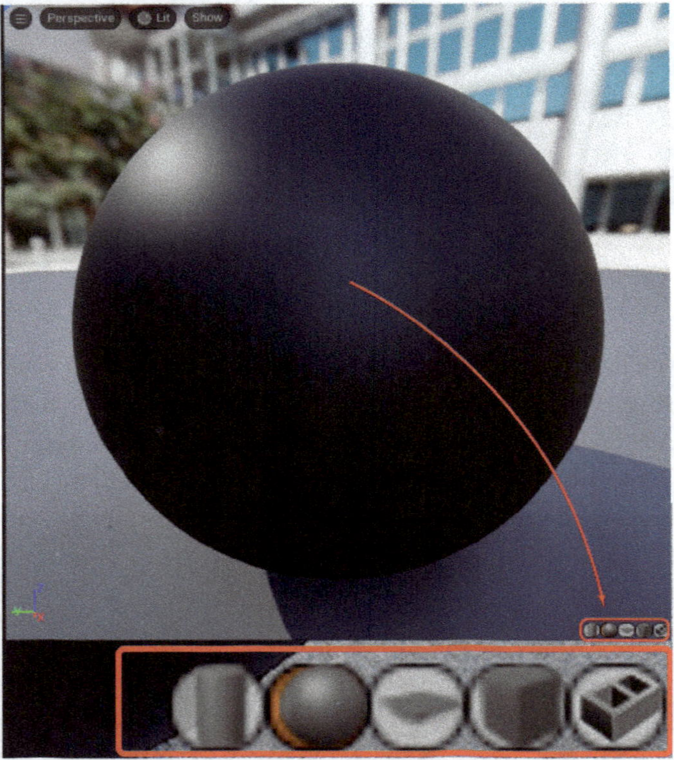

Figure 8.7 – Material Editor user interface: Viewport

These icons display basic primitives to better visualize the material being created. From *left to right*, they include **Cylinder**, **Sphere**, **Plane**, and **Cube**. The last icon, positioned all the way to the right, is used to visualize any Static Mesh selected in the **Content Browser**.

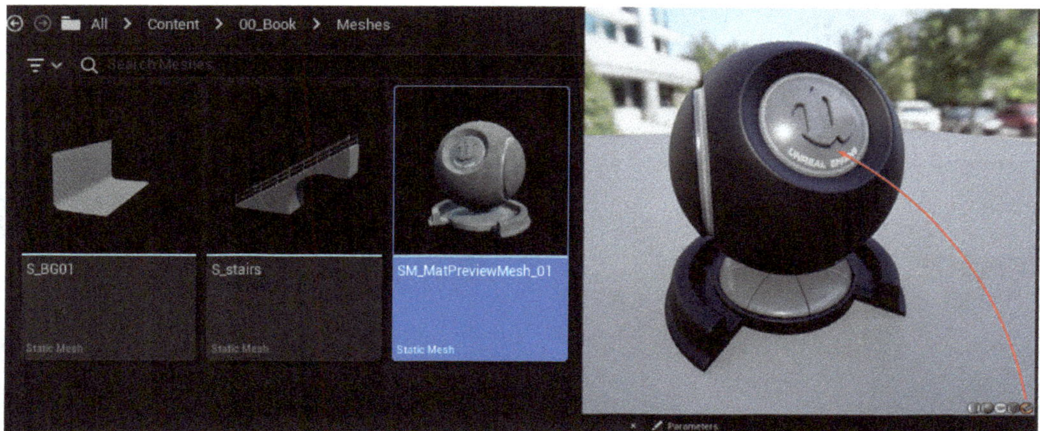

Figure 8.8 – Material Editor user interface: Preview custom Static Mesh

In the Material Editor, the material you're editing appears on **Element 0** of the Static Mesh. You can view this by opening the Static Mesh in the mesh editor and checking the **Material Slots** section. It shows how many materials are assigned to different parts of the Static Mesh. For instance, for **SM_MatPreviewMesh_01**, the material covers the entire surface, including the base.

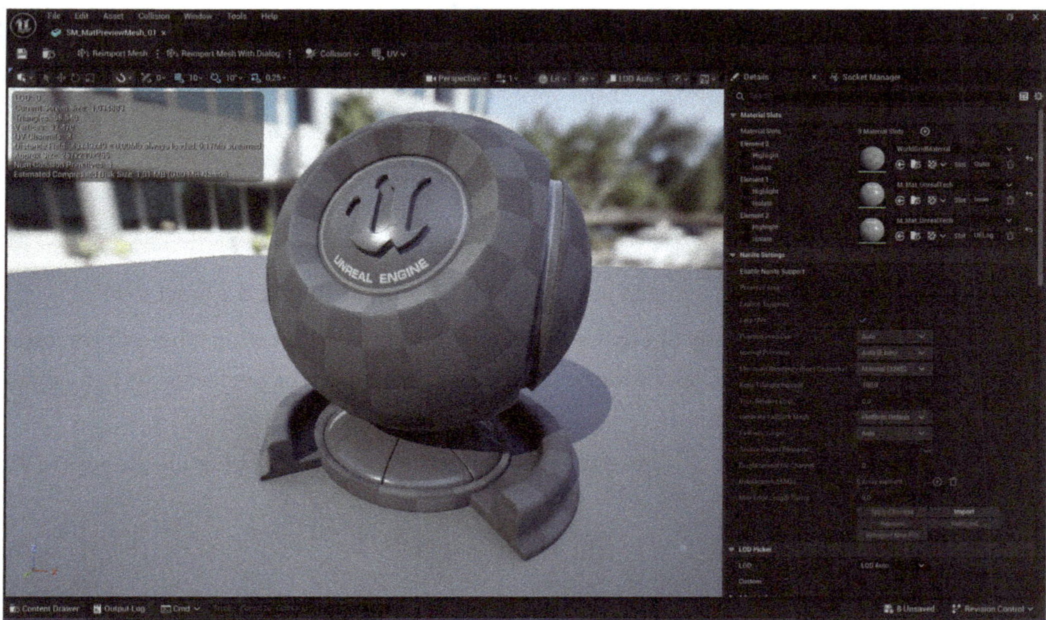

Figure 8.9 – Static Mesh editor: Material Slots

Details panel

In this area, all the properties of the expressions or functions selected in the Graph will appear, allowing you to make necessary changes.

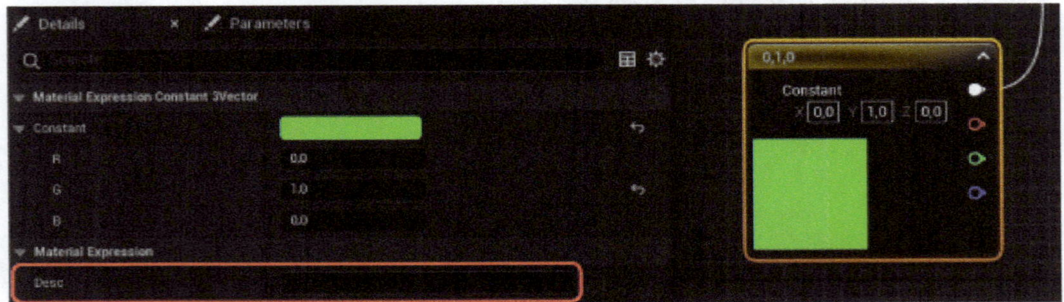

Figure 8.10 – Material Editor user interface: Details

Toolbar

This toolbar contains a series of icons, focusing on the most common tools used when working with materials. You need to double-click on any material to open this toolbar.

Figure 8.11 – Material Editor user interface: toolbar

Here's a list of these tools, from *left to right*:

1. **Save**: Saves every change made in the Material Editor, including the asset itself.
2. **Browse to Asset**: Directly opens the **Content Browser** to the location where the material is saved. This icon is found throughout Unreal Engine and is the quickest way to navigate between different locations.
3. **Apply**: If the material is assigned to an object in the scene, this applies all changes made in the Material Editor.

4. **Search**: Opens a **Search** tab in the Material Editor where typing the name of an expression, function, or comment displays a list.

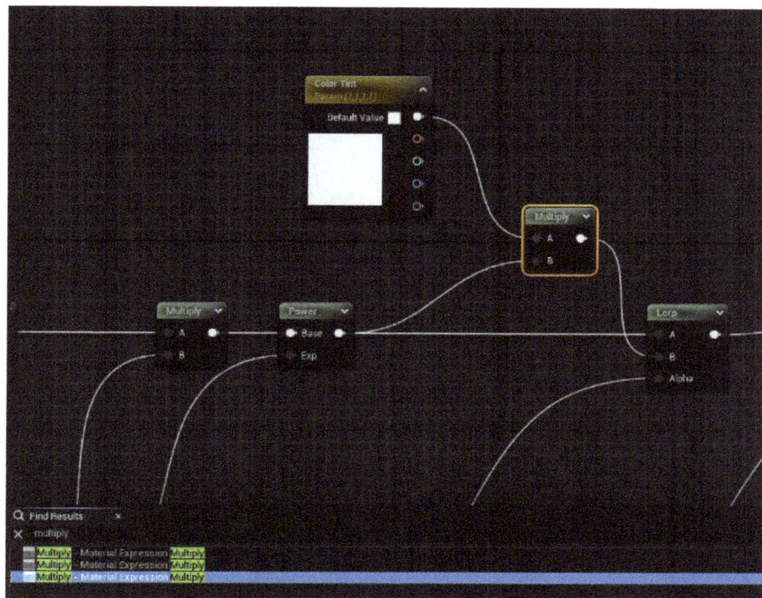

Figure 8.12 – Material Editor user interface: toolbar | Search

5. **Home**: Zooms to the main node.
6. **Hierarchy**: Lists instances created from the material. This will be explored further in the *Material Instances* subsection.

7. **Live Update:** Allows selection of preview types in nodes and Viewports. Useful for animating textures or masks within materials.

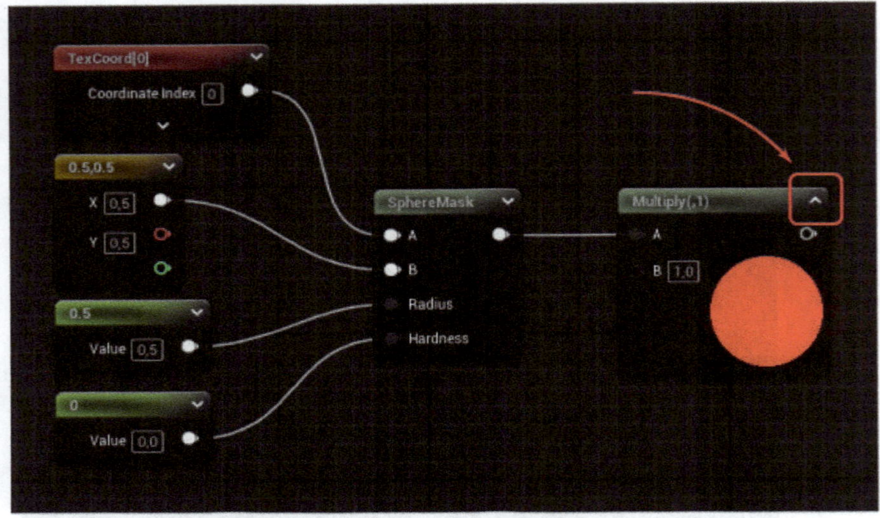

Figure 8.13 – Material Editor user interface: node preview

8. **Clean Graph:** Removes all nodes not directly or indirectly connected to the main node. Includes the **Hide Unselected Connectors** option, collapsing inputs and outputs in all nodes that are not connected.
9. **Preview State:** Modes for visualization and selection when working across different platforms and shader qualities based on hardware specifications.
10. **Hide Unrelated:** Quickly visualizes connections between selected nodes, useful in materials with extensive node networks.
11. **Stats:** Opens the **Stats** tab, covered in its respective subsection.
12. **Platform Stats:** Opens a tab displaying material statistics and compilation errors for different platforms used.

Stats

The **Stats** panel in Unreal Engine is crucial for material optimization. It includes **Instruction Count**, estimating rendering costs; fewer instructions mean lower costs. Compiler errors during node network compilation are flagged here.

As you can see, the **Material** interface in Unreal Engine is quite comprehensive. The tools we've explored so far allow us to view the construction (structure) of our material, add and remove nodes, and even access the **Stats** information, which can be used as a performance indicator in the future. With this in mind, let's configure our first material.

Working in the Material Editor

Understanding data representation and manipulation in the Material Editor is crucial for creating materials in Unreal Engine. Each input in the main node defines the physical attributes of the material and is designed to accept specific types of data, such as other material expressions or functions. Let's learn about some common data types frequently used in material creation.

Float

Float stores a single floating-point value that can be positive or negative and includes a decimal point. It is usually used as a power or intensity value that can be combined with other nodes. There are two material expressions commonly used to define a float:

- **Constant** (shortcut key *1*): This value remains constant after material compilation.
- **Scalar Parameter** (shortcut key *S*): Unlike a constant, a scalar parameter acts as a named variable that can be modified in a Material Instance after compilation or even during runtime.

Float2

Float2 stores two numerical values, for example, `(2.0, 3.0)`. In the Material Editor, the **Constant2Vector** material expression (shortcut key *2*) is used to define a float2. This is particularly useful when working with UV coordinates of textures or positions on the screen.

Float3

Float3 in Unreal Engine stores three numerical values, often used to represent the *red*, *green*, and *blue* color channels of a pixel's color. A common application of float3 is defining solid colors. The **Constant3Vector** expression (shortcut key *3*) is used to define a float3 in Unreal Engine. It includes a color bar in its details, and you can double-click it to open a color selector.

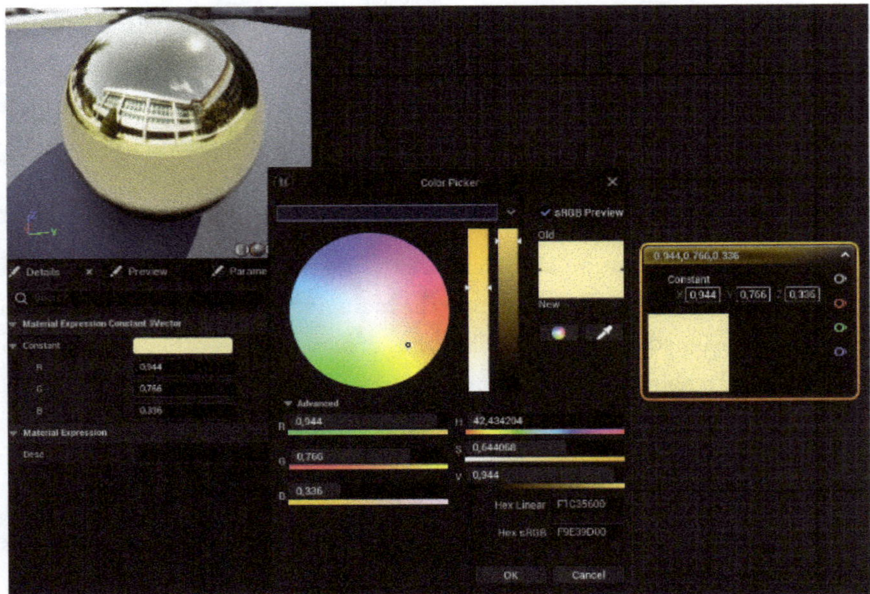

Figure 8.14 – Material Editor data type: Float3

Float4

Float4 stores four floating-point values, for example, `(50.0, 0.0, 100.0, 0.5)`. There are two commonly used material expressions to define a float4:

- **Constant4Vector:** Stores four constant values. Most commonly, **Constant4Vector** (keyboard shortcut *4*) is used to represent RGBA colors, including an alpha channel.
- **Vector Parameter:** Represents a parametrized float4. You can create a vector parameter directly from the palette.

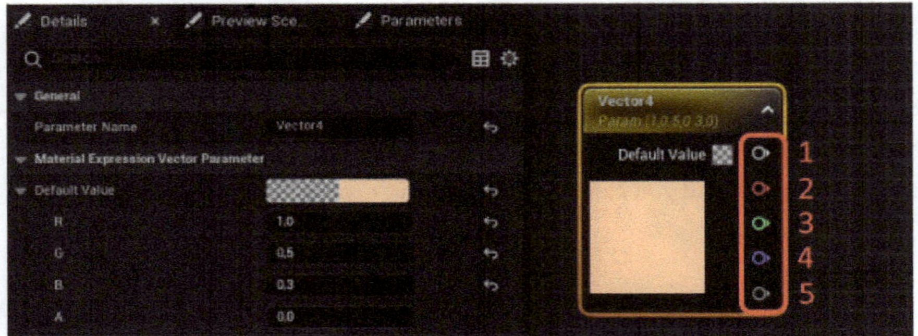

Figure 8.15 – Material Editor data type: Vector Parameter

Each channel is accessible through the five output pins as follows:

1. **RGB**: Returns the first three values of the float4 – in the example, `(1.0, 0.5, 0.3)`
2. **R**: Returns the value of the **R** channel only, `(1.0)`
3. **G**: Returns the value of the **G** channel only, `(0.5)`
4. **B**: Returns the value of the **B** channel only, `(0.3)`
5. **A (5)**: Returns the value of the **A** channel only, `(0.0)`

To work with all four RGBA values together, you would use the `AppendVector` expression to concatenate the last **A** channel.

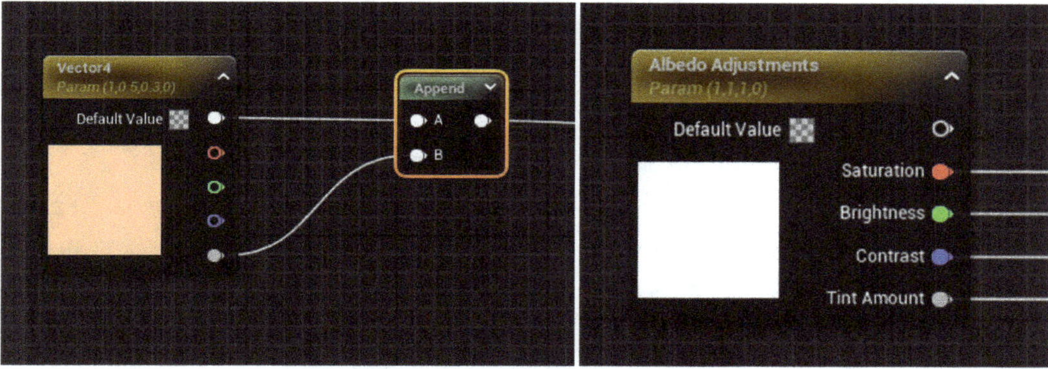

Figure 8.16 – Material Editor data type: RGBA

So far, we've worked with float expressions within the engine, observing how a float can behave both as a grayscale scale and as a single value indicating intensity or strength. By adding more values to **Scalar Parameter**, we are assigning channels that enable the construction of more complex values within the color palette, eventually including a fourth channel that allows us to control opacity. In the next section, we will explore the main properties that define PBR materials.

Overview of PBR materials

A PBR material in Unreal Engine closely follows physical laws to accurately depict how light interacts with surfaces. Unreal Engine currently employs the **PBR Metallic - Roughness** system, which encompasses three core properties: **Metallic**, **Specular**, and **Roughness**. In addition to these, specific inputs such as **Base Color**, **Normal**, and **Ambient Occlusion** play crucial roles in defining a PBR material's appearance and surface properties.

Let's explore the essential inputs required to create a PBR material.

Base Color

Base Color defines the material's primary color, representing diffuse light without shadows or specular reflections. It can be connected to a uniform color for consistent object coloring or textured to simulate materials such as wood or rock. This input also provides shader information on both the material's color/appearance and reflectivity, particularly relevant for metallic elements, which will be elaborated on further.

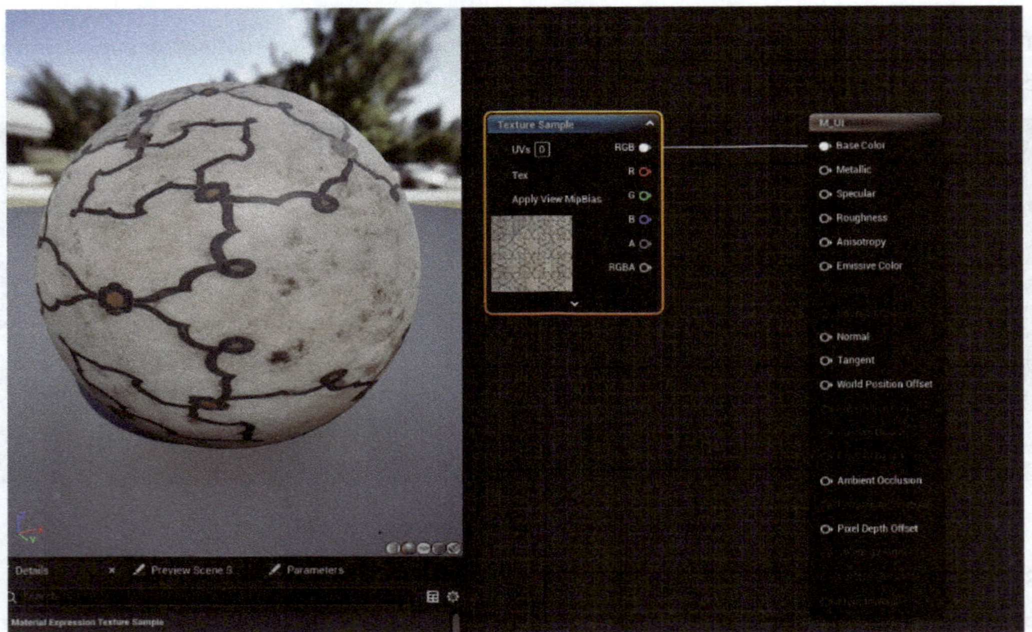

Figure 8.17 – PBR material: Base Color

Metallic property

The **Metallic** property in PBR determines whether the material is metallic (conductor) or non-metallic (dielectric). This parameter ranges from `0` to `1`, where `0` (*black* in a texture) indicates non-metallic, while `1` (*white* in a texture) indicates metallic.

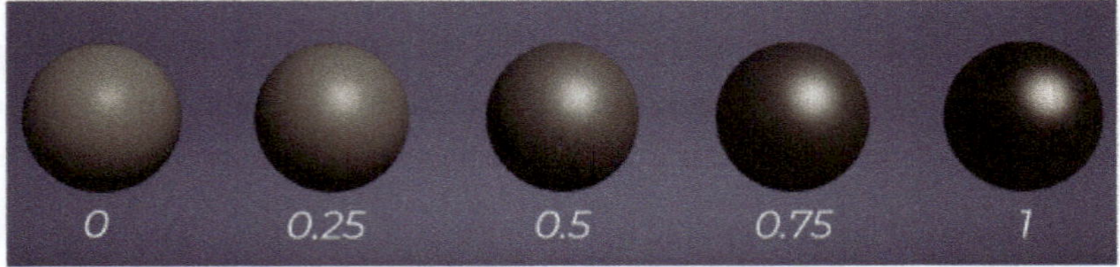

Figure 8.18 – PBR material: Metallic

Initially, materials should be categorized as either pure metals (`1`) or non-metals (`0`), avoiding intermediate values. Both metals and non-metals often coexist within the same material.

Specular

This input communicates to the shader the amount of light that a surface should reflect, with values ranging from `0` to `1`.

For non-metallic (dielectric) surfaces, light reflection typically ranges from 2–5% up to a maximum of 8–10%. In Unreal Engine, a **Specular** value of approximately `0.05` represents the real-world reflection of about 4–5% of incident light. Pure metallic materials reflect between 70% and 100% of incident light. When the **Metallic** value is set to `1`, the shader handles reflection internally. The exact reflectivity of a pure metallic material varies based on its **Base Color** input, as discussed in the preceding section.

Roughness

Roughness defines the surface texture of a material, affecting whether reflections appear diffuse or specular. Rough surfaces scatter light in many directions, creating diffuse reflections and a matte appearance. **Roughness** values range from `0` to `1`:

- A value of `0` (*black* when using textures) simulates a polished surface, resulting in sharp specular reflections

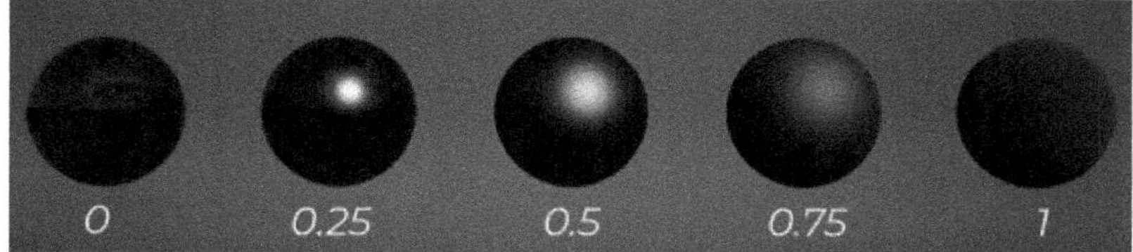

Figure 8.19 – PBR material: Roughness with Metallic = 1

- A value of `1` (*white* when using textures) simulates a rough or matte surface, leading to diffuse reflections

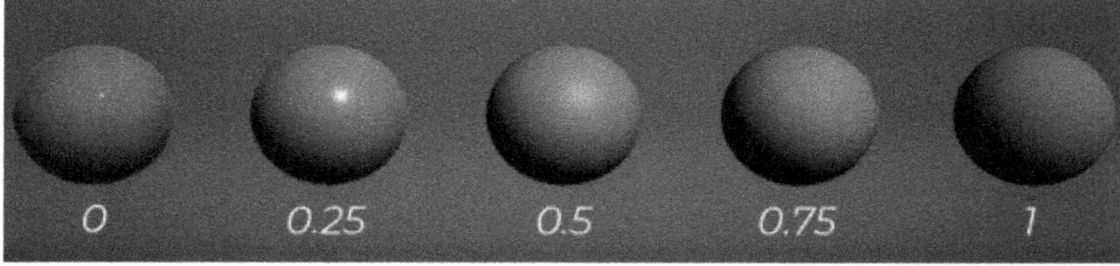

Figure 8.20 – PBR material: Roughness with Metallic = 0

Normal

The **Normal** input adds surface detail to a material, influencing how light interacts to create shadows and highlights. In Unreal Engine, it uses a bluish texture where each channel (**R**, **G**, and **B**) affects different aspects: **R** for horizontal detail, **G** for vertical detail, and **B** for depth.

Figure 8.21 illustrates this enhancement: the *left* object lacks a **Normal** map, while the *right* one, with a **Normal** map applied, shows increased detail without needing a high-polygon mesh:

Figure 8.21 – PBR material: Without a Normal map (left) and with a Normal map (right)

Ambient Occlusion

Ambient Occlusion simulates self-shadowing within surface crevices using a texture map ranging from *black* to *dark gray* (values near `0`) to near-white (values approaching `1`). These shadows indicate areas where light bounces less, creating darker regions. This effect is effective with static or stationary lighting, but is inactive with lights set to the **Movable** mobility state.

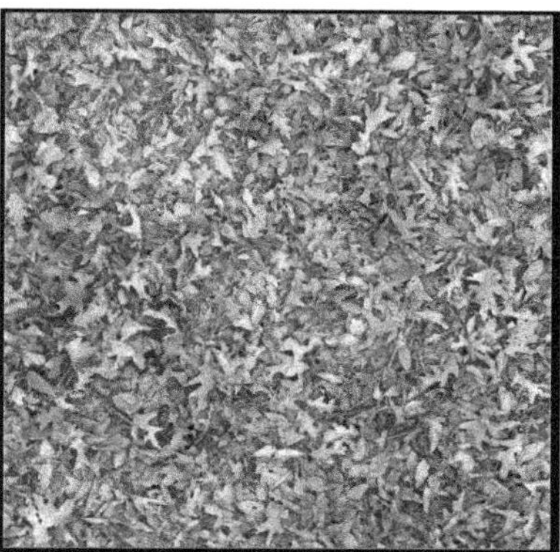

Figure 8.22 – PBR material: Ambient Occlusion

Understanding these nodes in PBR materials allows us to wield all possible control when creating materials. With this information in hand, let's move on to creating practical materials for our project.

Exercise 8.1: Creating a gold material

Using what we've learned so far, let's create a basic PBR material, specifically for gold:

1. First, ensure it's a pure metallic material by setting the **Metallic** input to a **Constant** node with a value of `1` (directly in the node's **Details** panel).
2. Next, apply the color using a **Constant3Vector** node, setting **Details** to **R** = `0.944`, **G** = `0.766`, and **B** = `0.366`.
3. Finally, for the **Roughness** input, connect another **Constant** node with a value of either `0` or `0.05` to add some imperfection to the reflections.

Et voilà! You now have your first perfect gold material ready to use:

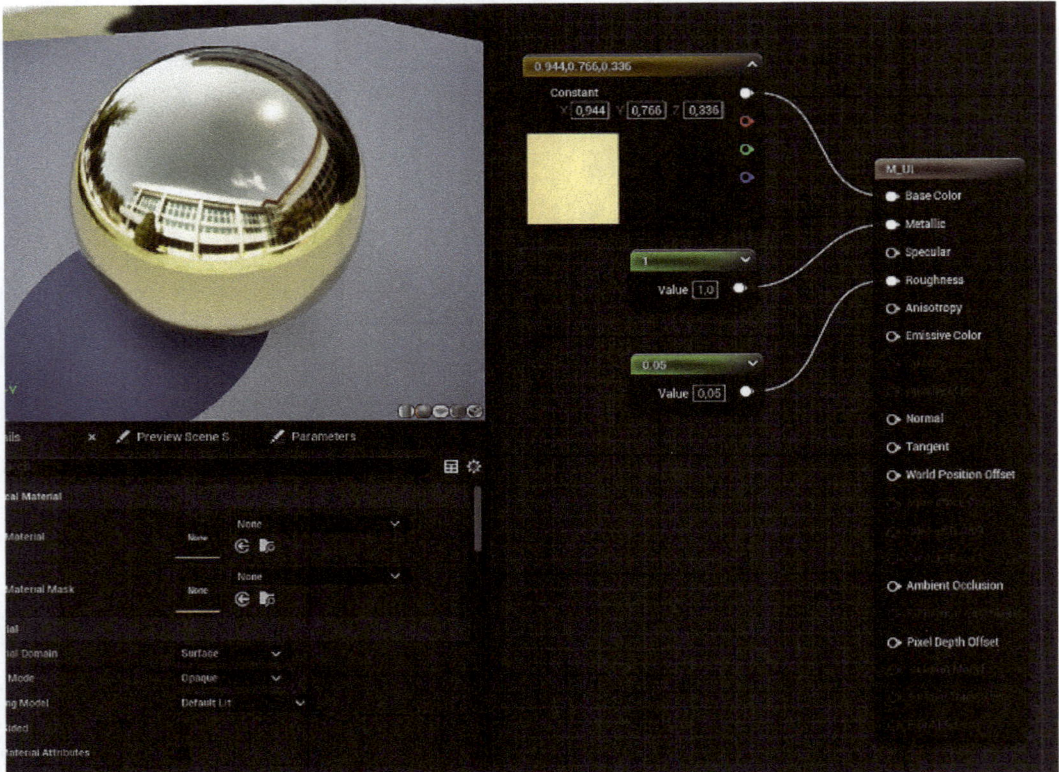

Figure 8.23 – PBR material exercise

Delving into texture implementation

We have seen in the previous exercise how it is possible to create a gold material using three simple nodes composed of floats (values). But this is not possible when we talk about 100% PBR materials, so we must understand the correct use of textures in Unreal Engine.

Formats and resolutions

We've used values for color (float3), roughness (scalar), and metallic level (float). These inputs also accept texture maps, which must meet specific criteria for file format and resolution. Unreal Engine supports various image formats, including JPG, FLOAT, JPEG, PCX, PNG, PSD, EXR, TIF, BMP, TIFF, TGA, and DDS.

Texture dimensions are crucial, as not all resolutions perform equally in the engine. Ideally, textures should have dimensions based on powers of two. In the following table, we can see the progression of texture resolutions in powers of two, a very useful property that Unreal Engine can leverage.

1 x 1	2 x 2	4 x 4	8 x 8	16 x 16	32 x 32	64 x 64
128 x 128	256 x 256	512 x 512	1,024 x 1,024	2,048 x 2,048	4,096 x 4,096	8,192 x 8,192

Table 8.1 – Texture resolution (in pixels)

Unreal Engine can handle dimensions that aren't powers of two, but using powers of two enables mipmaps. **Mipmaps** are smaller versions of the original texture at reduced resolutions.

But what is a mipmap? It's a version of the original texture at one-fourth its resolution, as you can see in *Figure 8.24*:

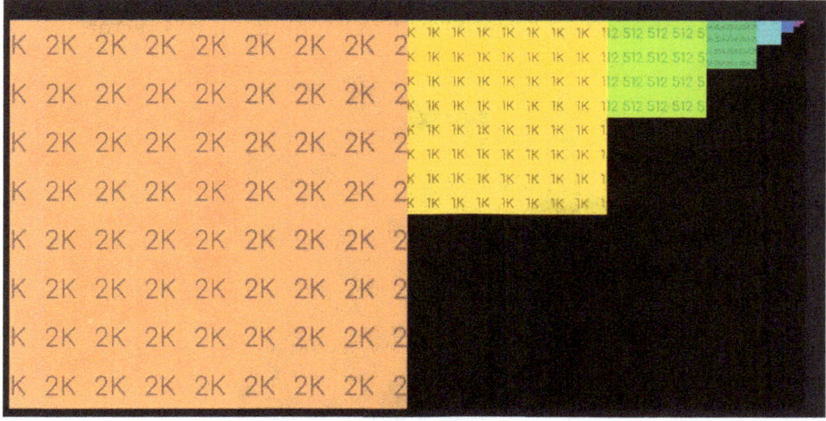

Figure 8.24 – Mipmaps of a texture

The engine creates smaller versions of textures, called mipmaps, to enhance rendering quality and reduce artifacts. These mipmaps are used to smoothly transition details between close-up and distant elements.

Figure 8.25 – Visualization of mipmaps on a Static Mesh

Important note

Textures don't necessarily have to be square; they can be rectangular as well, but they should always follow a power-of-two dimension: 4,096 x 1,024, 512 x 64, and so on.

Working with textures in the Material Editor

In Unreal Engine's Material Editor, handling textures is essential once they're imported into the **Content Browser**. The **Texture Sample** node (shortcut key *T*) is key to this process, enabling image channel manipulation (**R**, **G**, **B**, and **A**) such as handling a float4 vector.

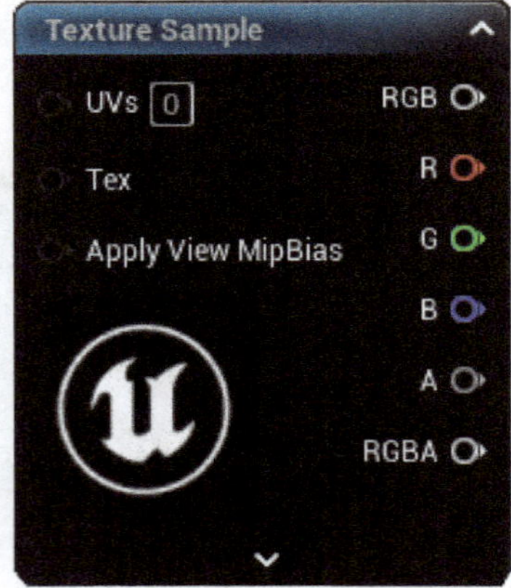

Figure 8.26 – Texture Sample expression

Let's connect this **Texture Sample** node to the **Base Color** parameter of our material to get the following result:

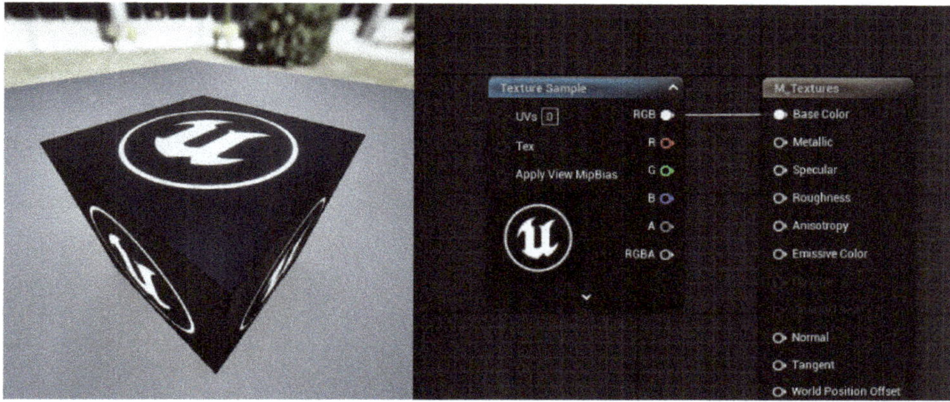

Figure 8.27 – Texture connected to the Base Color input

Working with textures brings an additional challenge as their visualization depends heavily on the object and how its UVs are laid out (see *Chapter 3* for details). To gain control over our textures, we utilize the **Texture Coordinate** node (shortcut key *U*), indicated by its *red* color.

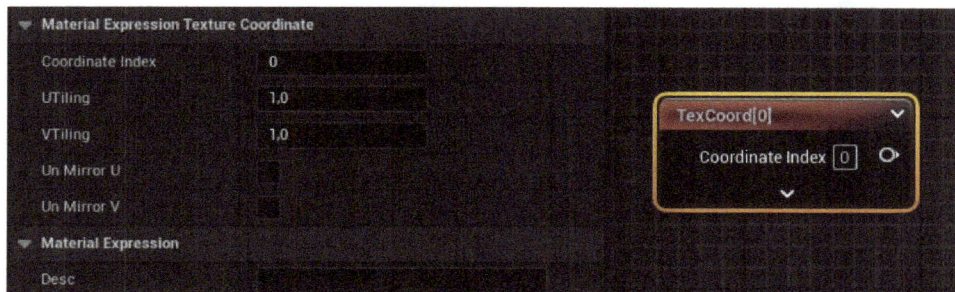

Figure 8.28 – Texture Coordinate

Adjusting the **UTiling** and **VTiling** parameters allows us to repeat the texture multiple times along the corresponding axis; for example, setting both to 2 results in the texture repeating four times (twice in both *U* and *V* directions). Hence, the default value for the **Texture Sample** node in its UVs input is **1**.

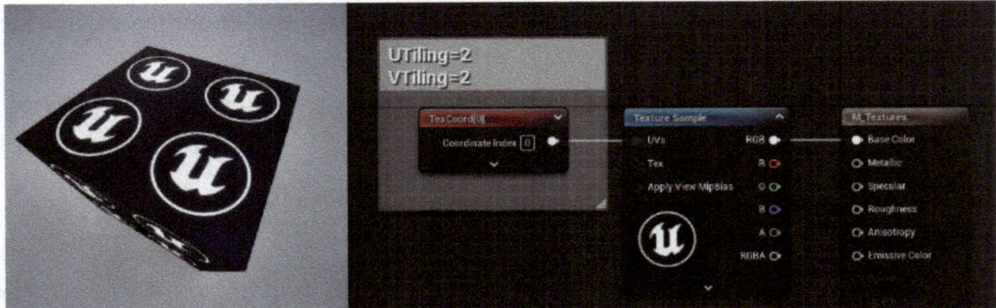

Figure 8.29 – Texture tiling

For greater utility, it's beneficial to manage these UV tiling values outside of this node, allowing us to incorporate them into a parameter. This approach lets us observe and adjust the UV tiling within Material Instances, which will be discussed in the *Material Instances* subsection of this chapter.

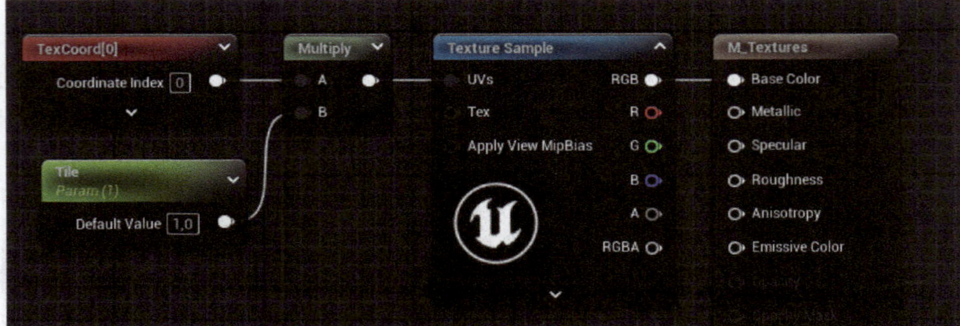

Figure 8.30 – Texture tiling construction

In this section, we've explored the use of textures for visualization in PBR materials, as well as the **Texture Coordinate** node to adjust the scale or tiling of textures on a surface. It's also important to note that the same **Texture Coordinate** node can be used for multiple textures within the same material. With this in mind, let's dive deeper into material workflows to understand how to manage and reuse materials throughout our projects without compromising performance.

Tip

If you'd like to explore more complex or ready-made materials, you can find a variety of examples in Fab and through Quixel Bridge, both directly accessible from the Epic Games Launcher. You can also open sample projects from the **Learn** tab in the Launcher to study advanced material setups and workflows used in professional environments.

Material workflows

Unreal Engine's Material Editor is one of six tools for material work, including instances, functions, layers, parameter collection, and HLSL. These tools are popular for their efficiency in quickly creating materials and updating properties as needed during development.

In the following sections, we will explore each of these tools in detail, discussing their features and how they can enhance the material creation process.

Material Instances

Material Instances offer a way to alter a material's appearance without costly recompilation. As materials grow more intricate, adjusting directly in the Material Editor can become time-consuming. Material Instances solve this by enabling modifications without recompiling, improving workflow efficiency, and potentially enhancing material performance.

Instances can be created from the material itself via *right-clicking* and selecting **Create Material Instance:**

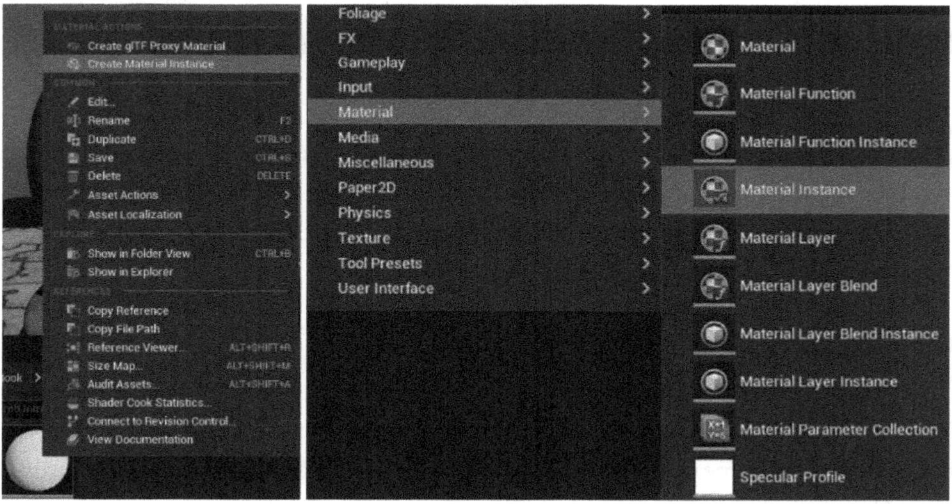

Figure 8.31 – Create Material Instance

Alternatively, you can create an instance from the **Content Browser** by *right-clicking* on the **Material** category and choosing **Material Instance**, as shown in *Figure 8.32*:

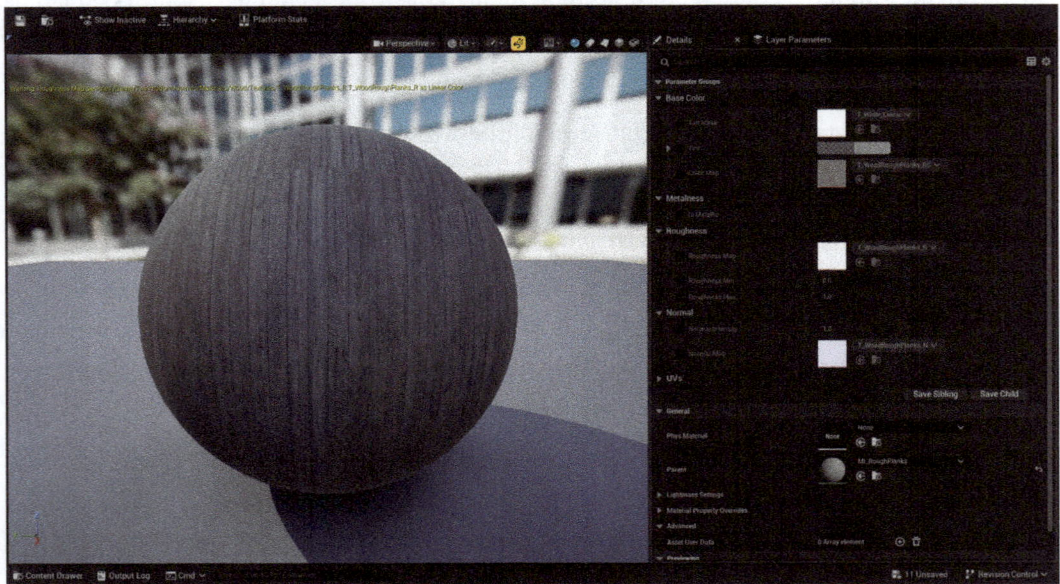

Figure 8.32 – Material Instance

Best practice involves creating a master material for each surface type and generating instances from it. This ensures that changes to the master material affect numerous scene objects instantly. Balancing the number of master materials and instances is critical; larger projects might use 20–50 master materials relied upon by many instances.

Texturing landscapes

When creating a scene, it's common to use an environment that needs proper texturing. Unreal Engine provides specific **Landscape** tools for importing heightmaps and sculpting terrain. Regarding texturing, any type of material can be applied to our landscape; however, to texture using layers and brushes, the material needs to be configured accordingly.

Let's begin by learning about the most common nodes to start painting layers on our landscape.

Common landscape material expressions

In the context of material setup for landscapes, we utilize nodes such as **Texture Coordinate** to manage texture display.

Specifically for landscapes, the following are the most common expressions.

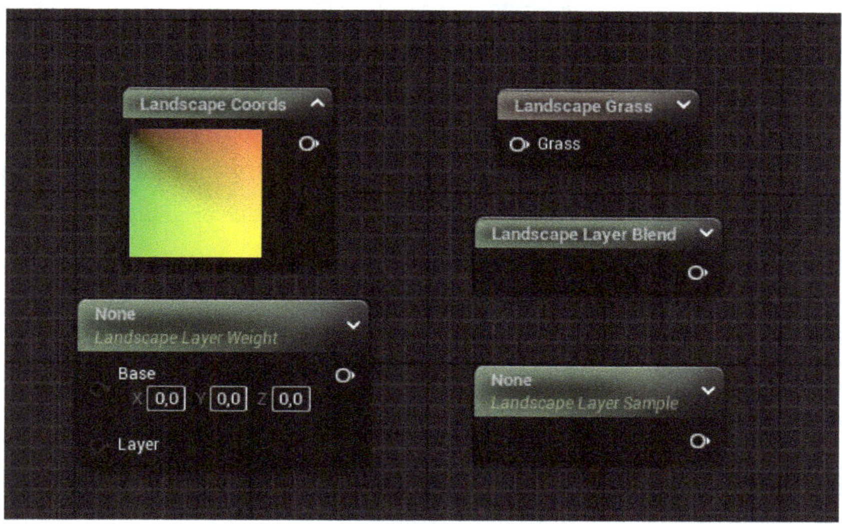

Figure 8.33 – Landscape material: common expressions

Among these, the **LandscapeLayerCoords** node offers tailored UV information. Additionally, nodes such as **Landscape Layer Weight** and **Landscape Layer Blend** facilitate the painting of layers on terrain surfaces.

In *Figure 8.34*, we can see the options available from the **Landscape Layer Blend** node in detail:

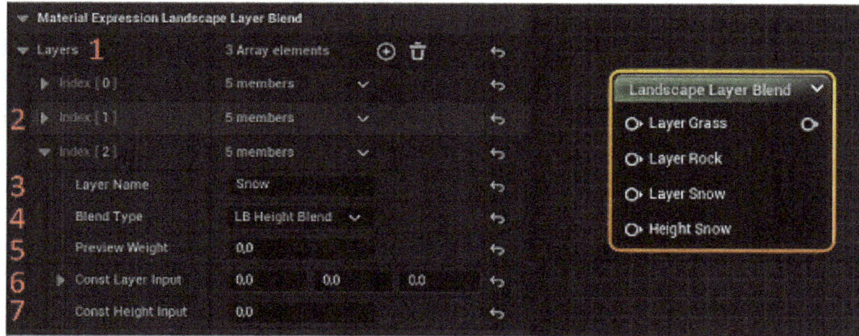

Figure 8.34 – Landscape Layer Blend

Here's what each option in the **Landscape Layer Blend** node means:

1. **Layers**: From the + icon, you can add layers that automatically appear in the node.
2. **Index [1]**: This is the collapsed layer view.
3. **Layer Name**: This is the unique name assigned to the layer. This name will appear in the **Paint** section of **Landscape Mode**. It is recommended not to use spaces in these names.
4. **Blend Type**: These are the different types of blends for painting between different layers. These can be **LB_AlphaBlend**, **LB_HeightBlend**, or **LB_WeightBlend.** If **LB_HeightBlend** is used, a new input, **Height 'layer name'**, appears where a texture can be connected; typically, a heightmap acts as a mask for a more precise transition between layers.
5. **Preview Weight**: This value indicates the weight of the layer to preview the blend exclusively in the Material Editor.
6. **Const Layer Input**: Here, you can enter a numerical value that is used as a color if you do not want to use a texture. It is mainly used to debug a layer if any issues arise.
7. **Const Height Input**: This can be used to provide a number as height if you do not want to use a texture.

The other two expressions, **Landscape Layer Sample** and **Landscape Grass Output**, usually go hand in hand, as shown in *Figure 8.35*:

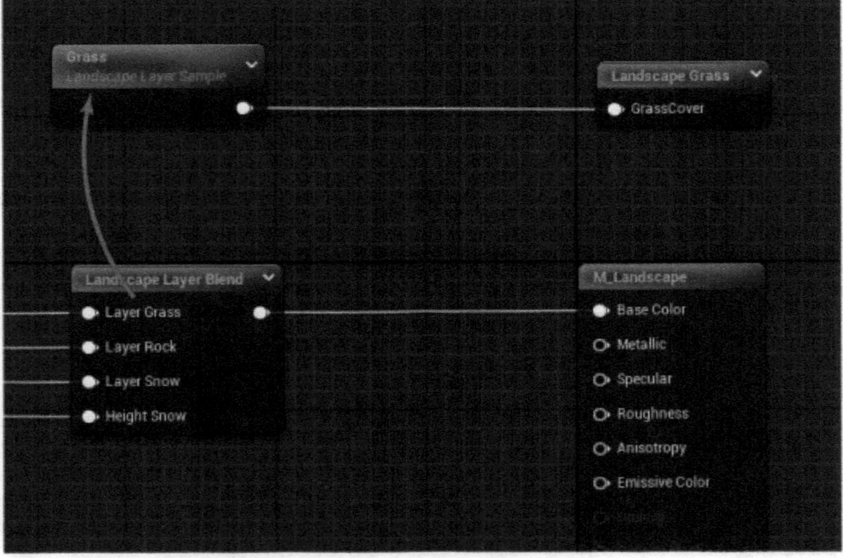

Figure 8.35 – Landscape Layer Sample and Landscape Grass Output

As shown in *Figure 8.35*, the **Landscape Layer Sample** expression takes values from layers with exact names. If you name it `Grass`, it will take the value from that layer. This expression is very useful for displaying vegetation through materials.

The **Landscape Grass Output** expression is an output, like the main node, responsible for procedurally generating 3D vegetation in those layers specified using the **Landscape Layer Sample** node.

Generating vegetation from landscape material

What type of vegetation will be generated from the landscape material? Clearly, we need to specify the type of vegetation and under what conditions it should be generated. This is where a new asset comes into play: **Landscape Grass Type**.

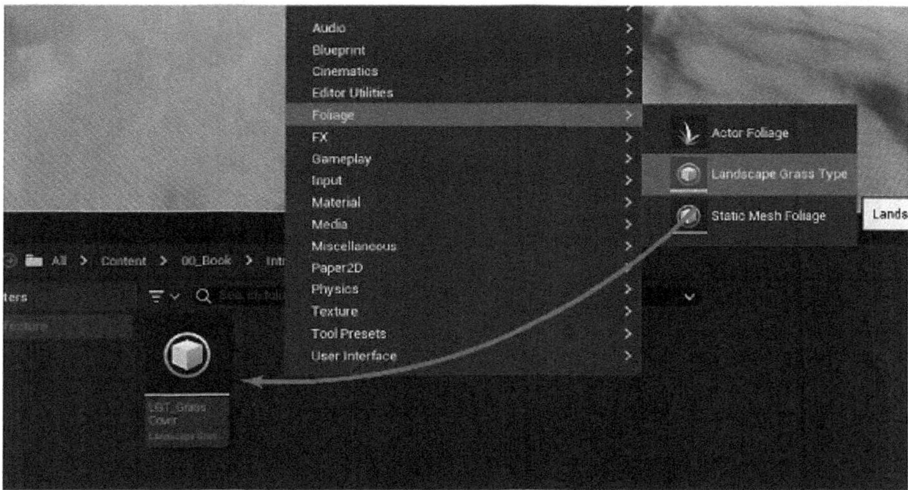

Figure 8.36 – The Landscape Grass Type asset

To create this asset, *right-click* in the **Content Browser** and navigate to **Foliage** | **Landscape Grass Type**. Once created, double-click (as with all assets in Unreal) to open the asset, and you'll find a series of properties very similar to **Static Mesh Actor**, which we saw in *Chapter 7*.

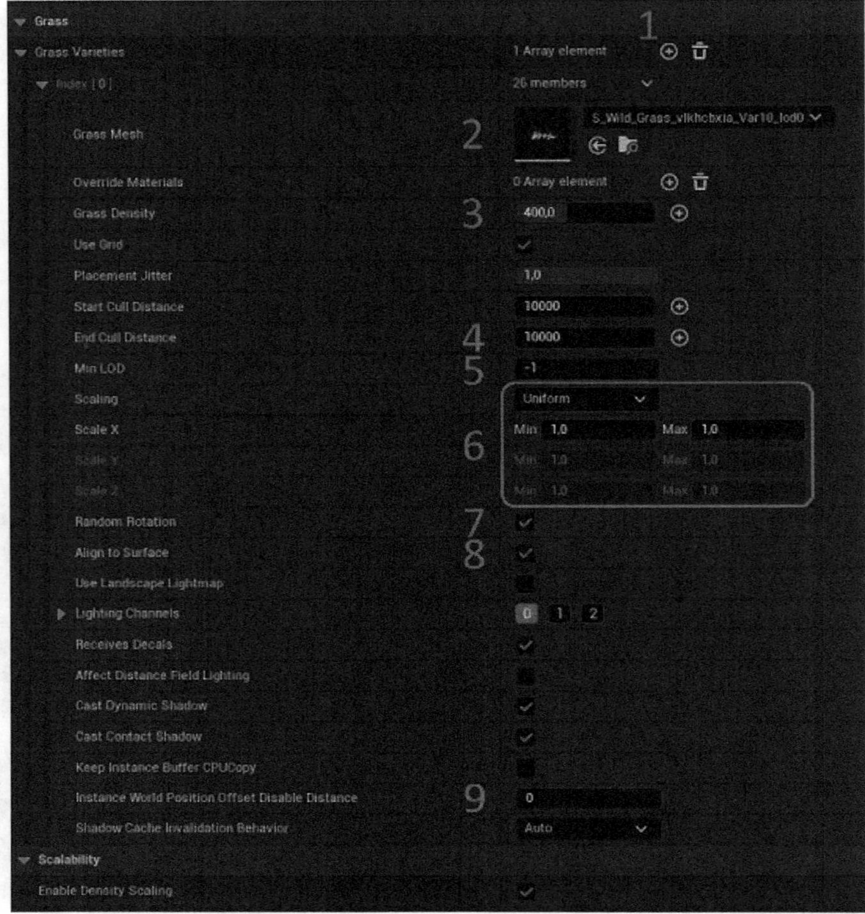

Figure 8.37 – Landscape Grass Type

Each **Array Element (1)** represents one vegetation type you add by clicking the + symbol. Within each element, you'll find the following options:

- **Grass Mesh (2)**: Assign the Static Mesh for the vegetation.
- **Grass Density (3)**: Number of instances generated per 10m^2 of terrain.
- **End Cull Distance (4)**: Rendering distance of the vegetation from the camera. This ensures that vegetation is only populated up to a specified distance from the camera, optimizing performance by not populating the entire terrain unnecessarily.
- **Min LOD (5)**: Minimum LOD used for generating vegetation.

- **Scaling (6)**: Scale variation applied to the vegetation to create visual randomness.
- **Random Rotation (7)**: Adds random rotation around the **Z** axis to each instance of vegetation for more natural variation.
- **Align to Surface (8)**: Determines whether vegetation aligns perpendicular to the terrain surface. Suitable for ground cover but may not be ideal for vertical objects such as trees.
- **Instance World Position Offset Disable Distance (9)**: Distance beyond which any simulated movement of vegetation (e.g., wind effects) is disabled to improve performance and avoid visual artifacts.

Once this asset is configured, it's time to apply it within the material. You should place it in the properties of the **Landscape Grass Output** node, where you will find a series of elements. By clicking the + button, you can add all the elements needed to create your vegetation.

Figure 8.38 – Landscape Grass Type in Landscape Grass Output

We can add a second element to display sediments or small rocks on the **Rock** layer.

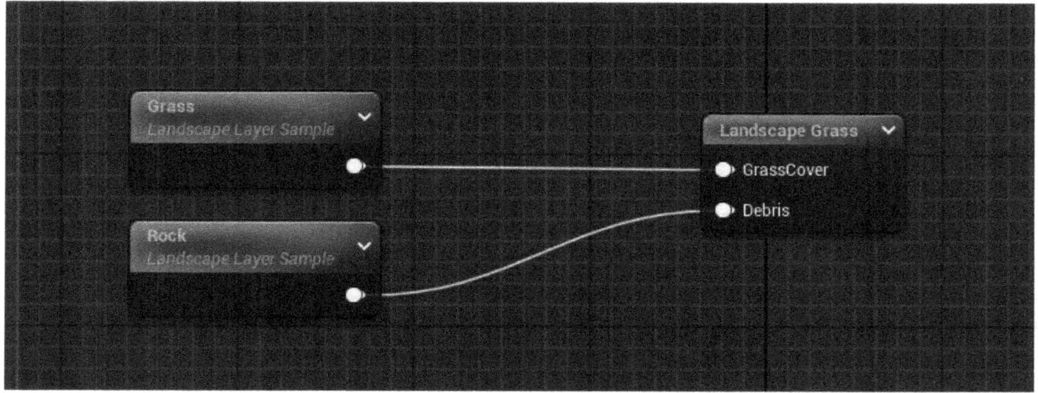

Figure 8.39 – Landscape Grass output: GrassCover and Debris

After exploring common landscape material expressions, let's create one using Megascans resources from *Chapter 2*.

Implementing landscape material expression

Using Bridge, import textures for grass, rock, and snow surfaces. Then, add these surfaces to the Material Editor by dragging their textures, each creating a **Texture Sample** node. Landscape materials often require many textures, but Unreal Engine limits each material to 16 texture samples.

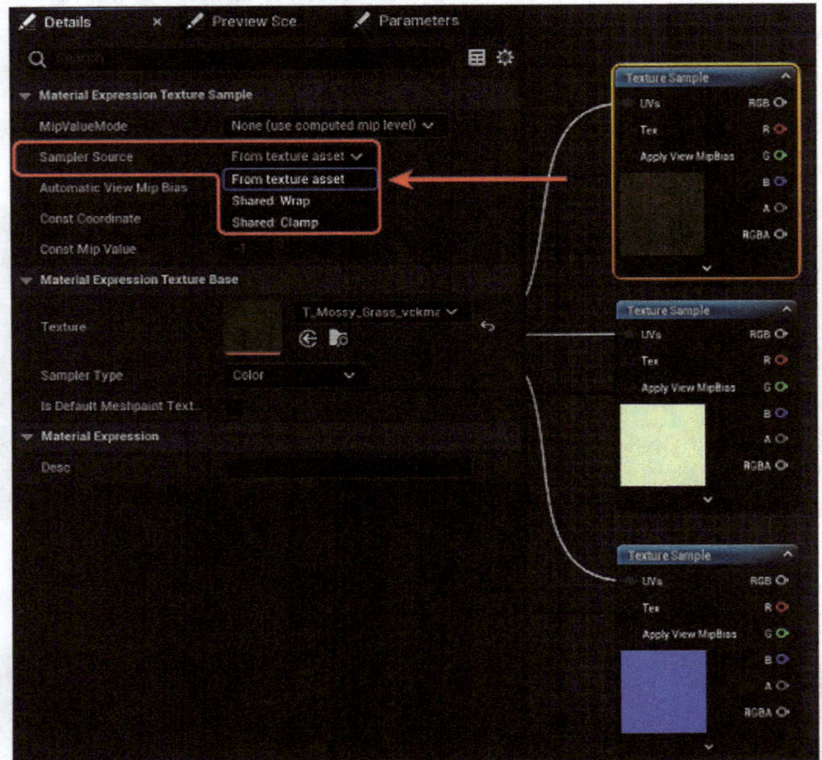

Figure 8.40 – Texture Sample: Shared Wrap

Adjust the scaling of textures for each surface using the **LandscapeCoords** node and a scalar parameter such as **Tile Grass.** This parameter, connected via **Multiply** nodes, ensures that textures adapt to the scene's scale. Each texture component, including normal maps and packed textures containing **Ambient Occlusion**, **Roughness**, and **Displacement**, should be connected accordingly.

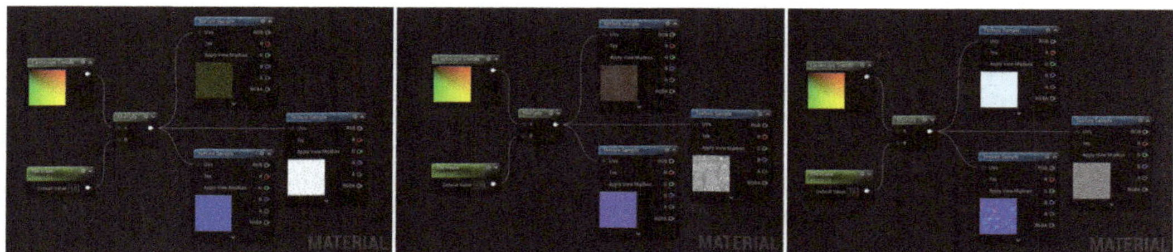

Figure 8.41 – Tiling set up

We'll use the **SetMaterialAttributes** expression to streamline data management for our textures. Each texture, or texture sample, supplies float data: **Base Color** and **Normal** as float3, and **Specular**, **Roughness**, and **Ambient Occlusion** as float. Connecting these textures to the node consolidates them into **Material Attributes**, which define our surface properties comprehensively. The expression's **Details** panel includes a + button for adding channels or inputs in the desired order as needed.

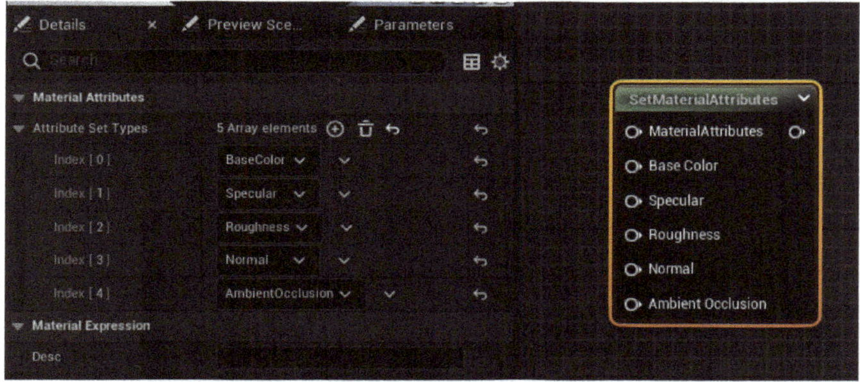

Figure 8.42 – The SetMaterialAttributes expression

Now, link **Base Color** and **Roughness** from the **G** channel of the packed texture, **Ambient Occlusion** from the **R** channel, and the **Normal** map. For **Specular**, connect a value of `0.15` (see *Figure 8.43*), which, while not strictly PBR, reduces shininess across the surface, creating a damp appearance on large terrains.

Note that **Tile Grass** is not a standard node; it is a **ScalarParameter**, and **0.15** is a **Constant** node.

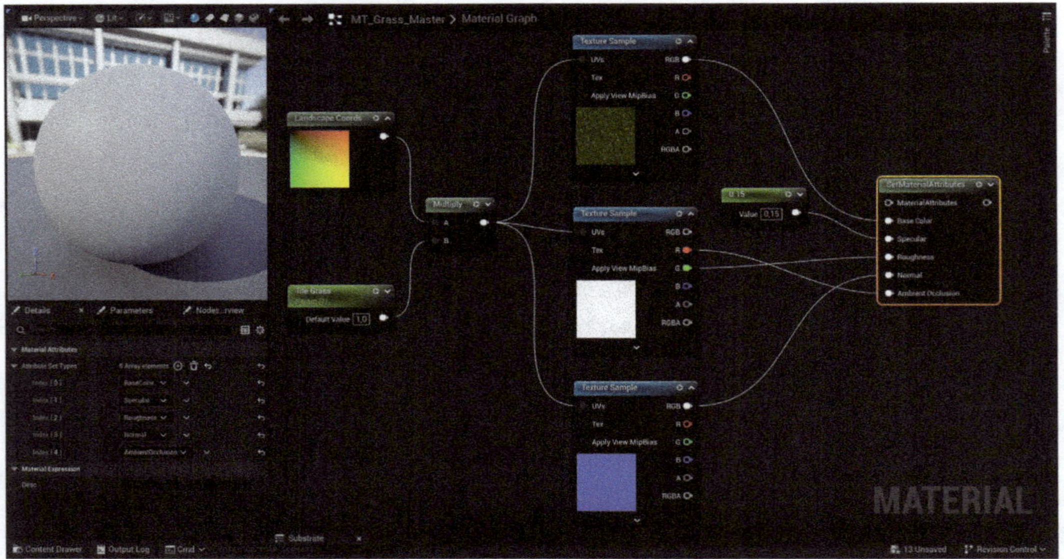

Figure 8.43 – SetMaterialAttributes connected

Each of these surfaces connects to **Landscape Layer Blend**. Additionally, the **Grass** and **Snow** layers are set as **LB_HeightBlend**, requiring another input for a **Height** texture. We utilize the **B** channel of the packed texture to make this connection, as depicted in *Figure 8.44*:

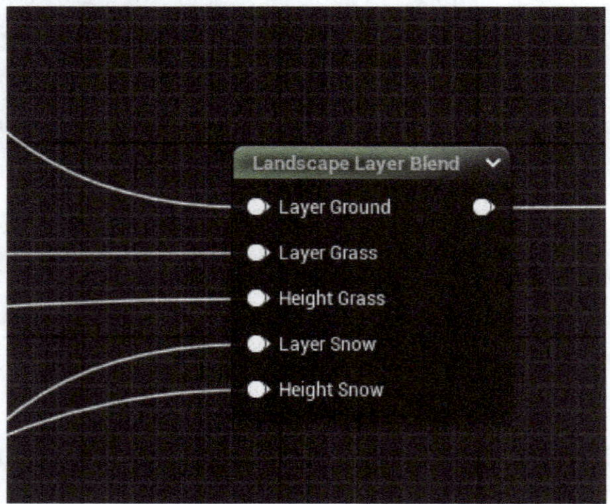

Figure 8.44 – Final SetMaterialAttributes

The final material setup will look as follows:

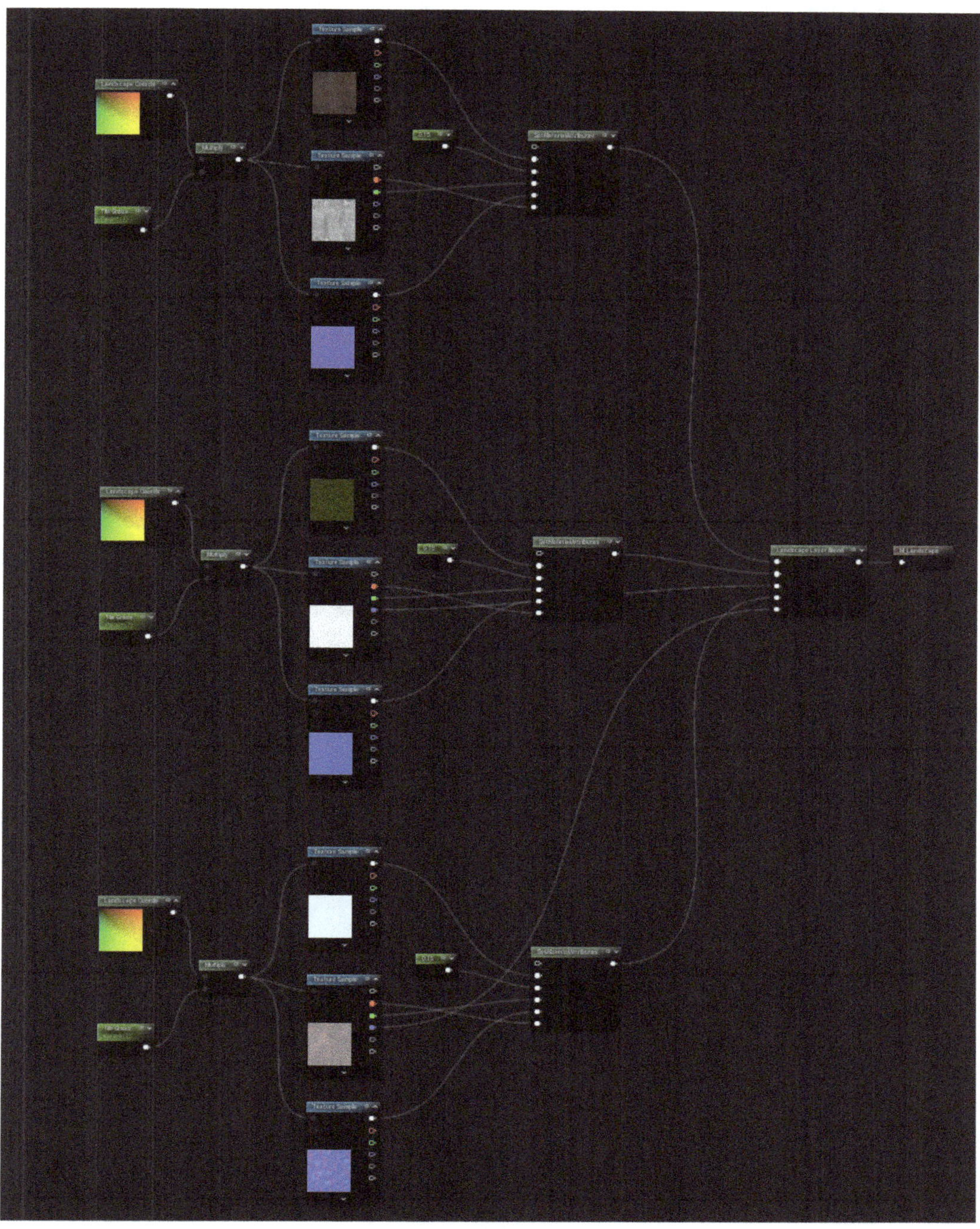

Figure 8.45 – Overview of the final material setup

As you can see, the main node isn't fully expanded, which is due to the **Use Material Attributes** property being enabled in the **Details** panel of the main node.

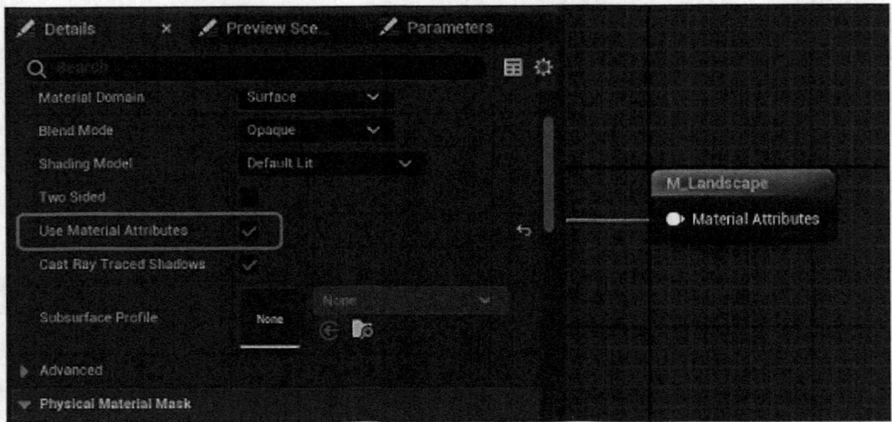

Figure 8.46 – Landscape material: Use Material Attributes

Once the material is created, it's best to create an instance to apply it to the landscape. In this case, select the landscape in the scene, and in the **Details** panel, assign the instance.

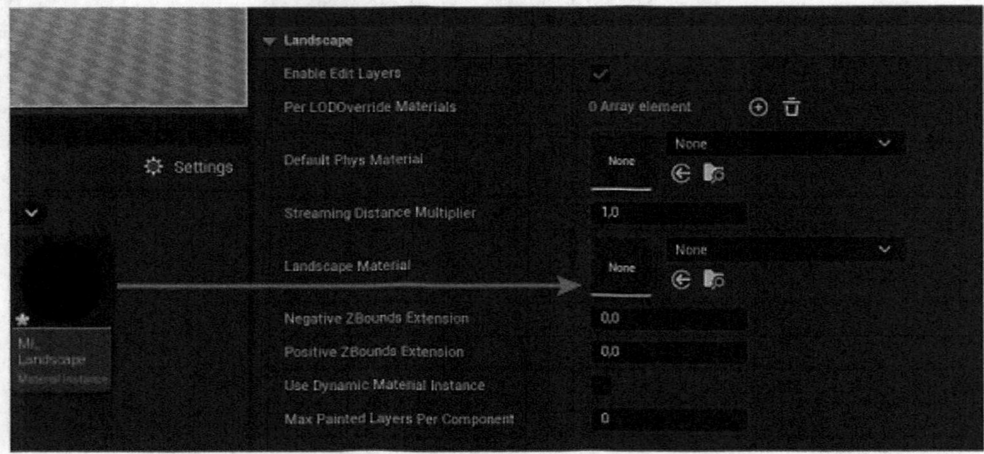

Figure 8.47 – Landscape Details

When assigning the material or instance, the landscape may appear *black*. This is normal because the landscape still lacks some assets to display the material correctly.

Figure 8.48 – Landscape material assigned to the landscape

These assets need to be generated from **Landscape Mode** (*Shift* + *2*). If you go to the **Paint** tab, you will see paint layers listed under **Layers**, each named according to the **Landscape Layer Blend** names we assigned.

Figure 8.49 – Paint layers

Currently, painting isn't available. On the right side, beside the layers, you'll find a + symbol. Clicking it reveals a menu for selecting how layers interact. Choose **Weight-Blended Layer (normal)**, the standard option allowing layers to blend like paint. A prompt will appear to save the necessary layer information for Unreal to paint on the landscape. Select a path or use the default option.

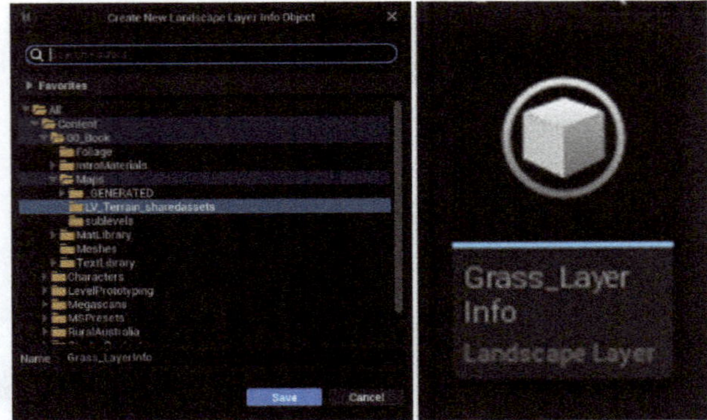

Figure 8.50 – Path info layers and a Layer Info asset

When applying the first layer, it may not cover the entire terrain automatically. Continue adding subsequent layers until the **brush** icon changes from *red* (indicating inability to paint) to *gray* (indicating ability to paint). Then, utilize Unreal's painting tools to add artistic detail to the terrain.

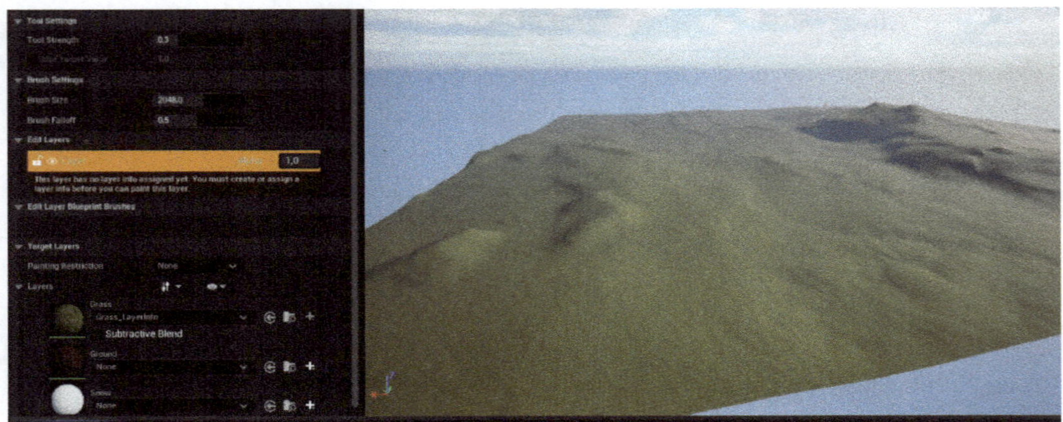

Figure 8.51 – Layer info created for Grass Layer

Finally, we can achieve a **Landscape** material that looks like this, in its most basic form:

Figure 8.52 – Final basic landscape texturing

In this section, we have put into practice everything seen throughout the chapter. We have created a **Landscape** material that consists of different types of surfaces, which allows us to use the painting tools to detail different surfaces as we like.

Summary

In this chapter, we delved into the intricate world of material creation within Unreal Engine, focusing particularly on its application in open world environments. We started by exploring the fundamental nodes and techniques used to texture landscapes, emphasizing the importance of preparation and optimization. Understanding how to utilize texture samples, landscape coordinates, and material attributes allows us to craft realistic and visually appealing terrains.

Moreover, we explored advanced concepts such as material functions and Material Instances, which streamline workflow and facilitate collaborative efforts among team members. These tools not only enhance efficiency but also ensure consistency across diverse materials and assets within large-scale projects.

Furthermore, integrating assets from Megascans into our materials enabled us to elevate the realism of our environments, demonstrating the seamless integration of high-quality textures and assets directly within Unreal Engine's ecosystem.

Finally, mastering the painting and layering techniques using **Landscape** layers provided us with the ability to transform our terrains into dynamic, artistically rich landscapes. By leveraging Unreal Engine's robust painting tools, we were able to achieve nuanced and visually captivating landscapes suitable for diverse open world settings.

In essence, understanding and effectively utilizing Unreal Engine's material system empowers developers and artists to create immersive and engaging open world environments, setting the stage for limitless creative possibilities in game development.

In the next chapter, we'll take a closer look at creating atmospheric lighting using Unreal Engine's environment lighting tools.

Subscribe to Game Dev Assembly Newsletter!

We are excited to introduce **Game Dev Assembly**, our brand-new newsletter dedicated to everything game development. Whether you're a programmer, designer, artist, animator, or studio lead, you'll get exclusive insights, industry trends, and expert tips to help you build better games and grow your skills. Sign up today and become part of a growing community of creators, innovators, and game changers.

`https://packt.link/gamedev-newsletter`

Scan the QR code to join instantly!

Part 3

Lighting and Post-Processing for Realism

In this part, you'll move on to examine how light and post-processing shape the overall visual tone of a scene. The part explains how to use **Environment Light Mixer** and related actors to create physically accurate and atmospheric lighting setups for open world environments. You'll also explore the principles behind dynamic lighting with **Lumen**, **Virtual Shadow Maps**, and **Nanite** for consistent performance and visual quality. The part concludes with post-processing techniques that refine your final image through **Color Grading**, **Exposure**, and **Bloom**, ensuring a cohesive and polished look across the entire scene.

This part of the book includes the following chapters:

- *Chapter 9, Create Your World's Atmospheric Lighting*
- *Chapter 10, Setting Up Your Post Process Volume*

9

Create Your World's Atmospheric Lighting

Lighting is crucial in shaping the mood and atmosphere of any virtual environment. In open world games, it adds emotional depth to scenes, guiding how players experience and interact with the world. Effective lighting can evoke emotions, from the warmth of a sunrise to the tension of a dark forest, making it a vital aspect of world-building.

In Unreal Engine, artists use tools to control light intensity, color, and shadows, enhancing both the visuals and emotional impact. These tools, including atmospheric effects and integrated lighting systems, help create dynamic, immersive experiences.

In this chapter, we'll focus on open world lighting in Unreal Engine, exploring the **Environment Light Mixer** and key Actors that enable physically accurate ambient lighting. We'll also cover performance-related technologies such as Nanite and Virtual Shadow Maps.

Topics to be covered include the following:

- Lighting in Unreal Engine
- Using the **Environment Light Mixer**
- Enhancing real-time rendering with Virtual Shadow Maps, Nanite, and Lumen

Technical requirements

To continue the development of this chapter, it is necessary to have a PC with **Unreal Engine 5.5** (or a later version) installed that meets the recommended requirements by Epic Games: `https://dev.epicgames.com/documentation/en-us/unreal-engine/hardware-and-software-specifications-for-unreal-engine`. Be sure to have active internet access on the system as well.

Lighting in Unreal Engine

In game development and virtual production, the quality and creativity of lighting can transform a flat scene into one that truly comes alive. Unreal Engine 5 (UE5) offers a robust set of tools and techniques that empower creators to achieve dynamic, realistic, and immersive lighting for any project.

In any 3D environment, lighting serves several key purposes:

- **Visibility**: Ensuring that objects and characters are visible to the player or viewer
- **Mood and atmosphere**: Establishing emotional tones such as the warmth of a sunset or the ominous darkness of a dungeon
- **Realism and immersion**: Increasing the scene's believability by replicating real-world lighting dynamics
- **Guiding the viewer**: Directing attention toward key elements within the scene

UE5 has transformed digital creation with groundbreaking features like **Lumen**, a fully dynamic global illumination system, and **Nanite**, a virtualized geometry technology that allows for unprecedented detail and complexity. These new technologies unlock new horizons in lighting, empowering creators to achieve levels of realism and performance that were once unimaginable.

Still, it is important to understand some key concepts and functions of lights within Unreal before starting any project.

Light mobility

Light mobility is a critical concept in Unreal Engine, defining how lights behave in terms of movement and adaptation. This chapter explores the different types of lighting mobility and their practical uses, and highlights the powerful Lumen Global Illumination system that distinguishes UE5 in real-time 3D rendering.

You can locate and select lighting mobility options within the **Details** panel of each individual light:

Figure 9.1 – Light mobility

Light mobility can be categorized into three primary types: **Static**, **Stationary**, and **Movable**. Each type has distinct characteristics and use cases, impacting both the visual quality and performance of your project. Let's take an in-depth look:

- **Static**: It is fully precomputed and integrated into the environment, remaining unchanged during gameplay. It's ideal for objects and environments that do not require lighting adjustments.
- **Stationary**: It provides a middle ground where lights can alter their color and intensity during gameplay while keeping static shadows. This option suits scenarios needing some dynamism without the computational demands of fully dynamic lighting.
- **Movable**: It is entirely dynamic, enabling both the light and its shadows to move and evolve in real time. This flexibility offers enhanced realism but requires higher computational resources.

The key features of movable lighting include the following:

- **Full dynamism**: Both the light and shadows can move and change in real-time, enhancing realism and responsiveness
- **Realistic interactions**: Perfect for interactive and immersive environments where lighting must dynamically respond to player and environmental changes
- **Versatility**: Ideal for dynamic elements such as flashlights, vehicle headlights, and any scenario requiring real-time interaction with light

Throughout our entire project development, we will exclusively utilize **Movable** dynamic lighting, which offers the advantages mentioned above.

Read more

Since our focus will remain on **Movable** lighting, you can refer to the Unreal Engine documentation on *Lighting* for detailed information on **Static** and **Stationary** lighting: `https://dev.epicgames.com/documentation/en-us/unreal-engine/light-types-and-their-mobility-in-unreal-engine?application_version=5.5`.

With **Movable** lights handling real-time updates, it's equally important to understand how Unreal Engine manages global illumination under dynamic lighting conditions.

Dynamic global illumination (**DGI**) in UE5 refers to a set of techniques used to simulate realistic lighting in real time, where light interacts with surfaces and dynamically changes based on the environment and objects within it. The most notable implementation of this is through a system called Lumen.

Exploring Lumen

UE5's **Lumen** system represents a significant leap forward in real-time **global illumination** (**GI**). Lumen provides DGI, allowing for realistic lighting in complex and changing environments without the need for extensive precomputation. This section explores how Lumen works and how to utilize it effectively.

Lumen is a fully dynamic GI system that simulates how light interacts with surfaces and volumes in real time. Unlike traditional baked GI solutions, Lumen responds immediately to changes in lighting conditions, geometry, and materials. Its key advantages include the following:

- **Immediate feedback**: Changes in the environment are instantly reflected in the lighting, enhancing creativity and iteration speed
- **Realism**: Accurate simulation of light bouncing off surfaces, capturing indirect lighting, reflections, and shadow nuances

Lumen leverages several advanced techniques to achieve its results, including the following:

- **Surface cache**: A system that stores surface lighting information to be reused and updated dynamically, ensuring efficient real-time performance
- **Software ray tracing**: A method for tracing light paths using software algorithms, enabling high-quality reflections and indirect lighting without the need for hardware ray tracing
- **Scene representation**: A dynamic representation of the scene's geometry and materials, allowing Lumen to accurately calculate light interactions as the scene changes

Lumen is particularly powerful for the following:

- **Open world environments**: Providing dynamic day-night cycles and realistic environmental lighting without extensive pre-baking
- **Interior scenes**: Achieving detailed and realistic lighting in indoor environments where lights and shadows change frequently
- **Interactive experiences**: Enhancing VR and AR applications with real-time lighting adjustments that respond to user interactions and environmental changes

Lumen stands out as the best option for lighting a scene due to its real-time capabilities, high visual fidelity, ease of use, performance efficiency, versatility across platforms, compatibility with high-detail environments through Nanite, and the enhanced creative freedom it provides.

After understanding the key concepts of Lumen, let's see what tools Unreal Engine makes available to us to illuminate our projects, such as the **Environment Light Mixer**.

Using the Environment Light Mixer

The **Environment Light Mixer** is an editor window that allows you to create and modify a level's environment lighting components, including sky, clouds, atmospheric lights, and sky lighting. For designers and artists, this tool provides a centralized location to efficiently edit these components, offering the flexibility to adjust the level of detail for the properties you need to access.

You can find the **Env. Light Mixer** window under the **Window** drop-down menu on the main toolbar, as shown in *Figure 9.2*:

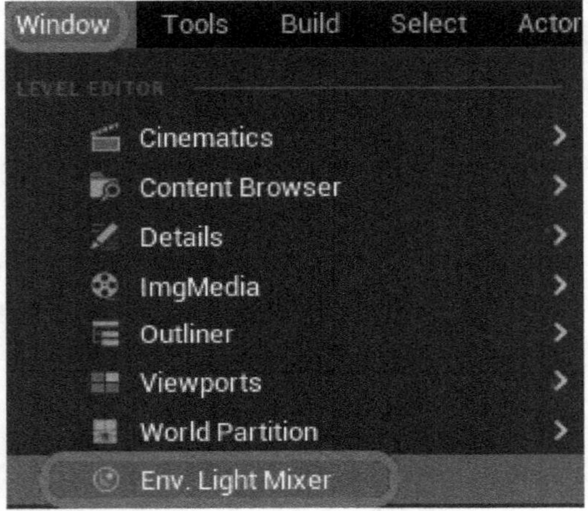

Figure 9.2 – Env. Light Mixer location

Once the **Env. Light Mixer** window is opened, we will see a window that does not contain any additional information (only if we have started with a new empty level):

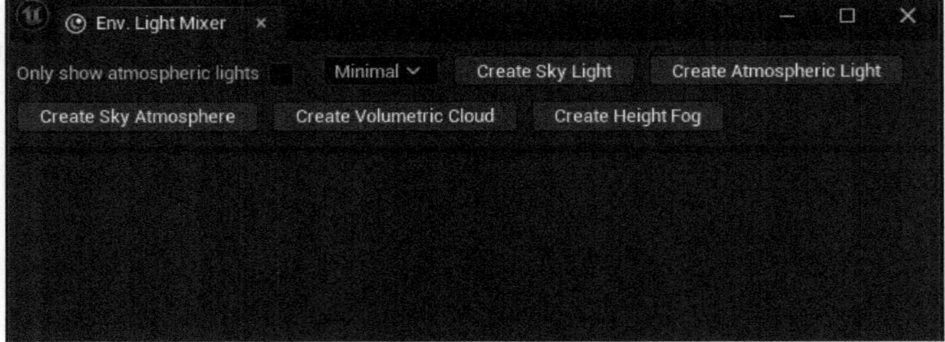

Figure 9.3 – The Environment Light Mixer, where you can directly and easily add all the Actors needed to set your environment's light system

The buttons at the top of the window allow us to add the different Actors necessary to create a basic lighting scheme in our project. Once added, we can control all their properties directly from this window, making it easier to manage and adjust the Actors responsible for lighting. Once added, our window should look like this:

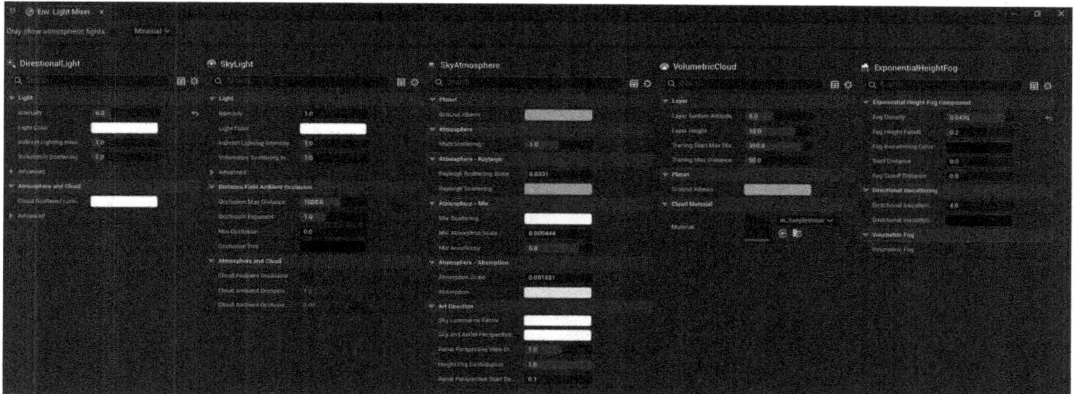

Figure 9.4 – The Environment Light Mixer allows you full control over every detail of the Actors

Unreal Engine's atmospheric Actors are designed to mimic the behavior of real-world lighting and atmospheric effects. By understanding the real-world counterparts, creators can better utilize these tools to achieve realistic and immersive environments in their projects.

Let's see which Actors are included in **Env. Light Mixer**:

- **DirectionalLight**: In Unreal Engine, this Actor simulates sunlight. It is a key light source that affects the entire scene uniformly, mimicking the parallel light rays emitted by the sun.
- **SkyAtmosphere**: This Actor in Unreal Engine simulates the scattering of light in the Earth's atmosphere, producing effects such as the blue sky, sunsets, and the transition of colors during different times of the day.
- **SkyLight**: This Actor captures the ambient light from the sky and applies it to the entire scene. It simulates the diffuse light that comes from the sky dome and affects areas not directly lit by the sun.
- **ExponentialHeightFog**: This Actor simulates atmospheric fog that increases in density with altitude, creating a realistic depth effect and softening the distant objects.
- **VolumetricCloud**: This Actor generates realistic clouds that can cast shadows and interact with light dynamically, affecting the lighting conditions of the scene.

Let's talk about these Actors in more detail in the subsequent sections.

DirectionalLight

This light simulates illumination from a source located at an infinite distance, resulting in all shadows being cast as parallel. This makes it the perfect option for replicating sunlight.

Light properties

Like other Actors, you can use this one with all different mobilities, allowing you to bake the lighting if necessary or get all the full advantages of Lumen with full DGI. These parameters can be adjusted in the **Details** panel of the Actor, giving you control over mobility settings and properties.

Let's talk about the most important qualities of this Actor:

- **Intensity**: Controls the total energy emitted by **DirectionalLight**, directly affecting the brightness of the sunlight in your scene. A higher intensity will result in a brighter, more pronounced sunlight effect.
- **Light Color**: Defines the color of the sunlight. This can be adjusted to simulate different times of day, such as warmer tones for sunrise or sunset and cooler tones for midday.
- **Source Angle**: Represents the angular size of the light source (sun) in degrees. By default, it is set to **0.5357** to match the average apparent size of the sun. Increasing this value will make the sun appear larger and soften the shadows.
- **Indirect Lighting Intensity**: Controls how much indirect (bounced) light is generated by **DirectionalLight**. This is crucial for outdoor scenes to create realistic soft lighting in shaded areas.
- **Volumetric Scattering Intensity**: Adjusts the intensity of volumetric scattering, influencing how much light is scattered through atmospheric elements such as fog or mist, contributing to the atmospheric depth of the scene.
- **Specular Scale**: Multiplies the strength of specular highlights, affecting how reflective surfaces respond to sunlight, enhancing the realism of materials such as metal or water.
- **Contact Shadow Length**: Defines the distance at which the screen-space ray tracing calculates contact shadows, producing sharper shadows where objects meet surfaces, which is particularly important for detailed outdoor environments.
- **Lighting Channels**: Specifies which lighting channels **DirectionalLight** will affect, allowing for greater control over how different objects or materials respond to the sunlight in the scene.

Another important aspect of controlling the final look of the directional lights is related to the visual behavior of the God rays, which we can control from the **Light Shafts** section.

Light Shafts

Also known as *God rays*, we can create a light shaft just by enabling the option in the **Details** panel, and in conjunction with **Volumetric Fog**, we can create interesting visual results in lighting, as we can see in *Figure 9.5*:

Figure 9.5 – Light shaft effect combined with Volumetric Fog

Light Shafts has its own section in the **Details** panel of **DirectionalLight**, as shown in *Figure 9.6*:

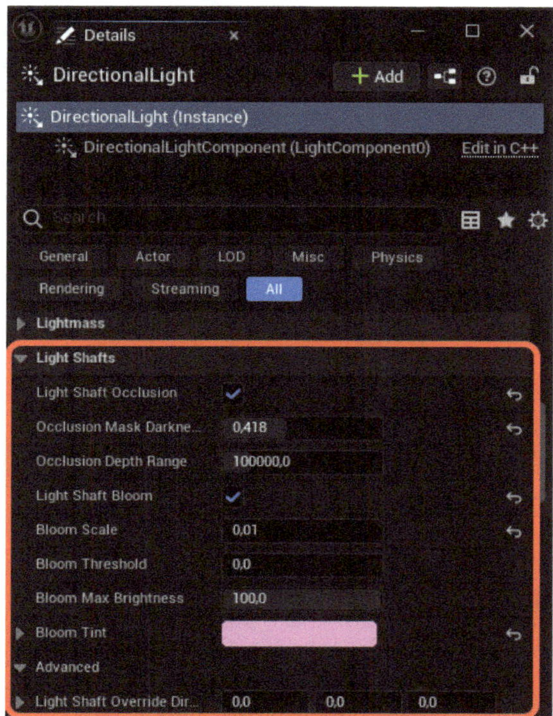

Figure 9.6 – Light Shaft details

In the **Light Shafts** section of **DirectionalLight**, we can try out the different light shaft methods available, **Light Shaft Occlusion** and **Light Shaft Bloom**, depending on the situation and the effect we want to achieve.

Light Shaft Occlusion is more effective when we have objects that directly cover the light source, while **Light Shaft Bloom** is more effective when the light source is visible in the scene, and we want to enhance its effect.

SkyLight

SkyLight captures the ambient lighting from distant parts of the level, such as the sky or far-off objects, and uses that information to illuminate the scene. This ensures that the sky's appearance, including its lighting and reflections, remains consistent throughout the environment, regardless of how the sky is generated, whether it's from a dynamic atmospheric system, layered clouds, a static skybox, or distant landscapes such as mountains. This consistency helps create a cohesive look across the scene by blending the lighting of distant elements with nearby objects.

Alternatively, you can manually assign a custom **Cubemap** to **SkyLight**, as shown in *Figure 9.7*. This feature allows for full control over the lighting and reflections, enabling you to use a specific image to dictate how the ambient light behaves in the scene. This is particularly useful in cases where the sky or background isn't directly tied to the lighting system, such as when using pre-rendered sky textures.

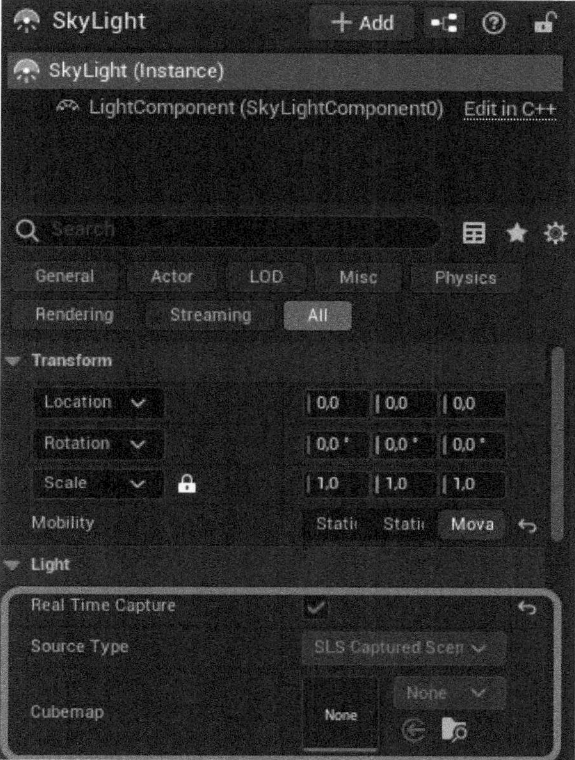

Figure 9.7 – SkyLight details

Additionally, **SkyLight** works seamlessly with Lumen for real-time GI, ensuring that lighting changes dynamically based on the environment or the time of day, offering a high level of realism for open worlds.

In the next section, we'll explore how to configure **SkyLight** to get real-time feedback on the overall look of our scene.

Movable Sky Light

When **SkyLight** is set to **Movable**, it functions entirely in real time without relying on precomputed lighting data. This means it captures lighting and reflection information from all objects in the scene, regardless of their mobility (static, stationary, or dynamic), and updates the lighting dynamically as the scene changes. This makes it ideal for environments where lighting conditions need to adapt in real time, such as outdoor open worlds with changing weather or time-of-day cycles.

Real Time Capture

The **Real Time Capture** mode provides dynamic and specular environment lighting, making it possible to perform dynamic time-of-day simulations with real-time reflections on scene elements.

This mode is available when the **SkyLight** mobility is set to **Stationary** or **Dynamic** and when **Real Time Capture** is enabled from the **SkyLight** component **Details** panel.

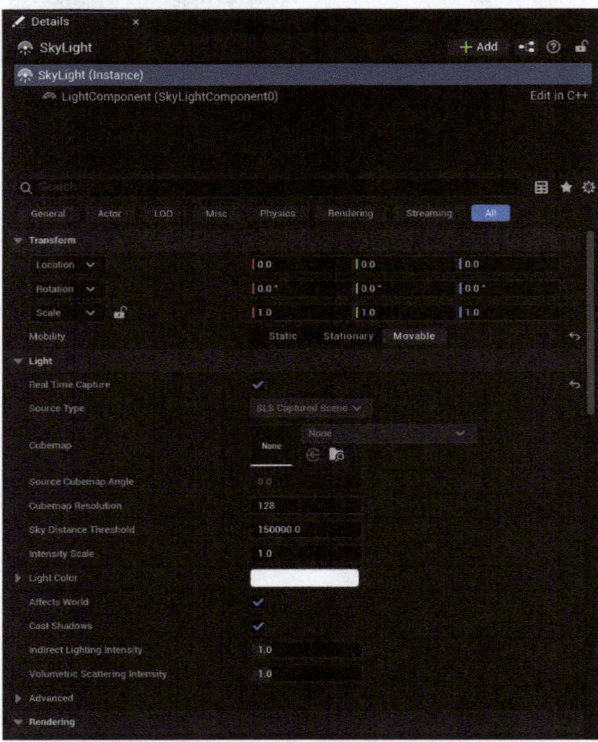

Figure 9.8 – SkyLight Real Time Capture allows you to see the impact of GI and reflections in real time

The last Actor involved in the creation of our outdoor lighting system is **SkyAtmosphere**. This works together with **SkyLight** and **DirectionalLight** to generate the sky dome in our scene. Let's see how it works.

SkyAtmosphere

The **SkyAtmosphere** component in Unreal Engine employs a physically-based rendering approach to create realistic skies and atmospheric effects. This versatile system can simulate Earth-like atmospheres, allowing for authentic time-of-day transitions, such as stunning sunrises and sunsets, as well as exotic extraterrestrial atmospheres. It provides an aerial perspective that facilitates smooth transitions from ground to sky to outer space.

Here are its key features:

- **Dynamic sky color**: The sky color adapts based on the sun's altitude, specifically how closely the vector of the dominant directional light aligns with the horizon. This results in natural color gradients as the sun rises and sets.
- **Control over scattering and fuzzy settings**: Users have full control over atmospheric density through adjustable scattering parameters, allowing for customized visual effects that suit various scenarios, from clear skies to dense fog.
- **Aerial perspective**: The system accurately models the curvature of the planet, providing a realistic transition from the ground to the sky and beyond, enhancing the immersive quality of the scene.

Additionally, the **SkyAtmosphere** system simulates light absorption using Mie Scattering and Rayleigh Scattering techniques. These effects contribute to the realistic color changes of the sky during different times of day by accurately depicting how light interacts with particles and molecules in the atmosphere.

The **SkyAtmosphere** Actor can be found in the **Place Actor** palette/menu under the **VISUAL EFFECTS** tab, as shown in *Figure 9.9*:

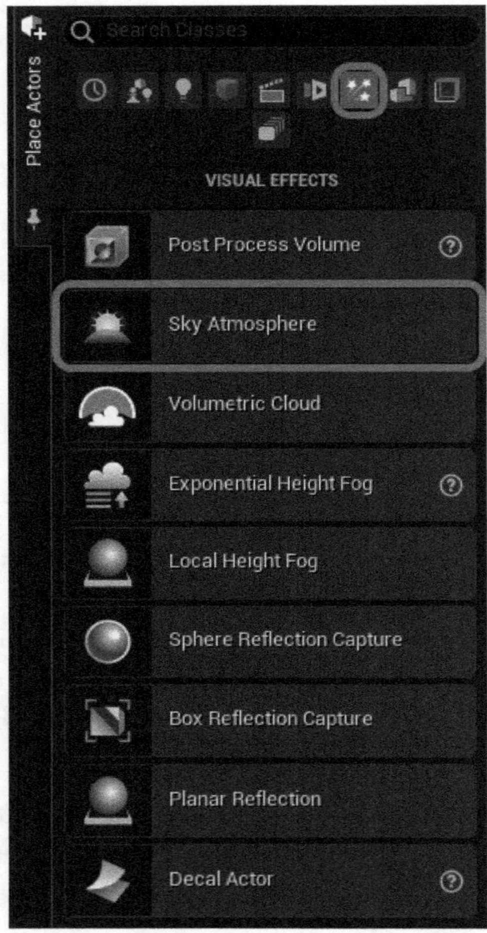

Figure 9.9 – SkyAtmosphere Actor location inside the VISUAL EFFECTS tab

Now that we know the main features, let's look at the sections involved in the process.

Rayleigh Scattering

In an Earth-like atmosphere, **Rayleigh Scattering** occurs when sunlight interacts with small particles dispersed throughout the atmosphere. The upper atmosphere is significantly less dense than the lower atmosphere, which is closer to the Earth's surface. This difference in density plays a crucial role in how light scatters and influences the color of the sky.

Adjusting the particle density in the atmosphere affects the extent of light scattering. Here's how:

- **Decreased scattering**: Lowering the particle density results in reduced light scattering, simulating an atmosphere that is 10 times less dense than Earth's. This creates a clearer sky with less blue hue, making the sun appear more intense.
- **Standard scattering**: This level maintains atmospheric density similar to Earth's, allowing for natural light scattering. This configuration produces the familiar blue sky during the day, along with realistic atmospheric effects.
- **Increased scattering**: Raising the particle density leads to enhanced light scattering, mimicking an atmosphere that is 10 times denser than Earth's. This results in a deeper blue sky and more vivid atmospheric effects, creating a more dramatic visual experience.

Let's see where these parameters are located in the **Details** panel of **SkyAtmosphere**:

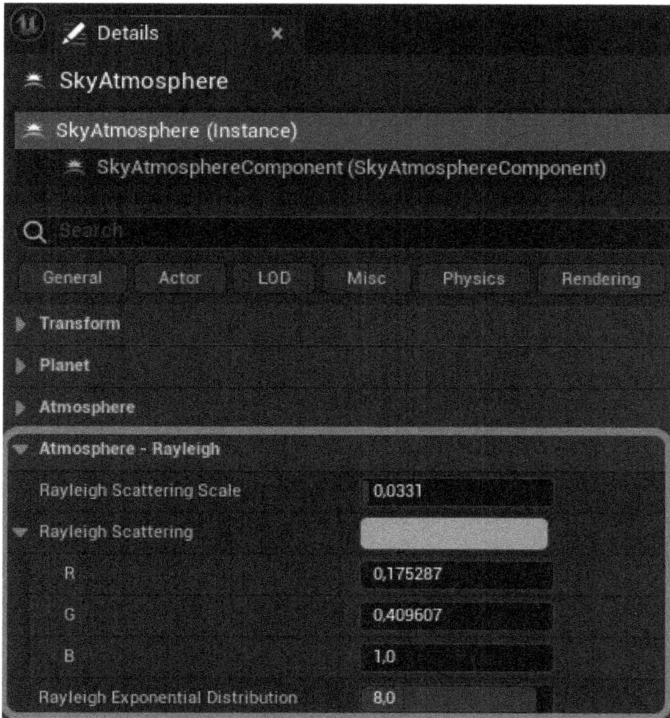

Figure 9.10 – SkyAtmosphere Rayleigh controls

In *Figure 9.11*, we can see our scene with the default values of **Rayleigh Scattering**, where, with a low value, we can see the *blue* color of the sky due to the low scattering of the atmosphere:

Figure 9.11 – Default Rayleigh Scattering Scale

In *Figure 9.12*, we see how altering the **Rayleigh Scattering** intensity changes the overall tone of the scene:

Figure 9.12 – Modified Rayleigh Scattering Scale

Mie Scattering

Mie Scattering occurs when light interacts with larger particles suspended in the atmosphere, such as dust, pollen, or pollutants. These particles, referred to as aerosols, can be naturally occurring or a byproduct of human activities.

Unlike Rayleigh Scattering, which primarily involves smaller particles, Mie Scattering tends to absorb more light, resulting in a hazy appearance of the sky. This phenomenon causes light to scatter predominantly in the forward direction, often creating bright halos around light sources like the sun.

Adjusting aerosol density can significantly influence the clarity and haziness of the sky. Here's how different levels of aerosol density affect the scattering:

- **Decreased aerosol density**: With a lower concentration of aerosols, the sky appears clearer with reduced haze. Light scattering becomes less directional, resulting in a more vibrant blue sky.
- **Default Mie scattering scale**: This setting represents a standard level of aerosol density, offering a balanced look that combines clarity with natural atmospheric effects.
- **Increased aerosol density**: Higher aerosol concentrations lead to a more occluded and hazy sky, characterized by pronounced forward scattering. This results in more significant light halos around sources such as the sun, enhancing the atmospheric effect.

We can find these parameters in the **Details** panel, in the **Atmosphere - Mie** tab, as we can see in *Figure 9.13*:

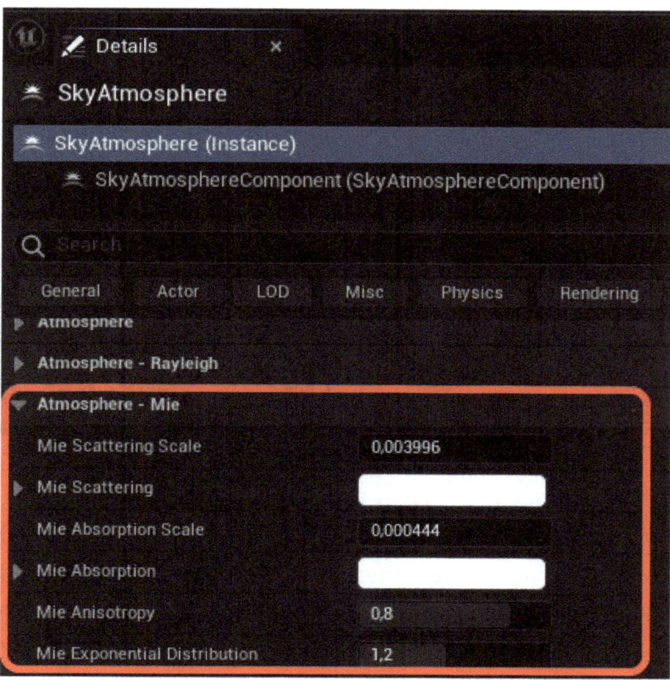

Figure 9.13 – Atmosphere Mie and Mie Scattering controls

The default value in a project should give us a result like that in *Figure 9.14*:

Figure 9.14 – Default Mie Scattering Scale

In *Figure 9.14*, we can see the default behavior of **Mie Scattering** in **SkyAtmosphere**. We can see the depth of the environment, and we see how the light source hits the trees in the scene directly.

If we increase the value, we can see the effect it has on the overall look of the scene, as well as the lighting:

Figure 9.15 – Modified Mie Scattering Scale

In *Figure 9.15*, we can see the same scene with a high **Mie Scattering** value. There is a feeling of fog in the environment, and we see how the atmospheric effects take center stage in the scene. Additionally, the light that previously reached the trees now does not affect the environment.

Art Direction

The **SkyAtmosphere** component offers artistic control, allowing you to customize the appearance of your project's sky and atmosphere to suit your creative vision.

The primary control is achieved through a **Color Picker** tool, which allows us to tint the sky with the desired hue and saturation. This adjustment is applied in addition to the current settings of **SkyAtmosphere**.

In *Figure 9.16*, we can see the color effect on the sky using the **Color Picker** tool in the **Art Direction** tab:

Figure 9.16 – Art Direction inside the SkyAtmosphere Actor

This section allows us to adjust the overall look of the scene, from modifying the sky color to controlling its visual contribution to the environment. These adjustments are designed to create effects that simulate atmospheres different from Earth's, such as extraterrestrial or fantasy environments.

Planetary atmospheres viewed from space

In addition to creating breathtaking atmospheres from a planet's surface, the **SkyAtmosphere** system in Unreal Engine enables the design of planetary atmospheres as seen from space. This feature allows for a seamless transition from the planet's surface, through its atmosphere, and into outer space, without needing complex configurations or additional setups. This creates a highly immersive experience, especially useful for space simulations or games involving planetary exploration.

Figure 9.17 showcases an example of a planetary atmosphere as seen from space:

Figure 9.17 – Planetary atmospheres

To configure **SkyAtmosphere** for a specific planet, you can find the relevant parameters in the **Details** panel under the **Planet** section. Here, you can adjust the planetary radius, atmospheric layers, and other important variables that control how the atmosphere behaves and appears when transitioning between the surface and outer space, as shown in *Figure 9.18*:

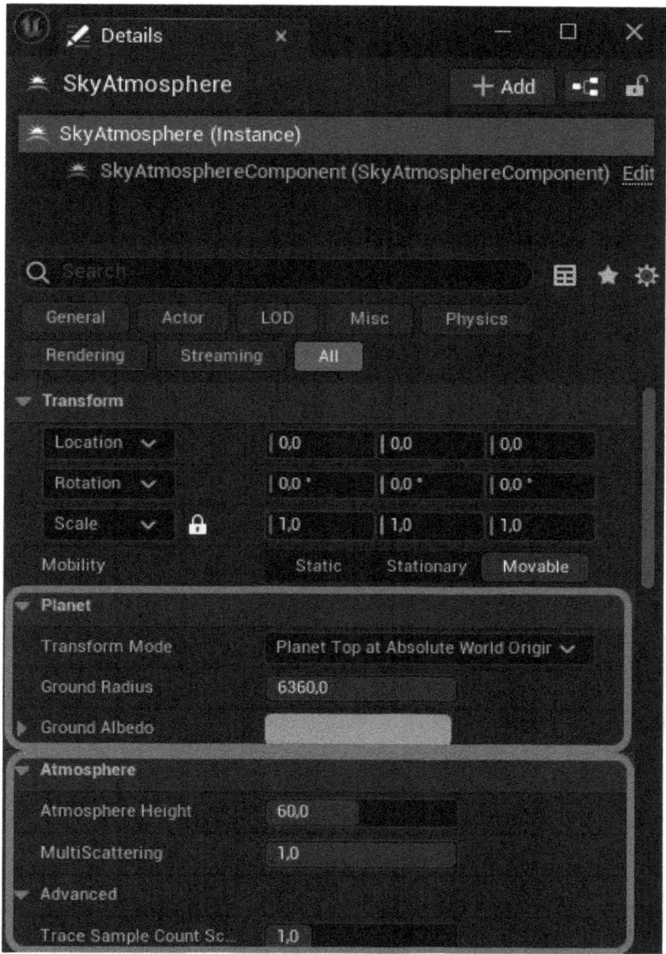

Figure 9.18 – SkyAtmosphere details

So far, we have discussed fog generated by **SkyAtmosphere**, focusing on how lighting behaves under various atmospheric conditions. Now, we will explore a different Actor called **ExponentialHeightFog**, which simulates fog accumulation in the lower parts of the scene.

ExponentialHeightFog

ExponentialHeightFog adds greater density to lower areas of a map and reduces it at higher elevations, with a smooth gradient that avoids abrupt cutoffs as altitude increases. This fog system also offers two distinct fog colors: one for the hemisphere facing the dominant directional light (or upward if none is present) and another for the opposite hemisphere.

Figure 9.19 illustrates the depth and spread of **ExponentialHeightFog** within a scene:

Figure 9.19 – Default ExponentialHeightFog

The effect is usually subtle, but when we compare it with the image without **ExponentialHeightFog**, we can see in *Figure 9.20* that the scene loses contrast:

Figure 9.20 – Not using ExponentialHeightFog

Like **SkyAtmosphere**, **ExponentialHeightFog** can be found in the **Place Actor** menu, in the **Visual Effects** category, as shown in *Figure 9.21*:

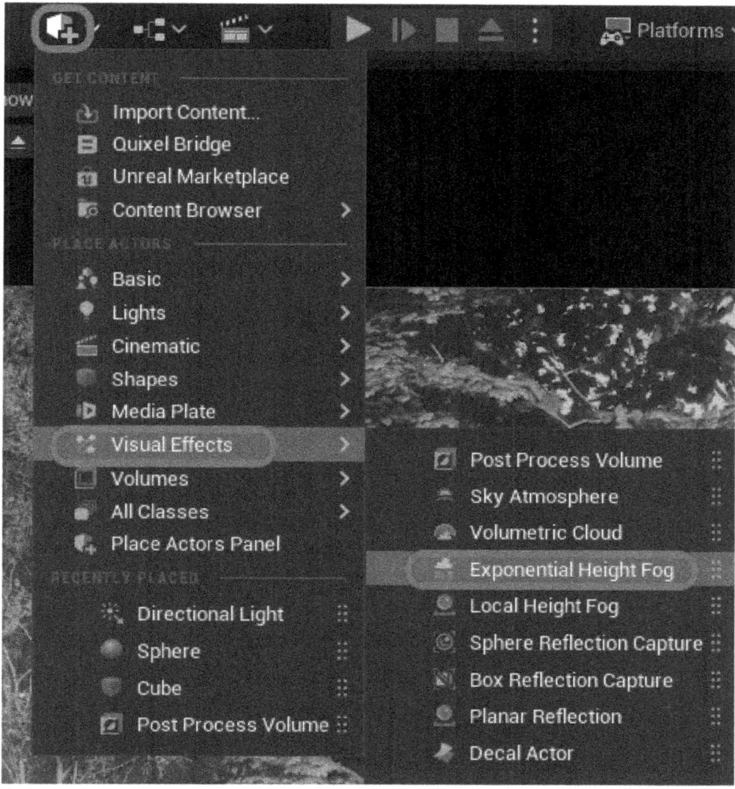

Figure 9.21 – ExponentialHeightFog location

Here you have some of the properties you will be able to use:

- **Fog Density**: Controls the overall density of the fog, determining its thickness across the scene.
- **Fog Inscattering Color**: Defines the main color of the fog, influencing how the light scatters within the fog.
- **Start Distance**: Sets the distance from the camera at which the fog begins to appear in the scene.

- **Volumetric Fog**: Enables **Volumetric Fog**, which provides a more realistic fog simulation. The resolution of this simulation can be adjusted via **Scalability Settings**.
- **Extinction Scale**: Modifies how much light is absorbed by fog particles in **Volumetric Fog**. Higher values make the fog more opaque by increasing light absorption.
- **Override Light Color with Fog Inscattering Colors**: When enabled, **Fog Inscattering Color** will replace **SkyLight's Volumetric Scattering Color** and **Directional Inscattering Color** for **DirectionalLight**. For optimal results, ensure that **Atmosphere Sun Light** is activated on **DirectionalLight**. However, keep in mind that this may produce non-physical volumetric lighting that might not match the lighting on other surfaces.

The performance cost of using **ExponentialHeightFog** is comparable to having two layers of constant density fog, but it comes with an optimization for **Start Distance**. By setting a start distance, the fog in the area directly in front of the viewer can be excluded, which improves performance by allowing for pixel culling through the Z-buffer.

Since we are discussing atmospheric effects such as **ExponentialHeightFog**, it's also important to cover another key component in Unreal Engine's atmospheric toolkit, **VolumetricCloud**.

VolumetricCloud

The **VolumetricCloud** component in Unreal Engine offers a physically based system for rendering clouds, using a material-driven approach. This enables artists and designers to create a diverse range of cloud formations for their projects. The cloud system is highly dynamic, supporting real-time time-of-day transitions, and seamlessly integrates with both the **SkyAtmosphere** and **SkyLight** components in real-time capture mode. Its scalability ensures that it can adapt to a variety of project needs, whether viewed from the ground, from the air, or transitioning from the surface to outer space.

We can add **VolumetricCloud** from the **PLACE ACTORS | Visual Effects | VolumetricCloud** panel, as we can see in *Figure 9.22*:

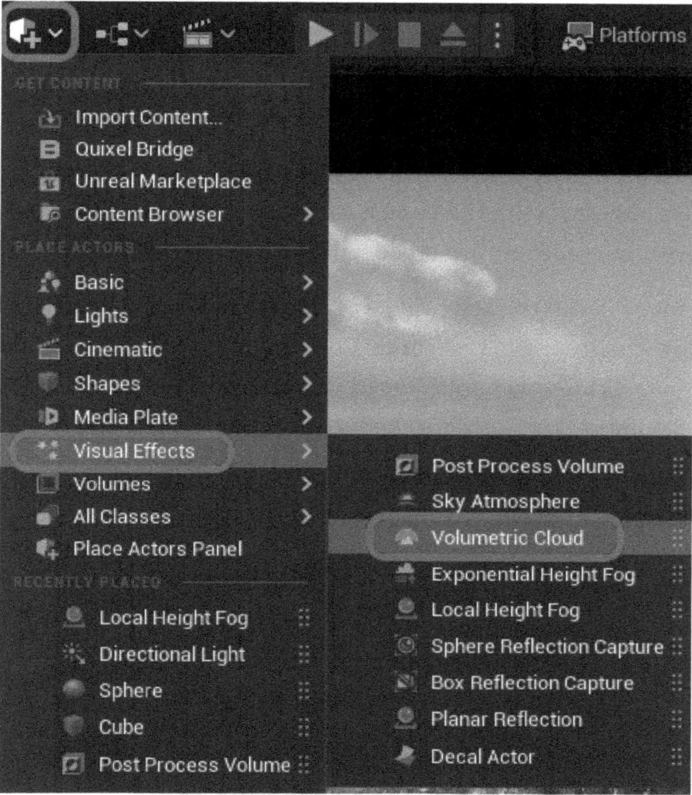

Figure 9.22 – VolumetricCloud Actor

Actor coverage depends on the needs of the project; we can get excellent details both from inside the atmosphere and outside of it, as we can see in this image of Volumetric Cloud on **Epic Games** (in the *Directional Light Interactions and Shadowing* section): `https://dev.epicgames.com/documentation/en-us/unreal-engine/volumetric-clouds?application_version=4.27`.

A key feature of **VolumetricCloud** is the ability to block light and cast realistic shadows onto surfaces below. The occlusion and shadowing of clouds are primarily controlled by atmospheric lights and the volume material used to represent the clouds. These settings allow you to customize various cloud behaviors, including creating sunlight shafts and simulating self-shadowing effects within the cloud masses.

The dynamic lighting system within Unreal Engine extends beyond just Lumen; it also incorporates two additional technologies that enable fully dynamic real-time lighting setups: Virtual Shadow Maps and Nanite.

Enhancing real-time rendering with Virtual Shadow Maps, Nanite, and Lumen

UE5 introduces groundbreaking technologies that elevate the realism and performance of 3D environments. This section explores two of these key innovations—Virtual Shadow Maps and Nanite—and their interplay with the Lumen GI system. Together, these technologies enable creators to achieve unprecedented levels of detail and dynamic lighting in real time.

Virtual Shadow Maps (VSMs) represent a new approach to shadow rendering in UE5, designed to improve shadow quality and performance. Conceptually, VSMs are essentially very high-resolution shadow maps, currently implemented with a virtual resolution of 16k x 16k pixels. To further enhance resolution for directional lights, VSMs utilize clipmaps.

You can find the **Virtual Shadow Maps** configuration options in **Project Settings** | **Rendering** | **Shadows** | **Shadow Map Method**, as we can see in *Figure 9.23*:

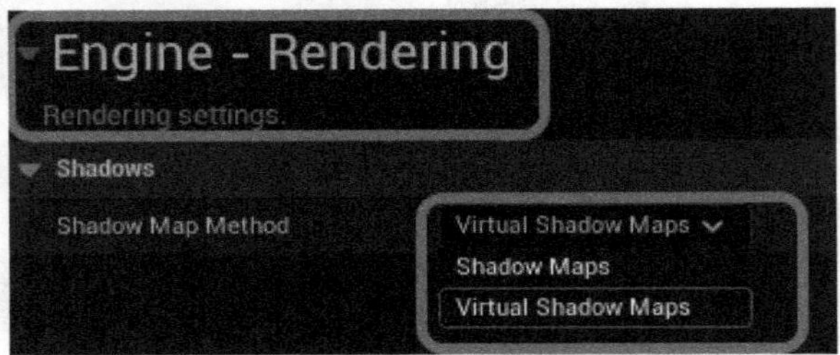

Figure 9.23 – VSM options in Project Settings

Traditional shadow maps often struggle with issues such as aliasing, low resolution, and performance overhead. VSMs tackle these challenges with a sophisticated method that splits the shadow map into tiles (or pages) of 128 x 128 pixels. Pages are allocated and rendered only as needed to shade on-screen pixels based on depth buffer analysis. This efficient system allows pages to be cached between frames, further improving performance, unless invalidated by moving objects or light.

Real-time rendering in UE5 demands a balance between visual fidelity and performance. The combination of Nanite, Lumen, and VSMs provides a powerful solution for achieving high-quality visuals without sacrificing performance. This section explores why it is a good practice to use these technologies together when working in real-time and how they enhance the overall rendering pipeline.

When used together, Nanite, Lumen, and VSMs significantly enhance the visual fidelity of a scene. Nanite provides intricate detail in geometry, Lumen ensures dynamic and realistic lighting, and VSMs deliver high-quality shadows. This combination results in environments that are visually stunning and immersive.

In *Figure 9.24*, we can see the **Ray Traced Shadows** options under **Project Settings** | **Rendering** | **Hardware Ray Tracing** | **Ray Traced Shadows**:

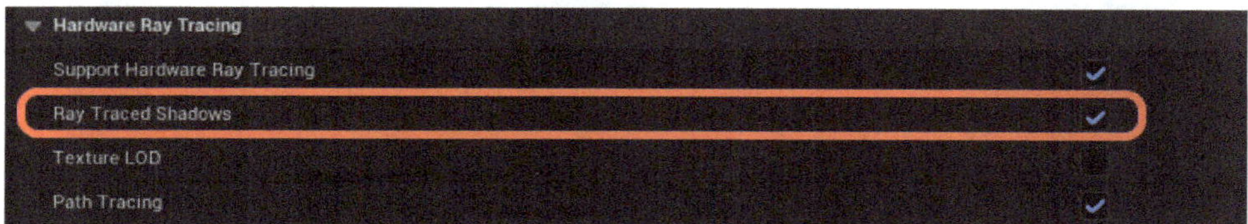

Figure 9.24 – Project Settings | Ray Traced Shadows

In *Figure 9.25*, we can see a scene with meshes and geometries that include **Nanite** receiving ray-traced shadows. Notably, some artifacts are visible in the scene, caused by **Nanite** utilizing an alternative mesh (**Nanite Fallback**) to project shadows onto the complex **Nanite** mesh. Unfortunately, this results in the visual issues we observe.

This phenomenon highlights the importance of understanding how Nanite interacts with other rendering technologies, particularly ray tracing. While Nanite allows for highly detailed geometries, the fallback system is necessary for shadow casting. This may lead to visual discrepancies, especially in intricate scenes where the shadow detail is critical for overall realism.

Figure 9.25 – Ray Traced Shadows enabled

On the other hand, if we maintain consistency in the use of technologies such as Lumen, VSMs, and Nanite, the difference in quality of the results is remarkable, as shown in *Figure 9.26*:

Figure 9.26 – Ray Traced Shadows disabled

The consistent application of advanced rendering techniques such as Lumen, VSMs, and Nanite significantly enhances the overall visual fidelity of a scene. By leveraging the strengths of Lumen for dynamic lighting, VSMs for high-quality shadow rendering, and Nanite for intricate geometry detail, creators can achieve a level of realism that elevates the viewer's experience. The seamless integration of these technologies not only improves visual quality but also ensures optimal performance in real-time applications.

Maintaining performance is critical in real-time rendering, especially for interactive applications such as games and VR. The synergy between Nanite, Lumen, and VSMs optimizes the rendering pipeline, ensuring that high-quality visuals do not come at the expense of performance. This collaboration streamlines the development workflow, allowing artists and developers to focus on creativity and iteration rather than manual optimization and tweaking.

Using Nanite, Lumen, and VSMs together in UE5 is a best practice for achieving high-quality, real-time rendering. These technologies complement each other, enhancing visual fidelity, optimizing performance, and facilitating a smoother development process. By leveraging their strengths, you can create detailed, immersive, and responsive environments that push the boundaries of real-time 3D rendering.

The following chapters will delve deeper into specific use cases and advanced techniques for maximizing the potential of these powerful tools. Specifically, for an in-depth discussion on optimizing scene lighting and performance testing, you can refer to *Chapter 12*.

Summary

Throughout this chapter, we've explored the various lighting tools available in Unreal Engine for outdoor environments. By combining these Actors—**DirectionalLight**, **SkyLight**, **SkyAtmosphere**, **ExponentialHeightFog**, and **VolumetricCloud**—it's possible to create different types of lighting. There is no single way to achieve the desired results, so I encourage you to experiment and explore different combinations to achieve a variety of outcomes.

In the next chapter, we'll discuss an Actor called Post Process Volume and its significance in determining the final look of our scene.

10

Setting up your Post Process Volume

The **Post Process Volume (PPV)** in Unreal Engine is a versatile and powerful actor designed to give developers full control over the visual representation of their scenes. It works by applying post-processing effects, such as **Color Grading, Bloom**, and **Depth of Field**, to achieve desired aesthetic results.

These effects can enhance realism, establish mood, and focus the player's attention on key elements within the game environment. The Post Process Volume can be set to either affect the entire level or be limited to specific areas, offering flexibility in how visual styles are applied.

In this chapter, we will cover everything from the fundamentals of setting up a Post Process Volume to advanced customization techniques. You'll learn how to configure key properties, understand the role of blending volumes, and leverage them for real-time, dynamic changes within your scenes. By the end of this chapter, you'll be equipped with the knowledge to effectively implement post-processing in your open world environments, tailoring the visual experience to suit your creative vision and gameplay needs.

Topics to be covered include the following:

- Exploring Post Process Volumes in Unreal Engine
- Color grading and tonemapping workflow
- Performance and frame rate considerations for Post Process Volume
- Exercise 10.1: Color adjustment in an outdoor scene

Technical requirements

To continue the development of this chapter, you'll need a PC with **Unreal Engine 5.5** (or a later version) installed that meets the recommended requirements by EPIC Games: `https://dev.epicgames.com/documentation/en-us/unreal-engine/hardware-and-software-specifications-for-unreal-engine`. Be sure to check that the system also has an active internet connection.

Exploring Post Process Volumes in Unreal Engine

To incorporate a **Post Process Volume** into your level, you can use the **Place Actors** panel. Once the volume is positioned in your level, the **Details** panel will grant you access to its properties and features, which are organized by categories based on their function and impact. The settings specific to the Post Process Volume dictate how it interacts with the scene and other overlapping volumes. For instance, enabling the **Infinite Extent (Unbound)** option allows the volume to influence the entire scene, while disabling it restricts the effect to a designated area. Additionally, when multiple volumes overlap, you can manage their interactions to create seamless transitions between different visual styles.

There isn't a single definitive approach to configuring and setting up the Post Process Volume. This is because it plays a key role in shaping the visual style of your project, which can be highly subjective. Therefore, we'll first cover the specific settings available and then delve into the general workflow, explaining how to correct the scene.

Post Process Volume can be found within **Menu** | **PLACE ACTORS** palette, in the **Volumes** category, as we can see in *Figure 10.1*:

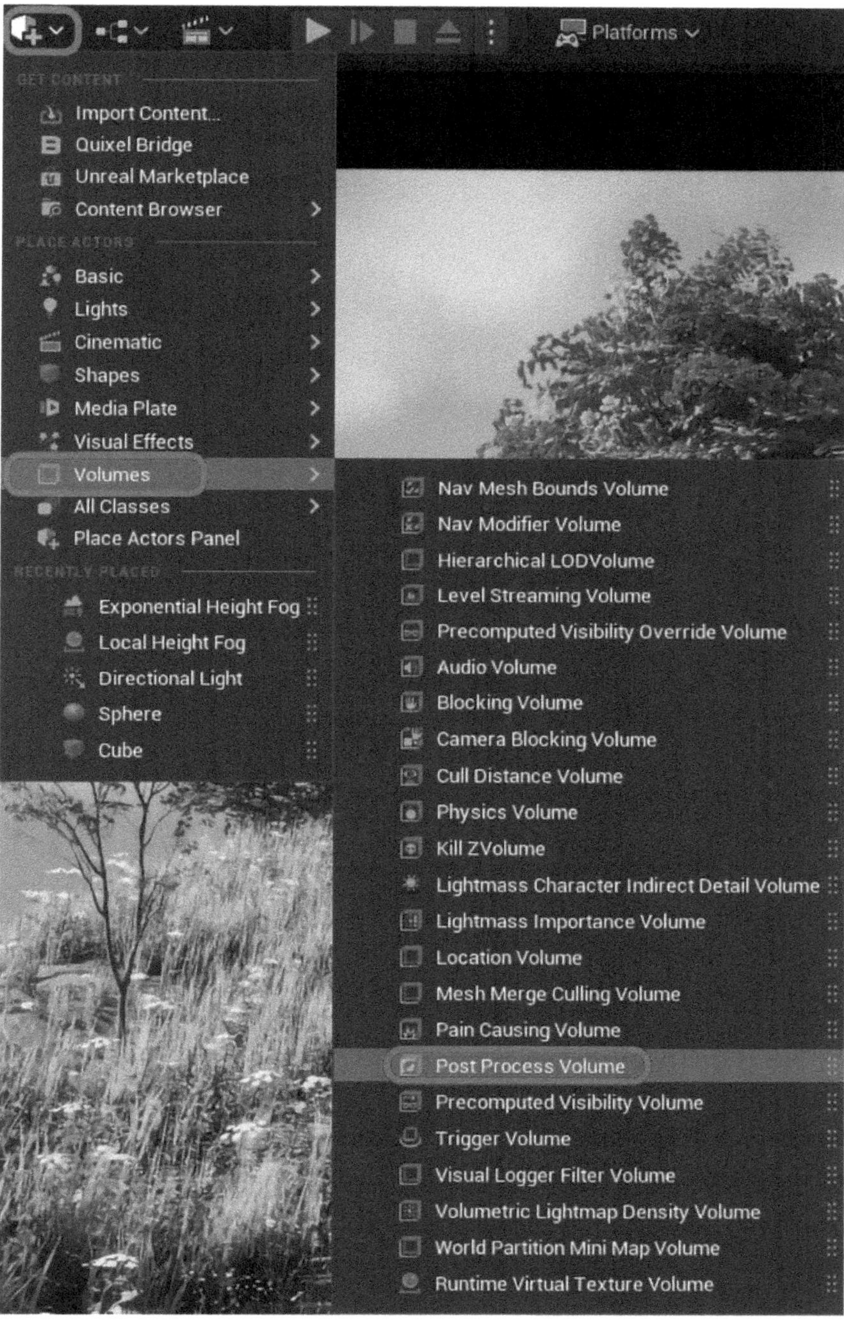

Figure 10.1 – Post Process Volume location

Once added to our level, we can see that the appearance of our Post Process Volume in the scene is that of a cube without faces, as shown in *Figure 10.2*. We can leave this anywhere in our scene without modifying it (if we want the configuration, we make to affect the entire level), or we can play with its position and scale to determine the area of effect that interests us.

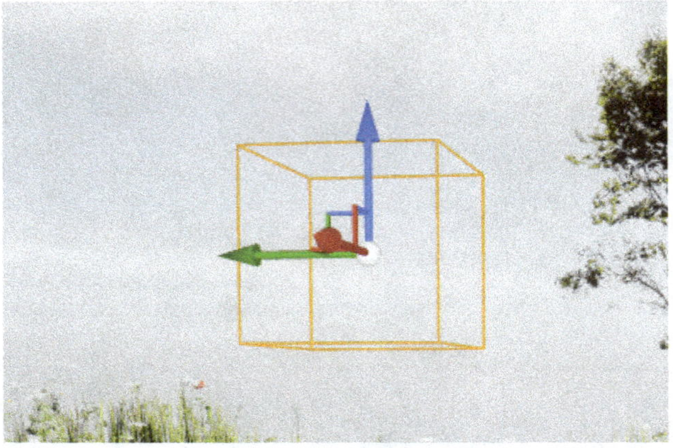

Figure 10.2 – Post Process Volume in the level

At first glance, the Post Process Volume may not seem to have a significant effect on the scene. However, the real power lies in the **Details** panel, where its properties come into play. Here, you can fine-tune a wide array of settings, such as exposure, contrast, and color correction, to shape the final look of your environment.

When to use Post Process Volumes

So, the question you might ask is: *Why use Post Process Volumes at all?* Post-processing is a fast, art-directable layer that lets you unify tone, guide the eye, and push mood without rebuilding lighting or materials. Let's have a look at some use cases.

- **Global look control:** A single unbound Post Process Volume to define the project's baseline tone mapping, exposure policy, and subtle color balance
- **Diegetic transitions:** Local Post Process Volumes for caves, interiors, underwater, dream sequences—any zone where perception should shift as the player crosses a boundary
- **Focus and readability**: Slight vignette, gentle local exposure, or restrained **Bloom** to increase subject clarity without over-brightening the whole scene

Let's also look at situations when we should be cautious about using Post Process Volumes:

- **Over-processing**: Heavy film grain, strong chromatic aberration, or aggressive vignette can fatigue players and reduce readability, especially in UI-heavy scenes
- **VR and fast-paced gameplay**: Effects that warp edges or add latency (for example, heavy DoF, intense lens effects) can harm comfort and responsiveness
- **Inconsistent art direction**: Too many local Post Process Volumes with conflicting settings create visual discontinuities

Now that we've seen where Post Process Volumes are useful and where they can cause issues, we'll examine their main strengths and limitations. Understanding these trade-offs will guide how you apply them across different scenes.

Here are the pros of using Post Process Volumes:

- Post Process Volumes are non-destructive, real-time, and highly art-directable. They support smooth blending and per-area look authoring.

Now, we'll dive into the cons of using Post Process Volumes:

- Some effects are not *free*; they cost GPU and can hurt clarity if overused.
- Complex overlaps require discipline (priority, blend radius, and weight management).

Like any visual tool, Post Process Volumes are most effective when used with intention. The goal is to support player experience, not overwhelm it. Hence, decide the *intent* of the look first (readability, mood, guidance). Then apply the minimum set of effects to achieve it. Finally, continuously test with movement, combat, UI, and varied displays.

Post Process Volume properties

The toolkit provided by **Post Process Volume** is extensive, making this actor (Post Process Volume) crucial for determining the visual appearance of your level. **Post Process Volume** also influences other aspects related to the overall setup of dynamic lighting, shadows, and path tracing.

In this section, we will focus specifically on the functions of the Post Process Volume and the features that impact the visual aspects of the scene.

If we go to the **Details** panel, we can see all the sections that this actor includes, as shown in *Figure 10.3*:

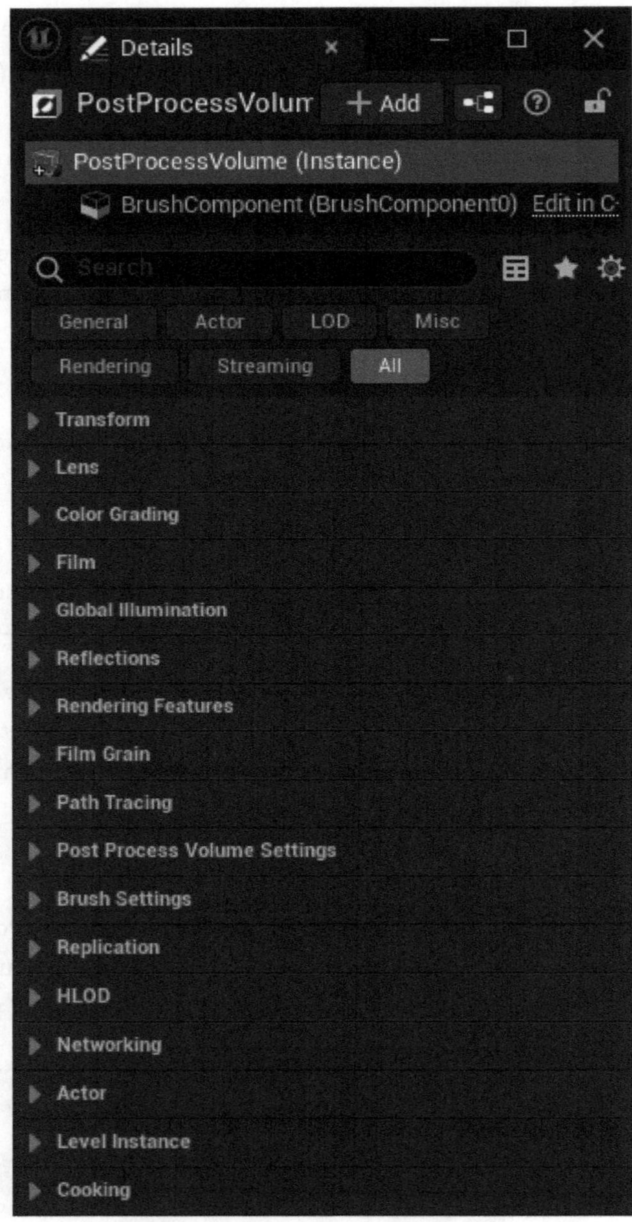

Figure 10.3 – PostProcessVolume properties in the Details panel

Among the properties shown in *Figure 10.3*, we will now focus on **Post Process Volume Settings** and explore the drop-down properties within:

- **Priority**: This property determines the priority level of the volume. In scenarios where multiple volumes overlap, the one with the highest priority takes precedence over those with lower priorities. If overlapping volumes share the same priority, the order in which they take effect is undefined.
- **Blend Radius**: This defines the radius (measured in world units) around the volume that is used for blending effects. For instance, as a player moves into a volume, the visual appearance can differ from the area outside the volume. The blend radius creates a transitional zone around the volume.
- **Blend Weight**: This controls the degree of influence the volume's settings have. A value of `1` applies the settings at full strength, while a value of `0` negates their effect.
- **Enabled**: This setting controls whether the volume affects post-processing. When enabled, its properties are applied and can blend with others. If not enabled, the volume has no impact on the scene's visuals.
- **Infinite Extent (Unbound)**: This option controls whether the physical boundaries of the volume are considered. When enabled, the volume influences the entire scene, regardless of its physical size. If not enabled, the volume only affects the area within its specified bounds. **Infinite Extent (Unbound)** is shown in *Figure 10.4*:

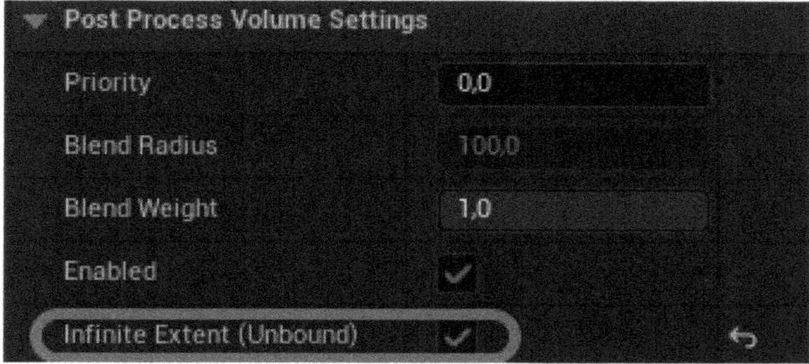

Figure 10.4 – Post Process Volume Settings

Features of Post Process Volume

In this subsection, we'll explore the key post-processing effects available in **Post Process Volume.** To test the impact of changing these values, we will use the control image shown in *Figure 10.5*. For each effect discussed in the following sections—such as **Color Grading, Bloom, and Exposure**—the adjustments will be applied to this image (if applicable), allowing us to observe how each setting influences the scene's visuals.

Figure 10.5 - Post Process Volume control image

With our base scene and a Post Process Volume selected, let's look at the properties included one by one, starting with the **Lens** section.

Note

Since this Post Process Volume is set to **Infinite Extent (Unbound)**, adjustments in the **Transform** section (**Location, Rotation, Scale**) are not required.

Lens section

The **Lens** category includes properties and settings that mimic typical real-world effects produced by a camera lens, as seen in *Figure 10.6*:

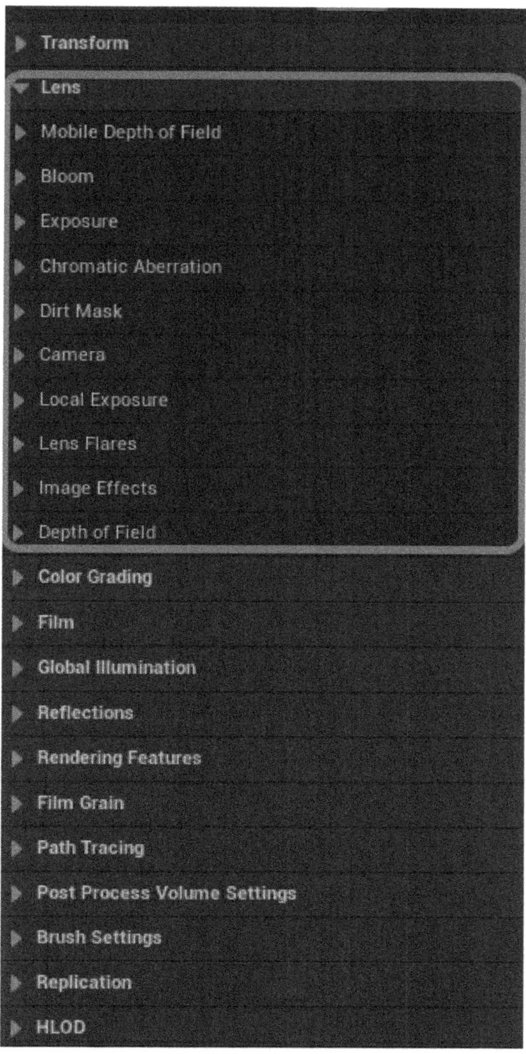

Figure 10.6 – Post Process Volume Lens settings

Let's take a look at these properties:

- **Mobile Depth of Field**: Much like real-world cameras, depth of field applies a blur to the scene based on the distance from a focal point, either in front of or behind it. This effect is commonly used in mobile applications and games to enhance visual depth and focus.
- **Bloom**: **Bloom** is a lighting artifact found in real-world cameras that enhances the perceived realism of a rendered image by creating a glow around lights and reflective surfaces. **Bloom** works in conjunction with other effects, such as lens flares and dirt masks, although those are not addressed by the general **Bloom** properties. In *Figure 10.7*, the **Bloom** effect is applied with an intensity of `0.2`; the image on the left shows the **Standard** method, while the image on the right illustrates the **Convolution** method:

Figure 10.7 – Bloom effects

- **Exposure and Local Exposure**: The engine automatically manages exposure, often referred to as *eye adaptation*, adjusting the brightness or darkness of the scene based on the current luminance in view. This effect simulates the way human eyes adapt to varying lighting conditions, such as transitioning from a dimly lit interior to a brightly lit exterior, or vice versa. The **Exposure** category offers properties to select the exposure method and to control how bright or dark the scene can become over a given period.

  Additionally, there's a feature called **Local Exposure**, which has its own set of properties. **Local Exposure** allows for fine-tuned adjustments to exposure within artist-defined parameters, utilizing an edge-aware data structure that preserves luminance detail. This is particularly valuable in high-contrast scenes, such as indoor environments with bright outdoor areas visible through doors and windows.

In *Figure 10.8*, you can see the scene's exposure (**Auto Exposure Histogram**); the image on the *left* has **Exposure Compensation** of -2, while the image on the *right* has +2 applied.

Figure 10.8 – Exposure – Exposure compensation

- **Chromatic Aberration**: Chromatic aberration is an effect that simulates the color shifts seen in real-world camera lenses. This phenomenon occurs when light rays enter a lens at different angles, causing the RGB colors to separate.

  In *Figure 10.9*, the effect of **Chromatic Aberration** is shown with **Intensity** of `3.0` and **Start Offset** of `0.8`. The effect is most pronounced at the edges of the image:

Figure 10.9 – Chromatic Aberration

- **Dirt Mask: Dirt Mask** is a texture-driven effect that enhances the **Bloom** in specific areas of the screen. It can be used to create the appearance of imperfections on a camera lens, such as dirt or dust. To see **Dirt Mask** in action, the **Bloom** effect must be active.

  In *Figure 10.10*, the **Dirt Mask** effect is demonstrated using the `T_ScreenDirt02_W` image (included in the engine) for **Dirt Mask Texture**, with **Dirt Mask Intensity** of `75`.

Figure 10.10 – Dirt Mask

- **Camera**: This category includes a set of properties that control the camera shutter and cinematic depth of field.
- **Lens Flare**: The **Lens Flare** effect is an image-based technique that simulates the scattering of light when viewing bright objects, due to imperfections in the camera lens. Similar to **Dirt Mask, Lens Flare** works in conjunction with the **Bloom** effect.

In *Figure 10.11*, the **Lens Flare** effect is applied to the scene with **Intensity** of `2.0`, **Bokeh Size** of `7.15`, and **Bokeh Shape** derived from the `Bokeh_5Sides` image (included in the engine).

Figure 10.11 – Lens Flare effect

- **Image Effects**: This allows developers to apply **Vignette** and **Sharpen** effects that alter the final rendered image in the scene.
    - **Vignette: Vignette** is an image-based effect that gradually fades the image towards the edges, creating a subtle borderless window, as we can see in *Figure 10.12*.
    - **Vignette Intensity**: This setting controls the darkening of the screen corners, enhancing the vignette effect. Higher values increase the amount of vignetting, while a value of 0 removes it.

Figure 10.12 – Vignette

So far, we have covered the Post Process Volume parameters corresponding to the **Lens** category (see *Figure 10.6*). Now, let's do an overview of the tools focused on **Color Grading**.

Color Grading section

The **Color Grading** and **Film** categories work in tandem to define much of the visual style of your project. The **Color Grading** category offers properties that enable color correction of the rendered scene, as shown in *Figure 10.13*:

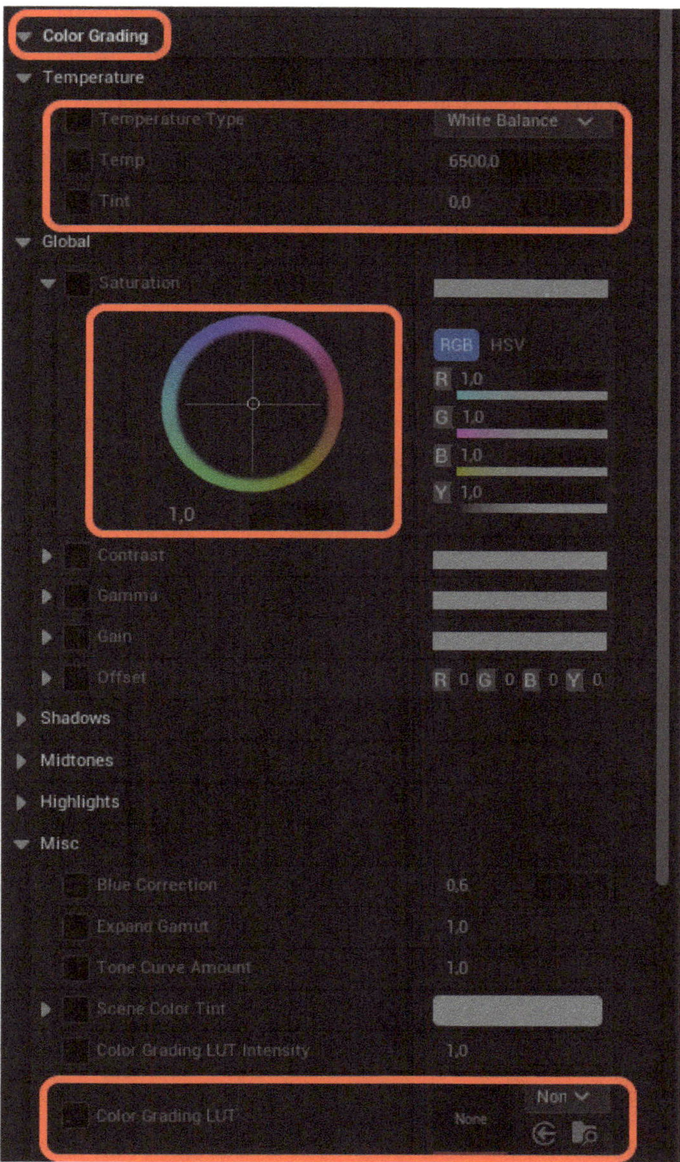

Figure 10.13 – Color Grading options for the Post Process Volume

Within the **Color Grading** category, you'll find properties that allow you to control contrast, color, saturation, and more, providing full artistic control over the appearance of the scene. The available settings include the following:

- **Color Temperature Control**: Adjust the overall warmth or coolness of the image.
- **Color Balance Properties**: These allow for adjustments to the global tones, as well as specific ranges, including shadows, midtones, and highlights.
- **Miscellaneous**: Additional options such as expanded gamut and **Look-Up Tables** (**LUTs**) for more advanced color grading.

The controls related to **Color Grading** are distributed across several tabs. You can adjust the temperature of the image, apply global adjustments, and fine-tune specific tones (**Shadows**, **Midtones**, and **Highlights**). Within these sections, you have the ability to modify the **Saturation**, **Contrast**, **Gamma**, **Gain**, and **Offset** of the image. Additionally, in the **Misc** category, you can find the settings for **Color Grading LUT**.

Next, we will explore the **Film** section.

Film section

The **Film** section allows you to adjust the image response properties, as if it were a photographic film. In *Figure 10.14*, we can see the available options:

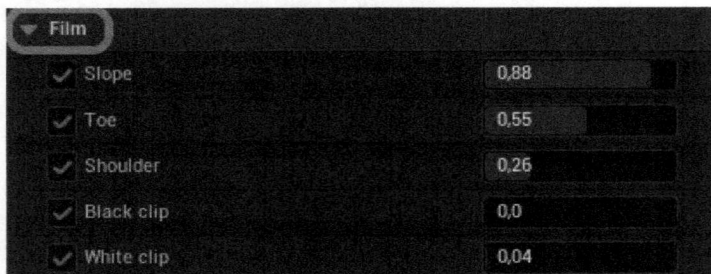

Figure 10.14 – Film options inside the Post Process Volume details

The **Film** category includes properties that adhere to the **Academy Color Encoding System** (**ACES**) standards, ensuring consistent color representation across various formats and displays. This helps maintain the integrity of the source material, reducing the need for adjustments when new mediums emerge. Let's take a look at the properties under **Film**:

- **Slope**: This controls the steepness of the S-curve used in the tonemapper. Higher values increase the steepness, resulting in a *darker* image, while lower values reduce the steepness, making the image *lighter*.

- **Toe**: This adjusts the dark tones in the tonemapper, influencing how the deepest shadows are rendered.
- **Shoulder**: This adjusts the bright tones in the tonemapper, affecting how the brightest highlights are displayed.
- **Black clip**: This determines the threshold where *black* colors start to lose detail and cut off their value.
- **White clip**: This sets the point where *white* colors begin to clip, causing them to lose detail. Adjustments to this setting are typically subtle.

In the next section, we will explore the different **Global Illumination** options available and their associated properties.

Global Illumination section

Another key feature of the Post Process Volume is its ability to let you choose the **Global Illumination** method to be used in the scene, as well as to adjust certain parameters related to visual quality and scene performance.

Important note

It's also important to note that when working on a new project in Unreal Engine 5, the default **Global Illumination** method used by the Post Process Volume will be **Lumen**.

The Post Process Volume settings for **Global Illumination** allow you to choose the type of dynamic global illumination to apply in your scene. Advanced properties provide options to adjust the intensity and color of certain global illumination methods, such as precomputed lighting. These are the primary global illumination methods available in the Post Process Volume:

- **Lumen Global Illumination and Reflections**: This method provides real-time global illumination and reflections, enhancing the realism of your scene. (Enabled by default in UE5.)
- **Screen Space (Beta)**: This technique uses screen space data to approximate global illumination effects, balancing performance and visual quality.
- **Ray Tracing Global Illumination**: This method leverages ray tracing technology for high-quality lighting and reflections, suitable for projects that prioritize visual fidelity.

- **Advanced**: In the **Advanced** section, you can adjust **Indirect Lighting Color** and **Indirect Lighting Intensity**. The *color picker* allows you to change the color of the indirect lighting, while the intensity setting lets you increase or decrease the amount of indirect lighting applied to the scene.

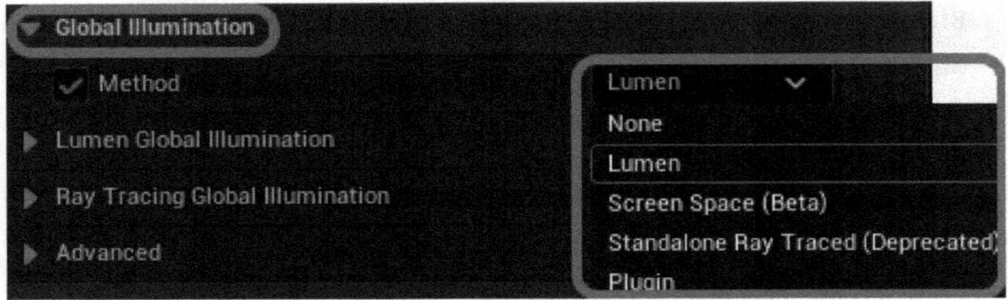

Figure 10.15 – Global Illumination options inside the Post Process Volume

Additionally, there is a **Film Grain** effect that can be implemented to alter the overall look of your scene.

Film Grain effect

Film Grain is an optical effect that simulates the look of processed photographic film. It can appear as tiny, randomized particles and adds a filmic look to the rendered frame.

Here are the key properties related to the **Film Grain** effect:

- **Film Grain Intensity**: Controls the overall strength of the grain effect; higher values make the texture more prominent.
- **Film Grain Intensity Shadows**: Adjusts how visible the grain appears in the darker regions of the image.
- **Film Grain Intensity Midtones**: Defines grain visibility in the midtone range, helping balance texture between dark and light areas.
- **Film Grain Intensity Highlights**: Sets how strong the grain appears in brighter portions of the frame.
- **Film Grain Shadows Max**: Limits the maximum grain intensity applied to shadow areas.
- **Film Grain Highlights Max**: Caps the maximum grain effect on highlights to avoid overexposure noise.

- **Film Grain Texel Size**: Determines the scale of the grain pattern; lower values create finer, denser texture, while higher ones yield coarser grain.
- **Film Grain Texture**: Specifies the texture asset used to generate the grain pattern for the filmic look.

In *Figure 10.16*, we can see the effect of **Film Grain** using the following settings: **Film Grain Intensity** set to 1 and **Film Grain Texel Size** set to 5:

Figure 10.16 – Film Grain details inside the Post Process Volume

One of the major advantages of using the Post Process Volume is the ability to make adjustments and see the results in real time within Unreal Engine. This real-time feedback allows you to fine-tune your scene's visual effects with precision.

Additionally, you can experiment with different transitions between properties of multiple Post Process Volumes by placing them within each other and correctly applying **Priority Order**. Next, we will discuss a workflow focused on color grading and tonemapping adjustments.

Best practices for overlapping and blending

The following best practices will help you structure and organize your Post Process Volumes more effectively:

- **Start global, then local**: Define a stable global Post Process Volume (unbound) for exposure and tonemapper. Add local Post Process Volumes only for specific perceptual goals.
- **Use Priority and Blend Radius deliberately**: Higher priority wins on overlap; set **Blend Radius** to `0` to avoid popping on entry/exit.
- **Limit the number of stacked volumes**: Too many overlapping Post Process Volumes complicate debugging and can create *muddy* looks. Prefer fewer, clearer regions.
- **Transition volumes between extremes**: Place an intermediate Post Process Volume between very bright and very dark areas to smooth exposure transitions (avoid eye-adaptation whiplash).
- **Document intent**: Add a one-line comment in the Post Process Volume's **Description** field about what it's for (e.g., `Cave cool/low-contrast`).

Once your Post Process Volumes are well structured and transitions behave smoothly, the next step is to refine the image itself. This is where color grading and tonemapping come into play.

Color grading and tonemapping workflow

At this point, we've covered the properties and settings available within the Post Process Volume. In this section, we'll discuss a straightforward workflow focused on color grading and tonemapping, which will enable you to efficiently work on color correction and initial image adjustments.

Color grading is the process of adjusting the color and tonal values of an image to achieve a desired aesthetic or mood. This involves altering the brightness, contrast, saturation, and hue of specific colors to create a cohesive look that enhances the storytelling of the scene.

Tonemapping, on the other hand, is a technique used to map the wide range of colors and brightness levels in a **high dynamic range** (**HDR**) image to a more limited dynamic range suitable for display. This process helps maintain detail in both bright and dark areas, ensuring that the final output appears balanced and visually appealing.

The workflow looks like this:

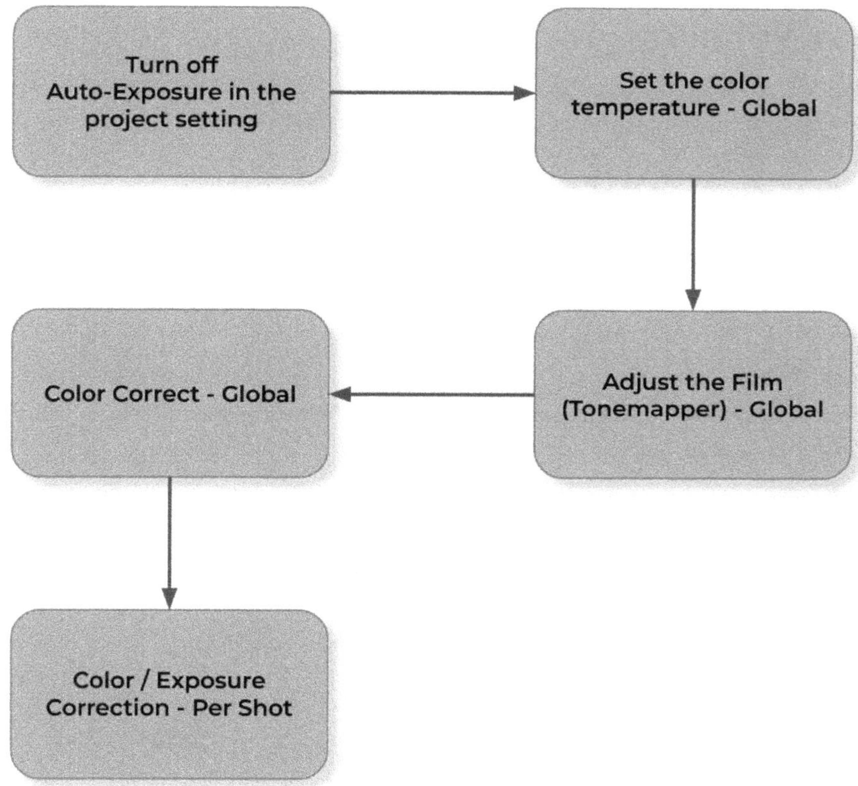

Figure 10.17 – Color grading and tonemapper workflow

These are the steps:

1. Turn off **Auto-Exposure** directly in the **Project Settings** (under the **Rendering** tab).
2. Set the color temperature in **Post Process Volume Details** (under **White Balance**).
3. Adjust **Film**, which is the main tonemapper; this will apply to the **Global** project.
4. Then, color-correct globally or per shot, as needed.
5. In case of some extra global color tuning, you can use the **Shadow/Midtones/Highlights** controls.

The parameters we have discussed have a substantial impact on the visual appearance of our scene. Achieving different looks and understanding which settings to modify requires time and a lot of practice. Before we move on to the exercise, let's have a look at performance and frame-rate considerations for Post Process Volume.

Performance and frame-rate considerations for Post Process Volume

Post effects run every frame. Some are *light* (cheap to compute) and others are *heavy* (costly). Knowing which is which helps you keep a smooth frame rate without sacrificing the look.

Using a mental model

Before optimizing, it helps to classify post-processing effects by their typical performance cost. Use the following as a mental model when deciding which to apply and at what intensity. This is especially useful for new or intermediate users:

- **Heavy hitters (use sparingly)**: **Ray-Traced GI**, **Circle DOF**, **Convolution Bloom**, high-quality **SSAO/SSGI**, and **Lumen** at high quality. While it is great for hero shots, it's risky for fast gameplay.
- **Middle weight (tune carefully)**: Default **Lumen GI/Reflections**, **SSGI**, **SSAO**, **Local Exposure**, **Motion Blur**. Often fine if values are conservative.
- **Lightweight (generally safe)**: **Color Grading (LUT)**, subtle **Vignette**, mild **Chromatic Aberration**, default **Auto Exposure**, **Sharpen** (low).

How to test quickly

Once you've identified which effects might impact performance, verify their actual cost in your scene. A quick, repeatable test will help you measure GPU impact objectively:

1. Make a baseline (target resolution and screen percentage). Run `Stat Unit` and `Stat GPU`.
2. Toggle one effect at a time in the Post Process Volume and watch the **GPU** column (per-pass time). If the frame time jumps, the effect is costly in your scene.
3. Re-test at a higher screen percentage (for example, 120–150%). If the cost grows a lot, that effect scales with resolution.
4. After changes, check UI/HUD readability and comfort (especially VR and competitive modes).

With performance considerations in mind, let's now shift our focus from optimization to creative control, applying these concepts in a practical color adjustment exercise. In the following exercise, we will apply the concepts learned about the Post Process Volume to create a specific aesthetic for our scene. We'll explore how each parameter influences the final output and experiment with various adjustments to enhance our project's overall visual quality. Let's get started!

Exercise 10.1: Color adjustment in an outdoor scene

Let's put the concepts we've learned about so far into practice by giving our scene a distinct look using a Post Process Volume:

1. First, we will add a Post Process Volume into our scene through the **Place Actors** menu. Let's set it to **Infinite Extent (Unbound)** so it will affect the whole scene, as we can see in *Figure 10.18*:

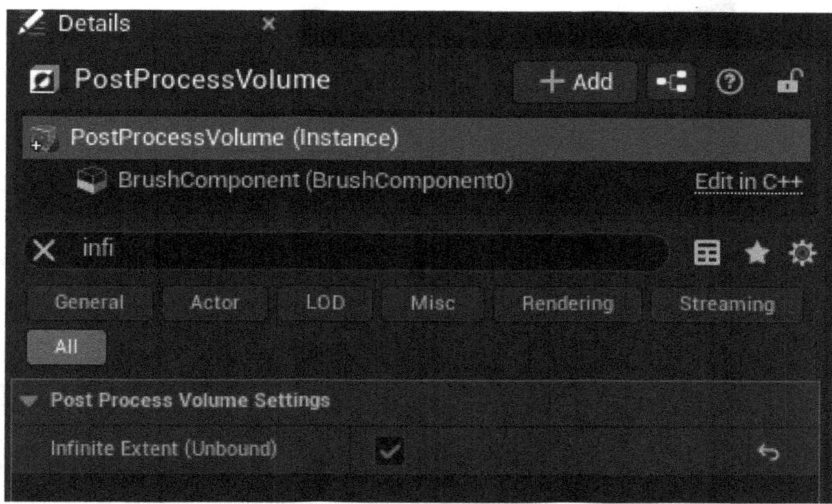

Figure 10.18 – Enable Infinite Extent

2. Let's adjust **Temperature Type** to **Color Temperature**, set **Temp** to `9800`, and adjust **Tint** to `0,048`:

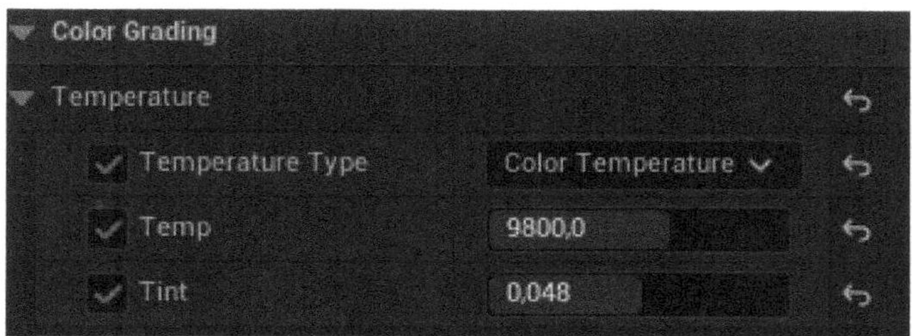

Figure 10.19 – Set the desired color temperature

3. Next, let's set the **Global** color correction to `1.1` and **Contrast** to `1.2`.

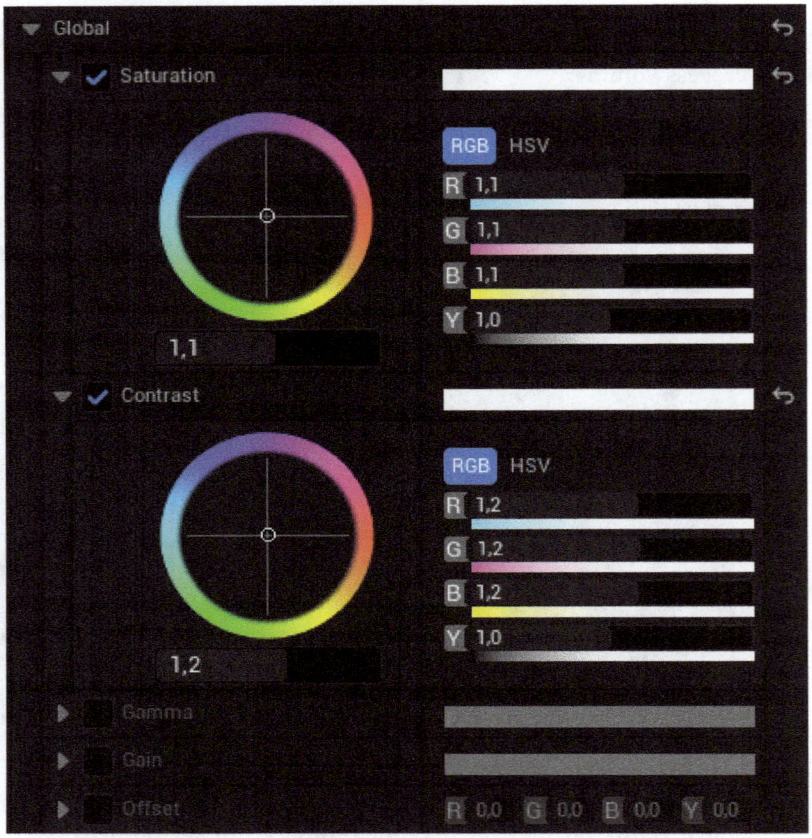

Figure 10.20 – Color adjustments

4. Let's now make some secondary changes to the Post Process Volume. We can add some **Bloom**, **Chromatic Aberration**, and other effects that will make our scene pop out. In *Figure 10.21*, you can see the additional adjustments made to the scene, adjusting **Bloom**, **Lens Flares**, **Chromatic Aberration**, and **Dirt Mask**.

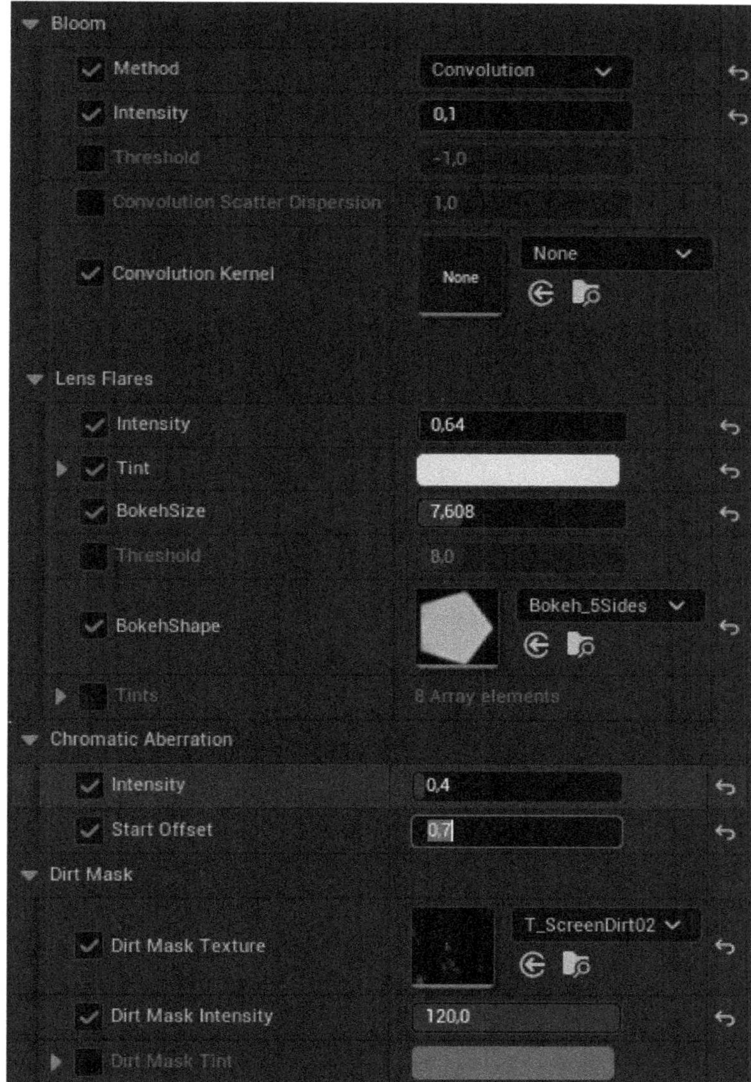

Figure 10.21 – Secondary adjustments

All these adjustments depend on the specific scene and the look you're trying to achieve. The key is to follow a structured workflow, as it is designed to contribute linearly to the final look of your project. This approach ensures that each step builds upon the previous one, leading to a cohesive visual style, as demonstrated in *Figure 10.22*:

Figure 10.22 – Final look of the Post Process Volume control image

When we talk about color adjustment, there is no single correct answer. In fact, two artists may produce completely different looks for the same scene due to the many factors at play. The key is to adhere to an organized workflow that doesn't hinder the subsequent steps as the project develops. This ensures a smoother creative process and allows for flexibility in achieving the desired aesthetic while maintaining consistency throughout the project.

Summary

In this chapter, we explored the significance of the Post Process Volume in shaping the visual aspect of our scene, as it plays a crucial role in defining the final look. We covered how it can impact the scene both locally and globally, how to blend different Post Process Volumes, and focused on the controls related to color adjustment. We also emphasized the importance of the Post Process Volume in managing scene lighting, and we tested all the controls within a workflow to develop the final look of our scene.

As a final recommendation, the Post Process Volume should always be present in your scene. It's a versatile actor that allows for simple adjustments to effects and lighting. Even during the development process, it's essential to make temporary adjustments to facilitate progress.

In the next chapter, we will delve into programming logic and Blueprints to implement automated tools for developing our environments.

Subscribe to Game Dev Assembly Newsletter!

We are excited to introduce **Game Dev Assembly**, our brand-new newsletter dedicated to everything game development. Whether you're a programmer, designer, artist, animator, or studio lead, you'll get exclusive insights, industry trends, and expert tips to help you build better games and grow your skills. Sign up today and become part of a growing community of creators, innovators, and game changers.

`https://packt.link/gamedev-newsletter`

Scan the QR code to join instantly!

Get This Book's PDF Version and Exclusive Extras

UNLOCK NOW

Scan the QR code (or go to `packtpub.com/unlock`). Search for this book by name, confirm the edition, and then follow the steps on the page.

Note: *Keep your invoice handy. Purchases made directly from Packt don't require an invoice.*

Part 4

Blueprints, Testing, and Optimization

This part focuses on the technical refinement and performance aspects of your Unreal Engine project. It starts by introducing programming logic through Blueprints, Unreal Engine's node-based visual scripting system used to create interactivity and reusable tools. You'll then learn how to evaluate and optimize your scene using profiling techniques that reveal performance bottlenecks in geometry, lighting, and materials.

The final chapter outlines best practices for maintaining balance between visual fidelity and efficiency, preparing your project for stable, high-quality real-time execution.

This part of the book includes the following chapters:

- *Chapter 11, Understanding Programming Logic and Blueprints*
- *Chapter 12, Optimizing and Testing Your Scene*

11

Understanding Programming Logic and Blueprints

The **Blueprint system** is a visual scripting tool that empowers both artists and developers to design and implement complex game functionalities without the need to write traditional code. This allows artists to create tools that can streamline and enhance the environment creation workflow, offering greater flexibility and efficiency.

Blueprints are based on a node-based interface, which simplifies the process of developing functionalities, eliminating the requirement for programming knowledge.

The classes defined within this system are referred to as **Blueprints**. These Blueprints enable the prototyping of any element that can be placed within a scene (or not), allowing it to participate in the game's functionality and be replicated as needed.

This chapter introduces you to Blueprint programming, covering the basic concepts and fundamental principles for its effective use.

These are the key topics to be covered:

- Basic concepts of programming with Blueprints
- Exploring Blueprint types
- Creating a Blueprint Class
- Exercise 11.1: Developing a tool for randomly placing Static Meshes
- Exercise 11.2: Creating Blueprints with components
- Debugging and optimizing Blueprints

Technical requirements

To continue the development of this chapter, you'll need a PC with **Unreal Engine 5.5** (or a later version) installed that meets the recommended requirements by EPIC Games: `https://dev.epicgames.com/documentation/en-us/unreal-engine/hardware-and-software-specifications-for-unreal-engine`. Be sure to check that the system also has an active internet connection.

Basic concepts of programming with Blueprints

Before we begin constructing our first Blueprints, it's essential to understand some fundamental concepts related to their operation and structure.

Nodes

Nodes represent actions, events, or functions. Each node has a specific purpose, such as moving an object, triggering an animation, or checking a condition.

Connections

Nodes are linked together through **connections** that define the flow of execution and data transfer. These connections are categorized into two main types: **execution wires** (represented by **arrows**) and **data wires** (represented by **lines**).

In *Figure 11.1*, we can see the anatomy of the connections of a node:

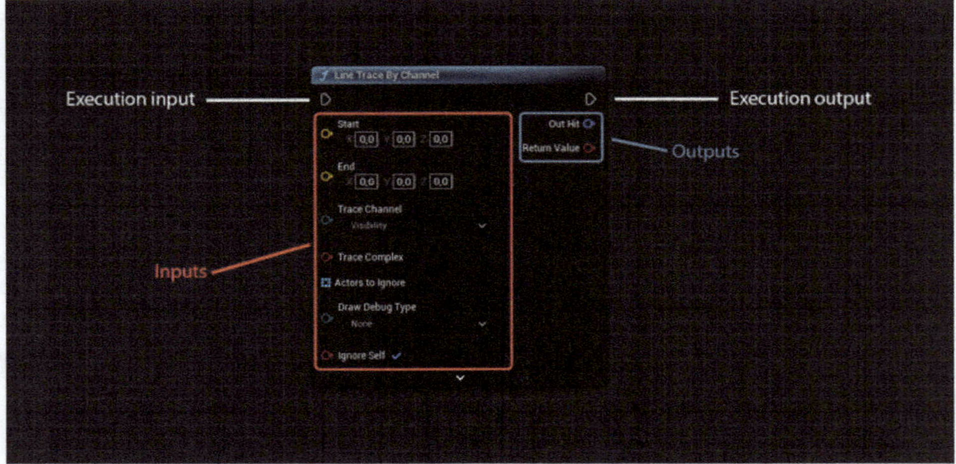

Figure 11.1 – Node connections

The construction of a Blueprint is done by joining different types of logic, called nodes, which are organized into categories. We can see them by *right-clicking* on the Blueprints workspace:

- **Execution flow**: The sequence of instructions that are executed in order by the processor.
- **Branching**: A split in the execution flow.
- **Variable**: A piece of data stored with a name that can be retrieved, modified, and operated upon.
- **Event**: A node that initiates an execution flow when triggered.
- **Function**: An execution flow that performs a specific task. It can receive parameters, return values, and may have restricted access.
- **Mathematical expression**: A mathematical operation collapsed into a single node.
- **Macro**: A set of operations grouped together to simplify reuse.

In *Figure 11.3*, we can see the basic construction of a Blueprint, where we can see the execution from an event and its execution flow until reaching the corresponding function.

Understanding the internal logic of Blueprints is important when creating and debugging projects. It is possible to use different types of Blueprints in our projects, which we refer to as *Blueprint types*.

Exploring Blueprint types

Let's look at some of the types of Blueprints available within Unreal Engine in the following sections.

Level Blueprint

A **Level Blueprint** is a level-specific type of Blueprint that contains logic and events affecting the entire level in which it resides. The Level Blueprint is directly tied to a particular level and is used to manage events and behaviors involving multiple actors or systems within that level.

Blueprint Class

Commonly referred to simply as a **Blueprint**, this type allows creators to easily develop functionalities. A **Blueprint Class** encapsulates data and methods, providing a modular and reusable structure for creating dynamic and interactive content. When defining a Blueprint Class, you can establish a set of characteristics and functionalities that will be inherited by all instances of that class, ensuring consistency and efficiency in game design.

Data-Only Blueprint

A **Data-Only Blueprint** is a Blueprint Class that contains only the code (in the form of node graphs), variables, and components inherited from its parent. These allow inherited properties to be adjusted and modified, but new elements cannot be added.

Blueprint Interface

A **Blueprint Interface** is a collection of one or more functions—just the names, without implementation—that can be added to other Blueprints. Any Blueprint that has the Blueprint Interface added will have access to those functions.

Blueprint Macro Library

The **Blueprint Macro Library** is a container that holds a collection of macros or standalone graphs that can be placed as nodes in other Blueprints.

Blueprint Utilities

A **Blueprint Utility** is an editor-only Blueprint that can be used to perform editor actions or extend editor functionality.

Now that we have a better understanding of the structure of Blueprints and their typology, let's start creating our first Blueprint Class.

Creating a Blueprint Class

The most common way to create a Blueprint Class is as follows:

1. *Right-click* in **Content Browser**.
2. Select the shortcut in the **CREATE BASIC ASSET** section or choose the **Blueprint Class** option from the **Blueprint** menu.

In *Figure 11.2*, we can see the Blueprint Class creation options from the **Content Browser**:

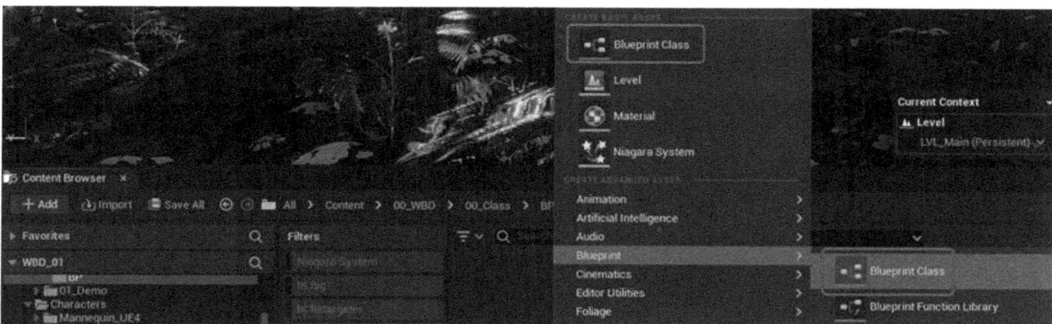

Figure 11.2 – Create Blueprint

Understanding Blueprint Class hierarchy

When creating a Blueprint, after completing *steps 1* and *2* of the *Creating a Blueprint Class* section, Unreal Engine will prompt you to select a base class for your Blueprint. A window will automatically appear, allowing you to choose the appropriate Blueprint Class (as shown in *Figure 11.3*). This step is crucial as it defines the core functionality and characteristics your Blueprint will inherit.

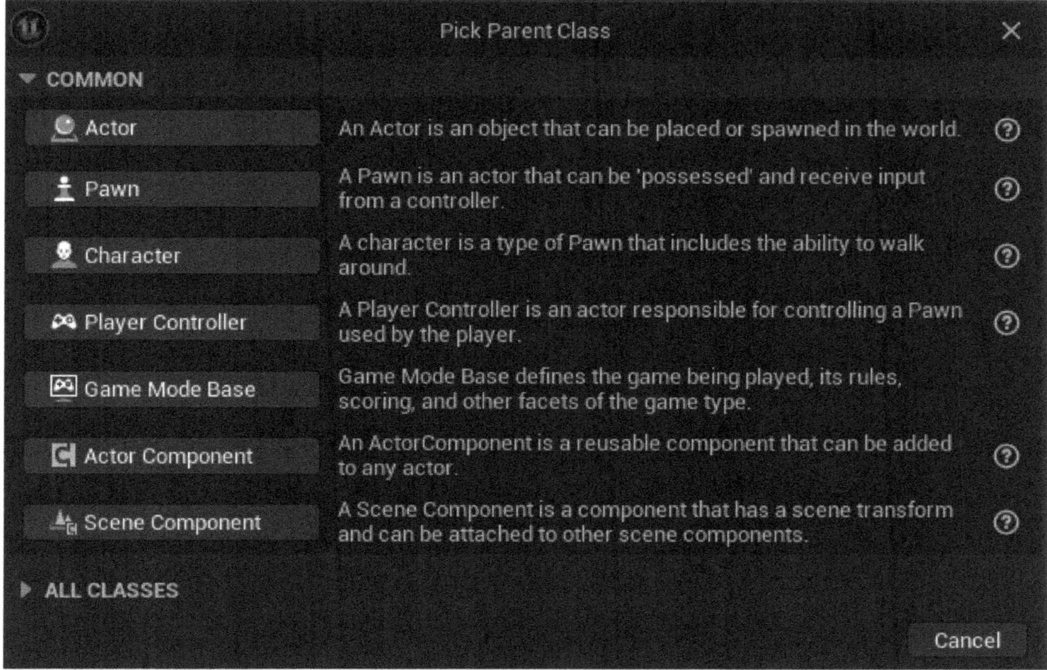

Figure 11.3 – Select the parent class

Unreal Engine uses an **object-oriented programming** (**OOP**) approach, meaning the engine is organized around discrete elements called objects. An **object** consists of properties, which can typically be viewed in the **Details** panel for the selected item in the level and often within the **Blueprint Editor** itself.

Objects are structured hierarchically into classes, which means an object inherits properties from its parent in the hierarchy. This allows objects to inherit attributes and behaviors from their parent classes, with the ability to modify or add new ones.

All Blueprint classes in Unreal Engine are inherited from the base class, `UObject`. The hierarchy follows this pattern: **Object >> Actor >> Pawn >> Character**.

For example, the `Character` class inherits properties and behaviors from the `Pawn` class, which inherits from the `Actor` class, and so on, all the way up to `UObject`.

In *Figure 11.3*, you can see a list of common classes. Under the **ALL CLASSES** section, you can find every class available in Unreal Engine.

The most used classes include the following:

- **Actor**: Contains a `Transform` component with data for position, rotation, and scale. It can be present in the scene from the start or spawned during runtime. It can also contain other components.
- **Pawn**: An Actor that can be possessed and receive input from a controller.
- **Character**: A type of Pawn with the ability to walk.
- **Player Controller**: An Actor responsible for controlling a Pawn.
- **Game Mode Base**: Defines the rules of the game.

For this chapter, we will focus on Blueprints of the **Actor** class, as they provide the most common functionalities. Selecting a class for your Blueprint will define its characteristics.

In this case, we will create an **Actor** class Blueprint, `BP_Rocks`, as it needs to be placed in the level and have components added to it.

In *Figure 11.4*, we can see how the newly created Blueprint Actor looks inside the **Content Browser**:

Figure 11.4 – Blueprint Class

As you can see, it is quite easy to create any type of Blueprint and assign different classes to them as needed. Now, let's see what is inside this new Blueprint.

Exploring the Blueprint interface

Double-click on the previously created Blueprint to access the Blueprint interface menu. Within this interface, we have the ability to define components, handle events, and organize and modularize processes for our Blueprints.

In *Figure 11.5*, we can see the structure of the editor, where you can visually script logic and manage the overall Blueprint setup:

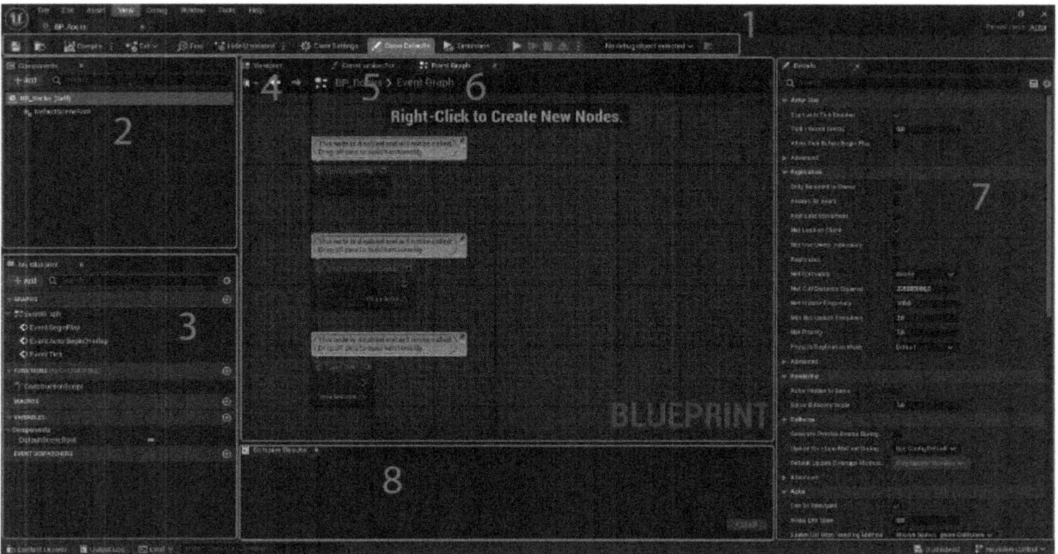

Figure 11.5 – Overview of Blueprint Editor

Let's look at a breakdown of the menus we have available:

1. **Toolbar**: Quick access to the most commonly used tools.
2. **Components**: A tab to add different types of objects to the Blueprint.
3. **My Blueprint**: A tab where you can create various elements, such as functions, macros, variables, and so on.
4. **Viewport**: This only appears in Blueprints for objects with spatial presence. It displays a prototype in the scene showing how a standard instance of the Blueprint would look in space.
5. **Construction Script**: A dedicated space for programming the Blueprint's constructor (and its instances).
6. **Event Graph**: Spaces dedicated to event programming, where the node system can be viewed.
7. **Details**: Shows the properties of the selected element, which can be modified.
8. **Compiler Results**: Displays the results of the Blueprint's compilation.

As you can see, the Blueprint interface is quite simple (very similar to the Material Editor interface). It is designed so that both artists and programmers can work in the same space without needing to write code to implement logic within the engine. With that said, let's move on to the next section, where we will develop a tool for randomly placing elements within our levels.

Exercise 11.1: Developing a tool for randomly placing Static Meshes

In this exercise, we will develop a tool to randomly place Static Meshes using a series of variables. This tool can be highly useful in environment creation, allowing you to quickly and randomly position elements in the scene. Let's get started!

Creating a Blueprint of the Actor class

The first step is to create a Blueprint of the Actor class, then place it in the scene (`BP_Rocks`). Follow these steps:

1. To place a Blueprint in the scene, simply drag it from the **Content Browser** into the level.
2. Now, open the Blueprint.

3. To create tools that work during environment creation, they need to function within the editor. For this, we'll use **Construction Script**. **Construction Script** allows you to create the logic necessary for the tool to function outside of scene execution. Enter the **Construction Script** tab to start.

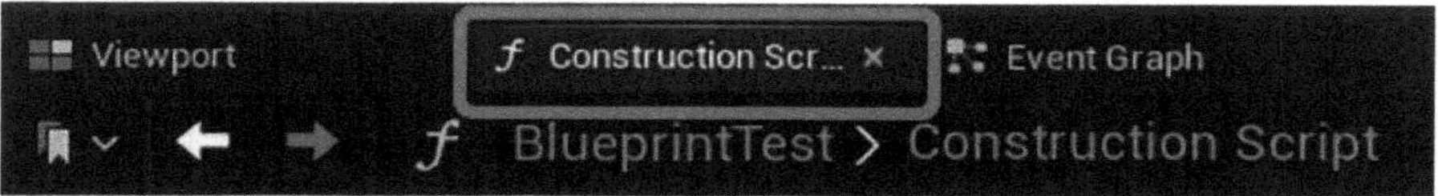

Figure 11.6 – Construction Script

Adding nodes

Before programming the tool, it's essential to understand a couple of concepts needed for this practice.

- **Loop (For Loop)**: Executes a loop for each index
- **Variable:** A variable allows storing a value that can be accessed later.

This tool will have the capability to define how many Static Meshes need to be created, and to establish that number, a node called **For Loop** will be used. **Loop Body** will execute a set number of times, defined by the integer values between **First Index** and **Last Index**. The **Index** pin *outputs* an integer specifying how many times the loop has been executed. The **Completed** pin is triggered after the last loop finishes.

In *Figure 11.7*, we can see the **For Loop** node and the nodes that compose it:

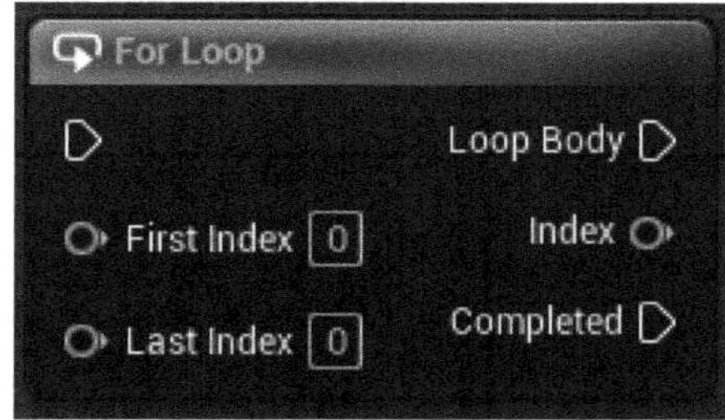

Figure 11.7 – For Loop node

Creating nodes in Unreal Engine is straightforward:

1. Simply *right-click* in **Graph** and a menu will appear listing the available nodes.
2. It's important to keep the **Context Sensitive** option enabled (as seen in *Figure 11.8*) to limit the search to nodes related to the Blueprint or node you are currently working with.

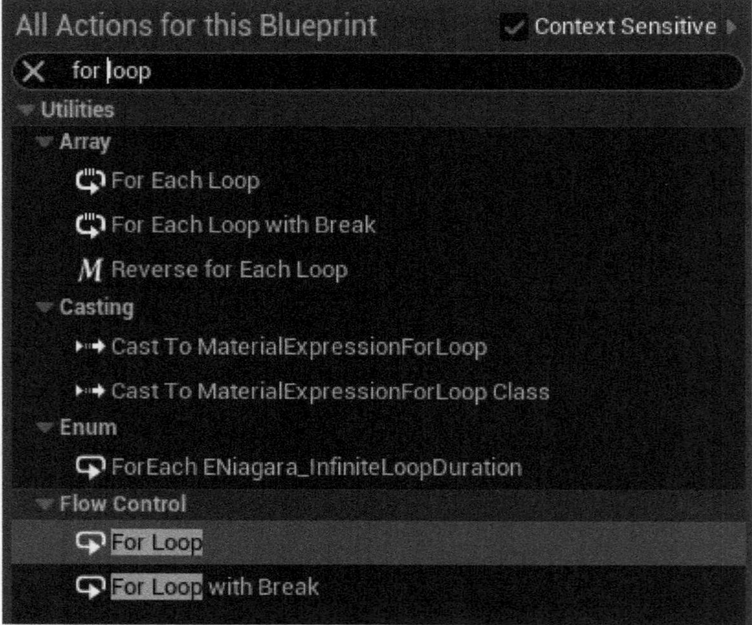

Figure 11.8 – For Loop – Context Sensitive

3. Another way to search for nodes is by dragging a wire (holding the *left mouse button*) and releasing it. After that, simply type the name of the node and press *Enter* to add it to **Graph**.

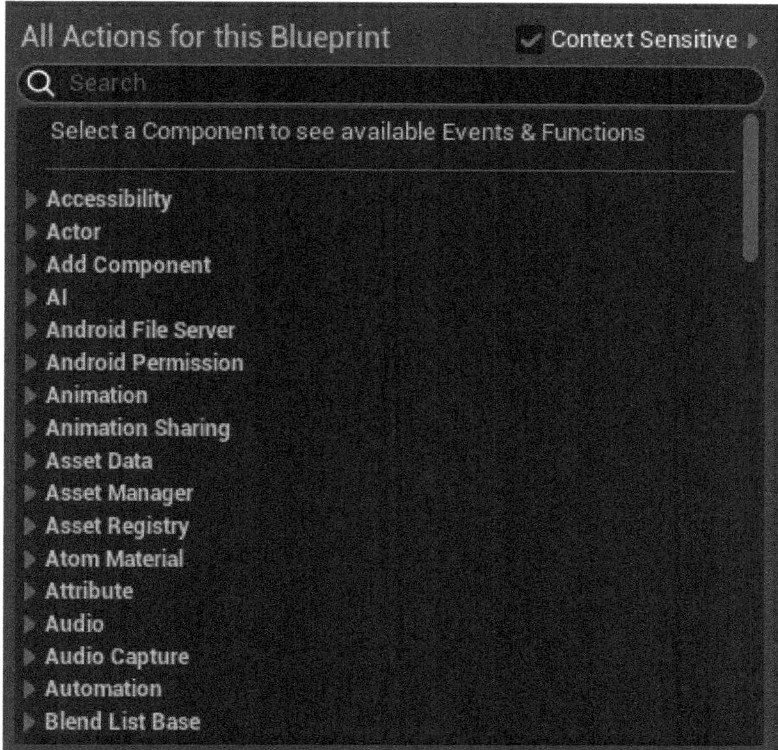

Figure 11.9 – Create node

4. Now, you need a node called **Add Static Mesh Component**, which allows us to access its transformation, meaning its location, rotation, and scale.

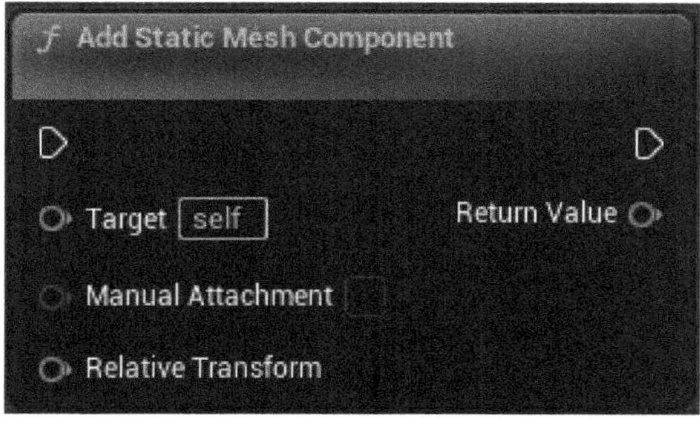

Figure 11.10 – Add Static Mesh Component

5. To access the location, rotation, and scale, the **Relative Transform** input needs to be separated. *Right-click* on the input to do this. Once the structure is separated, we will leave it like this (we will return to this struct to define the area of our tool). Next, we are going to define the mesh that we want to instantiate.

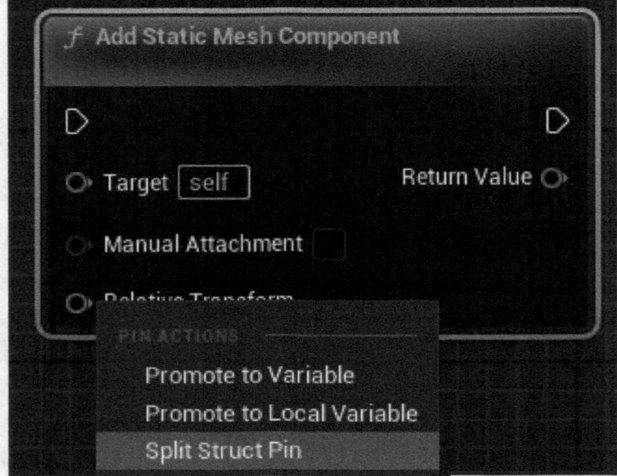

Figure 11.11 – Split Struct Pin

6. To add a Static Mesh, select the node and go to the **Details** panel.
7. In the **Static Mesh** section, choose the mesh you want to add.

Next, you need to create values that control the number of repetitions generated by **For Loop**, as well as the location, rotation, and scale of the created Static Meshes. This will be done using variables.

Adding variables

As previously mentioned, a variable can store different types of data, ranging from numerical and textual to vector data. Each variable will belong to a specific type and can only be of that type.

To create a variable in a Blueprint, there are several methods:

1. *Right-click* on the input to which you want to connect a variable and select **Promote to Variable**. This will automatically create a variable of the appropriate type needed for that input and connect it, as shown in *Figure 11.12*:

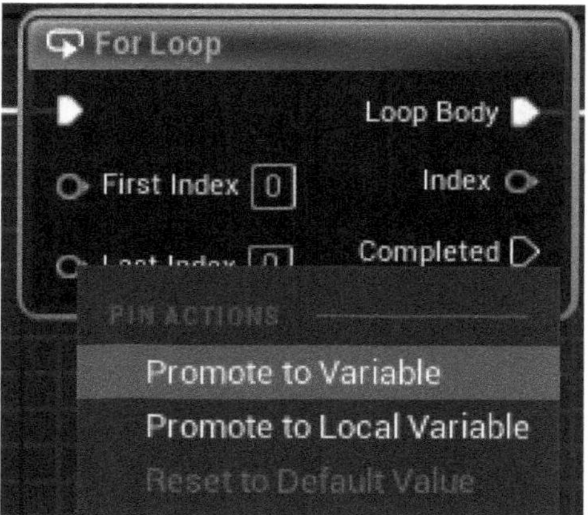

Figure 11.12 – Create variable

This is a simple way to create a specific variable depending on the node you are working with.

2. The other method is to create variables directly from the **My Blueprint** section (*3* in *Figure 11.5*), where you can manually create various types of variables. This gives you full control over the type and properties of the variables you need for your Blueprint logic.

   From the **My Blueprint** tab, click the **plus** (+) symbol to create a variable.

Figure 11.13 – Create variable

By clicking on the + sign, you'll see that there are different types of variables depending on the type of value they store, as shown in *Figure 11.14*:

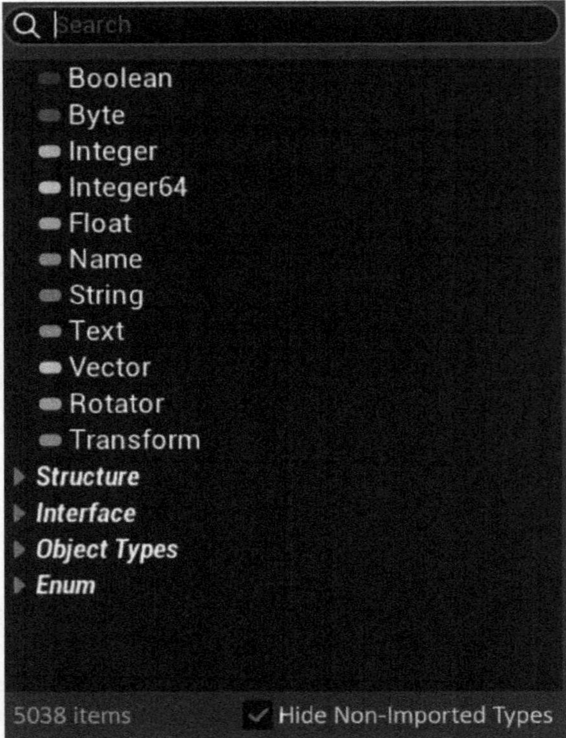

Figure 11.14 – Variable types

Here is a list of common variable types available in Unreal Engine.

- **Boolean**: True/False
- **Byte**: Uses 8 bits and represents values between 0 and 255
- **Integer**: Whole number
- **Integer 64**: Larger whole numbers
- **Float**: Real number
- **Name**: Text used to identify something within the game
- **String**: Text – comparing two name variables is faster than comparing two string variables
- **Text**: A string of text that is always visible and can be translated
- **Vector**: Describes the x, y, z position of a component
- **Rotator**: Describes the orientation in x, y, z
- **Transform**: Contains translation, rotation, and scale in 3D space

Knowing how to create variables and the types that exist, it is good practice to use them to store any values that may be needed later. This way, you can easily access and modify them when necessary.

3. For this exercise, we will create two **Float** variables that we will need for our Blueprint:

    - **Area**, with a default value of 500
    - **Scale**, with a default value of 1

    To set the default value, it is necessary to go to the **Compile** button to make the **Default Value** field visible. Additionally, we will enable the checkboxes for **Instance Editable** and **Expose to Cinematics**, as shown in *Figure 11.15*:

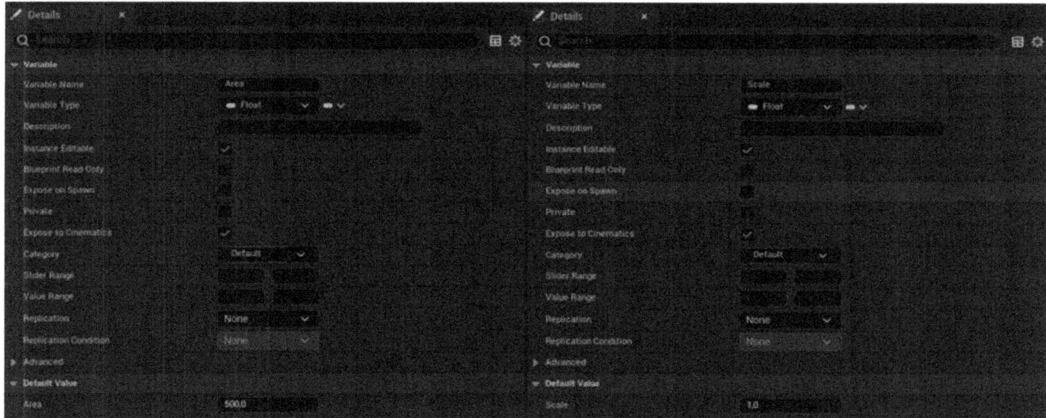

Figure 11.15 – Area and Scale variable configuration

With this, we will have the necessary variables created to complete our Blueprint.

4. If we go back to our **For Loop** node, in **Last Index**, we should have a variable created (as shown in *Figure 11.8*), where we can set the number of elements we want to distribute in space (set this value to 1).
5. To make the variables visible in the editor and allow their values to be changed without entering the Blueprint, simply enable **Instance Editable** in the **Details** panel.
6. It will also be necessary to connect **Construction Script** to the **For Loop** node, as shown in *Figure 11.16*:

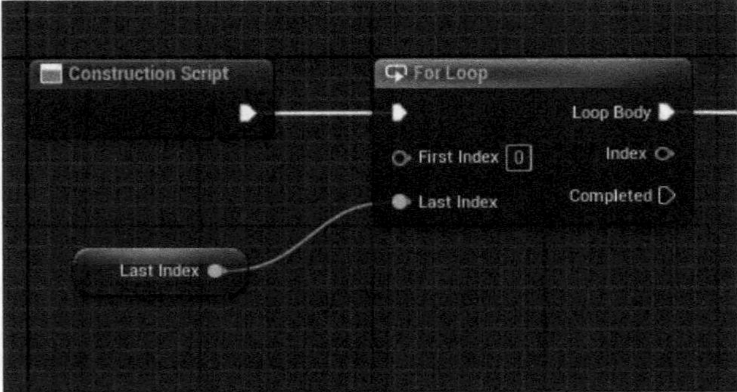

Figure 11.16 – Variable input

The next step is to control the *transform* where the Static Meshes are created.

Controlling the transform where the Static Meshes are created

For this, we'll use the variable created to store the position. However, since we want the position to be random and only affect the XY plane (i.e., the Z position won't be modifiable), this will allow us to control the area where the Static Meshes appear. Follow these steps:

1. To achieve this, the variable is multiplied (using the **Multiply** node) by a random value defined by the **Random Unit Vector** node.
2. After that, the resulting vector is separated (**Break Vector**) so that only the XY axes are affected.
3. Then, these must be combined again using a **Make Vector** node.
4. By using the XY nodes, the Static Meshes will be positioned within that plane.
5. This setup is then connected to the **Location** input of the **Add Static Mesh Component** node. This setup can be seen in *Figure 11.17*:

Figure 11.17 – Area distribution of the Static Mesh

6. The next step is to add the **Scale** variable and connect it to **Relative Transform Scale** of the **Add Static Mesh Component** node. This will allow us to configure the global scale of all Static Meshes created from the editor.
7. Finally, we can go to the **Add Static Mesh Component** node and select the Static Mesh we would like to instantiate.

With this, we will have completed the construction of our tool. The general structure of this setup can be seen in *Figure 11.18*:

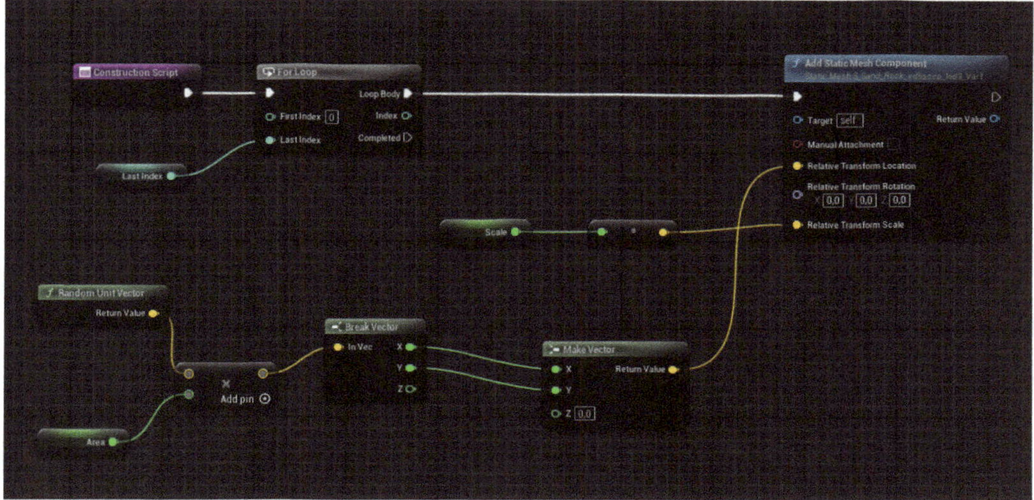

Figure 11.18 – Script finished

This Blueprint can be dragged and placed anywhere in the scene to randomly distribute the Static Mesh defined within the Blueprint. You can define the number of elements, the area of effect, and the global scale.

In *Figure 11.19*, you can see how the tool looks by default when added to a working level:

Figure 11.19 – Blueprint in the level

Now, if we go to the **Details** panel while selecting our newly created Blueprint, we can adjust the number of instances, the area, and the scale of the Static Meshes directly in the editor, as shown in *Figure 11.20*:

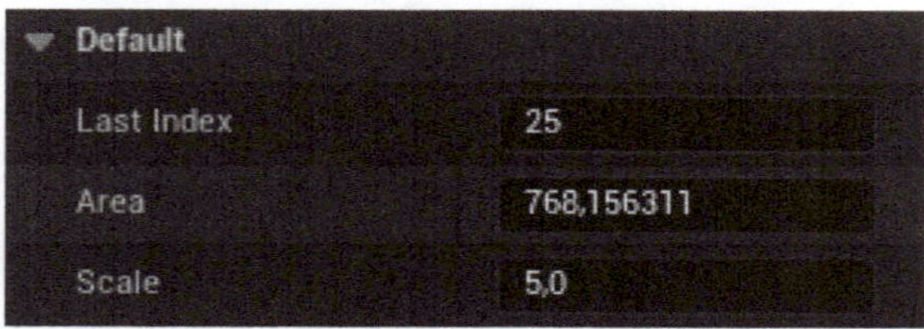

Figure 11.20 – Variables in the Details tab

In this exercise, we created a Blueprint tool in Unreal Engine to randomly place Static Meshes in a scene. We configured variables for instance count, area, and scale, and used nodes to manage mesh positioning and transformations. This tool streamlines environment creation by allowing quick adjustments directly in the editor, enhancing both flexibility and efficiency.

In the next exercise, we will work with components to modify various aspects of these elements.

Exercise 11.2: Creating Blueprints with components

In this exercise, we will focus on creating a Blueprint that incorporates various components to be used in the environment, and we will program the logic to modify some of their properties. This allows us to create containers for complex assets, making them easier to manage directly from the level.

Creating a Blueprint of the Actor class and adding components

1. Start by creating a new Blueprint of the Actor class. You can do this by *right-clicking* in **Content Browser** and selecting the shortcut at the top of the menu, or by going to the **Blueprint** section of the contextual menu (as shown in *Figure 11.2*). Name it `BP_Assembly_01`.
2. Once created, open the Blueprint and add the required components to build the asset. To add components, use the **Components** panel (located in the upper-left corner of the **Blueprint** menu) and click the **Add** button to search and include the needed elements.

   For this exercise, we will use the following components:

   - **Static Mesh**
   - **Niagara Particle System Component**
   - **Rect Light**

   To add a component, simply type its name in the search bar within the **Components** panel, as illustrated in *Figure 11.21*:

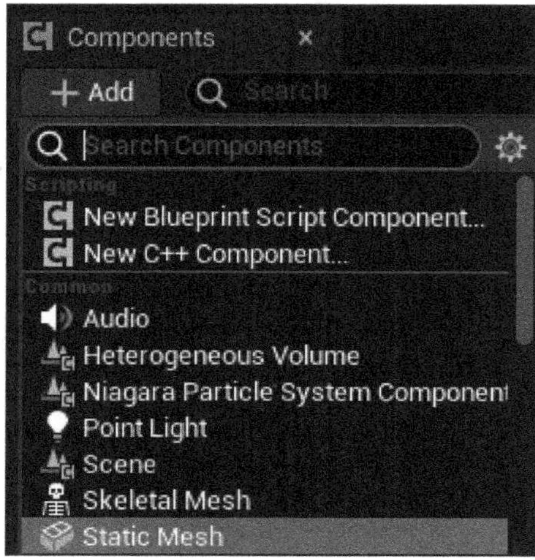

Figure 11.21 – Add component

3. Once the **Static Mesh** component has been added, it's necessary to select the specific Static Mesh Asset you want to include. This can be done through the **Details** panel. You can add as many Static Meshes as needed for the desired Blueprint composition.
4. As components are added to a Blueprint, a **hierarchy** is automatically created, allowing for better asset management. This hierarchy helps organize the asset structure. The hierarchy structure, as shown in *Figure 11.22*, can be modified by clicking and dragging components to move them up or down. The hierarchy is significant based on the operations performed, as changes made to the primary element will propagate to the elements below it.

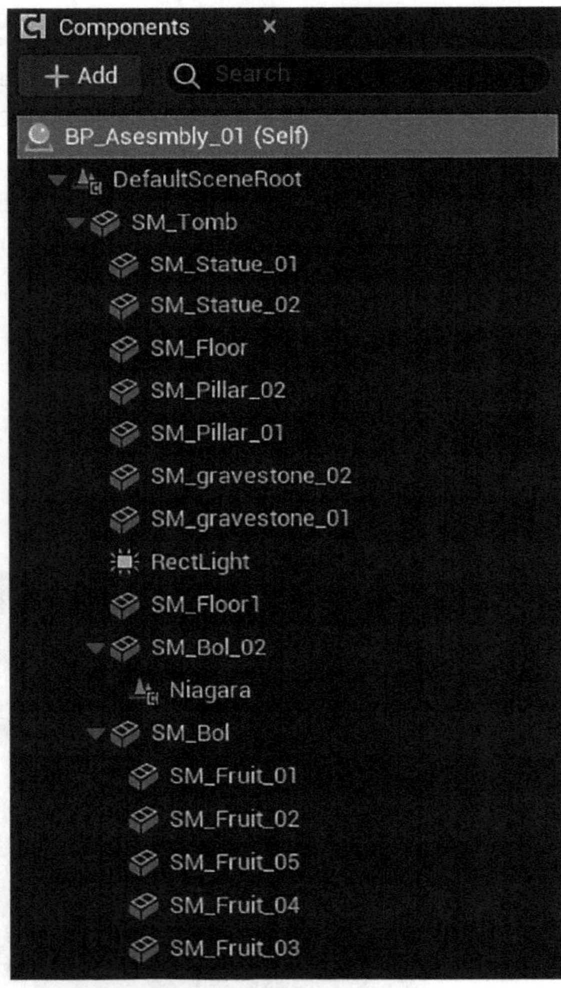

Figure 11.22 – Component hierarchy

Once the elements are created and configured (including **Rect Light**), the result can be seen in the **Blueprints Editor**, as shown in *Figure 11.23*:

Figure 11.23 – Final composition in Blueprint Editor

The final goal of this Blueprint is to provide logic and functionality to the **Rect Light** component, allowing us to later adjust its intensity directly from the editor.

To achieve this, once the desired components are created, we need to access the properties of these components. In order to modify their values, a reference must be created to the **Rect Light** element.

Creating a reference

A **reference** allows us to access the properties of a component to modify its values. Since we aim to adjust the properties of the components in the editor, all the programming will be done in **Construction Script**.

Creating a reference in a Blueprint is quite simple. Here's how to access the light properties for modification:

1. Drag the **Rect Light** component from the **Components** tab into **Graph**. This creates a **Rect Light** node, serving as a reference to the component, as shown in *Figure 11.24*:

Figure 11.24 – Component reference

2. With this reference, we can now access the properties of the **Rect Light** component that was added earlier. To modify the desired property, simply drag a wire from the reference node and search for the specific property. In this case, we will be adjusting the **intensity** and **color** of the light.

   When searching for a node from the reference (with **Context Sensitive** enabled), the options presented are relevant to the type of reference, as shown in *Figure 11.25*. This ensures that only appropriate properties and functions related to **Rect Light** are available for modification.

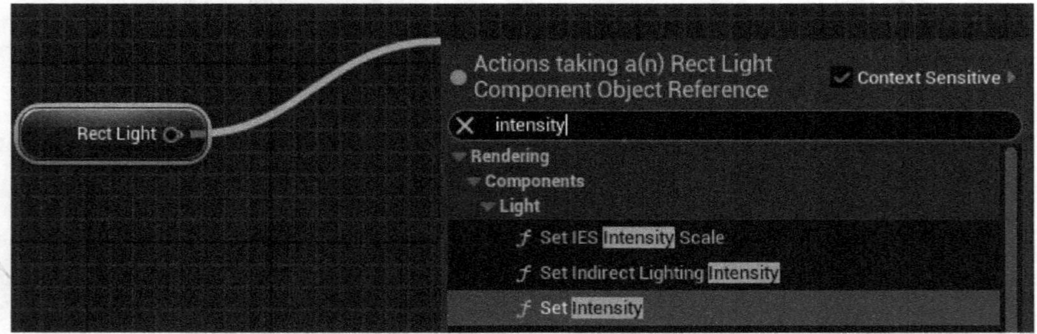

Figure 11.25 – Set intensity node

3. The nodes we need are **Set Intensity** and **Set Light Color**, both of which can be found by dragging from the **Rect Light** reference to configure the desired parameters.

   - For **Set Intensity**, we will need to create a variable to establish the new light intensity. This can be done by *right-clicking* on the node and selecting **Promote to Variable**, which will automatically create a **Float** variable connected to the node. After compiling, an initial intensity value must be set.

- The process for **Set Light Color** is the same, except we will be setting an initial color for the light. In both cases, it's important to compile before saving the Blueprint and to expose the values by enabling **Instance Editable** so they can be adjusted from the editor.

In *Figure 11.26*, we can see the final programming structure of this Blueprint:

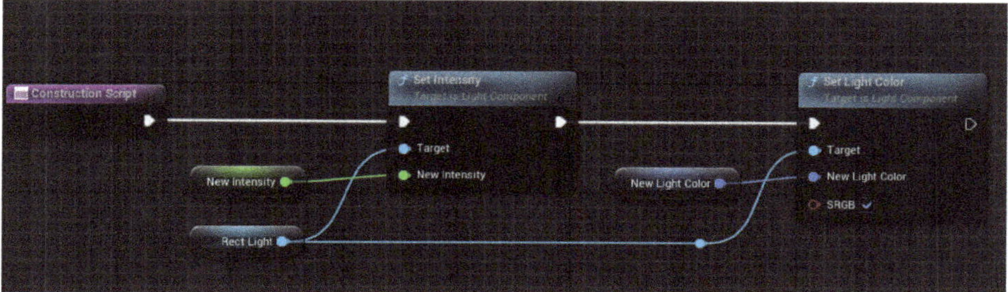

Figure 11.26 – Blueprint final assembly

With this simple programming, we can now modify the light's intensity and color directly in the editor, as shown in *Figure 11.27*:

Figure 11.27 – Blueprint in editor

Similarly, we could create logic to adjust other aspects of different components, such as changing materials, textures, particles, and more. This approach provides flexibility for asset customization within the editor, allowing for a more dynamic and efficient workflow.

In this exercise, we created a Blueprint of the **Actor** class and added various components, including **Static Mesh**, **Niagara Particle System Component**, and **Rect Light**. We configured the **Rect Light** component to allow adjustment of its intensity and color directly from the editor. By creating references and using nodes such as **Set Intensity** and **Set Light Color**, we made these properties editable. This setup enables easy manipulation of light properties and demonstrates how to extend similar functionality to other component aspects such as materials and textures.

Creating a Blueprint from Actors in the level

In some cases, it can be simpler to compose elements directly from the level Viewport. This approach allows for positioning, scaling, and designing the arrangement of Actors in the scene as desired.

Once the composition is finalized, it can be converted into a Blueprint, which is especially useful when certain assets or compositions need to be repeated throughout a project. Doing this manually can become tedious and repetitive, so creating a Blueprint from the Actors already placed in the level allows for easier reuse and centralized control, as well as the ability to program various functions, as shown previously.

Here's how to create a Blueprint from Actors in the level:

1. Select the assets in the level that you want to include in the Blueprint. You can do this either from the Viewport or **Outliner**.
2. Go to the **Blueprints** menu in the toolbar and choose the **Convert Selection to Blueprint Class** option, as shown in *Figure 11.28*:

Figure 11.28 – Convert selection to Blueprint

In the next exercise, we'll learn how to create a Blueprint from the Actors already placed in a level.

Exercise 11.3: Creating a Blueprint from the Editor

Sometimes, it's necessary to repeat certain assets or asset compositions throughout a project. Doing this manually can become tedious and repetitive. A quick and useful solution is to create a Blueprint from the Actors already placed in the level and convert the selection into Blueprints. This allows for controlling and programming various functions as we've seen previously.

Here's how to create a Blueprint from Actors in the level:

1. Select the assets in the level that you want to include in the Blueprint. You can do this either from the Viewport or the **Outliner**.
2. Go to the **Blueprints** menu in the toolbar and choose the option **Convert Selection to Blueprint Class**, as shown in *Figure 11.29*:

Figure 11.29 - Convert selection to Blueprint

Upon selecting **Convert Selection to Blueprint Class**, a window will appear as shown in *Figure 11.30*.

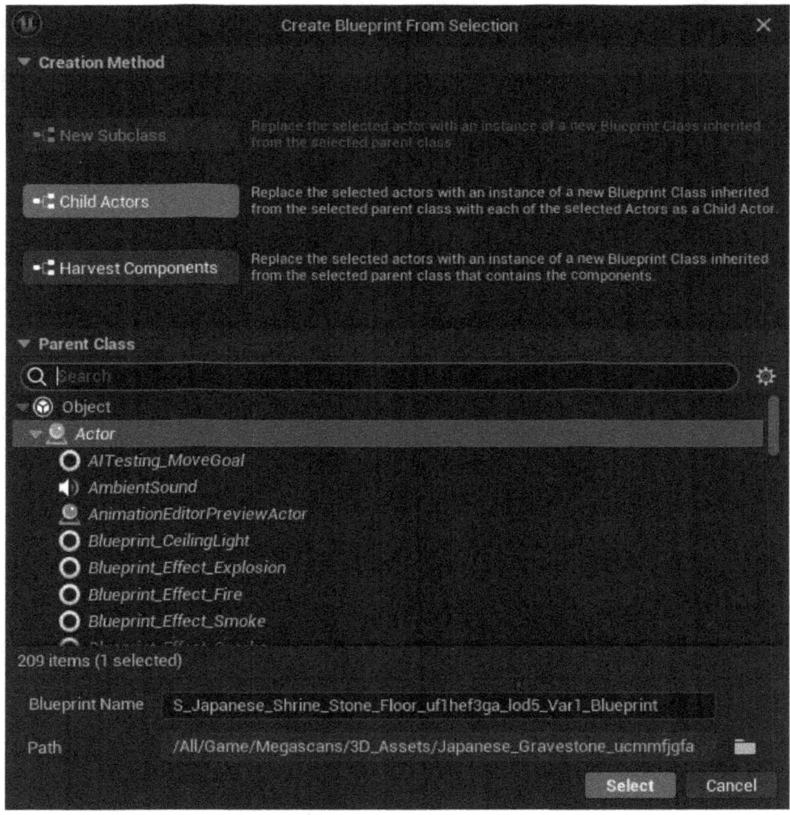

Figure 11.30 - Create Blueprint from Selection

In this window, you can choose how to create the Blueprint components:

- **Child Actors**: Creates a Blueprint with the selected assets as Child Actor Components.
- **Harvest Components**: Creates a Blueprint with the selected assets as components.

3. For this exercise, we'll use the **Harvest Components** method, as it simplifies modification and programming of these components. Name the Blueprint (e.g., `BP_SideWalk`) and select a path to save it within your project's content. This process results in a Blueprint composed of the selected assets in the level, making it easier to manage these elements as a single entity in the **Outliner**, as shown in *Figure 11.31*:

Figure 11.31 - Blueprint in the level

From this point on, you can use the Blueprint as many times as needed to achieve the desired design, allowing for quick repetition and iteration in the level. Once the Blueprint is created, it's easy to instantiate it multiple times in the level. In *Figure 11.32*, you can see the final result of this process:

Figure 11.32 - Final Level Assembly

In this exercise, we learned how to create a Blueprint from existing Actors in a level. By selecting the desired assets and using the **Convert Selection to Blueprint Class** option, we can quickly generate a Blueprint that combines these assets. We used the **Harvest Components** method to include the assets as components within the Blueprint. This approach simplifies managing and iterating on complex compositions, allowing for rapid duplication and adjustment in the level. The final result demonstrates how efficiently we can apply and reuse these Blueprints in our projects.

With the Blueprint workflows complete, let's turn our attention to maintaining and improving them through effective debugging and optimization practices.

Debugging and optimizing Blueprints

Debugging and optimization ensure that your logic runs efficiently and predictably across different scenarios. Small habits adopted early will save hours later in troubleshooting and performance tuning.

Let's have a look at some best practices:

- **Print String for flow checks**: Drop `Print String` at key branches to confirm execution order and parameter values during tests.
- **Breakpoints and stepping**: *Right-click* an execution pin and select **Add Breakpoint**. Play in the editor and step through to inspect values at runtime.

- **Watch values:** *Right-click* a data pin and select **Watch this Value** to see live updates while your graph runs.
- **Construction Script discipline**: Keep heavy loops out of **Construction Script**. Use cached results and expose only the **Instance Editable** variables you truly need to tweak in the **Details** panel. (You already did this in *Exercise 11.2: Creating Blueprints with components*, when exposing light controls.)

Next steps and Blueprint troubleshooting

Now, let's move on to practical next steps and additional learning resources to continue improving your Blueprint workflow.

- **Blueprint essential concepts (Epic):** This official documentation offers a concise path if you're new to visual scripting, ideally as a primer or refresher alongside this chapter's exercises: `https://dev.epicgames.com/community/learning/courses/QGD/unreal-engine-blueprint-essential-concepts/P7L/unreal-engine-introduction-to-blueprint-essential-concepts`.
- **Sample projects**: Explore Epic sample projects (for example, Lyra: `https://dev.epicgames.com/documentation/en-us/unreal-engine/lyra-sample-game-in-unreal-engine`) to see production-scale Blueprint patterns for input, UI, and gameplay scaffolding (great for naming and folder conventions).

Here are some good practices you can adopt while working with Blueprints:

- **Consistent naming**: Use `bIs`... for Booleans, `Max`... for limits, `Out`... for output pins
- **Keep graphs readable:** Use comment boxes, **Reroute** nodes, and one responsibility per function
- **Create a Function Library**: Start a Function Library for utilities you reuse across Blueprints

Troubleshooting Blueprint issues

Before wrapping up, here are answers to a few common issues you might encounter while working with Blueprints:

- *I can't find a node in the search.*
    - Enable **Context Sensitive** and drag from a compatible pin first; the palette then filters valid actions for that type.

- *My* **Construction Script** *doesn't affect gameplay.*
    - The **Construction Script** runs in the editor. Move runtime behavior to **Event Graph**, using **BeginPlay**, **Tick**, or custom events.
- *My placed instances don't show up.*
    - Check **Collision** settings on the target mesh, the area bounds math (XY plane versus Z), and confirm your loop's `Last Index ≥ First Index` (see the *Exercise 11.1* graph shown in *Figure 11.17*).

With these debugging and workflow practices in place, you now have a solid foundation for building, testing, and optimizing Blueprints efficiently.

Summary

In this chapter, we covered essential concepts and practical applications of Blueprints in UE5. We began with a basic understanding of Blueprint nodes, connections, and execution flow, including variables, events, functions, and macros. We then explored different Blueprint classes, such as Level Blueprint, Blueprint Class, Data-Only Blueprint, Blueprint Interface, Blueprint Macro Library, and Blueprint Utilities, learning how to create and utilize each for various purposes.

Through practical exercises, we developed skills in creating Blueprints, including the following:

- **Creating a Blueprint Class**: We learned how to create and configure Blueprints, set variables, and use loops to distribute Static Meshes randomly in a scene.
- **Creating Blueprints with components**: We focused on adding and managing different components such as **Static Mesh**, **Niagara Particle System Component**, and **Rect Light**, learning how to modify component properties using references and expose them for editing.
- **Creating Blueprints from the Editor**: We demonstrated how to convert existing level Actors into Blueprints, enabling easier management and replication of assets within the level.

In the next chapter, we'll explore optimization and scene testing.

UNLOCK NOW

12

Optimizing and Testing Your Scene

The creation of environments in Unreal Engine is primarily an artistic process. With planning and development, we can build extensive and realistic scenarios as required by our main objective. While artistry forms the foundation, technical understanding is just as important.

Throughout the development of each chapter, we have briefly provided tips and recommendations about specific aspects of the tools in use. Having explored the artistic side of world-building in earlier chapters, it's time to turn our attention to the technical layer that keeps those worlds running smoothly.

In this chapter, we will discuss optimization as a global concept that should always be present and can help us solve performance issues that arise in our projects. We will also address how to add a character to our environment to traverse the scene and evaluate it. In open world environments, the sheer scale, density, and long viewing distances amplify every performance cost: more objects in view, longer streaming paths, and heavier lighting and post-processing loads. Treat optimization as a continuous design constraint rather than a late-stage patch.

When we talk about real-time rendering, it is important to understand that compromises must be made during development to offset potential performance losses as assets are added to the project. These include polygon counts in Static Meshes, texture resolution, collision handling, and lighting complexity. Our goal should be to find a balance between the aspects of project development. The fundamental aspects are **performance**, **quality**, and **functionality**. In this kind of *Vitruvian Triangle*, there will always be trade-offs; we will always sacrifice one aspect to gain another.

Key topics that we will cover in this chapter include the following:

- Things to consider before starting a project
- Understanding real-time rendering
- Understanding profiling
- Best practices

Technical requirements

To continue the development of this chapter, you'll need a PC with **Unreal Engine 5.5** (or a later version) installed that meets the recommended requirements by Epic Games: `https://dev.epicgames.com/documentation/en-us/unreal-engine/hardware-and-software-specifications-for-unreal-engine`. Be sure to ensure you also have an active internet connection.

Things to consider before starting a project

Before starting a project, it's important to evaluate a few technical factors that will influence performance and stability. Consider the following points:

- Before starting a project, it is advisable to establish minimum requirements to ensure the project will be functional. Define the necessary framerate for the project to run correctly, normally expressed in FPS.
- Define the workflow to achieve that framerate, that is, which engine features and technologies we need to consider to maintain it, such as ray tracing, Lumen, or texel density.
- Remember that every feature or asset added to the project has a performance cost, so it is essential to ensure that whatever is added contributes meaningfully to the project.
- The target platform (Windows, Android, iOS, or game console) for which the project is intended is another very important factor to consider from the beginning, as it directly affects both the construction of the project and its optimization.
- Yet another important factor when optimizing a scene is the hardware on which it will run. It is essential to be aware of the minimum specifications required, since optimization and testing must be carried out based on those constraints. For this reason, the optimization must always go hand in hand with testing to ensure performance remains stable.

Before diving into the rendering process, it is necessary to review some key concepts; let's understand them in the next section.

Understanding real-time rendering

Unreal Engine is a **real-time rendering** engine, which means it must perform a large number of calculations on every frame to draw the necessary pixels on screen. These calculations are executed by both the CPU and GPU, each handling different parts of the rendering process in synchronization.

There are two rendering methods in Unreal:

- **Deferred rendering**: Renders material attributes into the **GBuffer** first and applies lighting in subsequent passes. It scales well with many dynamic lights and complex Materials, which is why it's the default for most content in this book.
- **Forward rendering**: Lights are evaluated during object rendering. It can offer lower overdraw and **Multisample Anti-Aliasing (MSAA)** support, making it attractive for certain stylized, VR, or mobile scenarios with limited light counts.

In this chapter, we will focus on *deferred rendering*, as it is the most widely used and performs best for most types of content.

Understanding how meshes are drawn: vertices, triangles, and pixels

Every 3D object in your scene is ultimately made of **triangles**. Each triangle is defined by three points in space called vertices. A **vertex** stores information such as position, normal direction, UV coordinates, and sometimes color or other per-vertex data.

When you see a **high-poly** mesh, what you are really seeing is "a mesh with a very high number of triangles," which also means a very high number of vertices. All those triangles stitched together form the visible surface of the asset.

In real-time rendering, the GPU receives those vertices, transforms them into screen space (what the camera sees), and then fills in, or **rasterizes**, the interior of each triangle into pixels. This is what ultimately becomes the image on your screen.

Why does this matter for performance?

- The CPU is responsible for preparing and submitting what needs to be drawn, that is, which objects are active, where they are, and whether they should be rendered this frame
- The GPU is responsible for taking the visible objects, processing their triangles, shading their pixels, and compositing the final frame

If a mesh has millions of triangles, the GPU has to process and shade them. Systems such as Nanite help by streaming and reducing triangle density intelligently, but the underlying cost is still tied to *how many triangles/pixels need to be drawn right now.*

Here's a handy mental model to keep in mind:

1. Vertices define triangles.
2. Triangles define the mesh.
3. The GPU shades the visible pixels of those triangles.

Understanding this chain makes it easier to interpret profiling data later in the chapter, especially when we talk about GPU time, triangle cost, and shadow cost.

In the next section, we will explain in simplified terms how Unreal's rendering process works and how to identify performance bottlenecks within each stage.

Diving into the rendering process in Unreal Engine

Before beginning optimization, it is extremely useful to understand how Unreal's rendering process works. This allows us to identify where optimizations should be applied to improve performance.

A lack of optimization can be as detrimental as over-optimization; therefore, knowing exactly where to optimize is essential for achieving the best possible balance between visual quality and performance.

We can divide the rendering process into three threads, which reflect calculations performed by both the CPU and the GPU:

- **CPU**: This is responsible for simulation and logic (animations, transforms, physics, AI, spawning, and collisions)
- **Draw (CPU)**: This is the command submission and visibility/occlusion work that prepares what the GPU will render
- **GPU**: This executes the rendering: depth pre-pass, lighting, post-processing, and composition

We'll explore these stages in detail in the *Exploring the rendering workflow* section.

To analyze how much time each stage consumes, Unreal provides real-time statistics. These help us measure the CPU (**Game**), **Draw**, and GPU threads and quickly spot bottlenecks before we dive deeper into the workflow.

You can view these performance statistics directly in the editor using several statistics commands. The most common are the following:

- `stat unit`
- `stat fps`

One of the simplest ways to activate stats in Unreal Engine is from the drop-down menu in the top-right corner of the Viewport (**eye** icon | **Viewport Stats** | **COMMON STATS**), as shown in *Figure 12.1*:

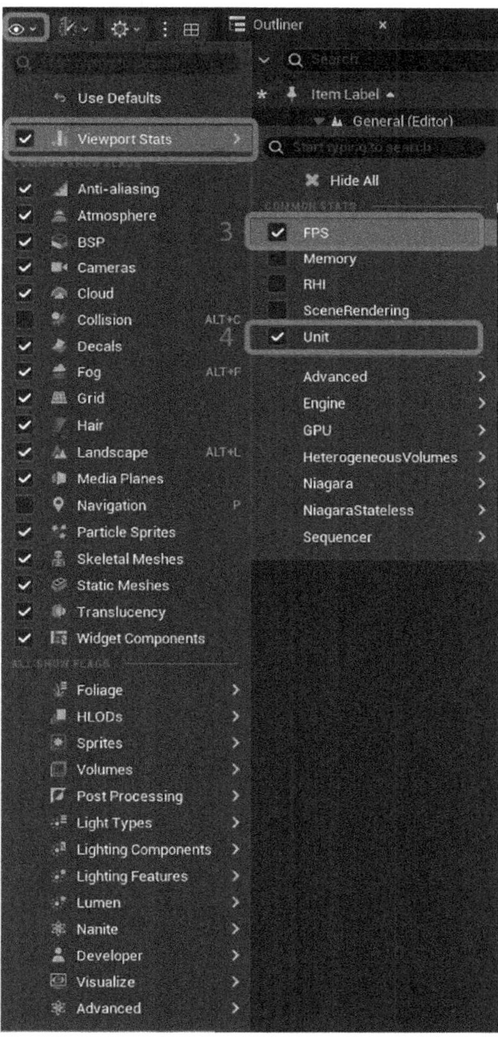

Figure 12.1 – Select stats

A summary of the selected stats should appear in the Viewport in the top-right corner, as shown in *Figure 12.2*:

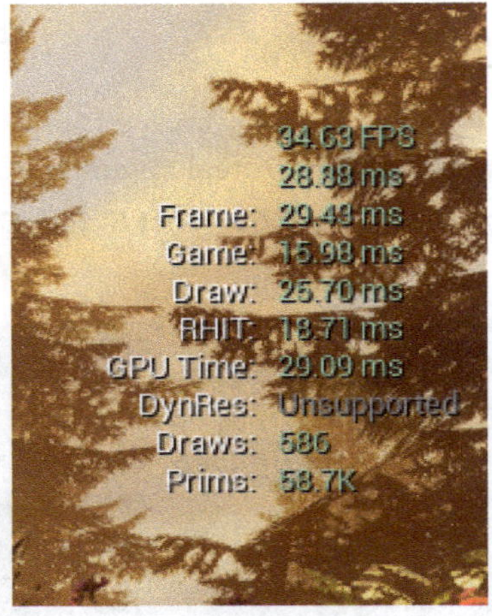

Figure 12.2 – Detail stats

We can also enable the stats through the following console commands, using the cvars (see *Figure 12.3*):

- `stat unit` shows per-thread times (ms) for CPU, Draw, and GPU, plus the total frame time, color-coded from *green* to *red* for quick triage.
- `stat fps` shows the current frames per second and frame time; use it to validate that your ms breakdown aligns with the observed FPS.

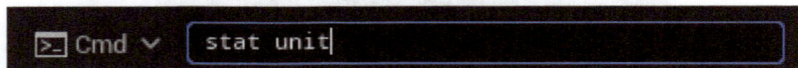

Figure 12.3 – Command console

With real-time timings visible, let's step through the rendering workflow to understand what each thread is doing and where optimizations have the biggest impact.

Exploring the rendering workflow

Now that we can see the calculation times of our system, let us go back to understanding the rendering process in Unreal Engine. The process consists of three stages (or *frames*), as illustrated in *Figure 12.4*:

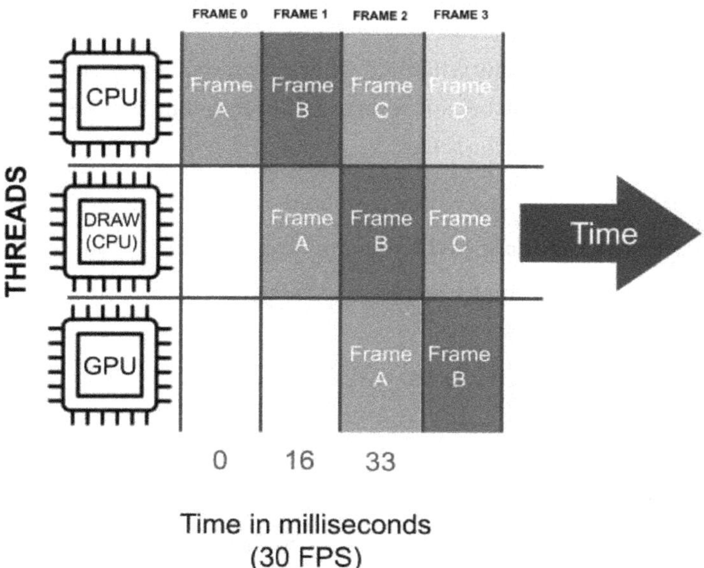

Figure 12.4 – Render workflow

In the diagram shown in *Figure 12.4*, we can see the following threads:

- **CPU**
- **DRAW (CPU)**
- **GPU**

These three threads are synchronized but do not start at the same time. Each is responsible for specific calculations so that by the end of the process, the corresponding frame is drawn.

Each stage of the process takes a certain amount of time (measured in milliseconds, or ms), which defines the framerate (in FPS) at which the scene is rendered.

Unreal Engine must render in real time all the information required to draw the number of pixels defined by the screen resolution. The higher the resolution, the more pixels need to be drawn in the same time. This is why rendering at high resolutions requires significant CPU and GPU power.

For example, at 30 FPS, rendering a single frame would take 33 ms. This is known as **latency**, that is, the time it takes to render one frame.

Let's now break down each thread of the rendering process to understand these in more detail.

Frame 0

Before rendering, Unreal must know what and where to render. Since this is real time, elements can constantly change position, so their location must be recalculated in every frame. This requires a series of logical calculations for the scene:

- **Animations**: They determine where animated objects will move
- **Object positions**: They define where each object is located in the scene
- **Physics**: They identify which objects are affected by physics and calculate the types of physics that apply to them
- **AI**: They calculate the behavior of AI to determine where AI-driven Actors will go or what they will do
- **Spawn, destroy, hide, unhide**: The engine must determine which objects will be spawned, destroyed, hidden, or unhidden
- **Collisions**: These checks identify how many collisions exist and the volume they occupy

All of these calculations must be processed by the CPU before rendering begins. The result is a complete set of transformations for all objects in the scene, frame by frame.

In the **Stat Unit**, these calculations are represented by the value of the **Game** thread, as shown in *Figure 12.5*:

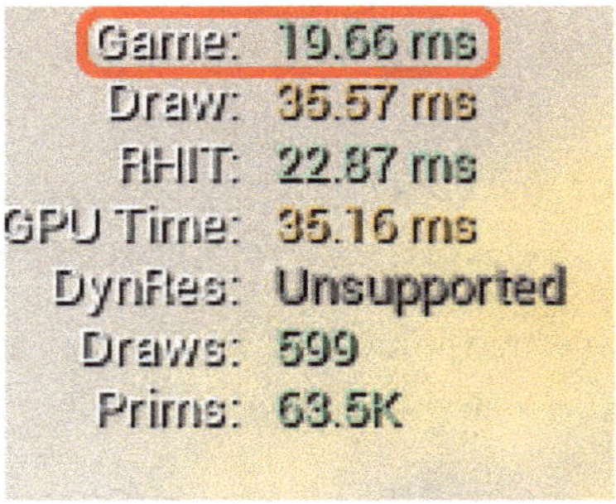

Figure 12.5 – Game thread

The values in the **Stat Unit** are expressed in milliseconds, which is a much more reliable measurement for interpreting performance changes.

Thanks to the color coding of the values, we can quickly identify whether they are acceptable or not, ranging from *green* to *red*.

Hence, with all these calculations, we are able to understand the behavior of the Actors in the scene.

Remember that a common source of performance issues comes from programming tasks and Skeletal Meshes with their animations. These operations consume significant CPU resources directly when building the scene. Developers should pay close attention to the **Game** thread, as spikes here are often the first sign of performance problems.

Frame 1

At this stage, we now have the transformations of the objects, but not all of them need to be rendered. We need to determine which objects should actually be rendered: those that will be visible in the current frame.

This process occurs partly between the CPU and GPU, though the CPU carries the heavier load of calculations.

To achieve this, Unreal begins an **occlusion process**, which creates a list of all visible objects. This check is performed at the object level, not per triangle, so it reduces GPU overdraw by skipping fully hidden Actors. However, each Actor still incurs a CPU/**Draw** thread visibility test, meaning thousands of tiny objects can shift cost to the **Draw** thread.

Since this process is complex, Unreal uses four different systems to generate the list of visible objects (**distance culling**, **frustum culling**, **precomputed visibility**, and **occlusion culling**). This is one of the mixed solutions that works very well with the deferred renderer. Each system is effective at handling specific tasks, and they are executed in order of *least* to *most* performance cost.

Let's look at each of these systems in order, starting with distance culling, the most straightforward and cost-effective approach.

Distance culling

Objects beyond a certain distance from the camera are not rendered. Each Actor has a parameter that defines the minimum draw distance (**Min Draw Distance**), which can be found in the Actor's **Details** panel, under the **LOD** section, as shown in *Figure 12.6*:

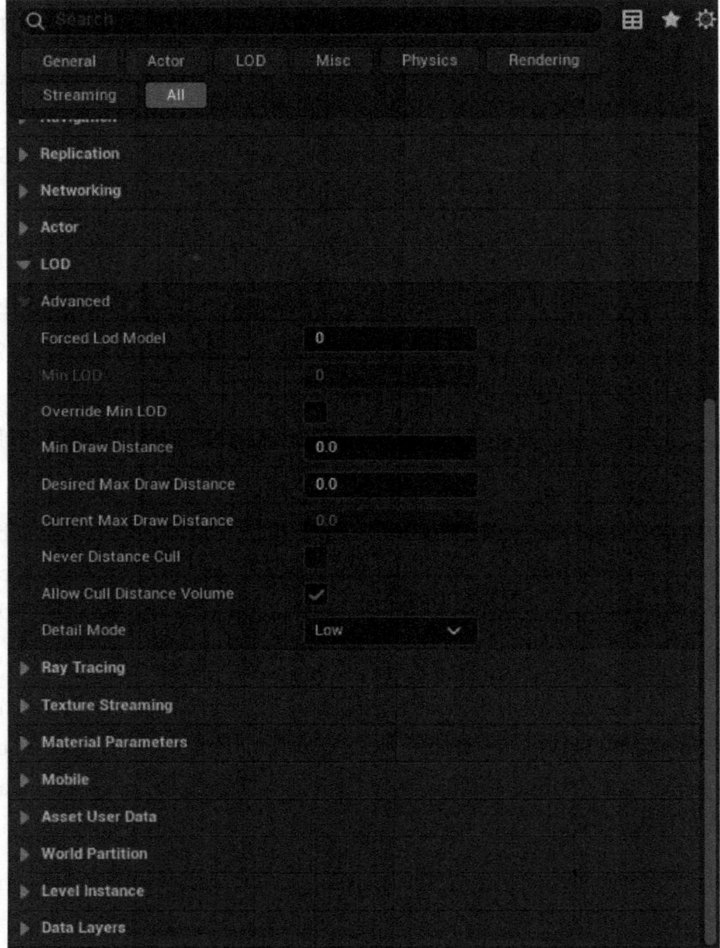

Figure 12.6 – Min Draw Distance

Note

The **Desired Max Draw Distance** parameter allows us to control the distance at which an Actor will stop being rendered.

Frustum culling

The frustum is a *truncated pyramid* (see *Figure 12.7*) that represents the camera's field of view. When an object enters this field of view, it is fully rendered. This culling is applied per object, not per triangle.

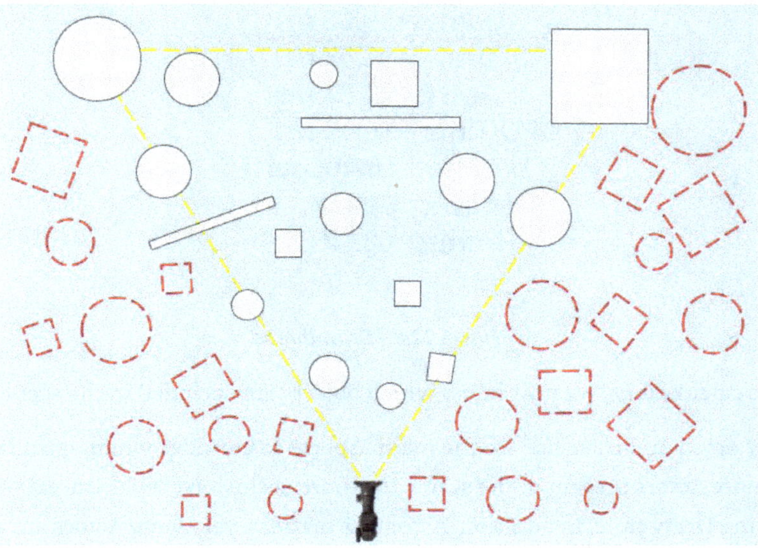

Figure 12.7 – Frustum camera

Note

All Actors outside the frustum that do not intersect with it will not be calculated or rendered in the frame.

Precomputed visibility

This method divides the scene into a grid, where each cell stores information about which objects are visible from that position. These cells are generated during the lighting build process.

Occlusion culling

This method checks the visibility of each object from the camera's point of view. It is the most expensive process and depends on the Actor's bounding volume. From the camera's position, Unreal must check each object in the scene to determine whether it is visible, partially visible, or completely hidden behind another Actor or Static Mesh.

By running all these processes for each frame, Unreal determines which objects are occluding others, ensuring that only the necessary pixels are rendered.

In the **Draw** thread, we can see the time required to calculate scene occlusion, as shown in *Figure 12.8*:

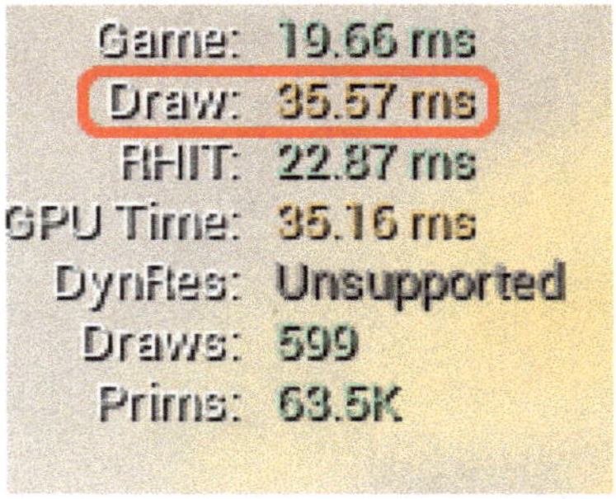

Figure 12.8 – Draw thread

With all these calculations, we now know which objects are occluded in the scene.

The *number of Actors* and their *size* are the main aspects to consider when optimizing the **Draw** thread. The more Actors present in the scene, the more occlusion checks Unreal will need to perform, increasing **Draw** time. In addition, Actor size matters: very large Actors are almost always rendered, while smaller ones are more costly to process due to the higher number of occlusion calculations required.

Frame 2

At this stage, we already know where the objects are and which ones are visible. Now begins the most complex step: rendering those objects.

However, before starting the rendering itself, there is an additional problem to solve. We need a **pre-pass**, because even though we know which objects to render and where they are, we do not yet know the order in which they should be rendered—specifically, which objects are closer to the camera than others.

The issue arises because Unreal renders objects one by one. If we render them without knowing their distance from the camera, we will repeatedly generate pixels in the same location, overwriting them with pixels that belong to only one object (due to occlusion between elements). This wastes performance.

To avoid this, a **depth pass** is created before rendering, which establishes the order of objects relative to the camera. This ensures that pixels belonging to objects hidden by others are masked and not rendered unnecessarily.

In essence, this process masks out the pixels that will not be visible, so only visible pixels are rendered. Furthermore, this is the stage where all the rendering passes are generated, which are then composited together to form the final image of the frame.

In the **GPU Time** thread, we can see the time it takes to draw the necessary pixels for the scene, as shown in *Figure 12.9*:

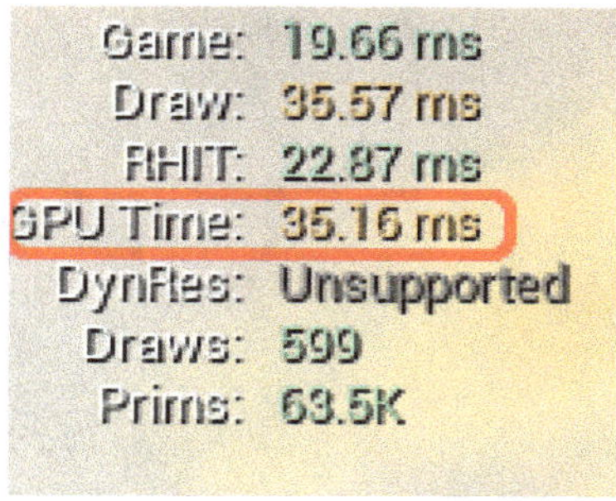

Figure 12.9 – GPU Time thread

When GPU thread times spike, this is often caused by high-resolution textures in materials as well as the resolution at which the scene is being rendered. These two aspects are key factors in optimizing the scene.

Post-processing effects applied to the render are another major contributor to GPU time, along with lighting and shadow calculations.

In open world environments, it is important to keep in mind that rendering large areas filled with objects requires the GPU to perform heavy calculations, consuming significant milliseconds per frame. For this reason, optimization in this thread is especially critical.

Draw calls

A **draw call** is a group of polygons that share the same properties—in other words, one object. Once this stage begins, the GPU starts rendering. The rendering process is carried out draw call by draw call.

Objects are rendered one by one into the GBuffer, which then combines the different images or render passes to produce the final frame.

To visualize the GBuffer passes, go to **View Mode** in the top-right corner of the Viewport, then select **Buffer Visualization** | **Overview**, as shown in *Figure 12.10*:

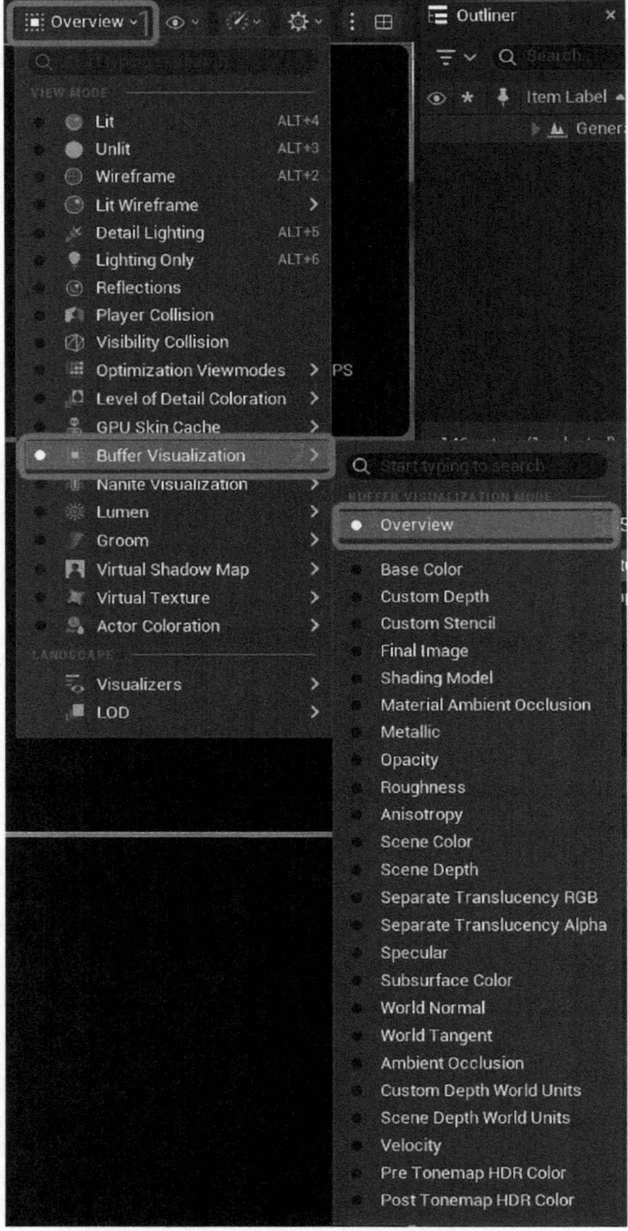

Figure 12.10 – Buffer Visualization menu

When enabled, this will display a new version of the Viewport showing the buffers separated from the final rendered image of the scene at that moment, updating in real time, as shown in *Figure 12.11*:

Figure 12.11 - Passes in the GBuffer and image composed

Draw calls have a significant impact on performance. In fact, now, the *number of draw calls* has a greater impact than the *number of triangles*. Reducing draw calls does not necessarily mean reducing scene quality. There are ways to optimize draw calls while still maintaining visual fidelity:

- Merge nearby Actors (**Tools** | **Merge Actors**) and, when safe, merge Materials to cut submission overhead
- Prefer **Instanced Static Meshes/Hierarchical Instanced Static Mesh** (**ISMs/HISM**) for repeated props instead of many unique Actors
- Use Material atlases and channel packing (R/G/B/A) to consolidate textures
- Cull small set dressing aggressively and rely on HLOD or World Partition proxies for distant clusters

The number of draw calls can be monitored in the **Stat Unit**, as shown in *Figure 12.12*:

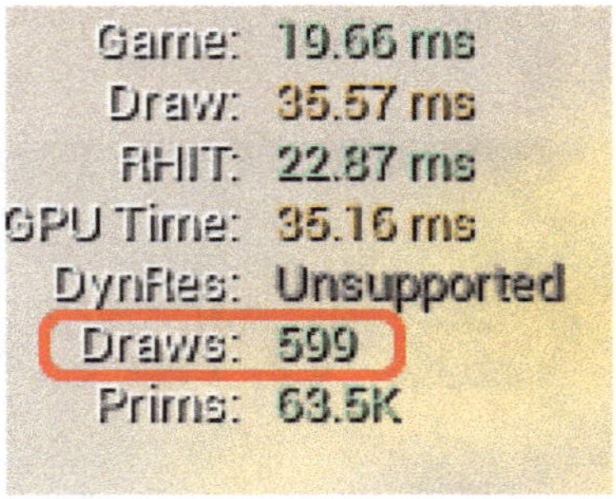

Figure 12.12 – Draw calls counter

The number of draw calls generated by an Actor is related to its materials, geometry, and lighting.

Note

Nanite geometries do not count as draw calls, but their *materials* do. This is an important detail to keep in mind.

With Unreal Engine's stats on screen and a clear grasp of the **Game** thread and draw calls, it's time to interpret the numbers and run our first profiling pass.

Understanding profiling

Profiling consists of measuring the time it takes the engine to complete a task, function, or group of functions. Once we know which thread is losing performance, it is time to investigate which parts of the scene are causing the times to spike and how we can solve these issues.

To do this, we begin profiling using the tools that Unreal provides to help identify what are known as *bottlenecks*.

Bottlenecks occur when the flow of information between the CPU and GPU is not continuous or homogeneous, which can cause slowdowns in data input and output. To detect these bottlenecks, different tools can be used. We have already learned how to use the **Stat Unit** to identify where performance is being lost.

Now we will explore other tools, such as **visualization modes**, which allow us to analyze how much it costs the engine to render different elements of the scene and, in turn, help us identify where optimization should begin.

Within the visualization modes, we have several types designed to identify performance issues in specific aspects of the scene, such as Materials and lighting.

Under **View Modes**, Unreal provides a suite of tools for review and diagnosis. *Figure 12.13* shows how to access **Optimization Viewmodes**:

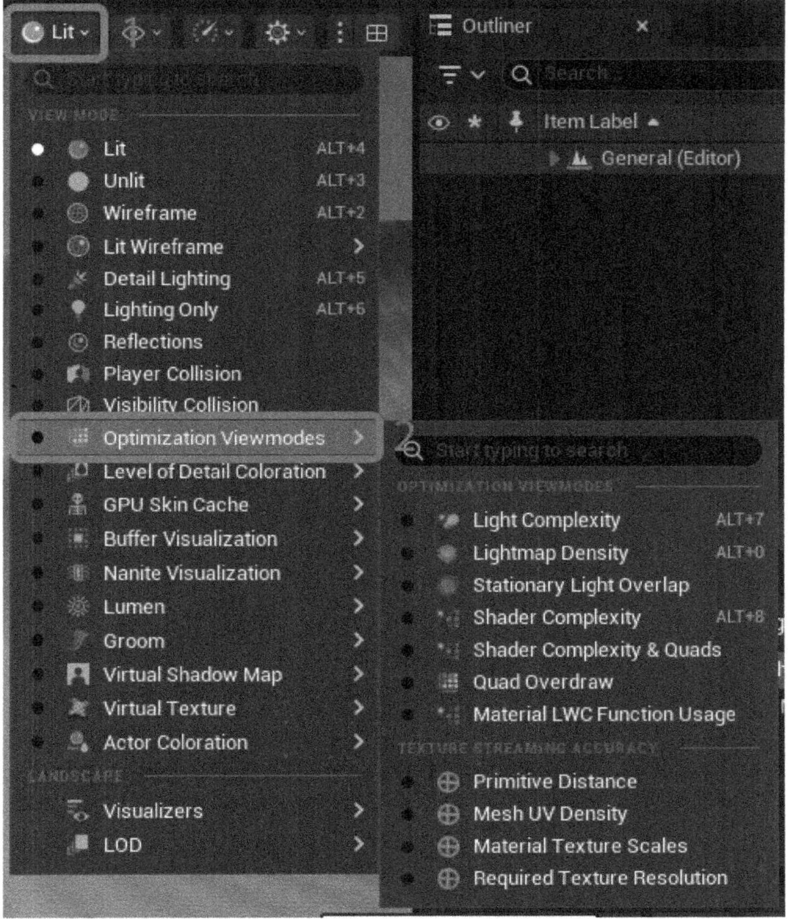

Figure 12.13 – View Modes

Among the options included in **Optimization Viewmodes**, we'll have a look at some of the most useful ones:

- **Light Complexity**: This mode allows us to visualize the number of dynamic lights in the scene and the overlap of their influence radii, which leads to increased complexity in real-time lighting calculations. The warmer the color, the more overlapping lights are present.

Figure 12.14 – Light Complexity mode

- **Shader Complexity**: This mode allows us to see the processing cost of each shader. The more *red* or *white* an area appears, the more instructions that shader is processing. It is best to avoid large *white* or *red* areas.

Figure 12.15 – Shader Complexity mode

In our case, using these modes allowed us to identify where the highest number of calculations related to lighting and Materials were occurring within this part of the project.

There are also more advanced tools available to identify where high computational costs may be taking place within the scene. These tools can be divided into two categories: **GPU Visualizer** and **Statistics**, which collect information from a captured frame and provide a detailed breakdown of how the frame was rendered.

Working with the GPU Visualizer

The GPU Visualizer captures information from a frame on the GPU to identify the processes taking place during that frame and the time each consumes.

Since it provides information on what is being rendered by the engine, the best way to obtain realistic data is to capture it at the final resolution. To do this, do the following:

1. Go to **Editor Preferences** | **Level Editor** | **Play** | **Game Viewport Settings**.
2. In **New Viewport Resolution**, set the resolution you want. This way, the capture will be made at the selected resolution.

To open the GPU Visualizer, there are two methods. You can do either of the following:

- Press *Ctrl* + *Shift* + ,
- Type `profileGPU` in the console

When the capture completes correctly, you'll see the **GPU Visualizer** window, illustrated in *Figure 12.16*:

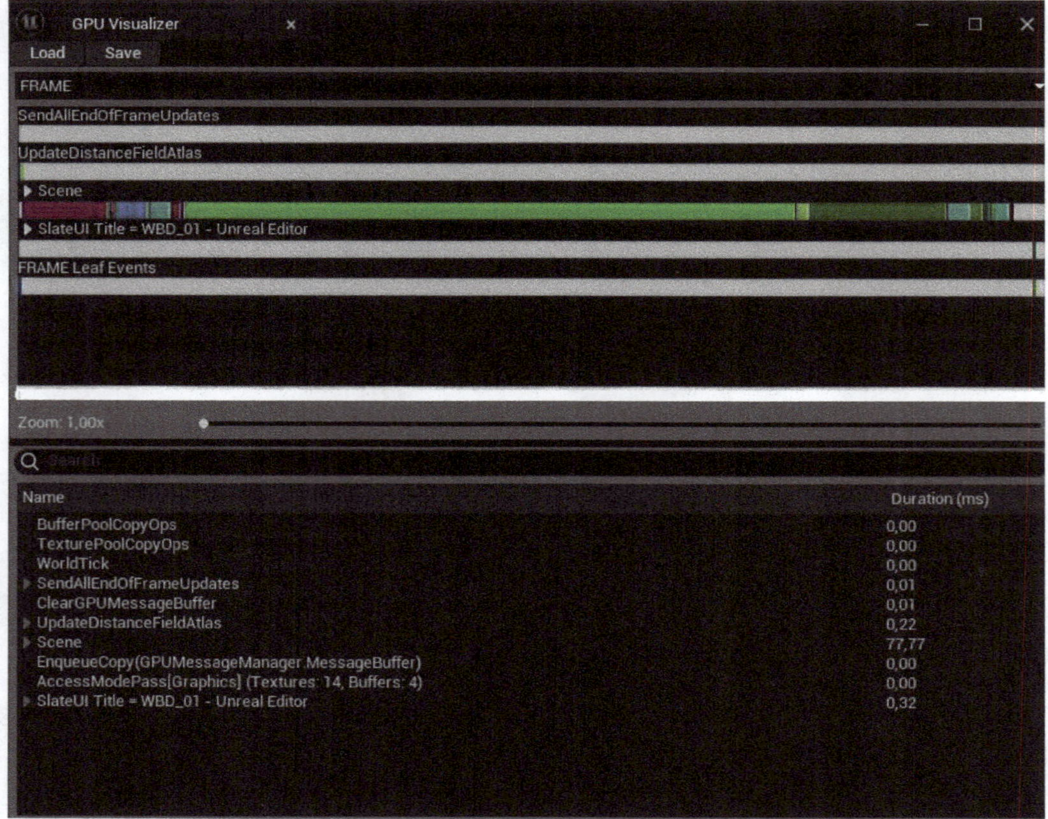

Figure 12.16 – GPU Visualizer

Inside the GPU Visualizer, two sections provide similar information but displayed in different ways.

At the top, there is a *visual representation with bars*, where each bar represents a process and the proportion of time it takes within the frame calculation:

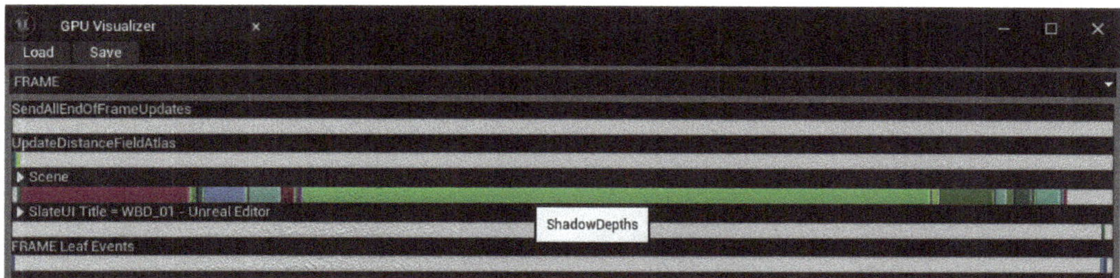

Figure 12.17 – GPU Visualizer detail

In the example shown in *Figure 12.18*, we can see that shadows take up the largest proportion of the frame's processing time, at **15.08** ms:

Name	Duration (ms)
Scene	25,96
ShadowDepths	15,08
RenderVirtualShadowMaps(Nanite)	14,95
Nanite::DrawGeometry	14,93
MainPass	14,38
SW Rasterize	8,78
HW Rasterize	4,25
PersistentCull	0,92
InstanceCullVSM	0,32
RasterBinCount	0,05
RasterBinScatter	0,04
RasterBinReserve	0,00
CalculateSafeRasterizerArgs	0,00
ClearBuffer(Nanite.RangeAllocatorBuffer Size=4bytes)	0,00
PostPass	0,50
BuildPreviousOccluderHZB(VSM)	0,02
CompactViewsVSM	0,01
InitArgs	0,00
ClearBuffer(Shadow.Virtual.CompactedViewsAllocation Size=8bytes)	0,00
NaniteFeedbackStatus	0,00
BuildHZBPerPage	0,00
BuildHZBPerPageTop	0,00

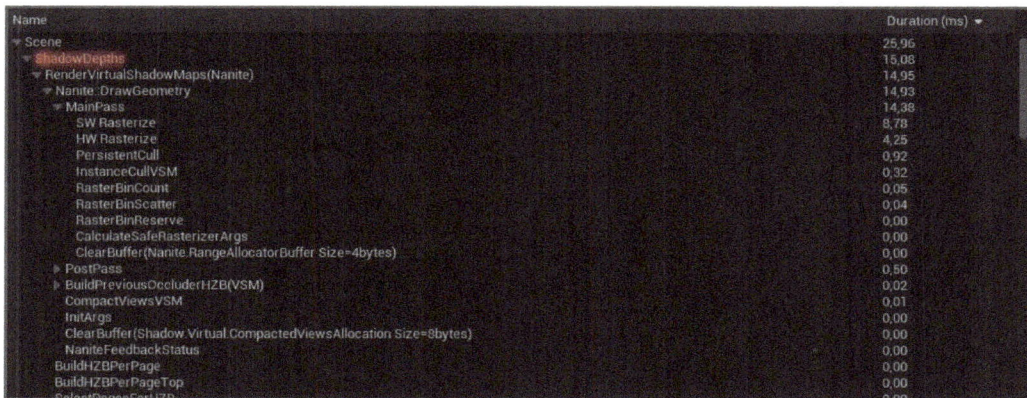

Figure 12.18 – GPU Visualizer detail

Note

UI numbers may appear with comma separators depending on the OS locale.

Here, we see that virtual shadows from Nanite meshes consume **14.95** ms of the total frame. With this information, we know that we need to start optimizing this part of the scene. In this case, the issue comes from the shadows generated by the landscape vegetation, as shown in *Figure 12.19* for your reference:

Figure 12.19 – Landscape detail

Although they are Nanite meshes, the large number of them generates a considerable number of shadows.

To minimize this cost, several strategies can be applied:

- **Reducing the number of plants**: In this case, they are foliage-painted/material-driven spawning, so it is necessary to adjust density in the corresponding Foliage Actor
- **Scaling up meshes slightly**: This way, they cover more space, reducing the total number needed
- **Caching shadows**: This is so that they are not recalculated constantly, for example, by baking the lighting and setting it to static

It is important to keep in mind that although Nanite allows us to work with very high poly meshes, it can introduce other performance issues, such as shadow calculations or material count.

When using Nanite meshes, it is recommended to enable **Virtual Shadow Maps** as the shadow mapping method to make shadow calculations more efficient.

To collect actionable performance data on scene assets, we'll begin with Unreal's **Statistics** tool, covered in the next section.

Auditing with Statistics and Resource Usage

To open **Statistics**, go to **Tools** | **Audit** | **Statistics**, which will display a window as shown in *Figure 12.20*:

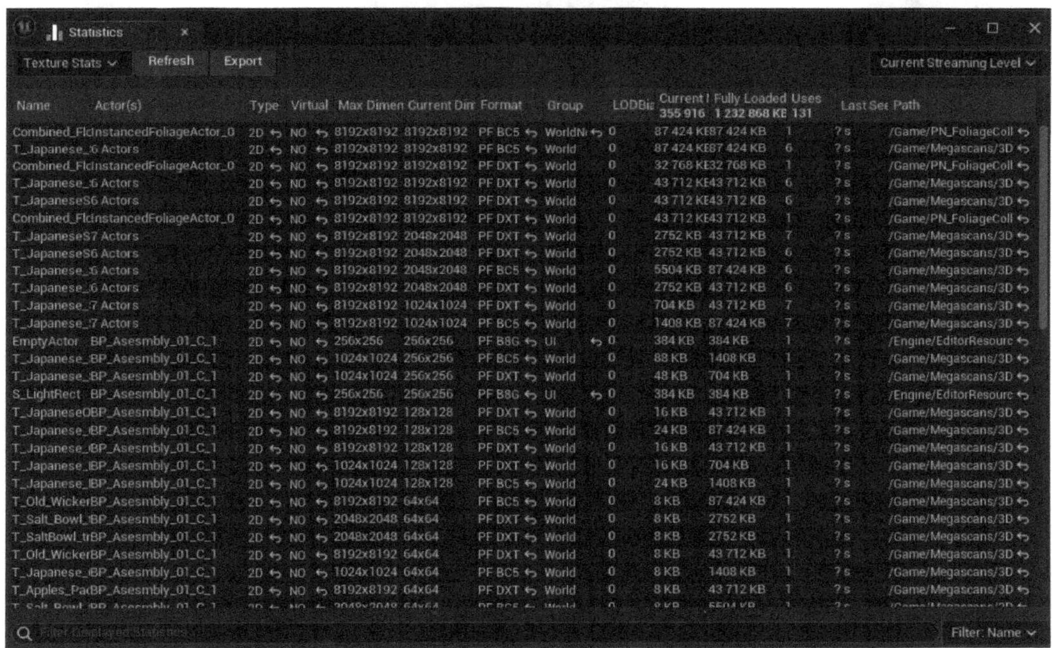

Figure 12.20 – Statistics tool

The **Statistics** window presents a sortable table of level assets grouped by type (Static Meshes, Skeletal Meshes, materials, textures, etc.). Each group lists per-asset metrics, such as triangles/vertices, material slots, LOD count, approximate resource size (memory), and instance count at the current level. You can filter, search, and sort columns to surface outliers quickly.

Using Resource Usage

This option provides a list of the assets used in the project, organized by categories and expressed as the total number of elements and their resource consumption.

To open **Resource Usage**, go to **Tools** | **Audit** | **Resource Usage**, which will display the following window:

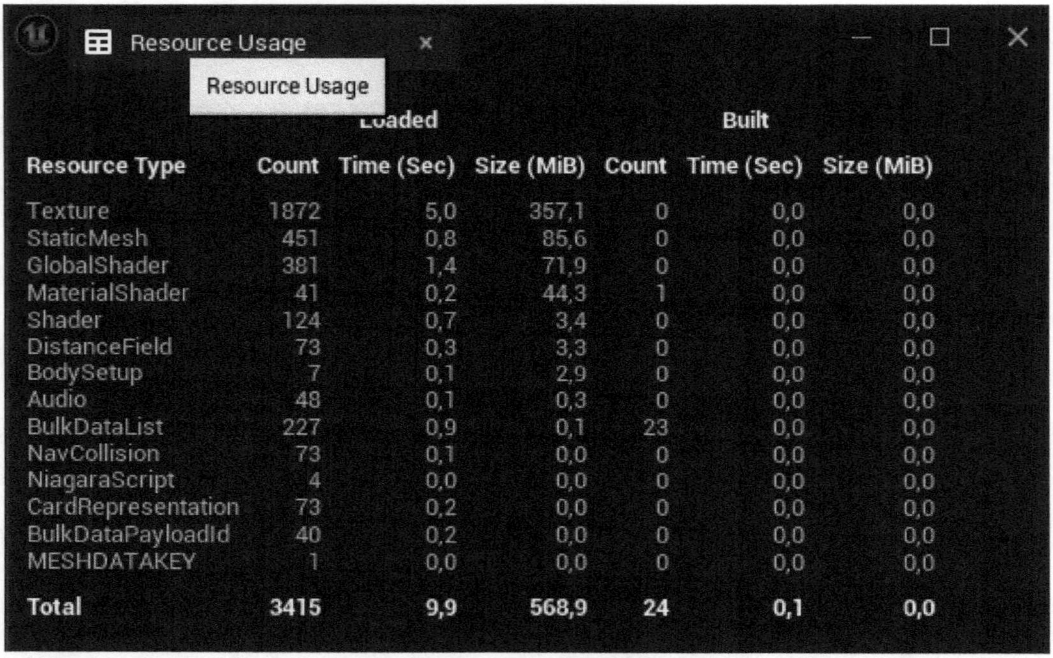

Resource Usage ×

Resource Usage

	Loaded			Built		
Resource Type	**Count**	**Time (Sec)**	**Size (MiB)**	**Count**	**Time (Sec)**	**Size (MiB)**
Texture	1872	5,0	357,1	0	0,0	0,0
StaticMesh	451	0,8	85,6	0	0,0	0,0
GlobalShader	381	1,4	71,9	0	0,0	0,0
MaterialShader	41	0,2	44,3	1	0,0	0,0
Shader	124	0,7	3,4	0	0,0	0,0
DistanceField	73	0,3	3,3	0	0,0	0,0
BodySetup	7	0,1	2,9	0	0,0	0,0
Audio	48	0,1	0,3	0	0,0	0,0
BulkDataList	227	0,9	0,1	23	0,0	0,0
NavCollision	73	0,1	0,0	0	0,0	0,0
NiagaraScript	4	0,0	0,0	0	0,0	0,0
CardRepresentation	73	0,2	0,0	0	0,0	0,0
BulkDataPayloadId	40	0,2	0,0	0	0,0	0,0
MESHDATAKEY	1	0,0	0,0	0	0,0	0,0
Total	**3415**	**9,9**	**568,9**	**24**	**0,1**	**0,0**

Figure 12.21 – Resource Usage tool

Resource Usage provides a high-level breakdown of your project's memory footprint, grouped by asset category (**Texture**, **MaterialShader**, **StaticMesh**, **NiagaraScript**, **Audio**, etc.), so you can see how much CPU RAM and GPU VRAM each group and individual assets consume. It lists per-asset "resource size" (including mip levels for textures, buffer sizes for meshes, and compiled shader memory for Materials), along with references and usage counts, letting you sort to find the top offenders quickly.

With the biggest memory offenders flagged in **Resource Usage**, the next step is to act. In the next section, we'll turn those findings into concrete fixes.

Best practices

Once we have identified the aspects of the project that may be causing performance losses, we must apply the necessary modifications to improve overall performance. In this section, we'll roll up our sleeves and improve performance holistically, tackling geometry, LODs, and materials so every change we make reduces draw cost, balances GPU time, and keeps memory within budget.

Geometry

If we have too many assets visible on screen, the time spent in the **Draw** thread will increase. We can optimize this in several ways:

- Convert Static Meshes to Nanite to minimize triangle calculations
- Merge meshes to reduce the total number of Actors in the scene

To merge Actors, use the dedicated tool. First, select the Actors you want to merge, then go to **Tools** | **Merge Actors**, as shown in *Figure 12.22*:

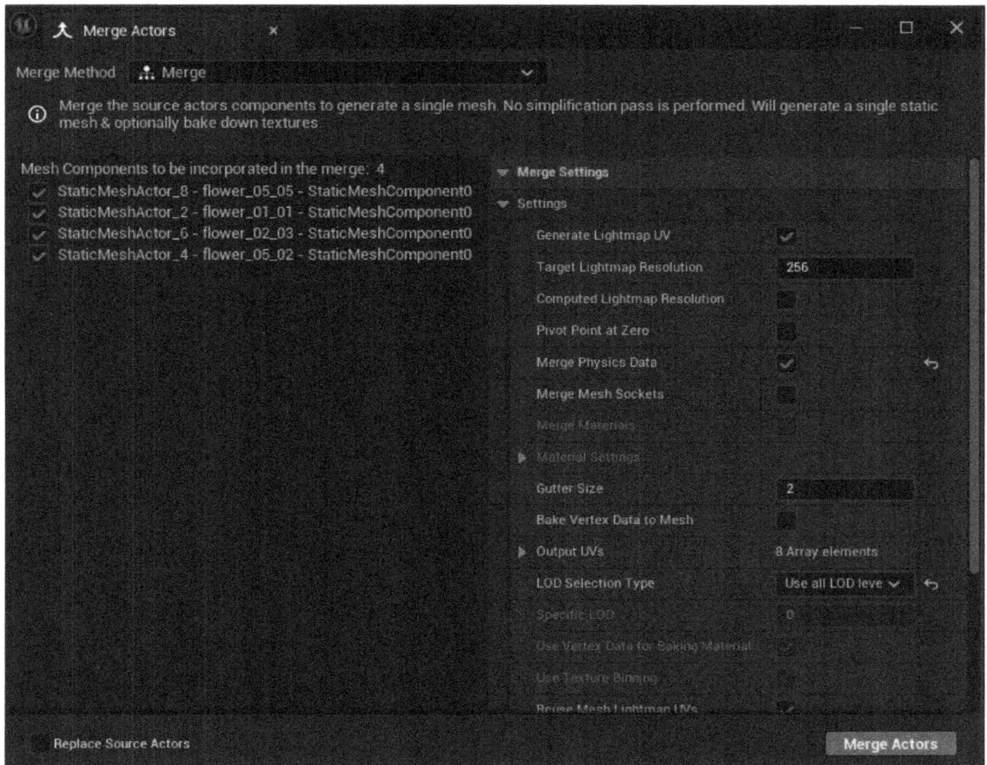

Figure 12.22 – Merge Actors

With the **Merge Actors** tool, we can combine Static Meshes and even their materials, giving us great flexibility when managing geometry.

To avoid occlusion problems, it is important to follow certain rules when merging geometries:

- Merge Actors that are close to each other, since merged meshes generate new bounds that encompass the combined volume and may affect occlusion
- Avoid merging very large objects, as these will always be rendered once on screen, which negatively impacts occlusion

If materials are merged, it is possible to define which texture maps should be merged, as well as their resolution. Keep in mind that texture resolutions will be reduced when combining several maps into a single one.

LODs

Continuing with geometry, we can use LODs to improve performance in non-Nanite Static Meshes (Nanite meshes already include their own internal LOD system).

LODs are simplified versions of the original meshes with a reduced triangle count. Unreal Engine swaps these meshes depending on the camera's distance: low-poly versions are used when the object is far away, and higher-poly versions when the camera is closer.

In open worlds, long sightlines and streaming make LODs vital. Pair per-mesh LODs with HLODs from **World Partition**, so distant areas collapse into lightweight proxies, cutting draw calls and overdraw. Set LOD distances by asset type (foliage versus architecture), use dithered transitions if needed, and strip shadows or complex materials on lower LODs to keep far content cheap while close-up detail stays sharp.

Generating LODs

LODs can be generated *manually* or *automatically*, either in Unreal or in external software. Let's examine both processes.

In Unreal, to automatically generate LODs, open the Static Mesh Editor (double-click the Actor in the **Content Browser**).

In the **Details** panel, under **LOD Settings**, you will find the following options (see *Figure 12.23*):

- **Number of LODs**: This defines how many LOD levels will be created
- **Auto Compute LOD Distance**: Disable this option to manually control distances

- **Apply Changes:** This generates the LODs. The distances at which LODs are displayed are defined automatically, but can be adjusted
- **Screen Size:** This defines the camera distance (based on percentage of screen coverage) at which each LOD is displayed

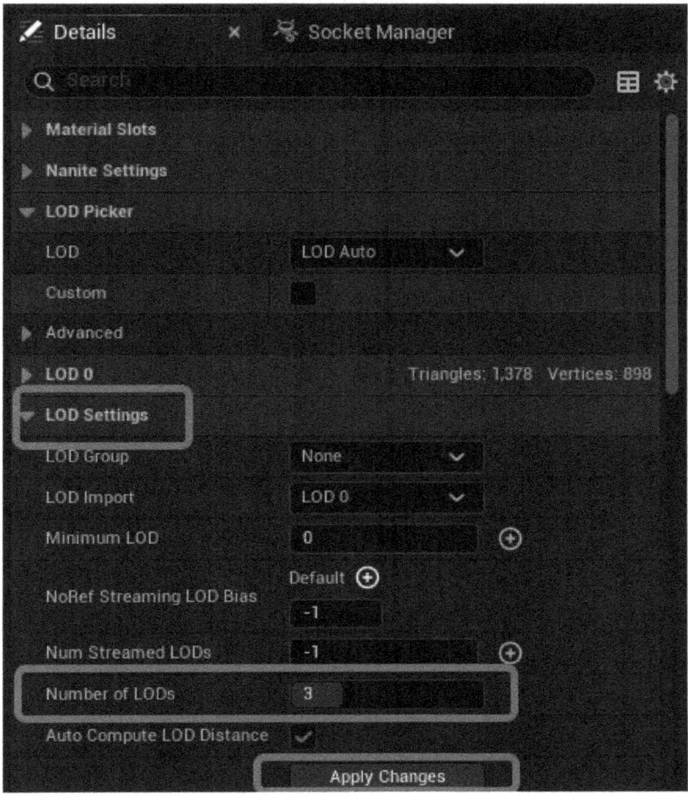

Figure 12.23 – LODs

Now, let's move on to how we can create LODs manually. There are two ways to create LODs manually:

- **Import LOD meshes**: After generating LODs automatically, use **LOD Import** to assign a specific mesh to each LOD slot
- **Reduction settings (per LOD)**: Control the triangle count of each mesh, defining the geometric density for each LOD level

Textures

When creating a Master Material, it is common to use specific textures tied to that material.

These textures are loaded into memory even if the material is not applied to any object in the scene. They are also loaded into memory even if Material Instances do not use them.

The best way to avoid this is to use a series of simple, low-resolution textures to minimize memory usage:

Figure 12.24 – Textures for Master Material

It is very important to use power-of-two textures whenever possible, because non-power-of-two textures have two drawbacks:

- Will not have mipmaps, which can cause moiré and flickering effects
- Will take up more memory space

The *compression format* of textures is also very important, as it directly affects both the visual quality and the memory footprint.

Take the following examples:

- **DXT1 Texture:**
    - 512x512 | 171 kB
    - 1024x1024 | 683 kB
- **ARGB8 Texture:**
    - 511x513 | 1,024 kB
    - 1023x1025 | 4,096 kB

There are two major types of texture compression:

- **Default**: This is block compression (4–8 bpp) that greatly cuts VRAM and bandwidth. It is good for color maps (albedo, ORM).
    - **Trade-off**: Blocky/banding artifacts on gradients or UI.
- **Grayscale compression**: This single-channel compression (4 bpp) is ideal for masks/height maps. It reduces memory versus storing the same data in RGBA.
    - **Trade-off**: One channel only; use channel packing (multiple masks in RGBA) if you need to minimize samplers rather than pure memory.

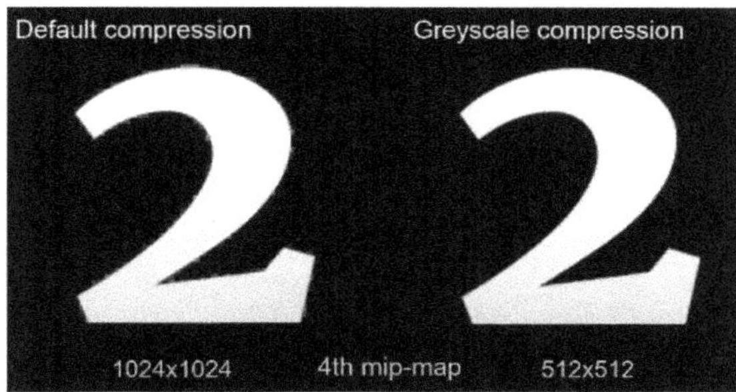

Figure 12.25 – Textures compression

Now that we've explored optimization strategies for geometry, LODs, and textures, let's see how these principles apply in practice by analyzing a scene.

Example: Scene analysis

Nanite is a geometry virtualization system that allows us to have a large number of meshes with very high triangle counts in a scene. However, they still affect performance in areas such as lighting and materials.

Because of this, care must be taken when using Nanite, especially when adding assets through the **Foliage** tool. While foliage placement is optimized by the tool, if those assets are also Nanite meshes, we could easily end up with very large amounts of geometry. The engine will then need to calculate, for example, the shadows cast by those assets, which can consume a significant portion of the frame's render time—even when using Virtual Shadow Maps as the shadowing method.

In the scene we are optimizing, we observed high calculation times in the following threads:

- **Draw:** 35.57 ms
- **GPU:** 35.16 ms

Additionally, the GPU Visualizer showed that **ShadowDepths** consumes the largest portion of render time, with **15.08** ms. Out of this, **14.95** ms are spent calculating the Virtual Shadow Maps of the Nanite assets in the scene:

Figure 12.26 – Virtual Shadow Maps render time

In this scenario, there are several possible solutions to reduce per-frame render times:

- **Reduce the number of Nanite assets:** For example, by removing assets with the **Erase** tool in **Foliage** mode.

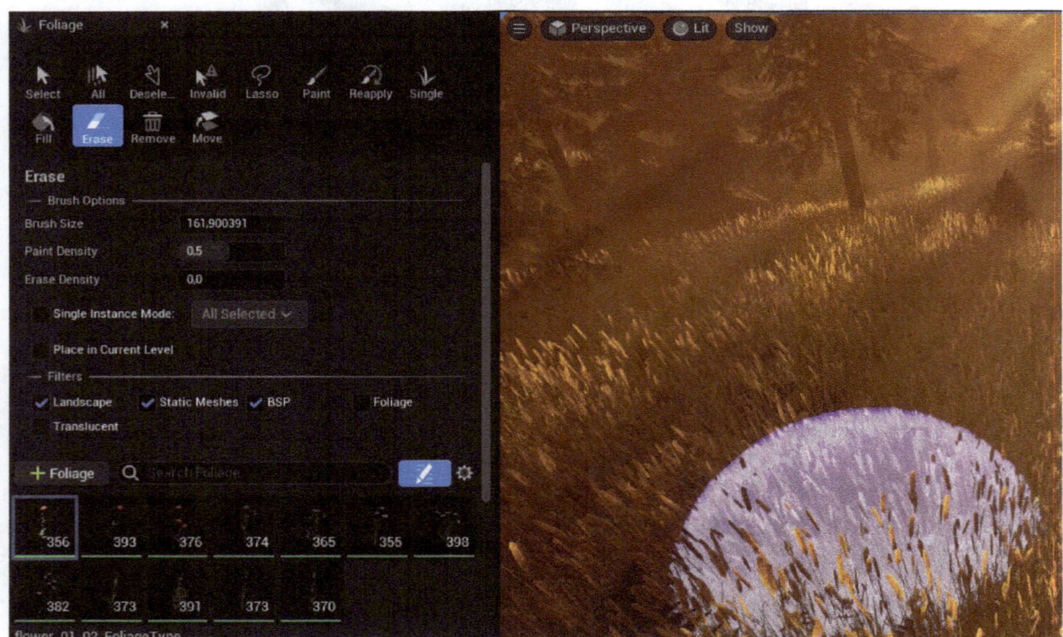

Figure 12.27 – Erase tool

- **Scale the assets:** This is so that they cover more space, allowing us to use fewer instances while achieving the same effect. This can be adjusted in **Foliage** mode as follows:
    1. Select the asset.
    2. Go to **Painting** | **Scale X**.

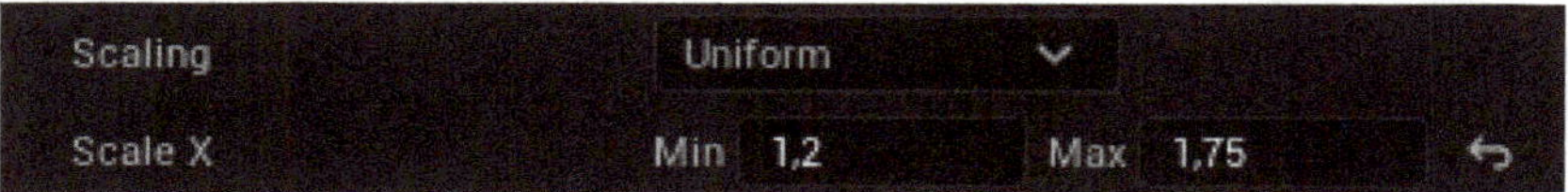

Figure 12.28 – Scale Foliage

- **Disable Nanite:** Disabling Nanite for the Static Meshes used in foliage allows us to control LODs. This way, we can define which LODs cast shadows, minimizing shadow calculations when those LODs are loaded. Follow these steps:
    3. Open the Static Mesh Editor | **Details**.
    4. Go to the **LOD** settings (usually the lowest LODs, i.e., least detailed).
    5. Disable **Cast Shadow**.

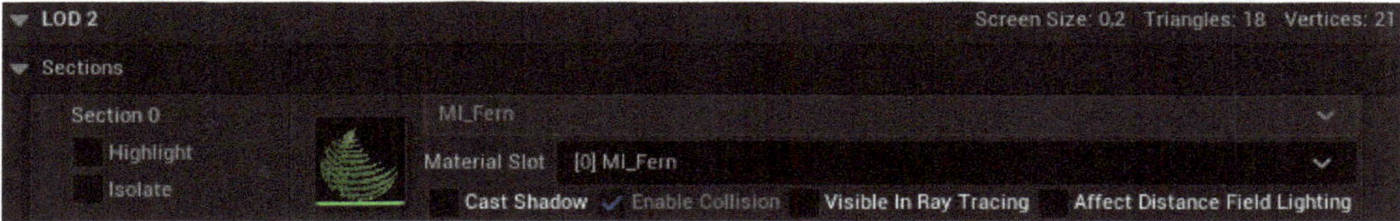

Figure 12.29 – LOD Cast Shadow

After reducing part of the foliage and scaling the remaining assets, we achieved significantly better performance metrics compared to the initial state. This was done without any noticeable loss in visual quality, as shown in *Figure 12.30*:

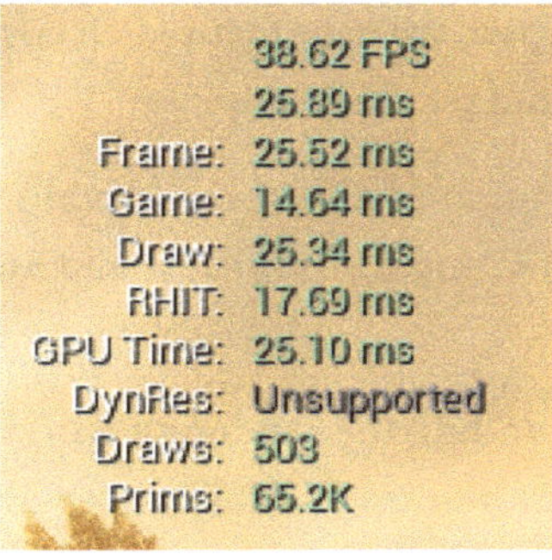

Figure 12.30 – Stat Unit of the optimized scene

Figure 12.31 shows the optimized foliage layout, demonstrating how performance improvements were achieved without compromising visual fidelity:

Figure 12.31 – Scene detail

Along the way, we've touched on many concepts you should already recognize, and taken together, they span the entire Unreal Engine workflow. Optimization is therefore an integral part of level development. By understanding how the engine works and consistently applying best practices, you can ship more complex projects without sacrificing performance.

Summary

Throughout this book, we have explored the artistic and technical aspects of building open worlds in Unreal Engine. In this final chapter, we have focused on ensuring that environments not only look good but also perform well and play correctly.

This chapter highlighted optimization as a key principle in real-time rendering. We examined the rendering pipeline (**CPU**, **Draw**, and **GPU** threads) and how to measure performance using Unreal's profiling tools.

The key topics included understanding the rendering workflow and identifying bottlenecks; managing draw calls, LODs, Nanite meshes, and foliage density; and profiling with the **Stat Unit**, GPU Visualizer, and **Optimization Viewmodes**. We rounded it off with best practices for geometry, textures, shadows, and memory usage.

So, before calling an area "optimized," run a quick scene analysis in the play context. Note any stalls on the **Game** thread tied to AI, animation, or overlap events, then reprofile at target resolution. This ties performance findings to real player interaction, not just synthetic timings.

Optimization and testing are not isolated tasks but ongoing processes that must be revisited throughout development. By combining technical profiling with practical gameplay validation, you will be able to deliver worlds that are not only visually stunning but also stable, efficient, and enjoyable to explore.

The journey ahead

This completes our journey through the creation of open world landscapes in Unreal Engine: from the artistic foundation of world-building, through technical optimization, to final gameplay validation. With these tools and practices, you are now equipped to create expansive, performant, and immersive worlds ready for players.

Any story, game, or cinematic requires a world in which to exist, so there are infinite possibilities of what we can develop. Take each of those possibilities as an opportunity to capture the spark you carry inside and turn it into a world others can step into!

13

Unlock Your Exclusive Benefits

Your copy of this book includes the following exclusive benefits:

- Next-gen Packt Reader
- DRM-free PDF/ePub downloads

Follow the guide below to unlock them. The process takes only a few minutes and needs to be completed once.

Unlock this Book's Free Benefits in 3 Easy Steps

Step 1

Keep your purchase invoice ready for *Step 3*. If you have a physical copy, scan it using your phone and save it as a PDF, JPG, or PNG.

For more help on finding your invoice, visit `https://www.packtpub.com/unlock-benefits/help`.

Note: If you bought this book directly from Packt, no invoice is required. After *Step 2*, you can access your exclusive content right away.

Step 2

Scan the QR code or go to `packtpub.com/unlock`.

On the page that opens (similar to *Figure 13.1* on desktop), search for this book by name and select the correct edition.

<packt> Search... Subscription 0

Explore Products Best Sellers New Releases Books Videos Audiobooks Learning Hub Newsletter Hub Free Learning

Discover and unlock your book's exclusive benefits

Bought a Packt book? Your purchase may come with free bonus benefits designed to maximise your learning. Discover and unlock them here

Discover Benefits Sign Up/In Upload Invoice

Need Help?

1. Discover your book's exclusive benefits

Search by title or ISBN

CONTINUE TO STEP 2

2. Login or sign up for free

3. Upload your invoice and unlock

Figure 13.1: Packt unlock landing page on desktop

Step 3

After selecting your book, sign in to your Packt account or create one for free. Then upload your invoice (PDF, PNG, or JPG, up to 10 MB). Follow the on-screen instructions to finish the process.

Need help?

If you get stuck and need help, visit `https://www.packtpub.com/unlock-benefits/help` for a detailed FAQ on how to find your invoices and more. This QR code will take you to the help page.

Note: If you are still facing issues, reach out to `customercare@packt.com`.

Other Books You May Enjoy

If you enjoyed this book, you may be interested in these other books by Packt:

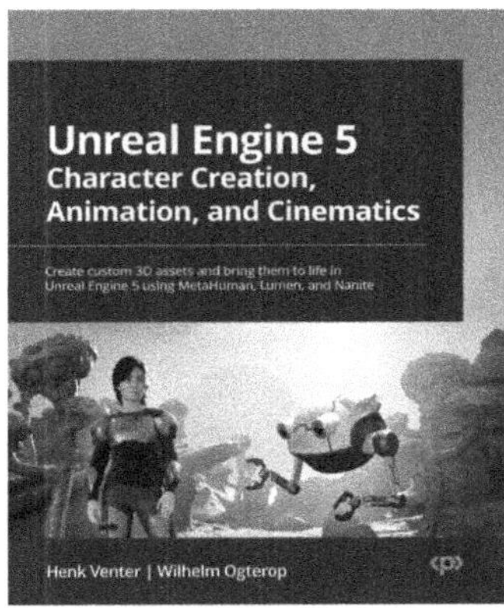

Unreal Engine 5 Character Creation, Animation, and Cinematics

Henk Venter, Wilhelm Ogterop

ISBN: 978-1-80181-244-3

- Create, customize, and use a MetaHuman in a cinematic scene in UE5
- Model and texture custom 3D assets for your movie using Blender and Quixel Mixer
- Use Nanite with Quixel Megascans assets to build 3D movie sets
- Rig and animate characters and 3D assets inside UE5 using Control Rig tools
- Combine your 3D assets in Sequencer, include the final effects, and render out a high-quality movie scene
- Light your 3D movie set using Lumen lighting in UE5

Blueprints Visual Scripting for Unreal Engine 5, Third Edition

Marcos Romero, Brenden Sewell

ISBN: 978-1-80181-158-3

- Understand programming concepts in Blueprints
- Create prototypes and iterate new game mechanics rapidly
- Build user interface elements and interactive menus
- Use advanced Blueprint nodes to manage the complexity of a game
- Explore all the features of the Blueprint editor, such as the Components tab, Viewport, and Event Graph
- Get to grips with OOP concepts and explore the Gameplay Framework
- Work with virtual reality development in UE Blueprint
- Implement procedural generation and create a product configurator

Packt is searching for authors like you

If you're interested in becoming an author for Packt, please visit `authors.packt.com` and apply today. We have worked with thousands of developers and tech professionals, just like you, to help them share their insight with the global tech community. You can make a general application, apply for a specific hot topic that we are recruiting an author for, or submit your own idea.

Share your thoughts

Now you've finished *Building Open World Landscapes with Unreal Engine 5*, we'd love to hear your thoughts! Scan the QR code below to go straight to the Amazon review page for this book and share your feedback or leave a review on the site that you purchased it from.

`https://packt.link/r/1835085571`

Your review is important to us and the tech community and will help us make sure we're delivering excellent quality content.

Index

Symbols

A

B

N

O

P

T

U

V

W

www.ingramcontent.com/pod-product-compliance
Lightning Source LLC
Chambersburg PA
CBHW072009230326
41598CB00082B/6893

* 9 7 8 1 8 3 5 0 8 5 5 7 8 *